Juvenile Justice Practice
A Cross-Disciplinary Approach to Intervention

Rodney A. Ellis, PhD
University of Tennessee

Karen M. Sowers, PhD
University of Tennessee

BROOKS/COLE

™

THOMSON LEARNING

Australia • Canada • Mexico • Singapore • Spain • United Kingdom • United States

Executive Editor: Lisa Gebo
Assistant Editor: Susan Wilson
Editorial Assistant: JoAnne von Zastrow
Marketing Manager: Caroline Concilla
Project Editor: Pam Suwinsky
Print Buyer: Robert King
Permissions Editor: Bob Kauser

Production Service: G&S Typesetters
Copy Editor: John Mulvihill
Cover Designer: Yvo Riezebos
Cover Images: Zephyr Images
Cover Printer: Webcom Limited
Printer: Webcom Limited

For permission to use material from this
text, contact us by
> **Web:** http://www.thomsonrights.com
> **Fax:** 1-800-730-2215
> **Phone:** 1-800-730-2214

ISBN 0-534-36795-X

For more information, contact:
Wadsworth / Thomson Learning
10 Davis Drive
Belmont, CA 94002-3098
USA
http://www.wadsworth.com

International Headquarters
Thomson Learning
International Division
290 Harbor Drive, 2nd floor
Stamford, CT 06902-7477
USA

UK / Europe / Middle East / South Africa
Thomson Learning
Berkshire House
168-173 High Holborn
London WC1V 7AA
United Kingdom

Asia
Thomson Learning
60 Albert Street, #15-01
Albert Complex
Singapore 189969

Canada
Nelson Thomson Learning
1120 Birchmont Road
Toronto, Ontario M1K 5G4
Canada

We dedicate this textbook to our own juveniles, Cody and Michael, who daily remind us of the joys, challenges, and tribulations of childhood and adolescence. We hope that this book will help practitioners who daily share in the joys, challenges, and tribulations of the juveniles in their care.

Contents

Chapter 9 An Evaluation Primer 228

Chapter 10 Current and Future Issues 257

Preface

During the last century a great deal of energy and money has gone into trying to help troubled juveniles. We have had a few successes. Looking back over the history of the juvenile justice system, however, we've probably had even more failures. Although the system was originally put in place to try to help youths, it has failed in many cases.

There is a great deal of talk today about improving the system. As we'll see later in this text, many experts have conflicting ideas about the steps that should be taken to make those improvements. One thing is clear, however: we must improve the professional expertise of the practitioners who work with troubled juveniles on a daily basis. This book is written to help accomplish that goal.

WHY DID WE WRITE THIS TEXT?

In a sense, this text was written for kids in the juvenile justice system. Please don't misunderstand our meaning. We know that few of those kids are likely to read the text, but we hope that many of the people who will work with them in the years to come will read it. We hope that by reading this text these practitioners of the future will be more aware of the system, more effective with their clients, and more active in promoting positive change within the system.

There are, of course, many texts written about juvenile justice issues. Why, then, was it important to write this book? The answer is that this book is unique. It supplies information and skill-building exercises across a range of practice never before covered in a single text.

The successful practitioner needs a broad range of knowledge about the roles and functions of various participants within the system. This book provides foundational knowledge across that range. The successful practitioner needs knowledge and skills about effective assessment, case management, and intervention. This book provides the basics of that knowledge and exercises to facilitate the development of those skills. The successful practitioner must be familiar with the current knowledge base regarding effective intervention. This book surveys that knowledge. The successful practitioner must have the knowledge and skills to work effectively with children and families of various racial and ethnic backgrounds, both sexes, and various developmental stages. The book provides a foundation in these areas. The successful practitioner must have the knowledge and skills to evaluate her own practice. The book offers basic guidelines for outcome evaluation with individuals and groups. The successful practitioner must also have tools that will allow her to remain current with state-of-the-art intervention. The book provides basic training in the development of those skills. Although many fine texts address many different juvenile justice issues, the authors are convinced that no other text provides such a broad range of material addressing so many of the issues central to successful juvenile justice practice.

FOR WHOM WAS THE TEXT WRITTEN?

The text, then, is written for the direct use of future and current practitioners in the juvenile justice system. It is written for clients in the sense that we believe it will help those practitioners be more effective in their work with clients. The book is most likely to be used in university or college courses in juvenile justice, treatment of adolescents and families, and criminal justice. It can be used in social work, criminal justice, and psychology programs. It might also be used in prelaw or law programs to make students who will work within the system more aware of the activities of other practitioners within that system. Although the book was designed for college settings, it is very practical and might also be used by state departments of juvenile justice to train and prepare their workers.

HOW DOES THE TEXT MEET THE NEEDS OF CURRENT AND FUTURE PRACTITIONERS?

This text addresses the needs of the textbook market in several ways. First, it is unique in its scope and content. No other book covers the wide variety of relevant and important topics covered in this text. Next, it is practical. It offers workable solutions to many of the real-life situations faced by professionals in their daily practice. Although it is current in terms of its inclusion of effective techniques and interventions, it recognizes its own mortality: It teaches students methods of staying current on both the latest in effective intervention and the shaping trends within the system. By applying the techniques described in the text, students and practitioners can establish relationships with and tap the resources of federal, state, and private juvenile justice organizations. Through contact with these resources, practitioners can ensure that they learn and employ state-of-the-art practices.

Each chapter contains learning activities and links to additional resources. Case studies are used to provide opportunities for role play and simulation activities. Sample interviewing tools and assessment instruments allow students to learn the basics of assessment, evaluation, and diagnosis. Helpful tables and graphs illustrate the relationships between the various entities and individuals who work within the system. These learning activities help bring the world of the practitioner to the classroom to optimize the learning opportunities of students.

WHAT ARE THE BENEFITS OF THIS TEXT?

A primary goal of this text is to equip instructors with the tools necessary to provide future practitioners with the broad base of knowledge and skills necessary for successful juvenile justice practice. Its primary benefit is the way in which it combines academic knowledge and practical experience to optimize the classroom environment for learning. Suggested activities also enhance the probability that the gains made during class will be successfully transferred to the practice environment. Each chapter is followed by specific activities, questions, and resources that will benefit both faculty and student.

No student workbook or faculty guide is available for this text as yet, but a myriad of excellent publications are available through the Office of Juvenile Justice and Delinquency Prevention and other agencies either free or at minimal cost. The book is written so that readings from these sources can be easily incorporated into both classroom and homework assignments. Resources from computerized databases and the Internet are also described in each chapter.

TO WHOM DO WE OWE AN ETERNAL DEBT OF GRATITUDE?

There are several people whose hard work and extraordinary dedication have helped to make this book possible. Nancy Meyer-Adams logged countless hours of research and proofreading. Gina Cox braved an onslaught of annual reports and new university catalogues to help with illustration and formatting the text. Faye Fillers, the best administrative assistant in the country, coordinated these activities, managing countless phone calls between the authors.

Shane Dixon contributed in numerous ways. He proofread text, coordinated communications with contributors, and wrote several pieces himself. Bernadette Brown also wrote a number of pieces and worked with contributors.

Bill Nugent, Charles Glisson, and David Dupper all took time from their busy academic and research schedules to offer important input in their areas of expertise. Several practitioners and other professionals contributed pieces describing their roles in the system. Their names are included with the pieces they wrote.

IN SUMMARY

We hope this book will be useful to those who use it, instructors and students alike. Most of all, we hope it helps the children . . . kids who for whatever reason have made bad decisions, and are at risk for making bad decisions, that may adversely affect both them and their worlds for years to come.

Chapter 1

◆

Practitioners in Juvenile Justice

CHAPTER OUTLINE

The Scope of the Problem
A Description of the Juvenile Justice Client
Roles of Practitioners
Future Trends in Juvenile Crime
Summary

Practitioners in the juvenile justice arena come from various backgrounds and play many different roles. Some have been trained in social work, psychology, or mental health counseling. Others have a background in criminal justice or a related discipline. Many enter the field with such diverse experience as business, history, or English literature.

Practitioners also fill a number of different roles. They may work for government agencies at the federal, state, or local level, for private not-for-profit agencies or for-profit agencies that specialize in services to delinquents. Some are case managers. Others are intake workers, counselors, or mental health technicians. Others are recreation specialists, tutors, educational specialists, or vocational trainers.

Juvenile justice professionals work in many settings, such as residential, daycare, or outpatient programs. They may also provide service in their client's home or community, in schools or churches, or as a part of parks and recreation programs. They may work in diversionary programs, alternative-to-suspension programs, treatment agencies, or many other settings.

Practitioners may work with youth with very specific problems, or juveniles with a wide variety of issues. They may serve at-risk children, truants, status offenders, violent offenders, sex offenders, gang members, and others. Delinquent clients may have additional problems in mental health, substance abuse, family relationships, or educational areas. Clients vary in age, race, ethnicity, gender, and level of cognitive and emotional development.

Juvenile justice workers must also interact with a wide variety of professionals. They must communicate with mental health professionals, child welfare personnel, substance abuse counselors, educational staff, vocational trainers, police agencies, and the court system. They often participate in interdisciplinary planning committees, refer clients for educational services, and testify in juvenile court.

Obviously, the juvenile justice worker faces a challenging task. Unfortunately, without sufficient training, she is likely to begin her career unprepared for her work. This book provides foundational knowledge for juvenile justice practice. It will help practitioners who plan to enter the field or those who are new to the field because it provides both this foundation and a list of resources to use to build on that foundation. It will also benefit seasoned professionals, since it can help them expand their knowledge base into unfamiliar areas.

The first chapter helps place the work of the juvenile justice practitioner in the context of the delinquency problem and society's response to it. First, it examines the scope of the problem. Second, it provides a profile of the typical client, focusing on the factors that tend to contribute to or maintain problem behavior. Third, it outlines the various roles practitioners play in treating delinquents. Finally, it examines likely future trends in juvenile crime and discusses potential responses by practitioners.

THE SCOPE OF THE PROBLEM

The juvenile justice system evolved in response to society's recognition of delinquency as a problem clearly distinguishable from adult criminal behavior. Prior to 1899, children were regarded as responsible for their actions to the same degree as were adults.

Children over the age of 5 who committed crimes were prosecuted in the criminal courts. Those who were convicted often experienced severe punishment, such as confinement with adults, whippings, public humiliation, and the death penalty (del Carmen, Parker, & Reddington, 1998). A series of reforms during the 1800s culminated in the creation of the first juvenile court in Cook County, Illinois, in 1899 (Krisberg, 1988). Children who entered the new juvenile system experienced an entirely different philosophy: an emphasis on treatment rather than punishment. The court's founders believed that youth developed delinquent behavior because of the influences in their homes and in society. They also believed that children could be saved from the effects of those influences. The goal of these reformers was to change, through rehabilitation, the behavior of youths who entered the system (Kelling, 1987). The Cook County system became a model for other jurisdictions. Today every state has a juvenile court. The juvenile justice system, including its case management system, diversionary efforts, and treatment programs, has developed in response to the court. The court's basic philosophy and approach, providing treatment to juveniles rather than punishment, has remained unchanged since 1899. Recently, however, several states have mandated a stronger, more retributive approach to juvenile crime. Many courts have taken an increasingly tougher stance in their dispositions as a result (del Carmen et al., 1998). This trend toward stronger consequences for juvenile crime will be discussed in greater depth in chapter 10.

The juvenile justice system has, unfortunately, been largely unsuccessful in meeting its goals. As the nation's population has grown and the frequency and severity of social problems including poverty, child abuse, and substance abuse have increased, the juvenile crime rate has remained alarmingly high. Although the overall juvenile crime rate decreased between 1994 and 1998 (Snyder, 1999), juveniles accounted for 17% of all violent crime arrests in 1998 (FBI, 1999).

Further, despite the decreases in juvenile crime rate of the last few years, the rates of some specific categories remain substantially higher than they were 10 years ago. For example, despite the fact that the number of arrests of juveniles for violent crimes decreased by 19% between 1994 and 1998, the rate of juvenile arrests for violent crime was 15% higher in 1999 than in 1998 (Snyder, 1999).

The recent decreases have reversed the trend of the previous ten years. Between 1985 and 1994 the number of offenses by a juvenile against a person (offenses such as assault, robbery, rape, or homicide) increased by 93%. Property crimes by juveniles increased by 16% for the same period, while drug offenses increased by 54%. Rates in specific categories also increased dramatically. Homicide cases climbed by 144%, aggravated assault increased by 134%, robbery cases were up 53%, and rape cases increased 25% (OJJDP, 1996).

Clearly, juvenile crime has a significant impact on the safety and economic well-being of Americans. The extent of its effect can be illustrated by reviewing information on juvenile crime rates and the cost of processing and incarcerating juveniles.

In 1996, persons under the age of 18 were arrested for 1,892,312 offenses, about 12.5% of all arrests made nationally. This was an increase of 35.4% from 1987. Of the total arrests made in 1996, 573,620 were for more serious crimes (these are called Crime Index offenses, a designation that will be discussed more fully in the next section), and 1,318,692 were for less serious, or Part II offenses (also described below). Among the Crime Index offenses, 2,039 arrests were for murder, 3,680 for forcible rape, 36,569 for robbery, 50,560 for aggravated assaults, 87,233 for burglary, 336,774 for larceny/theft, 50,212 for motor vehicle theft, and 6,553 for arson. Certain Part II offenses also occurred in substantial numbers; for instance, 154,762 arrests were made for other assaults, 93,139 for vandalism, 35,670 for carrying or possessing a weapon, and 142,922 arrests were made for a substance abuse violation. In addition, 132,747 youth were arrested for curfew violations and 128,118 for running away (Bureau of Justice Statistics, 1997). Table 1.1 provides a full report of all arrests for all offenses reported to the Federal Bureau of Investigation (FBI) for 1996.

Each of these arrests represented some form of cost to the system, the victims, and the offenders themselves. For example, the cost of incarcerating a single juvenile for one year was about $31,000 in 1995 (Bureau of Justice Statistics, 1997). During that year the average daily population of incarcerated juveniles was 3,400.

Table 1.1 Total Arrests of Persons under 15, 18, 21, and 25 Years of Age, 1996
[9,666 agencies; 1996 estimated population 189,927,000]

Offense charged	Total all ages	NUMBER OF PERSONS ARRESTED				PERCENT OF TOTAL ALL AGES			
		Under 15	Under 18	Under 21	Under 25	Under 15	Under 18	Under 21	Under 25
TOTAL	11,093,211	679,449	2,103,658	3,568,260	5,015,527	6.1	19.0	32.2	45.2
Murder and nonnegligent manslaughter	14,447	257	2,172	5,238	8,113	1.8	15.0	36.3	56.2
Forcible rape	24,347	1,423	4,128	7,293	10,591	5.8	17.0	30.0	43.5
Robbery	121,781	10,525	39,037	62,874	78,804	8.6	32.1	51.6	64.7
Aggravated assault	387,571	18,122	56,894	101,557	155,179	4.7	14.7	26.2	40.0
Burglary	264,193	36,859	97,809	141,612	169,722	14.0	37.0	53.6	64.2
Larceny-theft	1,096,488	155,287	370,607	517,982	624,549	14.2	33.8	47.2	57.0
Motor vehicle theft	132,023	14,473	54,813	77,882	92,471	11.0	41.5	59.0	70.0
Arson	13,755	4,887	7,302	8,573	9,574	35.5	53.1	62.3	69.6
Violent crime[1]	548,146	30,327	102,231	176,962	252,687	5.5	18.7	32.3	46.1
Property crime[2]	1,506,459	211,506	530,531	746,049	896,316	14.0	35.2	49.5	59.5
Crime Index total[3]	2,054,605	241,833	632,762	923,011	1,149,003	11.8	30.8	44.9	55.9
Other assaults	972,984	70,276	171,366	265,803	392,212	7.2	17.6	27.3	40.3
Forgery and counterfeiting	88,355	755	6,238	19,066	33,910	.9	7.1	21.6	38.4
Fraud	324,776	5,452	18,872	52,333	105,341	1.7	5.8	16.1	32.4
Embezzlement	11,449	63	958	3,046	5,071	.6	8.4	26.6	44.3
Stolen property; buying, receiving, possessing	111,066	8,099	30,189	51,518	66,642	7.3	27.2	46.4	60.0
Vandalism	234,215	46,353	103,333	136,519	160,884	19.8	44.1	58.3	68.7
Weapons; carrying, possessing, etc.	161,158	11,684	39,363	67,675	92,388	7.3	24.4	42.0	57.3

Prostitution and commercialized vice	81,036	140	1,104	6,644	17,110	.2	1.4	8.2	21.1
Sex offenses (except forcible rape and prostitution)	70,619	6,343	12,660	18,852	26,050	9.0	17.9	26.7	36.9
Drug abuse violations	1,128,647	26,705	158,447	345,349	512,174	2.4	14.0	30.6	45.4
Gambling	16,984	297	2,263	4,648	6,706	1.7	13.3	27.4	39.5
Offenses against family and children	103,800	1,879	5,850	13,091	25,772	1.8	5.6	12.6	24.8
Driving under the influence	1,013,932	341	12,814	81,867	228,015	[4]	1.3	8.1	22.5
Liquor laws	491,176	12,363	112,553	297,731	340,748	2.5	22.9	60.6	69.4
Drunkenness	522,869	2,414	17,111	58,499	122,961	.5	3.3	11.2	23.5
Disorderly conduct	626,918	53,726	159,951	250,591	338,871	8.6	25.5	40.0	54.1
Vagrancy	21,735	622	2,873	6,224	8,780	2.9	13.2	28.6	40.4
All other offenses (except traffic)	2,767,751	92,240	329,070	679,245	1,095,734	3.3	11.9	24.5	39.6
Suspicion	4,859	436	1,604	2,271	2,878	9.0	33.0	46.7	59.2
Curfew and loitering law violations	142,433	39,315	142,433	142,433	142,433	27.6	100.0	100.0	100.0
Runaways	141,844	58,113	141,844	141,844	141,844	41.0	100.0	100.0	100.0

[1] Violent crimes are offenses of murder, forcible rape, robbery, and aggravated assault.
[2] Property crimes are offenses of burglary, larceny-theft, motor vehicle theft, and arson.
[3] Includes arson.
[4] Less than one-tenth of 1%.

SOURCE: FBI, 1996

Multiplying the average cost of incarceration by the average daily population would probably not yield an accurate figure for the total expenditure for juvenile incarceration, but it certainly illustrates the tremendous costs associated with incarceration of juveniles.

Astonishing though these costs may be, they do not include the cost of the investigation and arrest, court hearings, case management, and other processing. They also omit the cost of services to those who are not incarcerated—for example, those who enter diversionary programs. Other costs are also created by services to families.

Costs to victims must also be considered. Since many juvenile offenses are robbery or property crimes, the total cost can be assumed to be substantial. In

---

Box 1.1 The Unified Crime Report and the National Crime Victimization Survey

The Unified Crime Report (UCR) is issued each year by the FBI. It summarizes information about the level of criminal activity that came to the attention of law enforcement agencies during the previous year. Law enforcement agencies across the country report specific data for 29 different types of crime. The information is compiled and organized by FBI staff, and the annual report is issued. The report includes arrest data as well as information on crimes cleared, characteristics of offenders, law enforcement agencies, and homicides. The eight most serious and frequent crimes are listed in a section called Part I, and are known as Crime Index offenses. Part I offenses are most often used in describing national crime levels. These crimes include homicide, forcible rape, robbery, aggravated assault, burglary, larceny-theft, motor vehicle theft, and arson. Part II offenses include the other 21 crimes. Since the UCR records only official crime, that is, crimes for which an arrest is made, it is thought to underreport the actual level of criminal activity (FBI, 1998; U.S. Department of Justice, 1995).

The National Crime Victimization Survey (NCVS) is prepared each year by the Bureau of Justice Statistics. In order to complete the survey, employees of the U.S. Bureau of the Census interview members of about 49,000 households. Every member of each household over the age of 12 is asked questions regarding specific crimes they experienced, whether or not the crimes were reported to the police. The survey includes information on rape, sexual assault, robbery, both aggravated and simple assault, burglary, theft, and motor vehicle theft. It does not collect data regarding homicides or commercial crime. From the data collected from the 49,000 households, inferences are made regarding the number of crimes reported in the general population.

The NCVS was intended to complement the UCR, since it is designed to detect crimes that are not reported to law enforcement. By considering the results of the two surveys together, authorities believe that they can obtain a much more accurate picture of the level of crime in the United States. Neither of the two methods considers another important method of data collection: asking youth themselves how many crimes they have committed. This method of data collection is discussed in greater detail in chapter 9 (U.S. Department of Justice, 1995).

1997, 408,772 arrests were made for property crimes. If each of these arrests cost the victims an average of even just $50, the cost for the year would be $20,438,600.

Perhaps the most disturbing cost is that of the disrupted life. Many juvenile offenders do not complete school and are not able to become productive members of society. Many of them go on to commit crimes as adults. For these individuals, there are the added costs of adult incarceration, ongoing treatment, government-supported medical care, and an ongoing life of crime. It is clear that juvenile crime substantially impacts the life of every citizen either directly or indirectly. It is equally clear that the need for trained practitioners in the juvenile justice system is great.

The statistics regarding juvenile crime used in this chapter were taken from reports prepared by the federal government. Most of these reports used two sources of information: the FBI's Unified Crime Report (UCR) and the National Crime Victimization Survey (NCVS). These two surveys are designed to be complementary, and represent the most complete set of official records regarding juvenile offenses in the country. More details about the UCR and the NCVS are offered in box 1.1.

Other methods of collecting information about the rate of juvenile crime are available to researchers and practitioners who wish to evaluate the effectiveness of their own programs. Each method has its own set of strengths and weaknesses. These methods, including self-report and report of significant others, will be discussed in chapter 9.

The high rate of juvenile crime suggests that the system has not been successful in either (1) preventing youths from initiating delinquent activity or (2) preventing them from continuing to engage in delinquent activity once the pattern has been established. This has led some experts to call for better programming, others to call for system reform, and still others to demand a return to a philosophy of incarceration and punishment. Whatever approach, or combination of approaches, is taken, it is clear that professionals in the system must develop a greater understanding of juvenile offenders, a greater ability to perform their roles within the system, and a greater capacity to treat their clients.

A DESCRIPTION OF THE
JUVENILE JUSTICE CLIENT

Understanding juvenile offenders begins with a review of what is currently known about them. Researchers have looked at youthful deviant behavior from various perspectives, and many of these perspectives are valuable for treatment. Based on these perspectives, profiles of various types of offenders can be developed. Based on those profiles, interventions can be more effectively structured. Some of the similarities are discussed in this section. These characteristics can be studied in greater detail by reviewing the publications listed in the reference section at the end of this chapter.

Understanding juvenile offenders involves more than identifying similarities, however. Practitioners must also learn to identify and adapt to differences among individual juveniles. Important differences result from various factors, including those related to race, ethnicity, gender, and developmental level. Many of the differences will be discussed in chapters 5 and 7.

In this section we'll look at some of the similarities among many offenders. Specifically, we'll examine five areas of similarity: demographic characteristics, types of offenses and offenders, risk factors, correlation between behavioral problems, and career patterns of criminal behavior.

Demographic Characteristics

Demographic characteristics refer to those features of persons commonly used as identifiers for groups in census, marketing, and other surveys. Categories of demographic data include such characteristics as age, race, sex, and socioeconomic status. These categories are useful in understanding which juveniles tend to commit what kinds of crimes.

Delinquents include persons under a specified age. By federal definition, children are no longer juveniles when they reach the age of 18. Some states, however, use different guidelines. For instance, Wyoming chooses not to prosecute youths as adults until they reach the age of 19. Connecticut, New York, and Vermont place the limit at 16. Georgia, Illinois, Louisiana, Massachusetts, Missouri, South Carolina, and Texas all give jurisdiction to the criminal court at age 17 (Sickmund et al., 1998). Many states allow juveniles of various ages to be prosecuted as adults for particularly persistent or severe offenses (Torbet & Szymanski, 1998).

Although children of various ages engage in some sort of unruly behavior, specific ages tend to be key for the development of problem behavior. Also, there are two general types of delinquents: those who develop conduct problems at a relatively early age and those who initiate delinquent behavior at a relatively late age (Patterson, DeBaryshe, & Ramsey, 1993). These two types will be discussed in greater detail under "Career Patterns of Criminal Behavior" later in this chapter.

For many youths, the factors believed to lead to delinquent behavior exist from very early in their lives, perhaps from before birth (Schorr, 1989). As these children progress through childhood, they often begin to show evidence of developing problems, such as excessive aggression or lying. During the late elementary and early middle school years, more significant problems begin to emerge. Children may begin to skip school, to run away from home, to abuse substances, and to shoplift. During late middle school and high school, the most severe problems, including violence, theft, school dropout, and promiscuous sexual behavior, sometimes emerge. The age at which problem behavior escalates differs for each youth. Some do not escalate in their problem behavior. Others stop altogether. Many, however, do escalate, and these youths constitute the group that commits the bulk of severe *delinquent offenses* (Henggeler, 1989).

Historically, older youths have committed both the most severe and the most frequent offenses. This pattern began to change, however, during the late 1980s and early 1990s. In 1984, youths under the age of 15 accounted for 25% of all violent crime arrests. By 1995 that percentage had increased to 30%. In 1995, 9% of all juvenile offenders arrested were under the age of 12. Youths ages 13 to 14 accounted for 25% of the juvenile arrests. The balance of the offenses were committed by youths between 15 and 18 (OJJDP, 1996).

White youth commit more crimes than other groups (67% in 1995). Blacks are the second most arrested group at 31%. The additional 2% of juvenile arrests are made of persons from other racial or ethnic groups (FBI, 1995). Although whites are arrested more often than are blacks, black youth are overrepresented in the system. This is evidenced by the fact that although blacks represent 31% of the total juvenile arrests, they constitute only 13% of the total population (Snyder, Sickmund, & Poe-Yamagata, 1996).

More males than females are arrested. In 1995, the FBI reported 1.5 million arrests of males and 511,000 arrests of females under the age of 18. Males are more frequently arrested for violent offenses, and females more frequently for larceny-theft (FBI, 1995). Females, however, are being arrested with increasing frequency and account for increasing portions of the violent crime rate (Poe-Yamagata & Butts, 1996).

Understanding the effect of socioeconomic class on delinquent behavior is a little more complex. The UCR and the NCVS offer little insight into this issue. Some studies use self-report measures (asking youth how many crimes they have committed). These studies have produced conflicting results. Both Hirshi (1969) and Johnson (1980) found that socioeconomic class made no difference in level of delinquency. Ageton and Elliott (1978), however, found that lower-class youth reported greater delinquent activity than did working-class and middle-class youth. Researchers have concluded that lower socioeconomic status can predict the development of delinquent behavior when other conditions are present (Dryfoos, 1990; Hawkins, Catalano, & Miller, 1992).

Types of Offenses and Offenders

Offenders can also be categorized by type of offense and by type of offender. Offenses are organized into classes according to their severity. The less severe are known as *status offenses*. This category includes such infractions as running away from home, skipping school, drinking alcohol, and *incorrigibility*. These are actions for which a youth can be held accountable, but for which an adult cannot be arrested. These offenses often result in less severe consequences and less strenuous treatment efforts than do the other category of offenses.

The second category is delinquency. *Delinquent offenses* include violent crime, property crime, and other offenses. Delinquency typically meets with more severe consequences and more intensive treatment than does a status offense. Consequences and treatment efforts also usually escalate as severity of delinquent offense increases.

Bartollas and Miller (1994) provide a different method of categorizing juveniles—by type of offender. They designate five general categories of offender: noncriminal, irresponsible, situational, drug and alcohol users, and chronic offenders. *Noncriminal offenders* are status offenders, whose actions are not criminal and do not substantially impact society as a whole. *Irresponsible offenders* include the mentally deficient (those who lack the capacity to know when they are doing wrong), those who are unaware of the laws they are breaking, and the naive (those who enjoy risk-taking, but are not able to understand potential consequences). The emotionally disturbed are also a part of this group. Emotionally disturbed children are those whose emotional problems tend to cause them to act out in an uncontrollable fashion. *Situational offenders* are occasional delinquents who commit criminal acts due to boredom, peer pressure, or a need for money. *Drug offenders* are those who use alcohol and illicit substances. *Chronic offenders* are those who commit serious, repetitive crimes and are of significant danger to society as a result of their behavior. The classification scheme developed by Bartollas and Miller (1998) can be useful during assessment and intervention. Its value will be discussed further in chapters 3, 4, and 5.

Risk, Need, and Protective Factors

Researchers have discovered that many delinquent youths have common characteristics usually not shared with nondelinquent youth. These have been termed *risk factors* because, when present, they are believed to increase the odds that individual youth will become delinquent. Other characteristics, known as "special needs" or *need factors,* do not directly produce risk, but increase the effect of the risk factors present. A third group of characteristics, known as *protective factors* tend to protect children against the development of delinquent behavior. Collectively, these groups of factors may be referred to as risk–related factors. Examples of risk factors include depression, aggressive behaviors, low levels of family support, and poor family management. Examples of need factors include the need for concrete services and learning disabilities. Protective factors include such characteristics as strong avocational interest and the presence of a mentor or role model (Dryfoos, 1990; Hawkins, Catalano, & Miller, 1992).

Risk-related factors can be best understood when placed within the context of the area of the youth's life in which they occur. For example, depression and aggressive behavior can be seen as primarily related to the individual, while low family support and poor family management are chiefly family issues (Ellis, 1998). Table 1.2 provides a partial list of risk-related factors. Table 1.3 then places some of those factors within the area of life in which they primarily occur. Understanding risk–related factors and the way in which they impact the youth and his systems can be very important to assessment and intervention. This will be discussed in more detail in chapters 3, 4, and 5.

Correlation between Problem Behaviors

Researchers have also noted a high correlation between various types of delinquent or problem behaviors. This means that adolescents who engage in one type of problem behavior are likely to engage in others as well. For instance, Elliot, Huizinga, and Menard (1989) found that youths who abused substances were also likely to commit delinquent acts. Bentler and Newcomb (1986) found a relationship between drug use and early sexual intercourse. Elliot and Morse (1987) found that sexual abuse and delinquency were related. Bachman, O'Mally, and Johnson (1978) discovered that many youths who use drugs also experience problems at school. These and other studies show us that the profile of the typical juvenile offender includes several categories of problem behavior,

Table 1.2 A Partial List of Risk, Need, and Protective Factors

RISK FACTORS

___ Early initiation of problem behavior
___ Low expectations for future success/
education
___ Anxiety or depression
___ Aggressive behaviors
___ Poor social skills
___ Minority status
___ High levels of nonconformity and
independence
___ Lower socioeconomic status
___ Low family support
___ Poor family management
___ Family models problem behavior
___ Truancy or school conduct problems
___ Poor academic achievement
___ Friends drop out of school
___ Strong peer influence
___ Problem behaviors among peers
___ Highly transient neighborhood
___ Criminal behavior and substance abuse
modeled

NEED FACTORS

___ Need concrete services: money, medical
help, etc.
___ Learning disabilities
___ Physical impairment
___ Hyperactivity or ADHD

PROTECTIVE FACTORS

___ Strong vocational or avocational
interest
___ High levels of self-esteem
___ Strong sense of control of environment
___ Good family relationships
___ Strong extended family
___ Good family management practices
___ Success in school
___ Prosocial friendship groups
___ Presence of a mentor or role model
___ Strong community organization
___ Prosocial norms and values in
community

Table 1.3 Risk-Related Factors by Life Area

RISK FACTORS

Individual
___ Early initiation of problem behavior
___ Low expectations for future success/
education
___ Anxiety or depression
___ Aggressive behaviors
___ Poor social skills
___ Minority status
___ High levels of nonconformity and
independence

Family
___ Lower socioeconomic status
___ Low family support
___ Poor family management
___ Family models problem behavior

School
___ Truancy or school conduct problems
___ Poor academic achievement
___ Friends drop out of school

Peers
___ Strong peer influence
___ Problem behaviors among peers

Community
___ High crime neighborhood
___ Highly transient neighborhood
___ Criminal behavior and substance abuse
modeled

NEED FACTORS

___ Need concrete services: money,
medical help, etc.
___ Learning disabilities
___ Physical impairment
___ Hyperactivity or ADHD

PROTECTIVE FACTORS

Individual
___ Strong vocational or avocational
interest
___ High levels of self-esteem
___ Strong sense of control over
environment

Family
___ Good family relationships
___ Strong extended family
___ Good family management practices

School
___ Success in school

Peers
___ Prosocial friendship groups
___ Strong relationship between parents
and peers

Community
___ Presence of a mentor or role model
___ Strong community organization
___ Prosocial norms and values in
community

including delinquency, substance abuse, school problems, and promiscuous sexual behavior.

The discovery that various problem behaviors so frequently occurred in the same youth led researchers to believe that there might be a common cause for those behaviors. Several studied the issue, and concluded that there is a common cause for all problem behaviors. They labeled this condition "problem behavior syndrome" (Jessor & Jessor, 1977; Donovan, Jessor, & Costa, 1988). Unfortunately, these researchers were unable to be very specific about what the common cause is. Other researchers have questioned whether the findings applied to all racial and age groups, and suggested there might be several causes instead of one (Gillmore, Hawkins, Catalano, Day, & Moore, 1991; Williams, Ayers, Abbott, Hawkins, & Catalano, 1996). Regardless of the form problem behavior syndrome appears to take, clearly all forms of juvenile deviant behavior are closely related. This has important implications for assessment and intervention, as will be discussed in chapters 3, 4, and 5.

Career Patterns of Criminal Behavior

Juvenile offenders can also be categorized by typical career patterns. Although the nature and frequency of criminal behavior varies greatly from youth to youth, two overall patterns exist. Researchers refer to youth who follow these patterns as *early starters* or *late starters*.

Early starters are youth who demonstrate antisocial behavior very early in their lives. Their problem behavior escalates as they grow older. An example of a typical early starter pattern is provided in box 1.2.

Box 1.2   Case Study: Ricky

Ricky is a 15-year-old white male who resides with his parents in an apartment in a lower-income neighborhood. He has no siblings, but is very close to his cousins Brad and Tiffany, ages 17 and 16. Brad is a dropout who is a member of a local gang. Tiffany is in school, but has problems with attendance and grades. She also spent six months in a drug treatment center.

Ricky's parents are both age 34. His father has been arrested several times on drug and assault charges. His mother is an active alcoholic.

Ricky has few friends. The ones he does have are frequently in trouble. One has dropped out of school, and one

is in a delinquency treatment facility. One positive influence is 40-year-old Roy, who operates a computer business near Ricky's school. Roy occasionally hires him to do odd jobs around the store.

Ricky's first brushes with the law were at age 7, when he was detained for breaking and entering. He has been in police custody at least 12 times since. When counselors have tried to help Ricky, his response has been, "I don't care . . . I do things my way."

Despite the negative influences around him, Ricky has positive self-esteem. He also has strong computer interest and skills.

Within the early starter pattern, another clear pattern exists. Some children who engage in problem behaviors at an early age (e.g., first grade) do so with sufficient frequency and intensity to warrant a diagnosis of *oppositional/defiant disorder* (ODD) based on criteria from the *Diagnostic and Statistical Manual of Mental Disorders,* fourth edition *(DSM-IV)*. Behaviors typical of these children include frequent defiance, deliberately annoying others, lying about misbehavior, becoming agitated easily, being excessively vindictive, and being frequently angry or resentful. About 50% of the children who might receive the *DSM-IV* diagnosis of ODD escalate in their behavior sufficiently to warrant a diagnosis of *conduct disorder* (CD) at a later age (e.g., seventh grade). Examples of criteria for conduct disorder are aggression or cruelty toward people and animals, destructiveness, theft, and disobedience to authority. Of those whose behaviors merit a diagnosis of CD during adolescence, about 50% go on to engage in sufficiently severe criminal behavior to justify a diagnosis of *antisocial personality disorder* (APD) as adults (Patterson, DeBaryshe, & Ramsey, 1993). The *DSM-IV* criteria for APD include frequent acts that are grounds for arrest, lying, impulsivity, excessive aggressiveness, disregard for safety, irresponsibility, and absence of remorse (American Psychiatric Association, 1994). More information is available about the *DSM-IV* in box 1.3. Late starters typically do not initiate delinquent behavior until their middle to late teens. They may engage in only a few delinquent acts, or in a brief flurry of deviant activities. They typically do not continue these activities into adulthood (Patterson, DeBaryshe, & Ramsey, 1993). Elena, described in box 1.4, has many of the characteristics of a late starter.

Box 1.3   The *DSM-IV*

The *Diagnostic and Statistical Manual of Mental Disorders,* fourth edition *(DSM-IV)* is published by the American Psychiatric Association. It represents the accumulation of many years of clinical and scientific observation of clients with various types of problems. Over the years common patterns have emerged that have allowed individual disorders to be identified. The *DSM-IV* is updated periodically in an effort to incorporate current knowledge into a diagnostic scheme that is useful for treatment.

Some of the disorders identified by the *DSM-IV* occur primarily in adults. Others occur most frequently in children and adolescents. For any individual to receive a diagnosis, he must meet a list of criteria designed to ensure that symptoms exist in sufficient frequency, severity, intensity, and diversity.

The *DSM-IV* is used primarily by psychiatrists, psychologists, social workers, and other mental health practitioners. It has been criticized for several reasons, including the tendency of clinicians to reify the diagnoses, the danger of labeling those who receive a diagnosis, and the inability of trained clinicians to make reliable diagnoses on many of the disorders. Despite these criticisms, the *DSM-IV* remains a frequently used tool.

Box 1.4　Case Study: Elena

Elena is a 16-year-old Hispanic female who resides with her parents and her 12-year-old brother in a three-bedroom suburban home. Elena's parents both work full-time jobs, but spend as much time with Elena as possible. Their parenting style is authoritarian, with the father as the dominant figure.

Elena struggles in school, but has managed to pass every year. Part of her problem is due to processing disorder, a learning disability from which she suffers.

Elena has two groups of friends. One group is composed of good students who are very involved both at school and in a church. The other group are "troubled" and have been known to smoke pot and shoplift.

Elena was recently arrested for shoplifting. Although she was not carrying drugs, she was with another girl who had a bag of cannabis. She denies having used drugs, but reports having used alcohol at parties.

Summary of Profile Information

In summary, the profile of the juvenile offender contains both similarity and diversity. There are many similarities. Delinquents are most often white, over the age of 15, and male. Other groups, however, have begun to engage in more problem behavior during the last several years. Delinquent youths often have common characteristics that apparently have predisposed them to their behavior, such as specific personal and family problems. Some have mental deficiencies or emotional problems.

Juvenile offenders are also strikingly diverse, however. Many are under the age of 16. A large and disproportionate number are black, and a growing percentage is female. Delinquents come from virtually all socioeconomic backgrounds and very different kinds of families. As chapters 3, 4, and 5 will show, these characteristics make working with the juvenile justice client exceptionally challenging.

ROLES OF PRACTITIONERS

Practitioners play many different roles in the juvenile justice system. Generally, those roles can be categorized as direct service, administrative, advocacy, advisory, evaluation and research, or policymaking. There are too many positions and roles to describe all of them in a single chapter. We will examine several roles, however, that are characteristic of each category. In chapter 2 we'll look at the ways in which practitioners who fill these roles and positions interact with members of other professions.

Practitioners in Direct Service

Direct service workers are those whose primary task involves daily interaction with and management of clients. *Direct service practitioners* usually work for one of two types of employers: state or private agencies. State agencies may be operated by either the executive or judicial branches of the government (Ezell, 1997). Private agencies are either not-for-profit (meaning that they are registered with the Internal Revenue Service as organizations that operate as a social service and do not attempt to make a profit) or for-profit. For-profit agencies are corporations that provide social services, but do so in order to make a profit.

Direct service workers typically provide one or more types of services, including assessment, counseling, case management, training, tutoring, or mentoring. Many practitioners in state agencies are case managers. Although the official title can vary from state to state (e.g., family services counselor, juvenile probation officer), the function of the position is similar between jurisdictions. The juvenile justice case manager supervises, brokers services for, provides surveillance of, advocates for, advises, and reports to the court on behalf of the clients. Depending on statutory and time restraints, the case manager may also provide some individual or family counseling. The case manager usually works primarily in the field, often visiting the homes, schools, and communities of the client. The role of a case manager in the juvenile justice system is illustrated by the life story in box 1.5.

Direct service practitioners may also work in one of several types of facilities. These facilities include detention centers, day treatment programs, and residential programs of varying levels of security. These settings often require practitioners to serve in multiple capacities, including monitoring, counseling, tutoring, and skills training.

Some jurisdictions have specialized programs in which direct service practitioners are employed. These programs include intervention initiatives for girls, school-based programming, and gang-directed intervention. Box 1.6 discusses an effective (school-based) alternative-to-suspension program.

Practitioners in private agencies also play many roles. In some jurisdictions, their employers contract with the state to provide the case management services traditionally provided by state employees. Similarly, they may work at in-house settings, such as day treatment or residential programs, operated by a private company that contracts with the government. Alternatively, juvenile justice workers may practice in school- or community-based prevention or intervention programs, intensive case management initiatives, aftercare projects, or programs that provide educational and vocational training. Such programs are usually funded by government dollars, philanthropic organizations, or contributions from individuals.

Practitioners in Administrative Roles

Mark Ezell (1997) offers an excellent list of positions held by administrators in the juvenile justice system. His list includes executives and managers in government and not-for-profit agencies, juvenile court administrators, chief probation officers, administrators and supervisors in detention and residential programs, and directors of specialized programs. Administrators in large organizations function at several levels, depending on the number of employees they supervise and the duties they perform.

Box 1.5   Life Story: Betty McBride

JUVENILE JUSTICE
CASE MANAGER

As a juvenile probation officer in a rural southeast Texas county, I received referrals about juvenile offenders (ages 10–17) from a variety of sources: police officers, school personnel, community agencies, and sometimes parents. Allegations ranged from minor behavior problems at school or home to status offenses (runaway, minor in possession of alcohol, truancy, etc.) to major felony offenses (murder, arson, burglary, etc.). My responsibilities began with assessing the circumstances of the case and determining the most appropriate action to be taken within the legal guidelines for juvenile offenders. This included decisions about custody.

I took custody of all juvenile offenders apprehended by police according to state law. Normally, misdemeanor or status offenders were released to their parents or legal guardian, while felony offenders were frequently incarcerated following a detention hearing. Because our county did not have a detention facility for juveniles, this necessitated transporting the offender to and from a juvenile detention facility in a neighboring county. Local police officers assisted in transporting dangerous or violent offenders.

After custody issues were resolved, decisions regarding disposition were examined. Possible dispositions ranged from "no action," to "counsel and release" (a one-time conference with the juvenile and his parent/guardian to discuss correcting the inappropriate or illegal behavior), to "informal adjustment" (an informal six-month probationary contract between the juvenile, his parent/guardian, and the probation officer), to "formal probation" imposed by the court, to "imprisonment" in the state juvenile facility until age 18.

My case management responsibilities included counseling juveniles and their parent/guardians, writing social histories, preparing court reports and recommendations, representing the juvenile probation department in court hearings, and supervising the juveniles on informal or adjudicated probation. I worked closely with the district attorney and police officers. Field visits were routinely made to the child's home and school to verify compliance with the terms and conditions of the probation order. Services were coordinated with other agencies, including mental health and child protection. Psychological testing or counseling was arranged as needed, and referrals were made to appropriate community resources, including emergency shelters or residential treatment facilities.

My advice to new practitioners in the juvenile justice arena is first to develop expert assessment skills using an ecological perspective—look at the big picture and consider how the child is affected by all the systems in his life. An understanding of the dynamics of child abuse and neglect is critical. Secondly, network, network, network. Know the parameters of other agencies serving children, understand their purpose and perspective, and develop relationships with these other professionals as you work together to serve juveniles and their families.

Box 1.6   In-School Suspension: Alternative-to-Suspension Program
Shane L. Dixon

Many schools are seeking a new solution to the old problem of misbehavior in schools. Some of these schools are turning to an old idea: in-school suspension. The use of in-school suspension allows the school a lot of leniency in its use of punishments, and it allows the school to reserve out-of-school suspension for those students who are causing severe problems in the school.

An example of an effective in-school program is the "In-School Suspension" program in Wilson County, Tennessee. With this program, when most students are reporting to their normal classes at the beginning of the day, the students in the in-school program are reporting to the one classroom that they will be staying in the entire day, except for a short break for lunch. These students are given the work that they would normally have to do in class, and the teacher assigned to the in-school classroom sees that the students do the work. This ensures that the students will not fall behind in their class work, which would further punish them for the offense that they had committed.

With the use of in-school suspension, many of the problems that were facing the school and the suspended student have been solved. Instead of getting a three-, four-, or five-day vacation from school, the student still has to come to school and do the work assigned to him or her. The biggest problem with suspending students in the past was that they did not get to make up the work they missed while on suspension, in effect punishing the student twice. Removing the student from school was almost certain to cause the student to make bad grades.

In-school suspension is beginning to solve this problem of not being able to complete class work and getting zeros for it. This program acknowledges that students need to be punished for the offense that they committed, but also that they need to be doing the work given to them. Students in in-school suspension are put into a very regimented classroom, where they are not even allowed to talk except at short intervals during the day, and at lunch, which they eat with just the other people in the in-school program and not with the rest of their friends. The classroom of an in-school suspension program is designed for completing the assigned class work, and not allowing the behavior that got the students there in the first place. This environment allows for students to be punished for their behavior once, while also making it possible for them to keep up in their work.

Patti (1983) identified three levels of administration: supervisors, program managers, and executives. Depending on the size of the agency, other terms may be necessary to describe other levels. An example of an *administrative practitioner* in a government agency is offered in box 1.7.

Ezell (1997) also includes a new and growing role in his discussion of administrative positions: that of consultant to the public defender's office. In such positions, practitioners are hired by public defenders to help prepare their cases and make recommendations for the disposition of juveniles.

I was asked to write about my experience as an administrator in juvenile justice in a large, urban area in the southeast part of the country. To explain my role, some history and background are necessary.

The juvenile justice agency I managed is centrally administered out of the state capitol, with local managers located in 15 geographic districts. The agency has statutory responsibility for the entire realm of juvenile justice services statewide: prevention, intervention, detention, and residential commitment services. Probation is included in the intervention services, unlike in many states where it is under the administration of the court.

Approximately 70–80% of the services are operated by private not-for-profit agencies, along with a handful of for-profit agencies. Probation and detention centers are operated by the state, and are managed locally. Planning for services is done on a statewide and local basis. The state prepares an agency strategic plan, and the district, with input from local system players, community leaders, and service providers, develops a local plan designed to meet local needs.

My responsibility as district manager was to manage a $25 million annual budget and oversee the planning and implementation of services for approximately 9,000 youths and their families. I had approximately 350 employees and 60 contracted programs under my span of management.

A typical day began with a 7:30 A.M. meeting. One such meeting included a group of CEOs from other organizations. This group met monthly to plan and collaborate on social service, education, health, and criminal justice issues. Following this, in a mid-morning session, I might meet with a contracted provider struggling to meet the performance objectives required in its con-

tract with us. Then, I might attend an 11:30 A.M. meeting of the county's Children's Services Board, a local advisory group that makes budget recommendations to the county commission for children and family services.

I might begin my afternoon in my office with a meeting with staff members on contractual or operational issues. Decisions would likely be made on awarding a contract, budget cutbacks, or developing a solution to an operational problem in a program. Perhaps a personnel problem would be discussed, or we might make decisions on a design for a new program. At 1:30 P.M., I might participate in a conference call with the central office in which I would receive a directive, participate in a discussion regarding policy implementation, or discuss a plan for operationalizing grant money. Around 2:30 or 3:00, I returned those phone calls determined to be of highest priority (generally the top 10). Most of these calls would require follow-up or action to be assigned to a member of my management team. Then around 4:30 I would read and respond to 30-plus e-mail messages. At about 5:00, I would begin to read mail, correspondence, incident reports, etc. At around 6:30 I would pack up to take home the large reports, statistical documents, etc., which required longer reading time. The next day was likely to be much the same.

A not-so-typical day might include a crisis in a program, a youth under community supervision that committed a heinous offense the previous evening, or a developing hurricane heading our way. In such situations, appointments would be canceled, emergency meetings called, and the situation handled as necessary.

To me, the best thing about being a juvenile justice administrator was that I got to use all the tools in the toolbox every single day. By tools, I mean the knowledge and skills I had accumulated through my education and experience. Flexibility and the ability to modify plans at a moment's notice were absolutely critical. Decisions needed to be made when time was short and relevant information was limited. In many cases I simply had to do the best I could, making sure that two things remained constant: (1) making the best decision for the juveniles and their families, the staff, and the community; and (2) making a decision that was right—morally, ethically, and legally. After these constants, I tried to plan carefully and strategically, Second to that, spend limited funds in a judicious manner, and keep the standards of the agency high.

In a role such as the one I filled, it is extremely important to have a sense of humor and not think you are more important than you really are. A system as large as the juvenile justice system has many players with many different roles. Some roles are adversarial to others, and with addition of the human element, some situations will require that you stop and laugh at your own absurdity as well as that of others. This will preserve your sanity and most certainly reduce stress.

As juvenile justice manager, I used all that I had learned in over twenty years—both in and out of the context in which I learned them. For example, while firing an employee I used the empathy I learned while a social work undergraduate student. I used my parenting skills with a misbehaving staff member. I had to use my mediation skills to resolve a dispute between two subordinates. My leadership style is eclectic; so I used different styles as varying situations occurred. Since I was appointed to serve at the pleasure of my boss, a member of the governor's cabinet, I learned quickly the ebbs and flows of politics and the influence this has over policy—good and bad policy. I also learned the importance of the "poker face." People will say the most outrageous things sometimes, and the ability to *not* respond saved me many times. My teachers called this a flat affect!!

I would like to offer a few thoughts on the role of juvenile justice workers in the future. The juvenile justice system is changing, and the ability of policymakers to focus on the facts and the information obtained from the data will be important in the new millennium. Policy set on rhetoric or on a knee-jerk reaction will not be good policy. Kids are more sophisticated than ever, and the demands on families are numerous. Working together with communities and neighborhoods will be important to give kids the tools they need for resiliency. Prevention starts with prenatal care and continues from there. We all have a role to play, and it must be done carefully and with others. Delinquency is a result of many factors, but can be reduced with careful planning, quality prevention services, and collaboration with other systems. Everyone has a role. No one is successful alone.

Practitioners in Advocacy Roles

Practitioners also play advocacy roles on several levels. The direct service worker may need to intervene on behalf of his client with the court, workers at other agencies, school officials, and others to ensure that the client is receiving effective and appropriate services. The administrator may need to perform similar tasks with the leadership at other agencies and may interact with community leaders and legislators to promote change in the service delivery or *policy* systems. Practitioners at any level can participate as citizens as voters, members of state and local committees, and through interaction with the press to advocate on behalf of their clients. Some practitioners also work outside the system, either on their own or as a part of organizations, to advocate for system reform.

Practitioners in Advisory Roles

Practitioners often serve the juvenile justice community in advisory roles. They may be members of local or state committees intended to improve or reform the system. They may sit on multidisciplinary teams that provide input to agencies on clinical matters or matters pertaining to *agency policy*. Some states provide opportunities for practitioners to perform such roles through advisory boards for district or regional administrators of government agencies. Often these states also have a state board, consisting of representatives from local boards. The state board may offer advice, direction, and/or policy input to the state juvenile justice agency or to the legislature. An example of a practitioner in an advisory role is provided in box 1.8.

Box 1.8   Guy Pierre, Juvenile Justice Board, Juvenile Justice Advisor

Guy Pierre is the prevention supervisor at The Starting Place, an agency that serves troubled teens in southeast Florida. His employment duties include supervision of five separate prevention programs for middle school children. In addition to his work as a juvenile justice administrator, Mr. Pierre serves his community as a juvenile justice advisor. The majority of his work in this role comes as a member of the community's Juvenile Justice Board.

The Juvenile Justice Board is composed of several members of the local community. Some of those members are a part of the board because of the positions they hold in the community. For example, members include the heads of the district's child welfare agency, the state's attorney's office, the county Department of Human Services, and local law enforcement. Other members, such as Mr. Pierre, are "at-large" members who have been selected to the board because of their capacity to represent the needs and interests of specific community groups. Mr. Pierre represents the interests of the West Indian and Haitian communities. He stresses the importance of this role because (as we will see in chapter 7) the needs of blacks who

have immigrated to this country recently are often different from those whose families have resided here for several generations.

Mr. Pierre and his fellow board members serve as an advisory organization for the district manager of the state Department of Juvenile Justice. They provide expertise in several areas, including recruiting and hiring, program development, and grant funding. Mr. Pierre reports that the board has been very effective in many of its efforts, including gang intervention, a truancy task force, cultural competency training, and innovative program implementation.

For those who would like to become involved as advisors to the system, Mr. Pierre recommends getting involved in public meetings and serving on community committees and organizations. By establishing contacts, rendering valuable services, and becoming known to the juvenile justice community, you will develop opportunities to become more involved. Mr. Pierre stresses the importance of the work that advisors do, and wishes to encourage you to both develop your expertise and invest the time and energy to get involved in this way.

Practitioners in Evaluation and Research Roles

Evaluation of program effectiveness has become increasingly important to juvenile justice programs over the last two decades. Funders are holding practitioners accountable for the success of their work with increasing frequency. Policymakers are examining new alternatives in prevention, treatment, processing, and prosecution. These alternatives need to be compared with traditional methods by researchers/practitioners. Recent research has also shown

---

Box 1.9   Bill Nugent, PhD, Researcher

Bill Nugent, PhD, is the coordinator of the PhD program at the College of Social Work at the University of Tennessee, Knoxville. Among his many other activities, Dr. Nugent specializes in research into juvenile justice issues. He offered these insights in a telephone interview.

When asked why he had chosen juvenile justice as an area for research, Dr. Nugent gave two reasons. First, he discussed its importance to society. He cited the high juvenile crime rate and the negative effects it has in areas such as public safety and cost to both the government and private industry. Dr. Nugent then stressed the importance of juvenile justice research to troubled youth. He underscored the role of research in helping children avoid or turn away from lives of crime: lives that may lead to hopelessness, imprisonment, or premature death.

When asked what he does in his research, Dr. Nugent described the path he follows in exploring juvenile justice issues. He begins by identifying an important problem or issue. One example of such an issue is what factors contribute to the development of delinquent behavior. Another example is whether a certain intervention is effective for certain types or ages of juveniles. He then formulates a research question about that issue, and conducts a literature review, that is, a study of any relevant research that has been published regarding the question. After the literature review,

he refines the question, designs the project, and conducts the research. He then analyzes the data, reports the results, and examines those results to see whether any new questions have emerged from the project.

Dr. Nugent cites the two issues mentioned above as critical questions in juvenile justice. One of those questions has to do with what kinds of problems in the lives of children tend to lead them into delinquent behavior. By recognizing these conditions, Dr. Nugent explains, practitioners can find ways to help children and families eliminate them or minimize their effects. The second question involves what interventions will work for specific categories of juveniles. As we will see elsewhere in this book, both the type of intervention chosen and the way in which it is administered are critical in juvenile justice practice.

When asked what advice he would give to those who want to become juvenile justice researchers, Dr. Nugent recommended that they study hard to learn as much about juveniles and research as possible. He stated that graduate school is a must: doctorate-level training is necessary for professional research. He recommended that throughout graduate school, research practitioners should focus on juvenile justice issues with particular emphasis on approaches taken by social work, psychology, and criminal justice.

that there are important differences, relevant to prevention and treatment, between offenders of different races and ethnicities, as well as between the sexes (Ellis, O'Hara, & Sowers, 1999; Vega & Gil, 1998). Researchers are needed to expand this growing field of knowledge. A researcher in the juvenile justice system describes his job in box 1.9.

Practitioners in Policymaking Roles

Practitioners at all levels may be involved in policymaking. Direct service workers, supervisors, administrators, researchers, advocates, and members of advisory boards have varying and vital perspectives on delinquency and the juvenile justice system. Each can offer her perspective to state and federal legislators and to the leaders of local human service organizations. Some practitioners become directly involved in writing proposed legislation. Administrators in state and federal agencies are often asked for their input on proposed legislation. Sometimes they actually draft statutes or portions of statutes that are proposed to lawmakers.

Summary of Practitioner Roles

Practitioners in the juvenile justice system play a variety of roles at a variety of levels. Each of those roles has evolved in response to a need in an ever-changing system. The system changes in response to changes in the patterns of juvenile crime. The next section discusses anticipated trends in juvenile crime that may impact the roles of practitioners of the future.

FUTURE TRENDS IN JUVENILE CRIME

Juvenile crime has shown several clear trends over the last two decades, including the following:

1. A rise in the proportion of crimes committed by youths under the age of 15 (Butts & Snyder, 1997)
2. An increase in the number of females arrested (Poe-Yamagata & Butts, 1996)
3. High rates of gang involvement (Howell, 1998)
4. Increased drug use (Butts & Snyder, 1997)
5. Overrepresentation of blacks (Butts & Snyder, 1997)

Many of these trends are expected to continue, and others may be generated by the projected growth of the juvenile population. For example, based on growth patterns, demographics, and the continued deterioration of social conditions for many children, Fox (1996) predicts an increase of more than 25% in juvenile homicides by the year 2005. Fox also believes that the same conditions augur a dramatic increase in the number of homicides by younger children.

If juvenile violence does increase, direct service practitioners and researchers will need to develop greater skills for working with youths who commit homicides. Administrators will need to develop programs, and to operate those programs effectively. Policy practitioners will face important decisions about alternatives for the disposition of such offenders. Evaluators will need to identify effective interventions, and must successfully communicate their findings to the public.

Crime by female adolescents can also be expected to continue to increase simply because of the projected growth of the adolescent population. Crime by girls is changing in other ways as well. For example, girls are becoming more violent. The growth in the aggravated assault rate for girls nearly doubled that for boys between 1989 and 1993. The increase in arrests for robbery was also greater among females than among males (Bureau of Justice Statistics, 1997).

Practitioners and researchers have recently begun to question the effectiveness of current intervention practice for females (Ellis, O'Hara, & Sowers, 1999; Belknap & Holsinger, 1998). Continued research in this area is vital if girls are to receive appropriate and effective intervention. Practitioners need to familiarize themselves with what is currently known about effective treatment of females and apply these techniques in their practice. They will also need to keep pace with new developments in practice knowledge.

Youth gang activity appears to have decreased slightly between 1996 and 1997. The 1997 National Youth Gang Survey (National Youth Gang Center, 1995) found an overall decrease in jurisdictions reporting active youth gangs during that period. Despite this decrease, nearly 75% of major cities, 33% of small cities, 56% of suburban counties, and 24% of rural counties reported gang activity. Practitioners must craft responses to this problem in multiple settings. Important areas of emphasis include regional responses, individual and group treatment methods, and policy development.

The use of alcohol and illicit substances has been increasing among adolescents since the early 1990s (Butts & Snyder, 1997). The strong correlation between crime and substance abuse makes this a vital area. Prevention programs must be improved and expanded. Treatment modalities appropriate for teens must be developed and evaluated. These activities constitute important roles for direct practitioners, administrators, and researchers.

Finally, the overrepresentation of black youth continues to be a problem (Butts & Snyder, 1997). The growth of the black juvenile population is expected to exceed that of the white juvenile population (Fox, 1996), which will increase the total number of black youth in the system rather than escalating overrepresentation. Overrepresentation is, at least in part, driven by racial bias at specific decision points in the processing of minority offenders. Practitioners at every level should work to see that such bias is eliminated. Additionally, researchers have noted important differences between various racial and ethnic groups with respect to prevention and treatment activities (Vega & Gil, 1998). Practitioners should familiarize themselves with these differences and adapt interventions accordingly.

Practice with juvenile justice clients can be both very challenging and very rewarding. Juveniles can be very demanding, and sometimes very disappointing. Many, however, can be helped to turn their lives around. An example of a juvenile who turned his life around is offered in the story of "Spencer" in box 1.10.

Box 1.10 Life Story: "Spencer," a Juvenile Justice Success Story

Rhonda Garrens, Community Prosecution
Coordinator, Office of the Knox County
District Attorney General

Rewards from working as a juvenile justice professional often come in the form of small but significant successes. The following story is about "Spencer," a youth from Knoxville, Tennessee. Spencer (not his real name) is just one example of how practitioners in the juvenile justice system can help make a difference in young people's lives.

Spencer was like many minority males who grow up in the inner-city housing projects of Knoxville. Raised in an atmosphere of poverty, drugs, and crime, and with no role models for educational or vocational motivation, he entered his teen years with no hope or plans for the future. Spencer grew up in a single-parent household, and had no relationship with his father. His mother was handicapped and supported her three sons with her disability payments. Spencer was very bright and intelligent, but he was a victim of the circumstances his family was forced to live in: a public housing project with the highest crime rate in Knoxville.

Spencer's older brother, whom he idealized, was killed in a gang-related shooting. Spencer himself drifted into the gang subculture and racked up a long record of delinquent adjudications. He was ultimately committed to state custody and placed in a juvenile institution. The staff at the institution saw the potential in Spencer, however, and he was placed in a special wilderness program where he received more individualized attention. He thrived in this atmosphere, and he did so well in his school work that he began taking college prep classes. He decided that he wanted to attend college and become an engineer. After he returned home, everyone was optimistic about his future. However, many of the old problems in Spencer's world were still there when he returned to it. Spencer became torn between his dreams of college and a bright future, and the facts of his life in the inner city. He was pressured to rejoin his old gang activities. Spencer cried out for help, and luckily he had people in his life who cared. His probation officer helped him get involved with a local minister who had grown up in the same neighborhood and operated a grassroots, faith-based mentoring program for young men. Spencer became very involved in the program, and he learned that he could survive his environment. Spencer is currently in college working toward his dream, and he also serves as a mentor to other young boys in the program that made such a difference in his life.

Many people in juvenile justice, law enforcement, the courts, the Department of Children's Services, and programs from the inner city worked together to help Spencer. Not all of our cases are as successful as Spencer's. But the saving of Spencer from drugs, gangs, incarceration, and most probably an early death was tremendously rewarding.

SUMMARY

Juvenile crime is an important and growing problem in American society. Youths who commit delinquent acts have both important differences and important similarities. Many of those characteristics have critical implications for successful treatment. Juvenile justice practitioners play multiple roles in an evolving system. The anticipated growth of juvenile crime is certain to bring important challenges to practitioners whatever role they play. To meet those challenges they must be able to interact successfully with other professionals, provide effective assessment and intervention, meet the needs of children of various backgrounds and of varying developmental levels, and effectively evaluate their practice.

ACTIVITIES FOR LEARNING

1. Box 1.2 is a case study of an imaginary juvenile justice client, Ricky. Ricky has several risk factors in several areas of his life. First, identify each factor and identify it as risk, need, or protective. Then, make an outline of the areas of life in which risk factors might occur. Finally, list each factor in your outline in the area of Ricky's life in which it primarily occurs. If you need a hint, look at the way the outline has been prepared in table 1.3.

2. Box 1.4 is a case study of Elena, another imaginary client. Perform the same activities for Elena that were described above for Ricky.

3. Compare the results of activity 1 and activity 2, then answer the following questions. How did the risk factors vary for Ricky and Elena? Which factors do you believe to be more important? How might the importance of specific factors vary because Ricky is male and Elena is female? What differences might there be because Maria is Hispanic and Ricky is not? What other information might a practitioner want to know about each?

4. Take another look at boxes 1.2 and 1.4. How well do Ricky and Elena fit the profiles offered in chapter 1. Why? Look at the categories offered by Bartollas and Miller (1994). Into which category do Ricky and Elena appear to fit? Do you have enough information to decide? If not, what additional information would you need?

5. Think about the descriptions offered in chapter 1 of the late starter and the early starter. Into which category does Ricky appear to fit? Into which category does Elena appear to fit? Which of the risk factors for Rocky may have contributed to his career pattern? Which factors may have been most important for Elena?

6. Think about the roles of practitioners described in the last section above. What might a direct service practitioner do for Ricky? for Elena? In what way might an administrator be involved in their lives? How might an advocate be needed? What might a policymaker or a researcher do for them or other youths like them?

QUESTIONS FOR DISCUSSION

1. The text clearly shows that the juvenile crime rate has been relatively stable for several years. Yet adult crime is decreasing. Why do you think this difference exists? What kinds of forces drive the juvenile crime rate? What forces drive the adult rate?

2. It seems that researchers know a lot about prevention of adolescent problem behavior. Why, then, have we not been successful in eliminating juvenile crime?

3. What kinds of activities do you think a case manager in the juvenile justice

system might perform? What kinds of information would she need in order to perform those duties?

4. Of the roles described in chapter 1, which interest you the most? Why? If you could choose to work in any of these roles in the system, what would that role be? Why?

5. The last part of chapter 1 described anticipated trends in juvenile crime. Which of those trends disturbs you the most? Why?

KEY TERMS AND DEFINITIONS

Administrative practitioners Workers who perform the management functions of an agency. Administrative practice occurs at many levels, from supervision of a few employees through management of an entire organization.

Agency policy The policies by which a social service organization operates. Informal policy exists more often at this level.

Antisocial personality disorder A condition identified by a diagnosis from the *DSM-IV.* It occurs in some persons over the age of 18 and is characterized by frequent acts that are grounds for arrest, lying, impulsivity, excessive aggressiveness, disregard for safety, irresponsibility, and absence of remorse.

Conduct disorder A condition identified by a diagnosis from the *DSM-IV.* It occurs in children under the age of 18, and most often in adolescence. It is characterized by aggression or cruelty toward people and animals, destructiveness, theft, and disobedience to authority.

Delinquent offense A deviant act committed by a juvenile for which an adult might have been arrested. "Juvenile" usually refers to an individual under the age of 18, but this definition varies in a few states.

Direct service practitioners Workers who directly interact with clients to provide, broker, or advocate for services. At the supervisor level, practitioners may engage in both administrative and direct practice activities.

Incorrigibility Unmanageable behavior in a juvenile, characterized by disobedience and defiance of authority.

Need factor (or special need) A characteristic of a youth or one of her social systems that enhances the risk of developing problem behavior. Need factors do not themselves create risk, but enhance the effect of other factors, known as risk factors.

Oppositional/defiant disorder A condition identified by a diagnosis from the *DSM-IV.* It occurs in children under the age of 18, and most often in middle and late childhood. It is characterized by frequent defiance, deliberately annoying others, lying about misbehavior, becoming agitated easily, being excessively vindictive, and being frequently angry or resentful.

Policy The laws, rules, or guidelines by which a group or affiliated groups operate. Policy may be either formal or informal, that is, written or unwritten. In this book, policy normally refers to guidelines at one of two levels: agency or social.

Protective factor A characteristic of a youth or one of her social systems that lowers the risk of developing problem behavior.

Risk factor A characteristic of a youth or one of her social systems that increases the risk of developing problem behavior.

Social policy The policies established by federal, state, and local governments to direct the activities of practitioners throughout a service delivery system.

Status offense A deviant act by a juvenile for which an adult could not be arrested but for which a juvenile can be detained.

REFERENCES

Ageton, S. S., & Elliott, D. S. (1978). *The incidence of delinquent behavior in a national probability sample.* Boulder, CO: Behavioral Research Institute.

American Correctional Association. (1990). *The female offender: What does the future hold?* Lanham, MD: ACA.

American Psychiatric Association. (1994). *Diagnostic and statistical manual of mental disorders* (4th ed.). Washington, DC: Author.

Bachman, J. G., O'Mally, P. M., & Johnson, J. (1978). *Adolescents to adulthood:*

Change and stability in the lives of young men. Ann Arbor, MI: Institute for Social Research.

Bartollas, C., & Miller, S. J. (1998). *Juvenile justice in America* (2nd ed.). Upper Saddle River, NJ: Prentice Hall.

Belknap, J., & Holsinger, K. (1998). An overview of delinquent girls: How theory and practice have failed and the need for innovative changes. In R. T. Caplin (Ed.), *Female offenders: Critical perspectives and effective interventions.* Gaithersburg, MD: Aspen.

Bentler, P. M., & Newcomb, M. D. (1986). Personality, sexual behavior, and drug use revealed through latent variable methods. *Clinical Psychology Review, 6,* 363–385.

Bergsmann, I. R. (1994). Establishing a foundation: Just the facts. In *1994 National Juvenile Female Offenders Conference: A time for change* (pp. 3–14). Lanham, MD: American Correctional Association/Office of Juvenile Justice and Delinquency Prevention.

Bureau of Justice Statistics. (1997). *Sourcebook of criminal justice statistics 1997.* Washington, DC: Author.

Butts, J. A., & Snyder, H. N. (1997, September). The youngest delinquents: Offenders under age 15. *Juvenile Justice Bulletin.* Washington, DC: Office of Juvenile Justice and Delinquency Prevention.

Caplin, R. T. (1998). *Female offenders: Critical perspectives and effective interventions.* Gaithersburg, MD: Aspen.

Chassler, S. (1997, February 2). What teenage girls say about pregnancy. *Washington Post Parade Magazine,* p. 3.

Del Carmen, R. V., Parker, M., & Reddington, F. P. (1998). *Briefs of leading cases in juvenile justice.* Cincinnati: Anderson.

Donovan, J. E., Jessor, R., & Costa, F. M. (1988). Syndrome of problem behavior in adolescence: A replication. *Journal of Consulting and Clinical Psychology, 56*(5), 762–765.

Dryfoos, J. (1990). *Adolescents at risk.* Oxford: Oxford University Press.

Del Carmen, R. V., Parker, M., & Reddington, F. P. (1998). *Briefs of leading cases in juvenile justice.* Cincinnati: Anderson.

Elliot, D., Huizinga, D., & Menard, S. (1989). *Multiple problem youth: Delinquency, substance use, and mental health problems.* New York: Springer-Verlag.

Elliot, D., & Morse, B. (1987). Drug use, delinquency, and sexual activity. In C. Jones (Ed.), *Drug use and adolescent sexual activity, pregnancy, and parenthood* (NIDA Research Monograph). Washington, DC: U.S. Government Printing Office.

Ellis, R. A. (1998). Filling the prevention gap: Multi-factor, multi-system, multi-level intervention. *Journal of Primary Prevention, 19*(1), 57–71.

Ellis, R. A., O'Hara, M., & Sowers, K. (1999). Treatment profiles of troubled female adolescents: Implications for judicial disposition. *Juvenile and Family Court Journal, 50*(4), 25–39.

Ezell, M. (1997). The administration of juvenile justice. In C. A. McNeese & A. R. Roberts (Eds.), *Policy and practice in the juvenile justice system.* Chicago: Nelson-Hall.

Federal Bureau of Investigation (FBI). (1995). *Crime in the United States.* Washington, DC: Author.

Federal Bureau of Investigation. (1996). *Crime in the United States.* Washington, DC: Author.

Federal Bureau of Investigation. (1998). *Unified crime reporting (UCR) summary system: Frequently asked questions.* Available: http://www.fbi.gov/ucr/ucrquest.

Federal Bureau of Investigation. (1999). *Crime in the United States: 1999.* Washington, DC: Author.

Fox, J. A. (1996, March). *Trends in juvenile violence: A report to the United States Attorney General on current and future rates of juvenile offending.* Washington, DC: Bureau of Justice Statistics.

Gillmore, M. R., Hawkins, J. D., Catalano, R. F., Day, L. E., & Moore, M. (1991). Structure of problem behaviors in adolescence. *Journal of Consulting and Clinical Psychology, 59*(4), 499–506.

Hawkins, J. D., Catalano, R. F., & Miller, J. Y. (1992). Risk and protective factors for alcohol and other drug problems in adolescence and early adulthood: Implications for substance abuse prevention. *Psychological Bulletin, 112*(1), 64–105.

Henggeler, S. W. (1989). *Delinquency in adolescence.* Newbury Park, CA: Sage.

Hirshi, T. (1969). *Causes of delinquency.* Berkeley, CA: University of California Press.

Howell, J. C. D. (Ed.). (1995). *Guide for implementing the comprehensive strategy for serious, violent, and chronic juvenile offenders.* Washington, DC: Office of Juvenile Justice and Delinquency Prevention.

Howell, J. C. D. (1998, August). Youth gangs: An overview. Juvenile Justice Bulletin. Washington, DC: Office of Juvenile Justice and Delinquency Prevention.

Jessor, R., & Jessor, S. E. (1977). *Problem behavior and psychosocial development: A longitudinal study of youth.* New York: Academic Press.

Johnson, R. E. (1980). Social class and delinquent behavior: A new test. *Criminology, 18,* 91–96.

Kelling, G. (1987). The historical legacy. In M. H. Moore (Ed.), *From children to citizens: Volume I* (pp. 25–48). New York: Springer-Verlag.

Krisberg, B. (1988). *The juvenile court: Reclaiming the vision.* Washington, DC: National Council on Crime and Delinquency.

Office of Juvenile Justice and Delinquency Prevention (1996, October). *Person offenses in juvenile court, 1985–1994* (Fact Sheet #48). Washington, DC: Author. (Butts, J. A.)

Patterson, G. R., DeBaryshe, B. D., & Ramsey, E. (1993). Adolescent limited and life-course anti-social behavior: A developmental taxonomy. *Psychological Review, 100,* 674–701.

Patti, R. J. (1983). *Social welfare administration: Managing social problems in a developmental context.* Englewood Cliffs, NJ: Prentice Hall.

Poe-Yamagata, E., & Butts, J. A. (1996, June). *Female offenders in the juvenile justice system: Statistics summary.* Washington, DC: Office of Juvenile Justice and Delinquency Prevention.

Schorr, L. B. (1989). *Within our reach: Breaking the cycle of disadvantage.* New York: Doubleday.

Schwartz, I. M., & Orlando, F. (1991). *Programming for young women in the juvenile justice system.* Ann Arbor, MI: Center for the Study of Youth Policy.

Sickmund, M., Stahl A. L., Finnegan, T. A., Snyder, H. N., Poole, R. S., &

Butts, J. A. (1998, May). *Juvenile Court Statistics 1995.* Washington, DC: Office of Juvenile Justice and Delinquency Prevention.

Snyder, H. N. (1999, December). Juvenile arrests 1998. *Juvenile Justice Bulletin.* Washington, DC: Office of Juvenile Justice and Delinquency Prevention.

Snyder, H. N., Sickmund, M., & Poe-Yamagata, E. P. (1996). *Juvenile offenders and victims: 1996 update on violence.* Washington, DC: Office of Juvenile Justice and Delinquency Prevention.

Torbet, P., & Szymanski, L. (1998). State legislative responses to violent juvenile crime: 1996–97 update. *Juvenile Justice Bulletin.* Washington, DC: Office of Juvenile Justice and Delinquency Prevention.

United States Department of Justice (1995, November). *The nation's two crime measures* (NCJ 122705). Washington, DC: Author. Available: http://www.ojp.usdoj.gov/bjs/pdf/ntmc.pdf.

Vega, W. A., & Gil, A. G. (1998). *Drug use and ethnicity in early adolescence.* New York: Plenum.

Weiss, F. L., Nicholson, H. J., & Cretella, M. M. (1996). *Prevention and parity: Girls in juvenile justice* (NCJ 161868). Indianapolis: Girls Incorporated.

Williams, J. H., Ayers, C. D., Abbott, R. D., Hawkins, J. D., & Catalano, R. F. (1996). Structural equivalence of involvement in problem behavior by adolescents across racial groups using multiple group confirmatory factor analysis. *Social Work Research, 20*(3), 168–177.

Wilson, J., & Howell, J. (1993). *Comprehensive strategy for serious, violent, and chronic juvenile offenders: Program summary* (NCJ 143453). Washington, DC: Office of Juvenile Justice and Delinquency Prevention.

Chapter 2

◆

Interdisciplinary Teamwork in Juvenile Justice

CHAPTER OUTLINE

Interaction with Clients
Interaction with Others in the Juvenile Justice System
Interaction with Law Enforcement Personnel
Interaction with Child Welfare Workers
Interaction with Mental Health and Substance Abuse Systems
Interaction with Educational Professionals
Interdisciplinary Cooperation and Teamwork
Summary

Practitioners in the juvenile justice system interact with a wide variety of professionals. Within the system itself are case managers, social workers, psychologists, psychiatrists, attorneys, and judges. Practitioners also interact with members of other systems, such as child welfare, law enforcement, mental health, and substance abuse. This chapter examines the way in which juvenile justice practitioners relate to other professionals in their own and other systems. First, it looks at the interaction between practitioners and their clients. Next, it examines the manner in which workers within the juvenile justice system relate to one another. Finally, it addresses the relationship between juvenile justice practitioners and professionals in other systems.

INTERACTION WITH CLIENTS

As we discussed in chapter 1, practitioners interact with clients by playing one or more of several roles. Depending on her role, the practitioner may have either a great deal of client contact, or virtually none at all. Direct service workers typically spend a great deal of their time with clients. Administrators, researchers, advocates, and advisors usually spend very little time in direct contact with clients. In this section, therefore, we will focus only on the interaction between direct practitioners and their clients.

Services

Practitioners provide five basic services to clients and their families. These services include assessment, prevention, intervention, treatment, and case management. The services performed by each practitioner depend in large part on the role the practitioner plays in the system. For instance, a social worker or psychologist who performs forensic evaluations for the court will probably provide only assessment services. A practitioner working in the truancy program of a private agency may provide assessment, prevention, intervention, treatment, or case management services.

Assessment refers to the examination of the client and his social systems to identify the problems that may contribute to his deviant behavior and the strengths that might be used to curb it. Assessment usually involves asking a series of questions about specific areas of the youth's life, such as taking family, educational, mental health, and substance abuse histories. Often, these questions are supplemented with reviews of various official and agency records. A narrative is then prepared summarizing the client's condition. The assessment questionnaire and narrative become the basis for prevention, intervention, or treatment activities, and is often used to guide judicial disposition. Assessment is often performed by social workers, psychologists, and psychiatrists.

After the assessment is completed, a plan is prepared. The plan is intended to facilitate the rehabilitation of the offender. Depending on the severity of the problem and the background of the worker, it may consist of prevention, intervention, or treatment activities.

Prevention activities are based on the risk-related factors discussed in chapter 1. In prevention planning, the worker targets the risk, need, and protective factors identified in the assessment. Her work attempts to minimize the effect of the risk factors and maximize the protective factors.

Intervention is a word that is used to describe a comprehensive approach to meeting a need or a group of needs of the client. Intervention might focus on a single area, such as school study skills. In other cases, it might be comprehensive, looking at multiple needs and strengths of the client.

Treatment is a term most frequently applied to clinical needs, such as a client with a *DSM-IV* diagnosis. It is often used in clinical settings such as adolescent psychiatric or substance abuse facilities. The term treatment is also used in other settings, and at times the distinction between intervention and treatment is not very clear.

Case management refers to the coordination of services to and on behalf of a client. Typically a case manager will identify services available in the community that can address the youth's needs and will see that the client is put in contact with those services. Often, the case manager is also responsible for determining whether those services are actually utilized.

Functions

Practitioners who provide different services perform different functions. For example, some workers provide assessment services. These individuals perform the four primary functions. They collect data from clients, interpret that data, organize the resulting information into a usable form, and communicate the information to some other individual. That individual might be a treatment

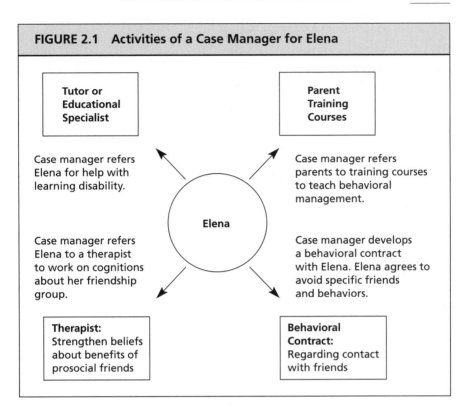

FIGURE 2.1   Activities of a Case Manager for Elena

Tutor or Educational Specialist

Parent Training Courses

Case manager refers Elena for help with learning disability.

Case manager refers parents to training courses to teach behavioral management.

Elena

Case manager refers Elena to a therapist to work on cognitions about her friendship group.

Case manager develops a behavioral contract with Elena. Elena agrees to avoid specific friends and behaviors.

Therapist: Strengthen beliefs about benefits of prosocial friends

Behavioral Contract: Regarding contact with friends

worker, a defense attorney, or a judge. Assessment personnel typically interact with clients briefly, often only for a single visit. These practitioners may work in the intake unit of the juvenile court, at private treatment programs, or as mental health evaluators for the court.

Other workers provide prevention, intervention, or treatment services to clients. These practitioners perform such functions as counseling, referral, and advocacy. In some instances, they may be required to provide information about client progress to other practitioners or the court. These workers have longer-term contact with the clients, and often come to know their families, friends, teachers, and other significant persons.

Case managers are probably the most frequent type of worker involved in direct services. These practitioners perform a very diverse and comprehensive group of functions. Their overall responsibility is seeing that the client's needs are met in an effective and timely manner while ensuring the safety of the community. Case managers may provide some services themselves, but more often they concentrate on linking clients and their families with existing resources in the community. An example of a case manager's work with Elena, the imaginary client in chapter 1, is seen in figure 2.1.

The functions of the case manager are nicely summarized by Woodside and McClam (1998). They refer to these functions as "roles," and describe them as advocate, coordinator, broker, colleague and collaborator, community organizer, consultant, counselor/therapist, evaluator, expediter, planner,

Table 2.1 Functions of a Case Manager[1]

Advocate—As an advocate a case manager becomes a voice for those who cannot speak or to whom others will not listen. For example: calling the principal of a school to ensure that a client gets a fair chance to do well in a teacher's classroom.

Broker—The case manager finds resources to meet as many needs of the client as possible, and connects the client with those resources. For example: linking a youth with weak social skills to a social skills training class and a prosocial source of activity (such as a school club or organization).

Coordinator—The case manager works with all service providers with which the client is involved to ensure service integration. For example: encouraging communication and collaboration between school personnel and a private psychologist working with a youth.

Colleague and collaborator—The skilled case manager must work closely with other professionals. For example: working cooperatively with mental health and substance abuse practitioners to ensure appropriate treatment.

Community organizer—Some case managers work with other community organizations to identify gaps in service in the community and to help develop those resources. For example: recognizing the need for a recreational program in a specific neighborhood and communicating that need to the funding arm of county government.

Consultant—A case manager with expertise in a given area may serve as an expert advisor to another worker. For example: a case manager with a child welfare background is asked to consult on a case involving a juvenile justice client in foster care.

Counselor/therapist—Sometimes the case manager provides direct counseling or therapy to the client and his family. For example: a case manager schedules one-per-week family therapy sessions to work on issues that result in family conflict.

Evaluator—A vital function in case management is assessment of the progress of the client and the effectiveness of the overall intervention. For example: using the Beck Depression Inventory to determine a 17-year-old's progress in overcoming depression.

Expediter—The case manager must sometimes help ensure that her client receives timely and effective service. For example: identifying alternative resources for a youth when the primary agency reports an extensive waiting list.

Planner—Case managers work with clients and their families to set goals, identify objectives, and specify outcomes. For example: helping a youth develop a study plan, including reviews and sample examinations, prior to sitting for the GED examination.

Problem-solver—Clients typically present with one or more problems, which case managers assist them in solving. They also attempt to help clients develop their own problem-solving skills. For example: a youth who encounters peers who encourage him to use drugs discusses ways to avoid contact and refusal skills with his case manager.

Record-keeper—Case managers must carefully document interactions with clients and providers. This facilitates future communication, case review, and judicial decision-making. For example: a case manger makes several calls on behalf of a client. She carefully documents the time, purpose, content, and outcome of each call in the client record.

Service monitor and system modifier—In order to ensure quality service, a case manager may need to affect the way in which the service system operates. This may be done through direct contact with other providers, or through interaction with her supervisor. For example: a case manager sees that many of her clients are unable to obtain medication because the psychiatrist at a provider is not available during evening hours. He brings the problem to his supervisor's attention, asking that she ask the provider to extend his hours.

Two additional functions of the juvenile justice case manager are *surveillance* and *monitoring*. These activities were discussed in greater detail in the text.

[1] The following functions were identified by Marianne Woodside and Tricia McClam (pp. 63–69). These authors used the word "role," but since that word is used in chapter 1 of this book to refer to more general combinations of activities, the term "function" has been used here.

problem-solver, record-keeper, and service monitor and system modifier. These functions are described more fully in table 2.1.

In addition to the functions described by Woodside and McClam, case managers often perform surveillance and monitoring functions with juvenile justice clients. Surveillance refers to both announced and unannounced telephone and personal contacts at home, school, work, and other sites. Its purpose is to ensure that clients are complying with the terms of their disposition. Monitoring refers to the process of ensuring that specific tasks are completed. One example of monitoring would be taking a urine sample to ensure that a drug offender has not begun to use again.

Other juvenile justice practitioners perform very specialized tasks. Psychiatrists perform mental health evaluations and dispense medication for mental and emotional disorders. Psychologists, social workers, educators, and others also perform diagnostic tasks in their areas of expertise. Any of these professionals may also provide counseling, training, or other service for clients and their families.

INTERACTION WITH OTHERS IN THE JUVENILE JUSTICE SYSTEM

In order to talk about the relationships between practitioners within the system, we must first define the system. Grisso (1998) identifies five components that he calls the most basic level of the system. Those components include (1) the laws governing the system, (2) the network of detention facilities and personnel, (3) the court system, (4) the attorneys who work within the system, and (5) the complex of treatment services that are available to delinquents.

The laws governing the system shape the system. They determine who is a juvenile, how youths are treated, procedures for processing, and guidelines for sentencing. Although most juvenile law is written at a state level, it is affected to some extent by federal laws and local ordinances. Federal laws provide broad guidelines that are made more specific by state statutes. Local ordinances often affect status offenses, such as curfew violations. All these rules are further clarified by case law, that is, instances where judges have made decisions about how to apply statutes to individual cases (del Carmen et al., 1998; Grisso, 1998).

Practitioners at every level work with law. Direct practitioners must comply with statutes in their interaction with clients. They must also be aware of these statutes as they are interpreted in the state's administrative code and their agency policies and procedures manuals.

Administrators work with laws by ensuring that agency policies and procedures comply with statutes. They also are given specific guidelines regarding the daily operation of their agencies and appropriate distribution of government funds both inside and outside the agency. Administrators may also provide feedback to legislators regarding proposed changes to legislation.

Advocates and advisors interact with the law by recommending revisions to current statutes, or attempting to force reluctant agencies to comply with important regulations. Advisors, for example, may be involved in committees formed by the governor or the legislature to draft proposed changes to legislation.

An advocate might telephone the head of a local agency that was refusing to comply with regulations. If unsuccessful, she might then go to a state legislator or to the press to attempt to compel compliance.

Evaluators and other researchers interact with the system of laws primarily by providing information needed to inform statute revisions, programming decisions, and funding distributions. A program evaluator, for instance, might examine the effectiveness of various programs to see which the state might require to be implemented. Another researcher might examine the process by which juveniles are detained, processed, and disposed, to identify reasons for the overrepresentation of black males in the system. Her findings might be used to develop legislation to correct this inequity.

The law gives the juvenile justice system its shape, but it also creates considerable diversity. Since the bulk of the law is created by each state, many differences exist between jurisdictions. This makes it very difficult to make specific statements that will apply to every jurisdiction. Certain characteristics are reasonably common, however. These commonalities are the focus of the next section. They include practitioners in state youth agencies, attorneys, the court system, and private providers.

Interaction with Juvenile Justice
Workers in State Agencies

Practitioners in state agencies perform many different tasks. Usually, they have primary responsibility for supervising and processing the clients who enter the system. Although there are many different positions within state agencies, basic categories of work responsibility are common to many jurisdictions. Some of those categories are case managers, detention personnel, treatment facility staff, supervisors and administrators, budgetary staff, quality assurance workers, legal personnel, and state-level support staff.

A large number of practitioners in the juvenile justice system are case managers. These workers are responsible for the day-to-day treatment and supervision of committed juveniles. In large part, their activities focus on ensuring that youths make appropriate contact with other practitioners. The activities of case managers are described in greater detail in the section above and in table 2.1.

Detention centers refer to those facilities designed to confine a juvenile under several circumstances: (1) prior to the initial adjudicatory hearing, (2) prior to disposition, or (3) prior to the implementation of the disposition (Regoli & Hewitt, 1997). They are secure facilities, meaning that there are physical measures such as locks and bars to prevent youth from escaping (del Carmen et al., 1998). These centers may be operated by state personnel or contracted to private providers. Detention facilities are often the offender's first point of contact with the juvenile justice system following arrest. Its role as an entry point makes detention a primary point of interaction between juvenile justice and law enforcement.

Detention centers have several different kinds of workers: secretarial staff, staff assigned to supervise the confined youth, and supervisory and administrative personnel. These staff normally have limited contact with other members of the juvenile justice system. Case managers may pick up a youth from the facility, or provide services to a youth who is there awaiting disposition. Some private providers provide counseling and educational services to detained youth. Agency administrators may interact with direct workers or detention administrators on behalf of individual youth or to improve interaction between agencies.

Treatment facilities employ many different types of workers. Some are responsible for supervising the daily activities of youth, such as recreation, education, and mealtime. Often workers in these positions have little clinical background and are hoping to gain sufficient experience to become employed as clinicians. Other workers perform therapeutic tasks, such as individual and group counseling, family counseling, and social skills training. Treatment facilities also need administrators.

Treatment facilities also vary in intensity and level of confinement. *Outpatient* programs provide counseling to individuals and families for between one and several hours per week. They are nonsecure and typically treat those who have committed offenses of lesser severity. *Day treatment* programs work with more frequent and severe offenders, providing daylong activities such as counseling, recreation, and education. Youths in these programs typically return home in the evenings. *Residential treatment* programs require that the youths actually live within the facility and feature varying levels of security, from "staff secure" or minimum security to "facility secure" or lockdown facilities. These programs usually serve the most severe and frequent offenders (Champion, 1998; Henggeler, 1989).

Depending on their level of management, administrators in treatment facilities may have both clinical and supervisory duties. Others devote all their time to the operation of the facility. Management duties often include such activities as scheduling, recruiting, hiring and training of personnel, interaction with outside agencies, and budget management. As with detention facilities, treatment centers may be state-run, or contracted to private providers.

Administrators interact with case managers and others with varying frequency depending on the level at which the administrator works. Those who supervise small staffs may interact daily or weekly with their employees. These interactions might consist of clinical supervision, discussion of agency or community resources, or consultation regarding personnel-related issues. Typically, the more employees supervised by an administrator, the less contact she has with either clients or direct workers. Higher-level administrators tend to spend a great deal of their time in meetings with other administrators.

The juvenile justice system also includes workers who manage budgets and agency finances. These workers also often handle payroll. Sometimes budgetary workers are trained in accounting. Others have basic accounting skills, and provide the results of their work to accountants or internal controllers for periodic review and processing. Interaction between direct service workers and budgetary personnel is relatively infrequent. Budgetary workers often interact with higher-level administrators, however, since their knowledge is critical for programming and planning.

Quality assurance (QA) personnel often work either for state agencies evaluating internal programs or programs operated by providers with state funds. These workers share some functions with evaluators, but their functions differ in several important ways. Evaluators usually focus on outcome; that is, they want to know whether the client's condition has improved as a result of intervention. QA personnel have some interest in outcome, but are also interested in process. Process refers to number of clients served, appropriateness of services delivered, compliance with agency policy, and client satisfaction. QA personnel are also less likely than evaluators to use experimental design and multiple measures.

Agencies also may employ legal personnel, either on-staff or contractually. A very large agency, such as a state youth authority, may have one or several employees who are attorneys. Others may contract with independent attorneys to provide specific services. Administrators most often interact with legal personnel when considering the degree to which plans or agency actions comply with statutes. Direct service workers interact with agency attorneys on individual cases, particularly in cases involving a dependency petition.

State youth agencies are often subdivided by region. A state-level staff provides either advice or supervision to regional staff. State-level staffs face multiple concerns on both the management and policy level. Direct service workers rarely interact with state-level personnel. Administrators within government agencies do so with varying frequency depending on their level and function. Administrators in private agencies typically communicate with state-level personnel on specific projects or as a part of state-level advisory committees.

Interaction with Guardians ad Litem and Attorneys for Youth

In some systems youth may be represented by one of three kinds of workers: guardians ad litem, attorneys ad litem, and attorneys employed by the offender or his family. These workers are involved at different points in the process, particularly in dependency-related cases and when juveniles face the potential for transfer to adult court (del Carmen et al., 1998). These terms are used differently in various states. Florida, for example, refers to paraprofessional volunteers as guardians ad litem. In some other states this title is used only for volunteer attorneys. In yet other states these attorneys are referred to as "court appointed special advocates."

Guardians ad litem are usually volunteers who work primarily within the dependency system. The *dependency* system is that branch of the juvenile court that attempts to protect children from abusive and neglectful families. In some jurisdictions judges hear both delinquency and dependency cases. In other areas, the two are separate.

The task of the *guardian ad litem* is to represent the interest of the child. This may be done in court, in interactions with private agencies, and at other points within the child welfare system. When a case involves a child who is dependent, the guardian ad litem may become involved. If so, her role will be to see that the child's rights and interests are protected as much as possible. She will want to see that the youth is protected from abuse and neglect, is adequately cared for, and has all his needs met, whether emotional, physical, psychological, or educational. Workers may encounter guardians in multidisciplinary planning sessions (discussed in detail below), through personal contact, or in court. Many guardians are very aggressive in their role. Despite the fact that juvenile proceedings are theoretically nonadversarial, many guardians become very animated in their efforts to protect children.

Attorneys ad litem are sometimes assigned by judges to represent children in either dependency or delinquency proceedings. These attorneys are responsible for protecting the legal rights of the children, to ensure that they are maintained in a safe environment and that the state acts responsibly on their behalf. Workers may encounter these attorneys under the same circumstances as guardians ad litem. Practitioners may also encounter attorneys who have been hired or appointed to defend youth who are facing possible transfer to criminal court. Under such circumstances the practitioner may have personal communication with the attorney, or may be questioned by the attorney in court. Guidelines for interacting with attorneys are provided in box 2.1.

Interaction with the Juvenile Court

Many of the decisions made regarding the fate of juvenile offenders are made in court. Once a youth has been arrested, or has been determined to be in need of services through "*intake*," judges determine process, treatment, and punishment. This section discusses various routes a youth may take through the system. It also describes the services that direct practitioners may provide at various points in the system.

It is important to note that many juvenile offenders are diverted from the system by law enforcement agencies. These juveniles are usually given referrals to community resources that provide assessment and intervention services. Other juveniles are diverted at intake or at other points in their interaction with the court.

Involvement with the juvenile court begins either soon after a youth is arrested or at the point of intake into the system. Arrested youth must appear before a judge for an adjudicatory hearing within 48 to 72 hours (depending on the state) after detention (del Carmen et al., 1998). Depending on the jurisdiction, police may refer a youth to either the intake division of the court or to the prosecutor's office for processing.

Some youths are referred to the court through schools, parents, or other sources. These juveniles go through intake without the initial involvement of law enforcement. Normally, these youths have committed less serious offenses, such as running away or truancy.

Intake workers must decide whether to dismiss the case, release the youth to her parents, or refer the youth to prosecutors (Champion, 1998). Juveniles who are released to parents may also receive referrals to counseling or other resources. This process is known as diversion. Diversionary alternatives exist at several points in the system, including at the point of arrest, at intake, and at adjudication.

Box 2.1 Guidelines for Interacting with Attorneys and the Court
Andrea L. Moore, Esq.

The process and language of the courts can often seem mysterious or intimidating to the new professional. Understanding what is happening and why can increase your effectiveness in communicating with the court. It can help you avoid the misunderstandings that sometimes confuse and intimidate new workers. The following five situations often form barriers to effective communication between caseworkers and the courts.

SITUATION 1

Too often professionals who appear in court are not trained in courtroom procedures or techniques. They may even lack a rudimentary knowledge of the legal system. The problem is compounded when overburdened prosecutors or public defenders do not have the time to adequately prepare each witness. If the first few court appearances are uncomfortable for the witness (in this case, a caseworker), it can set a pattern that may render the caseworker resistant and defensive in court and weaken the impact of her testimony. The following example illustrates the type of communication that may cause problems for the unprepared caseworker.

Attorney: "When did you last see the child?"
Case manager: "I had contact with the family just yesterday."
Attorney: "When did you last have contact with the child?"
Case manager: "The caregiver has kept me informed. We talk at least once a week."
Attorney: "When did you last have contact with the child?"
Case manager: "Your honor, do I have to keep answering the same question?

He is being rude to me just like he was outside the courtroom."
Attorney: "Your honor, move to strike the unprofessional outburst as nonresponsive. It is a simple question. Please instruct the witness to answer the question that was asked. Her outburst is wasting the time of the court. If she continues, she should be sanctioned or subject to being found in contempt of court."

The case manager in this example didn't listen to the question asked by the attorney. She appeared defensive and uncooperative, weakening her credibility with the court and others present. If she keeps it up, on this question or others, the court could threaten to hold her in contempt.

Human service professionals need to remember that the legal system is set up as an adversary model. Even though the juvenile justice system is intended to be nonadversarial, some of the characteristics of the system as a whole are sometimes reflected in the juvenile court. The attorneys each have clients with a particular point of view. Attorneys have a duty to zealously protect the interests of their client. They may scrap in court and be best friends out of court. The attorneys recognize that this is the way the system works. An uninformed observer or participant may be upset by the process.

SITUATION 2

The simple process of being sworn in as a witness is routine to attorneys, but sends an intimidating message to caseworkers: "If you aren't sworn, we can't rely on you to be truthful. If you aren't precise, your liberty could be at stake."

The swearing in of witnesses is meant to caution the person who might not otherwise tell the truth. All witnesses are sworn so that there is no appearance of discrimination against any one witness.

SITUATION 3

Attorneys need facts to prove a case. Caseworkers sometimes have difficulties distinguishing between facts and their own interpretations. Contrast the two answers below:

Answer #1

Attorney: "How did Mr. Smith appear?"
Caseworker: "He was angry."
Attorney: "Objection, your honor, calls for a conclusion by the witness. There are no facts offered to support the conclusion."
Judge: "Objection sustained."

Answer #2

Attorney: "How did Mr. Smith appear?"
Case Worker: "His face was red. He was raising his voice. He raised his hand and was gesturing and pointing while he was talking. He moved toward me in a manner that made me fearful he would strike me. I thought he was angry and not in control of his anger."

The second answer would be admissible because it contains facts observed by the witness and describes the witness's state of mind as created by Mr. Smith. The second answer carries more impact with a court or a jury. It takes longer. It requires a particular approach by the professional that may not be a part of her training, but it is the way of the legal system.

Expert witnesses may offer their opinions. Fact witnesses may not. Unless you are qualified as an expert witness by the court, you will be a fact witness, entitled only to offer facts based on first-hand knowledge.

Caseworkers may gather statements of others to form opinions that guide their actions. However, in a court of law these statements may not be offered for the truth of the matter or substance of the statements. In our legal system, the best person to testify is the person who made the statement so that he or she can be cross-examined on what was said. Hearsay (reporting the words of another) is not allowed in a court of law unless there is some special reason, such as admission of a bad act or crime. Let the lawyers worry about hearsay and exceptions. Caseworkers can help the process by sticking to facts within their personal knowledge.

SITUATION 4

Caseworkers generally focus on the present and the future. Lawyers generally look to the past for precedent in similarly decided cases and applicable laws. These differing approaches may contribute to a communication problem between the professionals.

SITUATION 5

Problems may also arise between caseworkers and the legal system when the caseworker wants to provide information to the court or others and doesn't know the prohibition on ex parte communication. Judges cannot talk about a particular case outside the courtroom or without all parties present. Even a simple letter or report must be provided according to the rules and made available to all parties, not just to the judge.

(continued)

Box 2.1 Guidelines for Interacting with Attorneys and the Court
   (*continued*)

SITUATION 6

Court orders to produce information to the court operate as subpoenas or releases of information. Problems sometimes arise when workers do not understand the function and nature of court orders. These orders are much like cement: the time to cure problems is

before an order is issued. The time to appeal is before the order becomes final. Once it is final, even an order with which the caseworker disagrees must be followed. Judges and lawyers use words like contempt frequently. If you conduct yourself in good faith and with respect to the court, you will not be subject to a contempt proceeding.

In this scenario, the intake worker is a juvenile justice practitioner either appointed by the court or employed by the state youth authority. Similarly, a youth who receives a referral to counseling is likely to see a practitioner employed by a private agency. These workers provide assessment or evaluation services, as will be described more thoroughly in chapter 3.

Youths who are arrested are also referred to the prosecutor's office. Here, variables related to the offense, the arrest, and the youth's background are reviewed and a decision is made about prosecution. Prosecutors have three alternatives: (1) charges may be dropped, (2) a delinquency petition may be filed, or (3) the youth may be transferred to criminal court.

If the prosecutor's office decides to pursue the case, a delinquency petition is filed with the juvenile court. When the youth is to be tried as an adult, the prosecutor may use one of several mechanisms depending on statute and circumstances. The options for transfer of juveniles to criminal court are discussed in table 2.2.

When a delinquency petition is filed with the juvenile court, it results in an adjudicatory hearing. At this hearing, a decision is made as to whether "proof beyond a reasonable doubt" exists that the youth committed the offense in question. If the judge determines that such proof exists, he schedules a dispositional hearing. At that hearing he may exercise one of several disposition options. His choice often depends on information gathered by a juvenile justice worker in a document called a predispositional report (PDR).

A PDR is provided to the judge prior to the dispositional hearing to help him make decisions regarding appropriate services for the offender. PDRs typically include such information as nature of the offense, developmental history, legal history, school history, family history, substance abuse history, and mental health history.

According to Champion (1998), judges have three categories of dispositional options: nominal, conditional, and custodial. Nominal dispositions consist of verbal reprimands and release into the custody of parents or guardians. Such dispositions are normally for first-time offenders and those who engage in minor offenses. Other youth may receive conditional or custodial dispositions.

Table 2.2 Transferring Juveniles to Criminal Court

Transfer Classifications	Definition
Discretionary Waiver	A juvenile court judge may waive jurisdiction and transfer the case to criminal court typically based on factors outlined in the *Kent* v. *United States* [383 U.S. 541 (1996): 566–67] decision.
Mandatory Waiver	A juvenile court judge must waive jurisdiction if probable cause exists that the juvenile committed the alleged offense.
Presumptive Waiver	The burden of proof concerning a transfer decision is shifted from the state to the juvenile. Requires that certain juveniles be waived to criminal court unless they can prove they are suited to juvenile rehabilitation.
Direct File	The prosecutor decides which court will have jurisdiction over a case when both the juvenile and criminal courts have concurrent jurisdiction. Also known as prosecutor discretion or concurrent jurisdiction.
Statutory Exclusion	Certain juvenile offenders are automatically excluded from the juvenile court's original jurisdiction. Also known as legislative exclusion or automatic transfer.
Reverse Waiver	A criminal court judge is allowed to transfer "excluded" or "direct filed" cases from criminal court to juvenile court for adjudication.
Once an Adult / Always an Adult	Once a juvenile is convicted in criminal court, all subsequent cases involving that juvenile will be under criminal court jurisdiction.

SOURCE: OJJDP, November, 1998, p. 3

Conditional dispositions place the youth on probationary status, usually under the supervision of the state youth authority. The juvenile returns to her home, but is required to participate in various programs or treatment alternatives. She might also reside in her home, but be required to spend her days in a day treatment program. In addition, she might experience curfew restrictions, electronic monitoring, drug testing, and scheduled and unscheduled visitation.

Custodial dispositions include incarceration in facilities of various levels of security. Some facilities make little effort to confine a youth who is determined to leave. Foster homes, some group homes, and camp ranches fall into this category (Champion, 1998). Others make varying levels of effort to confine a juvenile. These include "staff secure," where staff may attempt to dissuade or restrain a youth, and "facility secure," where buildings are locked and barred. Theoretically, only the most severe cases should be assigned to high-security settings. Unfortunately, some researchers estimate that as many as 50% of the youth in secure facilities were inappropriately placed (Butts & DeMuro, 1989). There are various explanations for this discrepancy, such as inappropriate judicial disposition and racial prejudice (Champion, 1998). Some of these explanations will be discussed in greater detail in chapter 10.

Table 2.3 Basic Juvenile Court Terminology

Term	Definition
Respondent	The juvenile accused of an offense
Intake	Initial processing point for many delinquents; decisions made whether to pursue case
Petition	The document filed with the court to allege delinquent acts
Hearing	An official appearance before a judge; may be adjudicatory, dispositional, or status
Adjudication	The process of deciding whether a youth committed the alleged offense
Finding	The court's decision, equivalent of verdict in criminal court
Disposition	The decision as to the consequences and treatment for the youth

Juveniles who receive conditional and custodial dispositions often have periodic reviews by the court. Practitioners who supervise the youth report to the court on their progress. They also make recommendations as to whether sanctions should be diminished, maintained, intensified, or discontinued. The court then decides which alternative to implement.

Youths who are released from the court's supervision may be offered voluntary or mandatory aftercare services. When services are mandatory, they really represent a form of parole, since the court maintains control through the practitioner. When they are voluntary, a youth is offered the opportunity to participate, and may be encouraged to do so. The court will take no action, however, should she choose not to comply.

Practitioners interact with the court in many ways. They serve as advisors for adjudicatory and dispositional decisions. They report on the offender's progress and compliance with the court's orders. They also may serve as a locator and a conduit for the expertise of mental health and substance abuse professionals.

Given the variety and importance of the roles of practitioners, it is clear that their ability to communicate with the court is very important. Unfortunately, many have problems in their interactions with the court. A basic list of court terminology is presented in table 2.3. An understanding of the structure of the court is also important. A diagram showing a simplified version of the path of a juvenile through the court is provided in figure 2.2.

Workers should be familiar with the basic terminology of both the legal and the law enforcement systems. They should also have good writing skills, since they prepare such documents as PDRs and other offender-management tools. They will also be required to present written progress reports at hearings. It is absolutely vital that the worker be totally honest with the court at all times. It is better, for example, to admit that tasks were forgotten and to promise rapid completion than to be dishonest. Serious consequences (including perjury charges) have resulted when practitioners failed to be forthcoming in court.

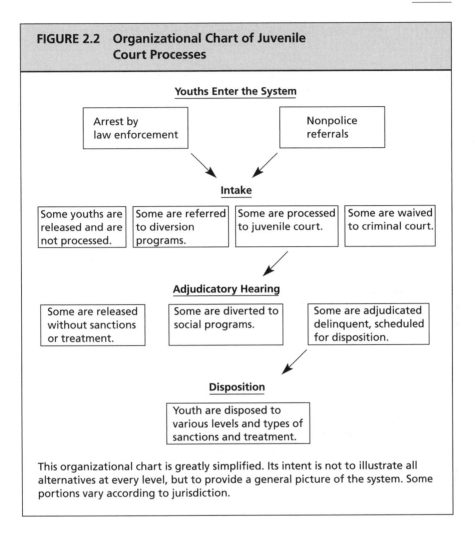

FIGURE 2.2   Organizational Chart of Juvenile Court Processes

Youths Enter the System

| Arrest by law enforcement | | Nonpolice referrals |

Intake

| Some youths are released and are not processed. | Some are referred to diversion programs. | Some are processed to juvenile court. | Some are waived to criminal court. |

Adjudicatory Hearing

| Some are released without sanctions or treatment. | Some are diverted to social programs. | Some are adjudicated delinquent, scheduled for disposition. |

Disposition

| Youth are disposed to various levels and types of sanctions and treatment. |

This organizational chart is greatly simplified. Its intent is not to illustrate all alternatives at every level, but to provide a general picture of the system. Some portions vary according to jurisdiction.

Interaction with Service Providers

Service providers who contract with the state to provide treatment and supervision services are also an important part of the system. Practitioners from the state youth authority interact with them in several capacities. Direct service workers broker services for clients, and may speak with assessment or treatment workers at their facilities. (Assessment in many private agencies is also called "intake" because it refers to the process of taking the youth into the facility. This is distinct from the term "intake" as it is used in the juvenile court.) They may also serve as mediators or advocates for clients when services are not being properly utilized or delivered. They may serve on multidisciplinary teams that plan treatment strategies. These teams will be discussed in greater detail in the last section of this chapter.

State administrators may interact with providers to purchase or monitor service delivery. They may also work with them to establish successful resource

Table 2.4 Basic Mental Health and Substance Abuse Terminology

Term	Definition
Psychopathology	The study of mental or emotional disorders. The term is also used to refer to specific disorders (e.g., "The juvenile evidenced significant psychopathology.")
Psychotherapy	The process of treating mental or emotional disorders through a verbal interaction between client and therapist
Disorder	A mental or emotional condition that significantly inhibits the psychological or social functioning of an individual
Exacerbate	The worsening of the symptoms of a disorder
Defense mechanism	A method by which a client diverts attention from his symptoms or condition during therapy
Pharmacotherapy	Treating a disorder with medication

networks in a community. Finally, they may serve in an advisory capacity to a provider or to a consortium of providers.

For interacting with service providers, a knowledge of rudimentary mental health and substance abuse terminology will be helpful. A few basic terms are listed in table 2.4. Several helpful publications are available from the National Institute on Mental Health and the National Institute on Drug Abuse.

INTERACTION WITH LAW ENFORCEMENT PERSONNEL

The law enforcement system is the most frequent point of contact for most youths who enter the juvenile justice system (Kratcoski & Kratcoski, 1995). Juvenile offenders may come to the attention of police through citizen complaints or through direct observation of the youth's behavior. When deviant acts are suspected or recognized, police may choose to ignore the youths, stop them for further questioning, or make an arrest. Actually, these choices can be further divided into six categories, identified by Champion (1998). These categories of choice are (1) ignoring behaviors they observe that are not the source of citizen complaints; (2) providing a warning to offenders; (3) taking juveniles into custody, then releasing them to their guardians; (4) taking juveniles into custody, then referring them to community resources for treatment in the custody of their parents; (5) taking youth into custody, filing charges, then processing them to intake (where they may be detained or released); and (6) taking youth into custody, filing charges that require processing as an adult, then placing them in adult facilities. Juvenile justice practitioners may be involved at several points in this process.

Practitioners often interact with law enforcement officers when police exercise option 4. Some police departments hire practitioners who work on staff to make referrals to community agencies and provide a limited amount of direct service. Others refer to case management programs specifically designed to handle offenders diverted by law enforcement. An example of such a program

---

Box 2.2   Police Referral Outreach/Intervention Program (PROP)

Bernadette Brown, MSW, Broward County
Commission on Substance Abuse

The Police Referral Outreach/Intervention Program (PROP) was founded in 1991 as a partnership between the Hollywood (Florida) Police Department (HPD), the Broward County Commission on Substance Abuse (BCCOSA), and The Starting Place (TSP). It was originally conceived as an early intervention program that would receive referrals from police officers regarding children who were recognized as being at risk for developing substance abuse problems. Officers would refer these youths who associated with delinquents or who committed specific status offenses to PROP rather than detaining them. PROP's high rate of success soon led to referrals of more serious offenders and to partnerships with other police departments.

Police officers who recognize at-risk youth complete a brief form containing contact information for each youth. PROP staff make contact within 48 hours and attempt to schedule an appointment within 72 hours after that. Participation is voluntary.

PROP counselors deliver a range of services to the juveniles and families who accept their services. Services include in-home individual and family counseling, referral for evaluation and treatment, linkage to sources of "concrete" services, and recreational activities. Counselors also do a limited amount of monitoring through contact with the juvenile and significant others.

PROP has served over 1,000 children since its inception. Its small size and limited budget have precluded formal scientific evaluation, but the HPD credits a 70% reduction in the recidivism rate among runaways to the PROP program.

---

is the Police Referral Outreach/Intervention Program (PROP) in Broward County, Florida. The PROP program is described in greater detail in box 2.2.

Practitioners also interact with law enforcement when the arresting officer uses option 5. Intake workers receive referrals from officers, then gather information to help make the decision regarding adjudication. A part of the information gathering is obtaining information from the officer about the circumstances of the arrest. The officer may also have some knowledge of the youth's home life or peer group. Detention officers may also interact with law enforcement if officers provide transportation to the facility. Detention workers need information on the youth's potential danger to self or others and any special needs she may have. A detention worker describes his work in box 2.3.

When communicating with law enforcement, it is important that practitioners be concise, direct, and to the point. Officers are trained to communicate in this manner, and appreciate others who express themselves similarly. It is also important to remember that the primary mission of law enforcement is protection of society, a somewhat different goal from successful intervention. Consequently, the motivations of officers may differ from those of practitioners. Additional tips on effective interaction with law enforcement personnel are included in box 2.4. An example of an effective partnership between law enforcement and juvenile justice practitioners is described in box 2.2.

Box 2.3   Life Story: Interview with a Detention Worker

Bernadette Brown, MSW

This interview was conducted at the Broward Detention Center (DC) in Fort Lauderdale, Florida. The DC is divided into four sections: B1, B2, B3, and G1. Each section is segregated by sex and by age. For example, B1 contains males ages 14 to 16. G1 is for girls between 6 and 18. Under special circumstances, young adults can be kept at the DC, but are isolated from the juvenile population. Detainees are placed at the DC because of a variety of charges. The most common charge is possession of drugs with the intent to sell.

Detainees are rotated within the facility daily to decrease "networking" with other detainees. Networking occurs when detainees' friends, associates, or family members socialize and bond with each other. This may lead to conducting illegal activities together or discussing the best illegal practices.

Nathaniel Green is a 30-year-old African-American male who is a detention center worker (DCW) II. Mr. Green's educational background includes a high school diploma and Department of Juvenile Justice training. He also has 12 years in the United States Army and has occupied administrative positions at the local health department. Detention workers are divided into two positions: DCW I, who maintain the security, health, and overall welfare of the detainees; and DCW II, a supervisory position of DCW I employees. Mr. Green has been a DCW for three years.

What Mr. Green likes most about his job is one-on-one contact with the detainees. He feels like a "big brother" or a mentor for them. He feels a strong sense of accomplishment from being able to model and teach appropriate behaviors to the juveniles he serves. He also reports enjoying the experience he gains working with youth, since juvenile delinquency is a difficult and persistent issue in social services. He believes that there is good future for workers in this area.

The least favorite aspect of Mr. Green's job is staffing problems. Low salaries and difficult working conditions sometimes make it hard to retain employees. Mr. Green reported that the average salaries of a DCW I and DCW II are $22,000 and $25,000, respectively. These salary levels not only impact the services delivered but may also affect staff morale. Low morale may lead to security problems. Workers may become relaxed and develop inappropriate relationships with detainees. Mr. Green reports that when rapport builds between a detainee and security staff, staff awareness and professionalism may decrease. Supervisors compensate through consistent training and active supervision.

When asked what improvements he would like see made at the DC, Mr. Green discussed three areas: staffing, the facility, and salary. He said that staff is vital to effective, secure service. Mr. Green underscored the importance of professional interactions with detainees and strict adherence to the rules. Second, Mr. Green would improve the facility. The center is more than 20 years old and has not been modernized. This sometimes creates security problems. For example, a group of detainees was able to escape due to a weak foundation in one area. Mr. Green also believes that sufficient salaries would decrease the current high turnover rate and boost the morale, loyalty, and professionalism of the staff.

Mr. Green has seen a number of difficult cases during his years at the DC. The most disturbing cases he has seen include a 6-year-old male charged with aggravated sexual offense against a young female and a 10-year-old male charged with aggravated battery against a 70-year-old woman.

The most positive case Mr. Green has experienced involved a 15-year-old African-American male, who was detained for dealing crack cocaine. The two developed a positive relationship during the youth's confinement and remained in contact after the juvenile was released. The youth is now 19 years old, working two jobs, and looking toward a much brighter future.

Box 2.4 Communicating with Law Enforcement

Perry S. Turner, Inspector General
Florida Department of Juvenile Justice
Chief of Police (retired),
South Miami Police Department

As an individual who has spent over 25 years in the criminal justice system, over 20 years in law enforcement, and the last 5 years in the juvenile justice arena, I say welcome to the most challenging facet of the criminal justice system: juvenile justice. As a juvenile justice professional, it is absolutely paramount that you develop a rapport with law enforcement officers. In developing this rapport, keep in mind what I call the three "C's" of success. They are communication, cooperation, and commitment.

COMMUNICATION

The best way to develop a rapport is to communicate, especially in person, with law enforcement personnel. Volunteer to ride with them so you can develop a one-on-one relationship. Be prepared to offer them assistance by bringing with you information on juvenile justice offenders that may be in their particular zone or grid. In addition, make available to them a list of juvenile justice programs such as diversion, intervention, prevention, after-school programs, and other relevant programs in your community. Your willingness to go the extra mile, so to speak, will bring you great rewards with your offer to share and assist in helping them do their jobs.

COOPERATION

Juvenile justice is a cooperative partnership effort. All the partners must work together and share information actively. The information accumulated by law enforcement personnel is absolutely vital to you and the other members of the juvenile justice system. Without that information, it may be difficult to help the juveniles with whom you work to reach their goals and objectives.

In dealing with law enforcement officers, it is especially important that you stress your commitment to public safety. Officers should be aware of the presence of the serious habitual offenders you supervise and should be given any other information relevant to protecting the public. Offer them your contact numbers: phone pager, radio numbers, or anything else that may be pertinent, so you can be of assistance

(*continued*)

Box 2.4 Communicating with Law Enforcement (*continued*)

to them in a cooperative effort. By establishing a rapport of communication and cooperation, you will see a domino effect among other law enforcement personnel. When problems or issues arise, they will be more likely to contact you first because of trust and your earnest desire to assist.

COMMITMENT

You will find law enforcement personnel share your commitment to ensuring that crime is reduced and quality of life improved for everyone in the communities they serve. This is the most important factor in shaping the mission and goals of law enforcement agencies. Commitment requires consistent and continual communication with law enforcement. You should touch base with officers at least weekly, so that the flow of communication, cooperation, and commitment can be maintained. Encourage other juvenile justice professionals to follow your example. Help to communicate an understanding that "we are all in this together." Someone once said "none of us are as smart as all of us together." Using this philosophy of the collective "we" will go a long way to ensuring your success with your law enforcement partners. Law enforcement is moving toward establishing community policing as a cornerstone of the delivery of modern-day services. You, as a professional and as a member

of your community, can play a vital and critical role in ensuring the success of your clients, the success of law enforcement agencies, and the success of the community.

In the juvenile justice arena, we have the opportunity to change the lives and attitudes of troubled youths on the front end. We can divert them from a life of crime, in all probability with a much higher success rate than in the adult system. Young people should be absolutely certain that if they are involved in criminal activity, they will be apprehended and that the consequences will be swift and sure. However, many at-risk or wayward youths can be helped and put on the right track. Effective communication, cooperation, and commitment by and between practitioners and law enforcement are keys to the process.

In the past, many states handled juvenile justice through a social services agency. Today approximately half of the 50 states have an autonomous Department of Juvenile Justice or similar agency. More states are joining this trend to address juvenile justice issues. This new movement provides greater credibility for juvenile justice, particularly in the eyes of law enforcement. It is likely that at least a part of your career will be in an agency such as this.

My best wishes to you as you enter into this most challenging and rewarding facet of our criminal justice system.

INTERACTION WITH CHILD
WELFARE WORKERS

The child welfare system is closely related to the juvenile justice system. In some states, the systems operate separately; in others they are a part of the same agency. In some jurisdictions, separate courts operate under the same statutes, but hear the cases separately.

Child welfare refers to that system that attempts to protect children from abuse, neglect, and abandonment. Federal laws establish broad guidelines, which are, in turn, made more specific by states. State statutes define abuse, neglect, abandonment, and risk (a condition sufficient to justify removal in some jurisdictions). They also specify conditions for which a child may be removed from a home, the process that is to be used for removal, and the processes and conditions for the children's disposition.

Child welfare workers and juvenile justice workers most often interact when a child is both dependent and delinquent, or is being considered for either disposition. When both workers are employed by the same agency, the situation is simplified. In jurisdictions where separate organizations manage child welfare and juvenile justice, interactions may become more complex.

One potential problem has to do with primary supervision of the client. The primary goals of the two systems are somewhat different. Child welfare personnel investigate allegations of abuse, neglect, and abandonment, and facilitate responses according to their findings. Allegations may be judged to be unfounded, which means that there is insufficient evidence to conclude that abusive conditions exist. Such investigations are closed with no further action. When problems are found, but the problems are insufficient to justify removal of the child, the family is offered services to improve conditions. When problems are severe, or the risk is great, children are removed from the home and receive one of three types of services: (1) support for improving the home and returning children to the parents; (2) support for the child along with adoption planning; and (3) support for the child in developing a competent, independent lifestyle. The selection of service type is guided by an overarching mandate: the primacy of the family and efforts to preserve it.

Juvenile justice workers have a different primary mandate. Their goal is the habilitation of the offender with sufficient support and supervision to allow that person to develop and maintain a prosocial lifestyle. They also are responsible for helping to protect the public from further delinquent acts.

The goals of the two types of workers are not inherently conflicting, but may be discordant in certain circumstances. For example, imagine a situation in which a child welfare worker believes that a formerly abusive family is capable of regaining custody of a child in an environment that is otherwise questionable. The juvenile justice practitioner may oppose this move because of neighborhood or peer influences that might negatively impact the child.

In communicating with child welfare personnel, the juvenile justice practitioner should be cognizant of the philosophical differences between the systems. She should also be familiar with the language of child welfare (examples are included in table 2.5) and particularly aware of any terms that are shared by

Table 2.5 Child Welfare Terminology

Term	Definition
Abuse	Injury or harm to a child by a caregiver that was not accidental
Neglect	Harm or risk of harm to a child when the caregiver fails to meet the child's fundamental needs
Abandonment	Ceasing to provide supervision and, in some cases, breaking off contact with a child
Risk	When conditions are such in the home that the probability of child maltreatment is very high
Foster care	Substitute homes for dependent children who are in government care and custody
Adoption	The legal process of becoming parent to a child whose biological parents' rights have been terminated

the systems but are used differently. The two share a concern for the well-being of the child. This commonality should be emphasized.

INTERACTION WITH MENTAL HEALTH AND SUBSTANCE ABUSE SYSTEMS

The mental health and substance abuse treatment networks are groups of government and private providers funded through federal, state, and local sources. The mental health network treats individuals and families with specific mental and emotional problems. Examples of people with mental health issues include a woman with schizophrenia or a family with an adolescent displaying the symptoms of conduct disorder.

Mental health agencies typically provide individual, family, and group counseling in outpatient, day treatment, residential, and community settings. They also normally offer psychiatric services either on-premises or through contracts with local providers. They may also contract with the court or with the youth authority to provide mental health evaluations for several purposes. These evaluations are discussed in greater detail in chapter 3.

Many mental health agencies receive the majority of their funding through the federal government. Some are the designated "community mental health center" for a specific geographical area. This geographical area is referred to as a "catchment" area (Thackeray, Skidmore, & Farley, 1979).

Juvenile justice workers may interact with the mental health system at several points during a youth's processing. These points include intake, preparation of the predispositional or other reports to the court, and treatment. Usually, the mental health professional will either conduct a mental health evaluation or administer some sort of treatment to the youth. Sometimes, when a youth has a sufficiently severe mental health problem, he may be committed to a psychiatric facility. In such cases the courts often order continued supervision by the case manager.

The mental health profession (like the other systems discussed here) has a language of its own. Although it is not likely that the practitioner will need to learn all mental health terminology, a basic familiarity can be critical. Many of

Table 2.6 Commonly Used Drugs and Their Street Names

Drug	Street Names	Signs and Symptoms
Alcohol	Booze	Rapid mood changes
	Brew	Impaired judgment
	Juice	Slurred speech
	Hooch	Loss of coordination
		Euphoria
		Unconsciousness
Cocaine	Coke	Dilated pupils
	Blow	Dry mouth or nose
	Caine	Frequent wiping of nose
	Snow	Excessive activity
	Nose candy	Argumentative
	Freebase	Talkative
	Rock	
Marijuana	Weed	Loud talk/laughter
	Sense	Drowsiness
	Dope	Forgetfulness
	Grass	Chronic red eyes
	Smoke	Odor like burning rope
		Mood swings
Hallucinogens	LSD	Nausea
	Acid	Dilated pupils
	Ice	Inability to concentrate
	Dots	Muscular relaxation
	Red devils	Hallucinations
	Angel dust	Euphoria
	Window pane	Anxiety
	Psychedelics	Flashbacks

SOURCE: Bernadette Brown, MSW, Broward County Commission on Substance Abuse

the terms used in the mental health system can be found in the *DSM-IV*, which was discussed in chapter 1. Mental disorders, psychological defense mechanisms, and other important conditions are described in that volume. Although extensive training is needed to use the *DSM-IV* for diagnosis, a basic understanding of its contents is necessary for the worker who has clients with mental health issues.

The diagnoses most often made of adolescent offenders include conduct disorder, attention deficit hyperactivity disorder (ADHD), substance abuse, substance dependence, affective disorders (such as depression and anxiety), personality disorders, and post-traumatic stress disorder (PTSD) (Grisso, 1998). Many also experience oppositional/defiant disorder, mental retardation, learning disabilities, or developmental disorders. Some of these problems, such as ADHD, are biological, and are treated principally with medication. Others are often a product of cognitive errors or emotional processing (e.g., depression).

These are treated primarily with psychotherapy or skills training. Some, such as mental retardation and learning disorders, are caused by genetic deficits and cannot currently be treated. Interventions for these conditions focus on teaching specific skills and strategies that will allow youth to cope with their conditions. Some disorders are treated with a combination of medication, psychotherapy, and skills training. Those who wish to learn more about mental health diagnosis and treatment should consult the "References" section at the end of the chapter.

The substance abuse treatment system serves juvenile justice clients in one of three ways: evaluation, prevention, and treatment. *Evaluation* refers to interviewing the youth and significant others to determine whether there is a need for treatment. It may also include a urinalysis. Prevention activities are used when a youth is perceived to be at risk of abusing substances or has already begun to experiment. Prevention usually involves some combination of education and intervention for risk-related factors. Treatment refers to interventions with youth who are actively using substances. It may include detoxification, outpatient, day treatment, residential treatment, or community-based services. Both prevention and treatment will be discussed more thoroughly in chapter 5.

Juvenile justice workers should also be aware of the language of the substance abuse treatment system. It is also important to know the names and street names of the various substances youths often use. A partial list of these is included in table 2.6.

INTERACTION WITH EDUCATION PROFESSIONALS

Another system with which practitioners often interact is the educational system. The primary point of contact is often with school social workers or counselors. Workers may also need to communicate with teachers or administrators to help clients with their educational progress.

Many delinquent youth also have problems with grades, attendance, and other school-related areas. Case managers are usually responsible for ensuring that the youth have ample opportunity to correct these problems. This may involve registering the youth for school, arranging for tutoring, obtaining materials like books or eyeglasses, arranging for physical or psychological evaluations, and other similar activities. In may also involve advocacy with teachers and administrators who are reluctant to permit youths to continue in school.

Administrators are often involved in coordinating services and arranging joint programs with schools. They may also become involved in advocacy efforts when the efforts of direct practitioners are unsuccessful. Mental health and substance abuse evaluators may interact with school officials to obtain records of evaluations by school personnel. Researchers are often interested in the effectiveness of school-based prevention and treatment programs.

It is important that the juvenile justice practitioner have some familiarity with mental retardation, learning disabilities, and developmental disorders. Although she should not attempt to diagnose or intervene with these disorders, she will need to understand how each affects a child's ability to learn. She will also need to know what resources are needed to help each child.

INTERDISCIPLINARY COOPERATION AND TEAMWORK

At times the practitioner may need to participate with other professionals in interdisciplinary teams. These teams may be ongoing, or may be formed on an ad hoc basis, to make a very specific set of planning decisions. The teams may deal with the issues of a single youth, or make advisory recommendations to programs, agencies, or decision-makers.

Platt (1994) defines a team as a group of two or more people who share a sense of purpose or purposes. The group must be synergistic; that is, it must be able to accomplish more than its individual members could have accomplished alone. In interdisciplinary teams, the potential for synergy is great. Various disciplines, such as psychiatry, psychology, social work, and education have specialized areas of knowledge and unique perspectives. Combining these perspectives can produce creative alternatives for intervention that no single discipline could have produced.

Effective teams have at least nine characteristics (Larson & La Fasto, 1989):

1. The team's goals are clear and specific.
2. The team is structured and composed in a manner that is consistent with the goals.
3. The members are committed to the team's goals.
4. The climate of team meetings is open, honest, and collaborative.
5. The team has established standards of excellence toward which it strives.
6. The team is recognized as an entity by others in the community and receives recognition for its accomplishments.
7. The leadership emphasizes the importance and role of the team.

As a team member, the practitioner's attitude and behavior are key components in helping to establish and maintain these characteristics. In a team composed of the members of several professions, the members must demonstrate and must work together with intention, mutual respect, and team commitment (Carlton, 1984). Members must be respectful of one another's professional body of knowledge, theoretical orientation, and professional problem-solving process (Julia & Thompson, 1994). Further, although the professions share some terminology, sometimes terms are used differently by different groups. Still other terms are used by one profession, but are unknown to another group. The practitioner must learn enough of the language of other professionals to be conversant, and must be able to ask questions when he does not understand. He must adequately prepare his contribution to the meeting, and must listen respectfully when the professional opinions of others are offered. Finally, he must be willing to yield to the professional opinions of those who have more expertise. Although he may become conversant in the fields of other professionals, he is unlikely to develop their expertise.

SUMMARY

Practitioners in the juvenile justice system play many roles and perform multiple functions. In fulfilling those roles they frequently interact with other professionals both within and outside their own system. Other systems include law enforcement, the child welfare system, the mental health and substance abuse systems, and the educational system. It is important that the practitioner learn the languages and roles of those other professionals. Further, she must learn techniques of interdisciplinary teamwork and interaction, and must apply them in her relationships with others.

ACTIVITIES FOR LEARNING

1. Figure 2.1 offers an illustration of the needs and proposed interventions for Elena, the imaginary client from chapter 1. Pretend that you are the case manager for Ricky, the other client described in chapter 1. Draw a similar diagram for Ricky, showing what services you would provide or recommend for him.
2. Look at the description of the duties of the case manager outlined in table 2.1. Which of these duties might a case manager assigned to Ricky expect to perform? Which might a case manager assigned to Elena perform?
3. Imagine that Ricky enters the juvenile justice system through an arrest by law enforcement. What course is Ricky likely to take through the juvenile justice system? Why? Use the Organizational Chart of Juvenile

Court Processes in figure 2.2 to plot your answer. Complete the same process for Elena.
4. Pick a role you think you would like to play in the juvenile justice system. Prepare a short questionnaire about the activities of someone who plays that role, asking them specific questions about their work. Locate a practitioner in that position and schedule a time to interview her.
5. Using figure 2.2, trace the likely progress of each case study from chapter 1 (Ricky and Elena) through the juvenile justice system. Is either likely to receive diversion services? If you were their intake worker, what would you recommend? Would either require confinement for treatment? If so, at what level?

QUESTIONS FOR DISCUSSION

1. Do you agree with the juvenile justice system's philosophy of emphasizing treatment over punishment? Why or why not?
2. Laws in many states mandate that juveniles be tried as adults for certain particularly serious offenses (such as murder or gang-related activity). Do you agree with this policy? Should prosecutors be given some leeway on such cases? Are the state legislators correct to set this policy?
3. Review the process by which a juvenile moves through the court system. What problems do you see? How might youths be handled better? Do prosecutors have too much power?

Do judges? Do judges have adequate training to make clinical decisions?
4. Clients who have both substance abuse and mental health problems sometimes "fall through the cracks" because neither system sees the condition it is designed to treat as primary. For example, a mental health intake worker might assume that a substance abuse problem must be addressed before mental health issues can be addressed. Likewise, a substance abuse worker might believe that the mental health issues need attention first. What would you do as a caseworker to ensure that your client receives the necessary services?

KEY TERMS AND DEFINITIONS

Assessment The process of examining multiple areas of the client's life and social systems to identify strengths and weaknesses relevant to his or her problem.

Case management A method of practice in which the worker performs multiple functions in the process of linking the client to needed resources in the community (see table 2.1).

Day treatment Treatment that requires the client to spend the majority of the daytime hours in the treatment facility, returning home at night.

Dependency The condition in which youths have been found to be abused, neglected, and abandoned, and are taken into the protective custody of the state.

Evaluation A component of assessment in which the needs of the client in a specific area of life such as substance abuse or mental health are examined.

Guardian ad litem An adult appointed by the court to ensure that the interests of a child in state custody are adequately represented (usually done in dependency cases).

Intake The initial stage of juvenile court processing. Information is gathered to determine whether the youth will be released, diverted, processed, or waived to criminal court.

Intervention A specific, comprehensive plan designed to facilitate change in the life of a client.

Outpatient Treatment that occurs in the office of the practitioner, usually once or twice each week for about one hour per session.

Prevention Activities that target risk-related factors in an attempt to help a youth avoid developing or continuing problem behavior. Risk factors and need factors are minimized, while protective factors are maximized.

Residential treatment Treatment in which the youth is removed from his or her home and required to reside at the treatment facility. Residential programs have varying levels of security, from staff secure (low) to facility secure (high).

Treatment A plan to address specific needs of the client. Most often used in psychiatric, psychological, and medical settings.

REFERENCES

Butts, J. A., & DeMuro, P. (1989). *Risk assessment for adjudicated delinquents.* Ann Arbor, MI: Center for the Study of Youth Policy, University of Michigan.

Carlton, T. O. (1984). *Clinical social work in health settings.* New York: Springer.

Champion, D. J. (1998). *The juvenile justice system: Delinquency, processing, and the law.* Upper Saddle River, NJ: Prentice Hall.

Del Carmen, R. V., Parker, M., & Reddington, F. P. (1998). *Briefs of leading cases in juvenile justice.* Cincinnati: Anderson.

Grisso, T. (1998). *Forensic evaluation of juveniles.* Sarasota, FL: Professional Resource Press.

Henggeler, S. W. (1989). *Delinquency in adolescence.* Thousand Oaks, CA: Sage.

Julia, M. C., & Thompson, A. (1994). Essential elements of interprofessional teamwork: Task and maintenance functions. In R. M. Castro and M. C. Julia (Eds.), *Interprofessional care and collaborative practice.* Pacific Grove, CA: Brooks/Cole.

Kratcoski, P. C., & Kratcoski, L. D. (1995). *Juvenile delinquency* (4th ed.). New York: McGraw-Hill.

Larson, C. E., & La Fasto, F. M. (1989). *Teamwork.* Newbury Park, CA: Sage.

Platt, L. J. (1994). Why bother with teams? In R. M. Castro and M. C. Julia (Eds.), *Interprofessional care and collaborative practice.* Pacific Grove, CA: Brooks/Cole.

Regoli, R. M., & Hewitt, J. D. (1997). *Delinquency in society* (3rd ed.). New York: McGraw-Hill.

Thackeray, M. G., Skidmore, R. A., & Farley, O. W. (1979). *Introduction to mental health.* Englewood Cliffs, NJ: Prentice Hall.

Woodside, M., & McClam, T. (1998). *Generalist case management.* Pacific Grove, CA: Brooks/Cole.

Chapter 3

◆

Juvenile Justice Assessment

CHAPTER OUTLINE

Purposes of Assessment
Components of Assessment
Specialized Assessment: Evaluation
Risk-based Assessment
Instruments for Assessment
Using Assessment for Intervention Planning
Summary

Assessment is a very important part of the process for juvenile justice clients and practitioners. In assessment the practitioner examines several dimensions of the youth's life: psychological, family, school, peer group, legal history, substance abuse involvement, and sexual history. Based on this information, the practitioner is able to make recommendations about disposition, treatment, placement, and termination. Assessment must be performed competently, since much of what a youth experiences in the system is determined by this process. To ensure quality the practitioner often relies on multiple resources, such as archival records, evaluations by other practitioners, and personal interviews.

Assessment may be referred to as evaluation, classification, or diagnosis. Although sometimes used interchangeably, the terms will have somewhat different meanings when used in this book. Evaluation will be used to refer to the examination of specific areas, such as mental health, substance abuse, or educational status. *Classification* incorporates many aspects of assessment, but does so with a specific intent. Its goal is to identify the offender with a specific group of other offenders who share similar characteristics. Classification is used to help determine level of treatment, degree of confinement, and appropriate terms of release. *Diagnosis* refers to the identification of mental health or substance abuse disorders such as depression or chemical dependency.

Assessment refers to a comprehensive process that may include evaluation, classification, and diagnosis. In assessment, the practitioner attempts to gain an overall picture of the condition of the client. This picture includes both resources and needs, strengths and weaknesses. Based on this assessment, the practitioner can devise a plan for the client.

This chapter contains six sections. First, we will discuss the purposes of assessment. Next, we'll review the components of assessment. Third, we'll look at evaluation, a special type of assessment. Fourth, we'll examine yet another specialized procedure: risk-based assessment. Fifth, we'll review several assessment instruments and discuss their use in practice. Finally, we'll describe using the information gained during assessment to plan intervention.

PURPOSES OF ASSESSMENT

Assessment is used for several purposes and at several points in the juvenile justice system. It is typically employed for one of four purposes: (1) planning of prevention, intervention, or treatment activities, (2) classification, (3) processing, or (4) termination of services. Assessment may be performed by the case manager or by some other worker. Typically, however, it is the case manager who collects the findings and recommendations from all sources and organizes them into a collective document.

Assessment for Prevention, Intervention, or Treatment

Assessment for prevention, intervention, or treatment focuses on identifying the needs and strengths of the juvenile and the social systems that affect him. Although procedures vary, assessment is often conducted using a psychosocial evaluation form or some other type of questionnaire. Questions are asked about demographic characteristics (gender, age, race, etc.), educational background, vocational training, legal background, family history, substance abuse history, psychiatric conditions, social issues, medical problems, and sexual history.

Assessment includes interviews with the offender, as well as with parents, siblings, and other significant individuals. In addition to conducting interviews, workers may inspect related documents like school records, psychological tests, or juvenile court records. Based on the results of the interviews and document inspections, a theory is developed as to the nature of the youth's problem. This theory is summarized in a narrative that also describes the basic conditions of the youth's life. The narrative and the supporting instrument become the basis for developing a prevention, intervention, or treatment plan. A sample assessment instrument along with a hypothetical narrative is included in figures 3.1 through 3.10.

Assessment for intervention is performed at several points in the juvenile justice system. It is often done by case managers when youths are assigned to their supervision. It is also done at the treatment facilities to which youth are referred. The information collected by intake workers at treatment facilities is often similar to that collected by case managers. There are often differences, however, depending on the service provided by the treatment facility. For instance, a youth who is suspected of using marijuana may be referred for a substance abuse evaluation. The questions asked of him would include other areas, but would focus on issues related to substance abuse. Similarly, a youth thought to have mental health issues would be referred for an evaluation focusing on mental health problems.

Assessment is sometimes performed at other stages. The case manager may request an assessment before a youth is transferred from one treatment facility to another. Often, an assessment is requested before a juvenile is released from supervision. Educational or vocational programs may wish to perform assessments or specialized evaluations before providing services.

Prevention activities are also preceded by assessment. These assessments focus specifically on the risk-related factors discussed in chapter 1. Prevention may occur at one of three levels: primary, secondary, or tertiary (Center for Substance Abuse Prevention, 1993a). It may also be directed toward specific problems (such as substance abuse, smoking, or risky sexual behavior) or toward problem behavior in general (Dryfoos, 1990).

Primary prevention activities occur before the youth has begun to engage in the targeted behavior. An example would be a drug abuse prevention program directed to children from high-risk families in high-risk communities. Secondary prevention refers to activities for youths who have begun to engage in problem behavior, but for whom the problem is not yet severe. For instance, a program might target girls who have recently become sexually active, but have not yet become pregnant or contracted a venereal disease. Tertiary prevention is essentially treatment, since it is directed to youths for whom the problem has become severe. It does not seek to prevent the initiation of problem behavior, but its recurrence. An example of tertiary prevention would be an aftercare program for residential treatment, in which workers attempt to prevent recidivism among the participants (Center for Substance Abuse Prevention, 1993a).

Prevention activities directed toward specific problems address limited risk factors. Although most risk factors appear to be related to one another, as well as to most types of problem behavior, certain factors are related to only one or two problem behaviors. For example, a highly transient family creates risk for dropping out of school, but may not be related to drug abuse (Dryfoos, 1990). A program intended to prevent children from dropping out of school, then, might attempt to stabilize the living arrangements of a family. A program to prevent substance abuse might focus on other factors.

Activities directed toward multiple problem behaviors target risk factors for all those behaviors. Using the example above, a program targeting dropout and substance abuse would address the risk factors associated with both. Some specialized programs, often known as aftercare, target risk factors for recidivism. That is, they are designed to prevent youth from returning to the problem behaviors in which they engaged prior to treatment. One example of such a program is the Intensive Protective Supervision Project (IPSP) (OJJDP, 1999) described in box 3.1. Several instruments have been developed for measuring risk for specific behaviors, for multiple problem behaviors, and for recidivism. Some of those instruments are described later in this chapter.

Box 3.1 Life Story: Intensive Protective Supervision Program (IPSP)

Office of Juvenile Justice and Delinquency
Prevention, 1999

The IPSP is an intensive risk-based program that provides community supervision as an alternative to institutional incarceration of juvenile offenders. It is used for status offenders under the age of 16 who are adjudicated and are disposed to protective supervision. Its goals include the reducing of problem behavior, preventing of recidivism and escalation of offense, and increasing socially appropriate behavior. Offenders usually have little prior history of delinquency. In the study reported here, they were also primarily female.

Offenders are assigned to case managers who provide intensive, risk-based services. The case managers typically have small caseloads to allow for intensive interaction with both the juvenile and her family. During frequent visits to the home case managers provide ongoing assessment, referral to services, support for parents, and modeling of appropriate behaviors. Each youth and family receives expert evaluation, individualized treatment plans, and an array of professional services.

IPSP has demonstrated many positive outcomes when compared with other services. These outcomes include:

♦ Only 7.1% of IPSP youth were referred to juvenile court for delinquency while participating in the program (25.9% of the control group were referred to the court).

♦ 65% of IPSP youth finished the program successfully.

♦ One year after leaving the program only 14.3% of IPSP youth had returned to juvenile court. This compared to 35.2% of the group that received standard services.

Ellis (1998) argues that all prevention programs should be comprehensive. That is, they should attempt to address all risk factors for all problem behaviors. He contends that interventions should be multi-factor (addressing all risk-related factors), multi-system (in every system of the youth's environment), and multi-level (utilizing all the resources of the community to ensure that needs are met). He designed the Truancy Intervention and Prevention Program (TRIPP), an intervention being implemented by the Broward Sheriff's Office in southeast Florida, following these principles. The TRIPP program is described in box 3.2.

Assessment for Classification

Assessment is also conducted for the purpose of classification. *Classification* refers to the process of identifying a youth with subgroups or categories of juveniles with whom that youth shares relevant characteristics. For example, based on tendencies toward violence, a youth might be designated for confinement at a high level of security. One example of a youth who might require careful classification is Andrew, described in box 3.3.

Classification occurs at several points in the juvenile justice system. In a sense, police officers do both assessment and classification when they determine whether or not they will arrest a youth. Based on the limited information they

Box 3.2 The Truancy Intervention and Prevention Program (TRIPP)

The Truancy Intervention and Prevention Program (TRIPP) is designed to reduce truancy among the youth of Broward County, Florida. It uses prevention techniques delivered through intensive case management (ICM) services to truant children who are detained by law enforcement. It is operated primarily by a law enforcement agency, in partnership with the school system, the district attorney's office, and several social service providers.

Truant youths detained by law enforcement officers are transported to a truancy center. At the center they receive a risk-based assessment using the Southeast Florida Risk Assessment Package (SFRAP). Risk, need, and protective factors are targeted by ICM teams lead by master's-level social workers or mental-health practitioners. The intensity of the intervention varies according to the youth's level of need and history of truant behavior.

Lower-level interventions provide referrals to willing parents. The most intensive interventions include weekly contact with children and families, individual counseling, referral to services, and possible prosecution of uncooperative parents.

Box 3.3 Case Study: Andrew

Andrew is a 17-year-old African-American male who has come for an assessment because he was arrested as one of four juveniles who robbed a convenience store. He was adjudicated delinquent, and has had several prior arrests, including shoplifting last year (adjudicated dependent), conspiracy to sell marijuana 18 months ago (diverted prior to adjudication), and possession of marijuana a little more than two years ago (diverted prior to adjudication).

Andrew resides with his mother in an older, lower socio-economic status community in a major city. He has not seen his father in several years and his mother is an active alcoholic. Because Andrew's mother is rarely sober, she offers him little in the way of guidance and support. He has no brothers or sisters.

Andrew was diagnosed with oppositional/defiant disorder at the age of 8. At 14, his diagnosis was changed to conduct disorder. He is also frequently depressed.

Andrew has not attended school in three weeks. He has been truant for most of the last two semesters, beginning last semester when he was suspended for 10 days. He chose never to return after that suspension. His grades have been poor (mostly Ds) since the third grade, and he is two years behind in school as a result. Despite his school problems, Andrew is very bright and has an uncanny knack for repairing anything mechanical.

Andrew denies being religious, and has not attended church "since I was a kid." He denies any history of physical or sexual abuse, but reports that "My father whipped me 'til I couldn't walk."

Andrew denies any suicidal ideation, self-mutilation, cruelty to animals, or fire-starting. He is very impulsive and is very aggressive at times, often starting fights with other teenagers and young adults. He has never taken any medication for psychiatric problems. He reports that he has few friends and that all his friends have trouble with the law.

Andrew denies using any drugs other than alcohol and marijuana. He reports having used alcohol three or four days per week since he was 9 years old. He reports having smoked marijuana almost daily since age 14. Andrew denies any history of medical problems.

Andrew reports that he has been sexually active since age 13. He reports being heterosexual, and has never experienced involuntary sex. He denies using any form of protection when engaging in sexual intercourse.

---

are able to assemble from the youth, witnesses, and their own observations, they decide whether a youth will be classified among those taken into custody or those not taken into custody.

Additional points of classification may include intake, disposition, and termination. Intake workers must decide whether youths will be classified with those who are released, those who are diverted, those who are processed as adults, or those who are processed as juveniles. Classification for disposition often focuses on specific problems or needs of the youth. For instance, before placing a youth in a residential facility, it would be important to know whether he has a propensity toward sexual offense. Specific questions need to be answered regarding the youth's need for treatment, his level of openness to treatment, and his degree of dangerousness to others. Once these questions have been answered, decisions can be made about whether to include the offender in a coed population and whether he requires specialized treatment.

The process of examining the youth's sexual behavior and propensities is a kind of evaluation. Table 3.1 contains guidelines suggested by Groth and Loredo (1981) for evaluating sexual offenders. Evaluations might be performed of a youth's aggressiveness, substance abuse, or suicidal ideation.

Assessment for Processing

Assessment is also conducted to help prosecutors and the court make decisions regarding processing. Some of its applications during processing were discussed in the above section about classification. Sometimes, however, other specialized information is needed. In such cases, mental health practitioners may be asked to perform additional specialized evaluations to determine whether the youth is competent to go through or to have gone through various stages of processing.

An example of an evaluation for processing would be when issues are raised about a youth's *competence* to stand trial. Should this happen, the court or a prosecutor may request an evaluation of the youth's competence before proceeding. Should the youth be found incompetent, the evaluator might also recommend an intervention to increase the youth's abilities. Similarly, a prosecutor may believe that a youth lacked the capacity to understand his *Miranda rights* at the time of his arrest. In such a case, a mental health or educational professional might be asked to evaluate the youth's capacity for understanding. Additional situations requiring evaluation for processing are discussed below.

Table 3.1 Guidelines for Evaluating Juvenile Sexual Offenders

Assessment Question	Important Issues
1. What is the age relationship between the persons involved?	The greater the age discrepancy, the more ominous . . . the . . . activities.
2. What is the social relationship between the persons involved?	Sexual advances towards a family member or towards a total stranger . . . would appear to be inappropriate.
3. What type of sexual activity is being exhibited?	Are the sexual acts consistent with the developmental level of the subject? . . .
4. How does the sexual contact take place?	Does it occur through mutual negotiation or . . . deception and enticement?
5. How persistent is the sexual activity?	Does it have a compulsive, driven quality?
6. Is there any evidence of progression in regard to the severity or frequency of the sexual activity?	Any indication of an increase in aggression over time . . . is nature ominous.
7. What is the nature of the juvenile's fantasies that precede or accompany his behavior?	The juvenile's sexual fantasies . . . need to be assessed in regard to the same issues . . . (as) his sexual offense.
8. Are there any distinguishing characteristics about the persons who are the targets of the juvenile's sexual activities?	Encounters with persons who are not physically, socially, intellectually, and/or psychologically equal to the subject should be suspect.

SOURCE: Groth and Loredo, 1981

Assessment for Termination

In a sense, assessment for termination might be categorized either with classification or with processing. It might be included with classification, since youths may be categorized with either those who will be released from supervision or with those who will not be released. Further, among those who are released, they might be classified with those who will not receive aftercare, those who will receive voluntary aftercare, or those who will receive mandatory aftercare (actually a form of probation or ongoing supervision).

Assessment for termination might also be seen as related to processing, since it represents what may be the final processing decision. However, since termination decisions are particularly important, they are being discussed here in a separate section. *Termination* is particularly important for several reasons: (1) because youth who are released from supervision may constitute a greater risk to the safety of the community; (2) because the timing and method of the termination may be vital to the youth's success; and (3) because the nature of the aftercare chosen for a youth may be vital to her success.

Assessment for termination requires several important decisions. First, the practitioner must decide whether the youth has been sufficiently rehabilitated to allow the court to terminate supervision. If this decision is yes, it leads to a series of other decisions. Workers must know whether a youth still constitutes any danger to the community. If she does, then measures should be put in place to offset that danger. For example, she should be referred to appropriate after-school or counseling programs.

Even when the juvenile is not a threat to the community, she may have significant problems that will inhibit her ability to function. These deficiencies could affect the probability of her returning to criminal behavior. One example would be a girl with a reading disability. If she is returned to the community with inadequate support, she may do poorly in school, become truant, and commit property crimes during school hours. When a juvenile is released from supervision, adequate supports must be in place to ensure that her new *prosocial* attitudes and skills are supported.

Workers must also determine how likely a youth's social systems and community are to support the positive changes he has made while in state custody. A frequent criticism of juvenile programs has been their failure to support youths who are returned to the community. Pre-termination assessment should look at each social system with which the youth interacts: family, school, peers, community, workplace, church, and any others relevant to specific youth. When those social systems appear to be unlikely to successfully support prosocial behavior, aftercare can be designed to address those issues. Intervention for various social systems will be discussed more thoroughly in chapters 4 and 5.

COMPONENTS OF ASSESSMENT

As mentioned above, assessment questionnaires (instruments) are often divided into several sections. These sections represent different dimensions of the juvenile's life. As the worker interviews the youth and other significant persons, she looks for indications of problems that may contribute to the problem behavior.

An example of such a problem would be a mental condition such as bipolar disorder (manic-depression) that could be treated with medication. Another example would be a juvenile who has experienced physical or sexual abuse. Counseling (and relocation to a nonabusive home) might be needed. The life dimensions usually examined during assessment include demographic characteristics, educational background, vocational training, legal background, family history, substance abuse history, psychiatric conditions, social issues, medical problems, and sexual history.

Demographic Characteristics

The first type of information collected by assessment workers is usually demographic characteristics. This section asks about such factors as address, age, gender, race, ethnicity, and family income. This information is used for statistical purposes, for classification, and for need identification.

When used for statistical purposes, demographic characteristics help to inform agency practice. Administrators may use them to determine whether they are under- or overserving a specific segment of the population (like blacks or Hispanics). They may also pair demographic data with outcome results to determine whether they have greater success with one subgroup than with another (e.g., success with females more than with males).

Demographic data is also used for classification. Treatment programs are often separated by age group. For example, one program may serve children up

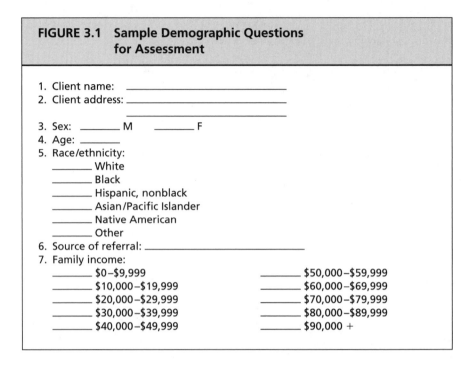

FIGURE 3.1   Sample Demographic Questions for Assessment

1. Client name: _____
2. Client address: _____
   _____
3. Sex: _____ M   _____ F
4. Age: _____
5. Race/ethnicity:
   _____ White
   _____ Black
   _____ Hispanic, nonblack
   _____ Asian/Pacific Islander
   _____ Native American
   _____ Other
6. Source of referral: _____
7. Family income:
   _____ $0–$9,999   _____ $50,000–$59,999
   _____ $10,000–$19,999   _____ $60,000–$69,999
   _____ $20,000–$29,999   _____ $70,000–$79,999
   _____ $30,000–$39,999   _____ $80,000–$89,999
   _____ $40,000–$49,999   _____ $90,000 +

to the age of 12. Another may work with 12- to 15-year-olds. A third program may target only older teens, ages 15 to 18. Knowing the age of the youth helps the courts and case managers make proper dispositional decisions. It may also help the case manager locate a program when the developmental stage of the youth does not permit placement with his own age group.

The third function of demographic data is need identification. Certain demographic characteristics are suggestive of certain needs. For example, although not all poor teens become delinquent, residence in neighborhoods with high crime, high transience, and low income is associated with risk of problem behavior (Dryfoos, 1990). Also, being a minority will not cause a youth to commit delinquent acts; however, it does subject juveniles to conditions that may lead to delinquency. Knowledge of such conditions will allow case management and treatment personnel to consider them when they devise interventions. A group of sample demographic questions is included in figure 3.1.

Educational Background

Educational problems are frequently associated with the development of problem behavior. Learning disabilities, mental retardation, and emotional and behavioral disorders sometimes contribute to delinquency. Some physical problems, such as hearing difficulties and vision problems, are also factors. The classroom or school environment may also generate impediments to learning, which, in turn, often contribute to conduct problems. Unsupportive teachers, overcrowded schools, and poor administration are all associated with behavioral problems (Dryfoos, 1990).

Any of these conditions may contribute to an assortment of educational difficulties. Initially, they often result in poor grades, which may negatively im-

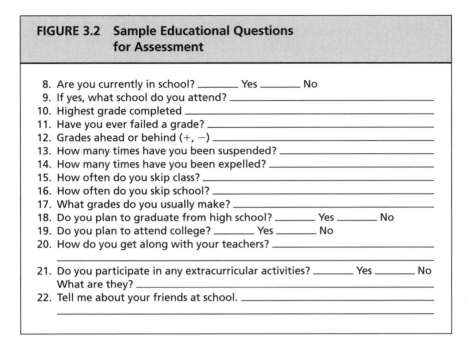

FIGURE 3.2   Sample Educational Questions for Assessment

8. Are you currently in school? _____ Yes _____ No
9. If yes, what school do you attend? _____
10. Highest grade completed _____
11. Have you ever failed a grade? _____
12. Grades ahead or behind (+, −) _____
13. How many times have you been suspended? _____
14. How many times have you been expelled? _____
15. How often do you skip class? _____
16. How often do you skip school? _____
17. What grades do you usually make? _____
18. Do you plan to graduate from high school? _____ Yes _____ No
19. Do you plan to attend college? _____ Yes _____ No
20. How do you get along with your teachers? _____
_____
21. Do you participate in any extracurricular activities? _____ Yes _____ No
   What are they? _____
22. Tell me about your friends at school. _____
_____

pact social relationships, expectations for future success, and self-esteem. These conditions may result in truancy, fighting, insubordinate behavior, and other problems. A properly structured intervention will address all facets of the problem: learning problems, peer relationships, and problems between the youth and the staff. A carefully completed assessment can help to identify many of these problems. Sample educational questions are included in figure 3.2.

Vocational Training

Some juveniles have stronger interests in the kinds of knowledge and skills that are developed through vocational training. In fact, a strong vocational interest is often very influential in helping a youth avoid developing problem behaviors (Hawkins, Catalano, & Miller, 1992). Assessment professionals should attempt to identify not only specific skills and knowledge, but also interests that may be developed. Sample vocational questions are included in figure 3.3.

Legal History

A history of legal involvement often predicts further involvement. Juveniles who commit more than one offense are likely to commit others (Jessor & Jessor, 1977). The kinds of offenses committed in the past may also be a clue to the nature of a youth's problems. For instance, a history of destructive fire-starting is often associated with a history of intensive physical or sexual abuse (Ellis, 1997).

A comprehensive history of legal involvement can be very important for a number of reasons. It can help intake workers determine whether charges should be filed. It can help judges decide the level of incarceration. It can help practitioners decide the types of treatment that are needed for each youth. Sample legal questions are included in figure 3.4.

(These questions might not be asked if the client reported intentions of completing high school or college in the education section in figure 3.2.)

23. Have you earned your GED? _____Yes _____No
24. Do you have any specialized vocational training? _____Yes _____No
25. What kind of work interests you the most? _____
    _____
26. What kind of work interests you the least? _____
    _____
27. What work experience do you have? _____
    _____
28. Have you ever had any kind of vocational testing? _____Yes _____No
29. If yes, what were the results? _____
    _____
30. Would you be willing to do some vocational testing to find out what kind
    of work you might be interested in? _____Yes _____No

---

31. What was the legal offense that caused you to have to come here today?
    _____
32. When did the offense occur? _____
33. Tell me about the circumstances of the offense. _____
    _____
34. What is the current status?
    _____ diversion   _____ being adjudicated   _____adjudicated
35. What other problems have you had with the law?

Offense	Date	Result
1.		
2.		
3.		

36. Has any other member of your family ever been in trouble with the law?
    _____ Yes _____ No
37. Explain who, what the trouble was, and when it occurred. _____
    _____

FIGURE 3.5   Sample Family History Questions for Assessment

37. What family members live in your home?

Name	Relationship	Age

38. What family members live elsewhere?

Name	Relationship	Age	Where do they live?

39. Are you adopted? _____ Yes _____ No
40. Do you live in a foster home? _____ Yes _____ No
41. What member of your family is the most supportive of you?
_____

42. What family member is the least supportive?
_____

43. How do you get along with the other family members?
_____

44. How many times have you run away from home? _____

Family History

The family is a key (perhaps the key) social system for developing children. Certain kinds of family problems, including poor parenting, high levels of family conflict, abuse and neglect, and parental modeling of criminal behavior (Hawkins, Catalano, & Miller, 1992), increase the likelihood that children will develop behavior problems. The family may also have physical needs, such as housing, food, or medical care, that increase stress levels in the home. Other issues may include parental substance abuse, physical or sexual abuse, and domestic violence.

When these kinds of problems exist in a home, they must be addressed in the intervention. Parent training, family counseling, and referrals for concrete services (help with housing, finances, etc.) can be arranged by the case manager. Judges need to be aware of parental substance abuse, child abuse, or domestic violence issues when considering out-of-home placement. A group of sample family-related questions are included in figure 3.5.

FIGURE 3.6   Sample Substance Abuse Questions for Assessment

45. Have you ever consumed alcohol? _____ Yes _____ No
46. Have you ever used any illegal drug? _____ Yes _____ No
47. Tell me about your drug use.

Substance	How often	Age first used	Currently using?

48. Do you think you have a drug or alcohol problem? _____ Yes _____ No
49. Does anyone else think so? _____ Yes _____ No   Who? _____
50. Has anyone ever suggested that you cut down on your alcohol or drug use?
    _____ Yes _____ No
51. Are you annoyed by suggestions that you should cut down?
    _____ Yes _____ No
52. Do you ever feel guilty about getting high? _____ Yes _____ No
53. Do you ever need an "eye-opener" (a little drink or hit of a drug) to start
    your day? _____ Yes _____ No
54. How many of your friends use drugs or alcohol? _____
55. Which members of your family use drugs or alcohol?

Name	How often

Substance Abuse History

Juveniles who abuse alcohol or other substances are often involved in other types of delinquent activity (Jessor & Jessor, 1977). Using those substances may substantially affect their ability to reason as well as their behavior. Clearly, this would have an effect on their rehabilitation.

Substance abuse assessment is usually conducted by a specialist who is trained to recognize the signs of abuse, even when a youth denies involvement. Case managers may request an evaluation, or the court may order it, based on the circumstances of the arrest or the results of the initial assessment. Since substance abuse assessment is so specialized, we will consider it a form of evaluation in this book. Sample questions related to substance abuse from an assessment instrument are included in figure 3.6. Substance abuse evaluation is discussed more thoroughly in a later section of this chapter.

History of Psychiatric Conditions

Specific psychiatric or social issues may be very relevant to a youth's disposition and treatment. For example, a juvenile who exhibits a mood disorder, such as the symptoms of bipolar disorder, may need to have his condition stabilized for treatment to succeed. A youth who suffers from explosive or impulsive disorders may need intervention to control her behavior.

**FIGURE 3.7   Sample Mental Health Questions
                for Assessment**

56. Have you ever received any treatment or medication for a mental or
    emotional condition?

Condition	Treatment	Date

57. Have you ever been to counseling? _____ Yes _____ No
    What happened? _____
    _____

58. Has your temper ever gotten you into trouble? _____ Yes _____ No
    Explain. _____

59. Has your appetite or weight changed recently? _____ Yes _____ No

60. Do you tend to act without thinking? _____ Yes _____ No

61. Have you lost interest in things? _____ Yes _____ No

62. Do you ever feel hopeless? _____ Yes _____ No

63. Have you ever cut or burned yourself intentionally? _____ Yes _____ No

64. Have you ever thought about or attempted suicide? _____ Yes _____ No

65. Have you ever harmed animals or started fires for fun? _____ Yes _____ No

66. Have you ever been physically or sexually abused? _____ Yes _____ No

---

Diagnoses of psychiatric conditions are generally made by mental health practitioners. A referral is often made to a private practitioner who contracts with the court or to a court-employed evaluator. Mental health status may also affect a juvenile's ability to complete certain stages of law enforcement and court processing. A case manager's assessment may raise questions about the presence of such disorders. Sample questions are included in figure 3.7. Diagnosis comes as a result of evaluation by a professional mental health practitioner. Such evaluations are discussed in greater detail in the section below.

Problematic Social Issues

Certain social conditions or problems may contribute to delinquent behavior. For example, a juvenile who associates with gang members often becomes gang involved. A lack of friends may signal social skill deficiencies, depression, and a propensity for delinquent behavior. Cruelty to animals often reflects an abusive past and signals the probability of future extreme deviant behavior (Asclone, Thompson, & Black, 1997).

Specific questions about these and other issues can be very helpful for disposition and treatment planning. They may be critical for appropriate placement or for identifying a need to be referred for mental health evaluation. Sample assessment questions for social issues are included in figure 3.8.

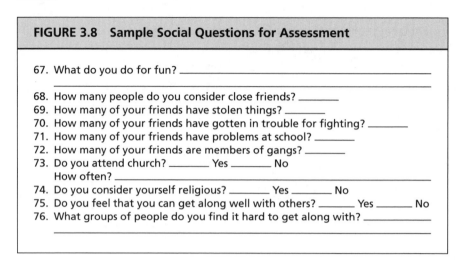

FIGURE 3.8　Sample Social Questions for Assessment

67. What do you do for fun? _____

_____

68. How many people do you consider close friends? _____
69. How many of your friends have stolen things? _____
70. How many of your friends have gotten in trouble for fighting? _____
71. How many of your friends have problems at school? _____
72. How many of your friends are members of gangs? _____
73. Do you attend church? _____ Yes _____ No
    How often? _____
74. Do you consider yourself religious? _____ Yes _____ No
75. Do you feel that you can get along well with others? _____ Yes _____ No
76. What groups of people do you find it hard to get along with? _____

_____

Medical Problems

Medical problems can compound treatment efforts and placement selection. Some conditions do not increase the likelihood that a youth will develop behavior problems, but strengthen the effects of other conditions. A diabetic youth, for example, may need access to insulin in the facility to which he is disposed. Children who suffer from ADHD can be treated medically, but are at risk for delinquent behavior if untreated. A good assessment identifies medical conditions the youth is known to have and recognizes the need for referral for diagnosis of unknown conditions. Sample medical questions are included in figure 3.9.

Sexual History

A youth's sexual history can be very important for disposition and treatment. Sexual offenders need to be separated from potential victims and need to receive services to help prevent them from re-offending. Sexual abuse survivors need treatment in a safe, nurturing atmosphere, where their issues can be explored and dealt with. Those who have become sexually active at an early age need counseling to avoid pregnancy and sexually transmitted diseases. Sample questions are included in figure 3.10.

Other Relevant Information

The assessment professional may uncover other information that is relevant to processing and treatment. For example, the juvenile may mention an adult relative or friend to whom he is close and whom he respects. This person would be a potential mentor, or someone to whom the youth could look for guidance. Mentors can be powerful deterrents to deviant behavior.

Additional relevant information should always be included either in a "comments" section of the assessment instrument or in the narrative summary. The narrative summary is written in paragraph form at the end of the assessment questionnaire. It recounts the findings of the assessment, including the diagnostic impressions of the practitioner.

FIGURE 3.9 Sample Medical Questions for Assessment

77. Has a doctor ever told you that you have any physical, mental, or emotional problems?

Problem	Duration	Date	Treatment	Doctor

78. Have you ever been hospitalized for a medical problem?
_____ Yes _____ No
79. Are you now under a doctor's care? _____ Yes _____ No
80. When was your last physical examination? _____
81. What were the results? _____
82. Are you now taking any medication? _____ Yes _____ No
What kind? _____
83. Do you have any physical handicaps? _____ Yes _____ No
What kind? _____

FIGURE 3.10 Sample Sexual History Questions for Assessment

84. How did you first find out about sex? _____
85. How old were you the first time you had sex? _____
86. Did you want to do it? _____ Yes _____ No
87. How old were you when you had your first voluntary sexual experience?
_____
88. Have you ever felt that someone had used you sexually?
_____ Yes _____ No
89. Are you sexually active now? _____ Yes _____ No
90. Have you ever been raped? _____ Yes _____ No
91. What is your sexual orientation? _____
92. How many sexual partners have you had in the last year? _____
93. When you have sex, what precautions do you use to ensure that you do not become pregnant or contract a sexually transmitted disease?
_____

SPECIALIZED ASSESSMENT: EVALUATION

Earlier in the chapter we took a brief look at evaluation. We said that for the purposes of this book, the word "evaluation" would be used to refer to a component of assessment in which a juvenile's need in a specific area is examined. This section discusses several different types of evaluation: mental health, substance abuse, risk of violence, risk of harm to others, risk of sexual offense, educational, psychiatric, and medical.

These evaluations are normally conducted by specialists. Licensed psychiatrists, psychologists, social workers, licensed mental health practitioners, education professionals, or physicians most frequently perform evaluations. Juveniles are typically referred by the court, the defense attorney, or the case manager.

Mental Health Evaluation for Treatment

Mental health evaluation may be conducted to help plan appropriate treatment for a youth. An important component of these evaluations is identifying mental and emotional problems that may contribute to the youth's problem behavior. At least three categories of conditions may be present. These include (1) disorders that may predispose a youth to problems, (2) disorders that may interact with other conditions to produce problems, and (3) disorders that are, by definition, behavioral problems.

Disorders that may predispose a youth to problems include such conditions as bipolar disorder and ADHD. Neither of these conditions causes a youth to engage in problem behavior, but conditions produced by each may contribute to developing such behavior. For example, in the manic phase of bipolar disorder, a youth may feel invincible, and may believe that he is entitled to lie or steal. The youth suffering from ADHD may be irritating and aggressive because she cannot contain her restlessness, and may start or provoke fights as a result. Each can often be successfully treated with medication.

Disorders that interact with other conditions include learning disabilities, mental retardation, and pervasive developmental disorders. Many youths who suffer from these disorders do not develop behavior problems. When other conditions (e.g., any of the risk factors for problem behavior discussed under prevention) are present, the youth's risk for delinquent behavior may increase dramatically. Although these diagnoses are often made by psychiatrists and psychologists, they may also be identified by educational specialists.

Disorders that are, by definition, behavioral problems include oppositional/defiant disorder and conduct disorder. These disorders are actually descriptions of the behaviors of youth who have developed specific levels of antisocial behavior. More specific descriptions of each disorder are included in chapter 2.

Grisso (1998) lists four important assessment questions that must be answered in performing a mental health evaluation for rehabilitation (treatment). He suggests that these might be used as an outline for an evaluation. Certainly, all these components, listed below, should be present in a good evaluation.

1. What are the youth's important characteristics?
2. What needs to change?

3. What modes of intervention should be applied toward the rehabilitation objective?

4. What is the likelihood of change, given the relevant interventions?

These guidelines make it clear that, although identifying disorders is important to evaluation, it is only a part of the overall process. When disorders are identified, they should be placed within a social context (question 1). The effects of the context should be considered when recommendations for intervention are made (question 3). An example would be a 14-year-old who has begun to manifest the symptoms of conduct disorder. Although his disorder may not be the direct result of his home environment, conditions there may exacerbate it. If, for instance, the parental management style is very loose, certain behavioral interventions, consistently applied, may help. Interventions that focus on the youth's condition but ignore the family, however, would likely be less effective.

Mental health evaluations are conducted by psychiatrists, psychologists, social workers, and other mental health professionals. In some jurisdictions the evaluators must be licensed by the state. In others, they can operate under the license of the agency that employs them. Evaluations typically include a series of interviews with the client and significant others, a review of available records, and may include a series of diagnostic tests. These tests are discussed in greater detail in the section below.

The mental health practitioner usually provides the referring person or agency with a summary report of her findings. If she has found diagnosable conditions, she will describe them. She may also make recommendations for treatment. If she suspects problems outside her area of expertise, she may suggest a referral to a physician or an educational specialist.

Mental Health Evaluation for Competence

A juvenile's competence for processing may become an issue at various points during his progress through the system. These points include his arrest (ability to understand Miranda rights), ability to stand trial, and appropriateness for waiver into criminal court (Grisso, 1998).

Understanding of Miranda rights usually becomes an issue prior to the adjudication hearing. Although a competence evaluation rarely occurs at the time of arrest, it does occur in response to the arrest. If a youth chooses to waive her Miranda rights, and her competence to make that decision is questionable, an evaluation may be requested. The request for an evaluation may come from the judge, the defense attorney, or the prosecutor. As with evaluation for treatment, the competence evaluation may be performed by a psychiatrist, psychologist, social worker, or other mental health practitioner approved by the court.

Grisso (1998) divides evaluation for competence to waive Miranda rights into four dimensions: functional abilities, causal factors, interactive components, and judgmental aspects. Functional abilities refer to the youth's capacity to comprehend, understand the importance of, and process information related to the decision. The examiner must determine the degree to which those abilities exist. Causal factors are conditions that affect a youth's functional abilities, including lags in cognitive development or various mental disorders. The issue is which of these are present and how they may impact functional abilities. Interactive components include the circumstances of the youth's waiver. Coercive interrogation of a youth whose functional capacities are limited may affect competence. Judgmental aspects refer to insights and opinions offered by the practitioner to help the court make judgments about competence.

Practitioners may also be asked to make decisions about a youth's capacity to stand trial. At issue are the respondent's ability to understand the nature of the process he faces, to communicate with his attorneys, and adequately assess and choose between the options facing him. His ability to perform these tasks may be affected by insanity, mental or emotional disorder, mental retardation, or by the youth's developmental stages. Some insight into the probability of incompetence can be gained from looking at related factors, such as age, diagnosis, and history of remedial education (Cowden & McKee, 1994). Further information can be gained through interviewing and diagnostic testing.

The evaluation report should include nine components:

1. Identification of the youth and the charges
2. Listing of the assessment methods used
3. Description of what the youth was told about the purpose of the evaluation
4. Social, clinical, and developmental history
5. Mental status data, including any psychological testing data
6. Interpretation of the data, including clinical or developmental explanations for any serious deficits in competence abilities
7. Recommendations for remediation of deficits if the youth is found incompetent (Grisso, 1998, p. 123)

Based on the findings of the evaluator, the court may decide to drop the charges, divert the youth to treatment, or continue with processing.

The third type of competence evaluation is a waiver to criminal court. The most important issues in this type of evaluation are the probability that the juvenile will harm others and the likelihood that he can be successfully treated in the juvenile system (Grisso, 1998). Factors indicating possible future danger to others include the following:

1. A persistent history of behaviors harmful to others
2. Individual factors such as anger management problems, impulsivity, and mental or emotional disorders
3. Family factors such as high levels of conflict and violence
4. A history of physical or sexual abuse
5. History of alcohol or substance use
6. Peer-related factors like gang membership or involvement with other violent peers
7. High levels of stress with low levels of perceived support
8. Community factors like high levels of violence and criminality

Several instruments are available for assessing risk of violent behavior. Some of these are described in the section on assessment instruments later in this chapter.

Amenability to treatment variables is described in the section above entitled "Mental Health Evaluation for Treatment." Much of a youth's ability to accept treatment has to do with personality factors and the presence or absence of cognitive and mental disorders. Environmental factors can be very important, however, and must be considered when evaluating this dimension.

Substance Abuse Evaluation

Substance abuse evaluations attempt to determine whether juveniles are using alcohol or other substances, the degree to which they use those substances, and the level of impairment they experience as a result. Ultimately, the purpose of assessment is to make recommendations for treatment. Substance abuse assessment should examine the following areas of the youth's life: history of alcohol or drug use, history of over-the-counter drug use, medical history, mental health history, family history, school history, vocational history, dependency or delinquency history, sexual history, peer relationships, gang involvement, interpersonal skills, leisure-time activities, neighborhood environment, and home environment. Assessment instruments will be discussed below. In addition to interviewing both the youth and significant others, the practitioner may administer a urine test (Center for Substance Abuse Treatment, 1993b).

Evaluation for Risk of Violence

Evaluation for the risk of violence was discussed above within the context of waiver to criminal court. An assessment of the degree of risk for violence may be needed for other reasons. Intake workers may need to know the level of risk before deciding whether to release or detain a youth. Judges need to know the propensity toward violence before making dispositional decisions. Case managers, in planning treatment, require a sense of whether or not anger management or other interventions are needed. Risk evaluation helps practitioners in these and other areas.

Evaluation for Risk to Self

Risk to self includes such harmful behaviors as suicidal ideation, self-mutilation, and eating disorders. Two of these conditions, suicidal ideation and *self-mutilation,* involve deliberate attempts to harm oneself. The third, *eating disorders,* is not an attempt to harm the self, but an indication of other factors, such as deficient perception of body composition and appearance.

In order to assess *suicidal ideation* (thoughts of suicide), the evaluator must examine (1) degree of suicidal intent; (2) current stressors; (3) ideas about death and dying; (4) family history; (5) degree of impulse control; (6) history of previous attempts; (7) coping skills and resources; (8) risk of suicidal actions; (9) ideas of family and support group about suicide, death, and dying; and (10) attitudes of family and support group about seeking help (Freeman & Reinecke, 1993). Similar factors are important for self-mutilation. In this case particular attention must be given to patterns of escalation.

Issues to be explored with juveniles with eating disorders include (1) personal habits, such as under- or overeating, purging, bingeing, or constant dieting; (2) individual factors such as low self-esteem and perfectionism; (3) family factors, such as parental alcoholism, depression, over-involved mothers and marginally involved fathers; (4) social isolation; and (5) problematic perceptions of body appearance and cognitions about eating (Zastrow & Kirst-Ashman, 1993).

Juveniles who harm themselves need particularly supportive environments and specific therapeutic intervention (Ellis, O'Hara, & Sowers, 1999). Identification of these conditions facilitates effective disposition and intervention planning. Instruments for evaluating risk of self-harmful behavior are discussed later in this chapter.

Evaluation of Sexual Offenders

Guidelines for the evaluation of sexual offenders were discussed in a previous section. Such evaluations are important for the safety of the community, the protection of other youth with whom the offender may be confined, and treatment planning for the offender. Instruments for assessment are listed below.

Educational Evaluation

Educational evaluation is conducted to determine whether a juvenile has physical, mental, or emotional conditions that negatively affect her ability to learn. A few of these conditions were described briefly in the section on assessment. Specific tests are used by school psychologists and educational specialists to identify these problems. When a youth has difficulties understanding written or verbal communication, performing mathematical calculations, or performing age-appropriate learning functions, evaluation by a specialist should be considered. Practitioners should be cautious about labeling juveniles and drawing conclusions about the nature of a youth's learning problems. Only qualified specialists with extensive training are qualified to make those kinds of decisions. It is also important to realize that many persons with learning disabilities can learn in nontraditional ways, and can be very successful. This makes referral to specialists essential. For example, read the story of Wendy Moore in box 5.5 (see chapter 5).

Medical Evaluation

Many juveniles who enter the juvenile justice system are in need of medical or dental care. Some of the conditions they experience negatively affect their mental and emotional condition, their ability to function in school, their ability to interact socially, and their general health well-being. Before any diagnosis of a mental or emotional disorder is given, physical causes should be ruled out. If there is evidence of any physical symptom, the youth should be evaluated by a physician.

RISK-BASED ASSESSMENT

This section will describe the basic techniques of risk-based assessment. These techniques are different from those used for other assessments because they focus on specific factors identified by research as related to risk. Risk-based assessment focuses on identifying risk-related factors (risk, need, and protec-

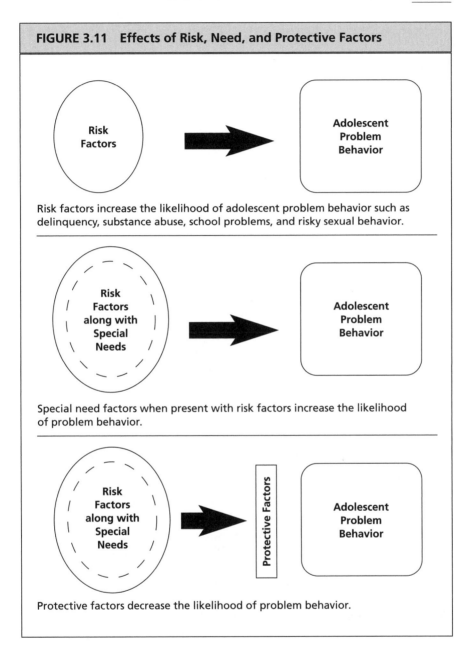

FIGURE 3.11   Effects of Risk, Need, and Protective Factors

Risk Factors → Adolescent Problem Behavior

Risk factors increase the likelihood of adolescent problem behavior such as delinquency, substance abuse, school problems, and risky sexual behavior.

Risk Factors along with Special Needs → Adolescent Problem Behavior

Special need factors when present with risk factors increase the likelihood of problem behavior.

Risk Factors along with Special Needs → Protective Factors → Adolescent Problem Behavior

Protective factors decrease the likelihood of problem behavior.

tive factors). Once those factors have been identified, interventions can be developed.

Risk-based assessment and intervention is based on the risk, need, and protective factors described in chapter 1. Risk factors increase the probability that a juvenile will engage in problem behavior. Need factors compound the effects of risk factors. Protective factors mediate the effects of risk factors; that is, they decrease the probability that a youth will become delinquent or develop other problems (see figure 3.11).

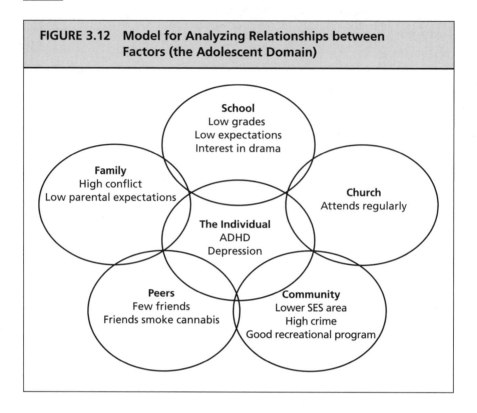

FIGURE 3.12   Model for Analyzing Relationships between Factors (the Adolescent Domain)

Assessment of risk requires that the practitioner focus on these factors. This might mean that some characteristics that would be ignored in assessment for treatment might be included (such as community transience or individual rebelliousness). Other characteristics that would be the focus of treatment (such as conduct disorder) might be only a single component of a prevention plan. In primary and secondary prevention, these differences are more pronounced. In tertiary prevention (really a form of treatment), prevention may simply be viewed as a very comprehensive form of treatment.

Risk assessment is done through interviews, reviews of the juvenile's records, and on-site visits to home, schools, and other locations. A good risk-based assessment carefully looks for all three types of factors and the relationships between those factors. For example, a youth might have school problems but high levels of interest and skill with computers. This youth might benefit from time with a respected uncle who is in the computer business (OJJDP, 1995).

Risk assessment must also include factors in all social systems. Many interventions have focused only on the family or on the school. These interventions often ignore serious problems that occur in other systems. A good assessment considers all systems. This assessment can then become the basis for comprehensive intervention.

Assessment begins with a comprehensive list of risk and protective factors. It might be arranged as a checklist, similar to the one discussed in chapter 1 and illustrated in table 1.3. Once the factors have been identified, they should be reviewed and any relationships between them identified. A model for review-

Box 3.4   Case Study: Maggie

Maggie is a 12-year-old white female who resides with her mother in a lower socioeconomic, high-crime area of a major city. Her father visits frequently, usually to fight with her mother. She has four older sisters who also reside in the home. They frequently argue with each other and with their mother. Maggie's assessment is because of her increasing truancy.

Maggie has attention deficit hyperactivity disorder (ADHD), but her mother has been unable to afford medication. Maggie is also moderately depressed, feeling very lonely and isolated. She does not feel loved or wanted at home. She also feels alienated from the

few friends she does have because they recently began to smoke pot. Maggie does not wish to smoke, but thinks she may need to start to keep her friends.

Maggie has several problems in school, including nearly failing grades and a strong lack of interest in most of her classes. She reports that she does not expect to do well in school. She does report an interest in drama, and did well this year in a drama class.

Maggie attends church regularly and is marginally involved in the youth group. She has also visited an excellent recreation program at a local park twice in the last six months.

ing and analyzing factors throughout the social systems is offered in figure 3.12. In this figure the risk factors for Maggie, the case study described in box 3.4, are written onto a systems map. After the factors have been mapped, a narrative describing the relationships between risk-related factors can be prepared.

INSTRUMENTS FOR ASSESSMENT

There are many different kinds of assessment and evaluation instruments. Some are easily given and interpreted. Some are very complex and difficult. Some can be administered by any practitioner. Others require special training or certification. This section describes several instruments often used for assessment or evaluation in the juvenile justice system.

Instruments for General Assessment

Many different instruments are used to perform general assessments. Most are not standardized, and most follow the format included in figures 3.1 through 3.10. Based on the answers to specific questions or groups of questions, the practitioner may determine that an evaluation of some dimension is needed. Instruments for these dimensions are described below.

Instruments to Assess Risk

Several different instruments have been designed to assess risk of problem behavior. Many are basically quantitative; that is, they assign a numerical value to the youth's level of risk. Others include a quantitative component, but also attempt to identify individual factors and describe the relationships between them.

One example of a quantitative instrument is the Michigan Youth Services Delinquency Risk Assessment Scale (MYSS) (OJJDP, 1994). The MYSS contains 11 questions about different dimensions of problem behavior. It focuses on delinquency (excluding, for example, sexual behavior and many school problems). Juveniles are given scores on each question based on the severity of their problem in the dimension represented by that question. A higher score represents a higher degree of risk.

A second example of a quantitative instrument is the Alaska Youth Services Needs Assessment Scale (AYSNAS) (OJJDP, 1994). This questionnaire contains 13 questions and is somewhat more comprehensive than the MYSS. It covers more dimensions and offers a broader range of potential scores than does the MYSS. Like the MYSS, a higher score is indicative of a greater degree of risk.

The Southeast Florida Risk Assessment Package (SFRAP) is actually a group of instruments. A practitioner can use these instruments to obtain not only an estimate of degree of risk, but also to specify risk-related factors and to analyze the relationships between those factors.

The first instrument in the SFRAP is the Comprehensive Checklist of Risk-Related Factors (CCRF) (Ellis, 1998), similar to the list included in table 1.2. Factors identified on the checklist are then mapped onto the Adolescent Domain (AD), pictured in figure 3.12. A third instrument, the Comprehensive Risk Description (CRD) is then used to record the relationships observed between the factors in narrative form. The fourth part of the SFRAP is the Systemic Competence Rating Scale (SCRS), which allows the practitioner to quantify the degree to which each social system with which the juvenile interacts is capable of supporting prosocial behavior. The final section draws from and is similar to the MYSS and the AYSNAS. It helps the worker assign a quantitative value to the juvenile's level of risk. It also considers the effects of race, culture, and ethnicity, since these are significant issues in southeast Florida. None of these scales have been scientifically tested, and, since they deal in risk, cannot be used for prediction. They are useful, however, for clinical purposes, and can help the practitioner gain an idea of the client's level of need and risk.

Instruments to Evaluate Mental Health Status

Several instruments are available to use in evaluating mental health status. Many of these are available only to persons who are licensed to administer and interpret them. These include the Minnesota Multiphasic Personality Inventory (MMPI), the Millon Adolescent Personality Inventory scale (MAPI), the Thematic Apperception Test (TAT), and several others (Hoge & Andrews, 1996). Others, such as the Beck Depression Inventory (BDI) (Beck, 1979) and the Clinical Anxiety Scale (CAS) (Fischer & Corcoran, 1994), are available to all practitioners. Many can be found in books like *Measures for Clinical Practice,* second edition (Fischer & Corcoran, 1994).

Instruments to Evaluate Substance Abuse

The Center for Substance Abuse Treatment (CSAT) offers both training information and a sample instrument for the evaluation of adolescent substance abuse. They are available in the publication *Screening and Assessment of Alcohol- and Other Drug-Abusing Adolescents.* It includes the Adolescent Problem Severity Index, a structured screening interview guide, which asks specific questions about substance abuse and many other dimensions of the juvenile's life. The CSAT recommends that urinalysis be conducted as a supplement to the interview.

Instruments to Evaluate the Risk of Specific Behaviors

The tools described above for assessing risk of problem behavior have not been normed or statistically tested. They are also based on risk factors that are correlated with problem behavior, but have not been shown to cause deviance. They cannot, therefore, be regarded as scientific instruments that predict which youths will become delinquent.

Some of the evaluation instruments for specific problems that are discussed here are predictive. Others, like the general risk devices, are useful as screening tools, but their validity has not been tested. Both types are used by clinical experts to identify those youth who are likely to engage in specific behaviors. These behaviors include violence, suicide, eating disorders, fire-starting, and sexual offense.

Several tools are available for determining the likelihood that a juvenile will be aggressive. Some of these have been statistically tested. Others have not. A review by Wiebush, Baird, Krisberg, and Onek (1995) is a good resource for an overview of several of these instruments.

A number of tools are also available for determining risk of suicide. One example is the Suicidal Ideation Questionnaire, designed by Research Psychologists Press/Sigma (Reynolds, 1988). Reynolds (1991) also offers a school-based assessment instrument.

Practitioners who wish to assess youth for the presence of eating disorders have a number of alternatives. One, designed by Garner (1996), is called the Eating Disorder Inventory–2. This 64-item instrument has been normed and tested in several clinical trials. Those who wish to test specifically for bulimia might use the Bulimia Test (BULIT) (Smith & Thelen, 1984). Other tools for anorexia and compulsive overeating can be found in *Measures for Clinical Practice,* second edition (Fischer & Corcoran, 1994).

Instruments for Educational Evaluation

Many different instruments are used to test for learning disabilities and other educational problems. A good resource for understanding those disabilities is *Exceptional Children: An Introduction to Special Education* (Heward, 1996). Youth who need educational testing should be referred to an expert in that field.

Other Useful Tools

Practitioners may need to assess their clients in any of several dimensions, including attitudes toward deviant behavior, family functioning, and social and communication skills. Diagnostic tools are available for many of these purposes. Several are described by Kalfus (1995) in *Handbook of Adolescent Psychopathology: A Guide to Diagnosis and Treatment.* Others are identified in *Assessing the Youthful Offender,* by Hoge and Andrews (1996).

USING ASSESSMENT FOR INTERVENTION PLANNING

Assessment becomes the basis for planning intervention, the topic discussed in chapters 4, 5, and 6. In juvenile justice practice, intervention has two purposes: (1) rehabilitation of the offender, and (2) ensuring the safety of the community.

In some cases, for example, when the balanced and restorative model is applied (see chapter 5), there may be a third purpose. That third purpose is the restoration of losses to the victim (restitution).

Various components of the assessment are used to plan the different elements of the intervention. Rehabilitation (treatment) planning uses many parts of the assessment. Problems often exist in multiple areas: individual, family, school, peer group, and other social systems. Counseling, tutoring, training, and other activities may be included in treatment.

Ensuring community safety normally involves more specific areas. Practitioners are concerned about propensity toward violence, the likelihood of sexual offense, the probability that the youth will elope (run away), and other issues. Interventions in these cases may include secure confinement, electronic monitoring, or frequent supervisory visits.

Restitution involves requiring the perpetrator to restore whatever was taken to his victim. The legal history portion of the assessment addresses this issue. Where possible, a youth may be required to do work directly for the victim, to earn money from other employment to repay the victim, or to perform community service tasks.

SUMMARY

This chapter has reviewed the process of assessment with juvenile justice clients. Assessment has several purposes, including treatment, classification, processing, and termination of services. It can be divided into several components, such as the client's demographic characteristics, educational and vocational backgrounds, legal history, family experiences, substance abuse history, psychiatric conditions, social issues, medical problems, and sexual history. At times, additional information may be needed about specific dimensions of a youth's life. This information is usually collected and analyzed by an expert in that dimension in a process known as evaluation. Various instruments exist to help assessment and evaluation workers complete their tasks. Their work then becomes the basis for structuring interventions. Chapters 4, 5, and 6 discuss the many components of intervention.

ACTIVITIES FOR LEARNING

1. Box 3.3 contains the case study of Andrew, a 17-year-old boy. Figures 3.1 through 3.10 contain groups of sample questions that are typically included on assessment questionnaires. Imagine that you are a juvenile justice practitioner who is interviewing Andrew. Answer the questions from the questionnaire. Would you recommend any specialized evaluations for Andrew? If so, what would they be?

2. In the first section of the chapter we discussed the three levels of prevention: primary, secondary, and tertiary. What level of prevention would you recommend for Maggie, the juvenile described in box 3.4? What level would be appropriate for Andrew, described in box 3.3?

3. Draw a copy of the Adolescent Domain, pictured in figure 3.12. Map Andrew's risk-related factors onto your copy. Then write a short narrative describing the relationships between those factors. Which are likely to affect the others? Which generate risk? Which are special needs? Which may offer Andrew some protection?

QUESTIONS FOR DISCUSSION

1. What kinds of specialized evaluations might you seek for Maggie? Does every juvenile need specialized evaluation? What kinds of characteristics suggest that a youth might need assessment for violent behavior? For sexual offense? For educational problems?

2. Suppose you were conducting an assessment of a juvenile and she reported a history of sexual abuse by her father (who was still living in her home). What steps would you take? (Hint: You need to think about several

areas: protection from future abuse, appropriate treatment for the juvenile, parent training for the mother, etc.)

3. Why is collecting information on vocational interest and training important to an assessment? How might that information be used in treatment planning?

4. Why is the classification of juveniles for treatment important? How might the decision to place a juvenile in a high-security facility affect the outcome of treatment?

KEY TERMS AND DEFINITIONS

Classification The process of identifying juveniles with other groups of juveniles who possess similar characteristics. This may be done for several reasons, including grouping youths appropriately for confinement or treatment or effectively designing interventions.

Competence The ability or capacity to perform an act and to understand the consequences of that act. For example, to waive the right to an attorney and to understand how that may affect adjudication.

Eating disorders Mental or emotional disorders that affect the sufferer's patterns of food consumption and retention. Includes anorexia nervosa, bulimia nervosa, and compulsive overeating.

Miranda rights A group of legal rights that a suspect must be made aware of at the time of arrest. For example, the accused is not required to respond to the questions of law enforcement and has the right to have an attorney present during questioning.

Prosocial Conforming to the acceptable patterns of society.

Self-mutilation Engaging in self-harmful behaviors such as cutting oneself.

Suicidal ideation Having suicidal thoughts, that is, thinking about or considering suicide.

Termination Ending a period of supervision or treatment.

REFERENCES

Asclone, F. R., Thompson, T. M., & Black T. (1997). Childhood cruelty to animals: Assessing cruelty dimension and motivations. *Anthrozoos, 10*(4), 170–173.

Beck, A. T., Rush, A. J., Shaw B. F., & Emery, G. (1979). *Cognitive therapy of depression.* New York: Guilford Press.

Center for Substance Abuse Prevention. (1993a). *Prevention primer: An encyclopedia of alcohol, tobacco, and other drug prevention terms.* Washington, DC: Author.

Center for Substance Abuse Treatment. (1993b). *Screening and assessment of alcohol- and other drug-abusing adolescents.* Washington, DC: Author.

Cowden, V. L., & McKee, G. R. (1994). Competency to stand trial in juvenile delinquency proceedings: Cognitive maturity and the attorney-client relationship. *University of Louisville Journal of Family Law, 33*(3), 629–660.

Dryfoos, J. G. (1990). *Adolescents at risk: Prevalence and prevention.* New York: Oxford University Press.

Ellis, R. A. (1997). *Gender differences in behavioral and psychosocial correlates of substance abuse among adolescents in residential treatment.* Unpublished doctoral dissertation, Florida International University.

Ellis, R. A. (1998). Filling the prevention gap: Multi-factor, multi-system, multi-level intervention. *The Journal of Primary Prevention, 19*(1), 57–71.

Ellis, R. A., O'Hara, M., & Sowers, K. (1999). Treatment profiles of troubled female adolescents: Implications for judicial disposition. *Juvenile and Family Court Journal, 50*(3), 25–40.

Fischer, J., & Corcoran, K. (1994). *Measures for clinical practice: A sourcebook* (2nd ed.). New York: Free Press.

Freeman, A., & Reinecke, M. A. (1993). *Cognitive therapy of suicidal behavior.* New York: Springer.

Garner, D. M. (1996). The Eating Disorder Inventory-2. In L. I. Sederer & B. Dickey (Eds.), *Outcomes assessment in clinical practice* (pp. 92–96). Baltimore: Williams & Wilkins.

Grisso, T. (1998). *Forensic evaluation for juveniles.* Sarasota, FL: Personal Resource Press.

Groth, A. N., & Loredo, C. M. (1981). Juvenile sexual offenders: Guideline for assessment. *International Journal of Offender Therapy and Comparative Criminology, 25,* 31–39.

Hawkins, J. D., Catalano, R. F., & Miller, J. Y. (1992). Risk and protective factors for alcohol and other drug problems in adolescence and early adulthood: Implications for substance abuse prevention. *Psychological Bulletin, 112*(1), 64–105.

Heward, W. L. (1996). *Exceptional children: An introduction to special education.* Englewood Cliffs, NJ: Prentice Hall.

Hoge, R. D., & Andrews, D. A. (1996). *Assessing the youthful offender: Issues and techniques.* New York: Plenum.

Jessor, R., & Jessor, S. L. (1977). *Problem behavior and psychosocial development: A longitudinal study of youth.* New York: Academic Press.

Kalfus, G. R. (1995). Behavioral assessment in adolescents. In V. B. Van Hasselt and M. Hersen (Eds.), *Handbook of adolescent psychopathology: A guide to diagno-sis and treatment* (pp. 243–264). New York: Lexington Books.

Office of Juvenile Justice and Delinquency Prevention (OJJDP). (1994). *Juvenile intensive supervision: Planning guide.* Washington, DC: Author.

Office of Juvenile Justice and Delinquency Prevention. (1995). *Guide for implementing the comprehensive strategy for serious, violent, and chronic juvenile offenders.* Washington, DC: Author.

Office of Juvenile Justice and Delinquency Prevention. (1999). Intensive Protective Supervision Project. *Blueprints for violence prevention* [Online]. Available: http://www.colorado.edu/cspv/blueprints/promise/index.html.

Reynolds, W. (1988). *Suicidal ideation questionnaire: Professional manual.* Lutz, FL: Psychological Assessment Resources.

Reynolds, W. (1991). A school-based procedure for the identification of adolescents at risk for suicidal behaviors. *Family and Community Health, 14,* 64–75.

Smith, M. C., & Thelen, M. H. (1984). Development and validation of a test for bulimia. *Journal of Consulting and Clinical Psychology, 52,* 863–872.

Wiebush, R., Baird, C., Krisberg, B., & Onek, D. (1995). Risk assessment and classification for serious, violent, and chronic juvenile offenders. In J. Howell, B. Krisberg, J. D. Hawkins, & J. Wilson (Eds.), *A sourcebook: Serious, violent, and chronic juvenile offenders* (pp. 171–212). Thousand Oaks, CA: Sage.

Zastrow, C., & Kirst-Ashman, K. K. (1997). *Understanding human behavior in the social environment* (4th ed.). Chicago: Nelson-Hall.

Chapter 4

◆

Interventions with Youths and Families

CHAPTER OUTLINE
Three Priorities in Intervention
General Principles of Effective Intervention
Sanctions, Monitoring, and Supervision
Family Counseling
Parent Training
Summary

Successful interventions with juvenile justice clients typically address three priorities and include several components. Priorities refer to the overall goals of the intervention. The three primary priorities of intervention are rehabilitation of the offender, protection of the community, and restitution to the victim.

Interventions also often include multiple components. By components, we mean that the intervention may include several separate but coordinated initiatives that address different problems. For example, an intervention for Andrew, the young man described in box 3.3 (see chapter 3), might include individual counseling for his conduct disorder, substance abuse treatment and parent training for his mother, tutoring for school problems, substance abuse treatment for Andrew, and other components.

In this chapter we'll look at all three priorities and two components. As we discuss the priorities, we'll investigate various methods of monitoring, supervising, and administering sanctions. The two components discussed in this chapter are the individual and family components. These are perhaps the most critical dimensions of a youth's life, and require a great deal of emphasis in many interventions. Chapter 5 will discuss other components.

THREE PRIORITIES IN INTERVENTION

As mentioned above, the three priorities in intervention are (1) rehabilitation of the offender, (2) protection of the community, and (3) restitution for the victim. Not all interventions attempt to meet all three priorities. There is, however, increasing evidence that when interventions consider all three issues, the effectiveness of the intervention is enhanced (Galaway & Hudson, 1996). This section reviews each priority, discusses the philosophical basis for each, and offers examples of how each might be applied in an intervention.

Intervention Priority 1: Rehabilitation

The juvenile justice system was originally conceived as a nonadversarial, treatment-oriented environment. Systemic abuses subsequently led to a series of court decisions that guaranteed offenders certain "due process" rights but gave the court greater structure and a more adversarial atmosphere (del Carmen et al., 1998). Also, recent "get tough" trends in many states have brought a greater emphasis on retribution and punishment to their court systems (Torbet & Szymanski, 1998). Nevertheless, the primary mission of the juvenile court remains the treatment and rehabilitation of the offender.

Intervention Priority 2: Protection of the Community

A second priority of the intervention is the protection of the community. The court often attempts to ensure, through the practitioner, that the community is protected from any future delinquent acts by the offender. Several alternatives may be used, including incarceration, active and frequent surveillance, and electronic monitoring. These and other alternatives will be discussed in the section on individual intervention.

Intervention Priority 3: Restitution to the Victim

Restorative justice, that is, ensuring that the offender makes some form of restitution to his victim, is a growing trend in juvenile justice. *Restitution* may be required in several forms, including direct repayment, performing work for the victim in lieu of repayment, or community service. Often face-to-face negotiation is conducted in the presence of a mediator. This process, often referred to as victim-offender mediation (VOM), shows a great deal of promise as an effective intervention with delinquent youth.

The Balanced and Restorative Approach

Historically, many interventions have emphasized either of the first two priorities, but few have emphasized all three. Recently, however, practitioners and researchers have begun to encourage the use of all three in planning and implementing interventions. This comprehensive method is often termed the balanced and restorative approach (BARA) (Bazemore & Day, 1996).

BARA emphasizes three goals: accountability, competency, and public safety (see figure 4.1). Accountability refers to identifying the obligation created by the offense and ensuring that the perpetrator is held responsible for it. In traditional justice models, the offender is seen as accountable to the state, and sanctions are administered accordingly. In BARA, the obligation and the response focus on responsibility to the victim.

Competency means that the offender returns to the community competent to interact successfully and prosocially with her social systems. This does not mean merely refraining from future delinquency. It also means performing bet-

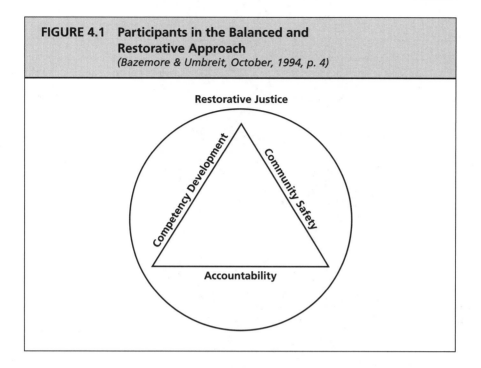

FIGURE 4.1 Participants in the Balanced and Restorative Approach
(Bazemore & Umbreit, October, 1994, p. 4)

ter in school, family, and other environments. Public safety refers to ensuring that the community is not further injured by delinquent activity on the part of the offender. In BARA this is accomplished by involving parents, employers, teachers, and others in the supervision of the offender. The practitioner develops relationships with these persons and emphasizes positive development in the youth through collaboration with them.

Ellis (1997) argues that, although BARA represents an improvement over *retributive justice* (also called the retributive model), it lacks one important goal: systemic competence. Systemic competence refers to the ability of the social systems with which the youth interacts to support his new, positive behaviors. Interventions that support systemic competence are discussed in this chapter and in chapter 5.

Victim-offender mediation plays a central role in BARA. Its proponents believe that by involving the offender, the victim, and the community, the effectiveness of the intervention is enhanced. For a summary of the role of each, see table 4.1.

GENERAL PRINCIPLES OF EFFECTIVE INTERVENTION

Researchers have been evaluating delinquency programs since at least the 1950s. Many of their discoveries have been discouraging. In fact, during the 1970s and early 1980s, some experts began to develop the philosophy that "nothing works" (Lösel, 1996). Recently, however, a series of studies called "*meta-analyses*" have

Table 4.1 The Balanced and Restorative Approach

CRIME VICTIMS	OFFENDERS	CITIZENS, FAMILIES, AND COMMUNITY GROUPS
◆ Receive support, assistance, compensation, information, and services.	◆ Complete restitution to their victims.	◆ Are involved to the greatest extent possible in rehabilitation, community safety initiatives, and holding offenders accountable.
◆ Receive restitution or other reparation from the offender.	◆ Provide meaningful service to repay the debt to their communities.	◆ Work with offenders on local community service projects.
◆ Are involved and are encouraged to give input at all points in the system as to how the offender will repair the harm done.	◆ Face the personal harm caused by their crimes by participating in victim offender mediation or other victim awareness programs.	◆ Provide support to victims.
◆ Have the opportunity to face the offenders and tell their story.	◆ Complete work experience and active and productive tasks that increase skills and improve the community.	◆ Provide support to offenders as mentors, employers, and advocates.
◆ Feel satisfied with the justice process.	◆ Are monitored by community adults as well as juvenile justice providers and supervised to the greatest extent possible in the community.	◆ Provide work for offenders to pay restitution to victims and service opportunities that allow offenders to make meaningful contributions to the quality of community life.
◆ Provide guidance and consultation to juvenile justice professionals on planning and advisory groups.	◆ Improve decisionmaking skills and have opportunities to help others.	◆ Assist families to support the offender in obligation to repair the harm and increase competencies.
		◆ Advise courts and corrections and play an active role in disposition.

SOURCE: Bazemore & Day, 1996, p. 9

allowed practitioners and researchers to draw several preliminary conclusions about the types of interventions that are effective. Many experts feel that these conclusions are sufficient grounds for developing a series of new programs structured using this information (Lösel, 1996). The next two chapters will provide basic information on how the juvenile justice practitioner can use the information gained from various studies and meta-analyses to structure effective intervention. The information will be organized according to the biological and social systems relevant to the offender: individual, family, peer group, school, and community.

Individual Counseling and Related Services

Individual counseling and related services are an important component of many interventions. In the past, individual counseling has often been used with juveniles, sometimes alone, and sometimes in combination with other components. Because of frequent recidivism among those who received it as a solitary form of intervention, many scholars have questioned its effectiveness (Henggeler, 1989). Others have found some forms of counseling to be very effective when applied in combination with other intervention components (Lösel, 1996). The meta-analyses help to sort out which methods are most effective.

One meta-analysis (Andrews et al., 1990) and several individual studies (Lösel, 1996; Patterson, Reid, & Dishion, 1992; Ross & Fabiano, 1985) have suggested that cognitive-behavioral techniques are particularly effective for troubled youth. Cognitive-behavioral techniques refer to a fairly broad range of practices. Examples include reality therapy, rational-emotive therapy, and cognitive therapy. Cognitive-behavioral counseling focuses on cognitive and behavioral factors as primary causes of deviant behavior. Faulty ways of perceiving the self, the world, and the future, and related behavioral contingencies are seen as the root of *dysfunctional* behavior. The therapist uses *empirically supported* procedures to alter those perceptions and contingencies to make them support prosocial behavior. Very specific techniques are used to recognize problem *cognitions* (thoughts, ideas) and to challenge and replace those thoughts. Behavioral techniques such as role play, modeling, and experimental activities are frequently employed (Zarb, 1992).

A therapist might choose to use cognitive-behavioral therapy with Maggie, the 12-year-old girl described in box 3.4 (see chapter 3). One goal of the therapy might be to increase Maggie's level of self-esteem, since she was described as moderately depressed, lonely, and isolated. If the therapist could help Maggie improve her self-esteem and become less depressed, Maggie might gain the confidence to develop new friendship groups. The case manager or therapist might also provide social skills training and might link Maggie with more positive groups. This combination of intervention techniques could be very powerful.

In cognitive-behavioral therapy, the therapist would attempt to establish rapport with Maggie, then would join with her in collaborative goal-setting. If they agreed that improved self-esteem was a desirable goal, they would work to uncover any dysfunctional ideas that Maggie has about herself. These ideas might be something like, "I'm worthless and incompetent," "My condition

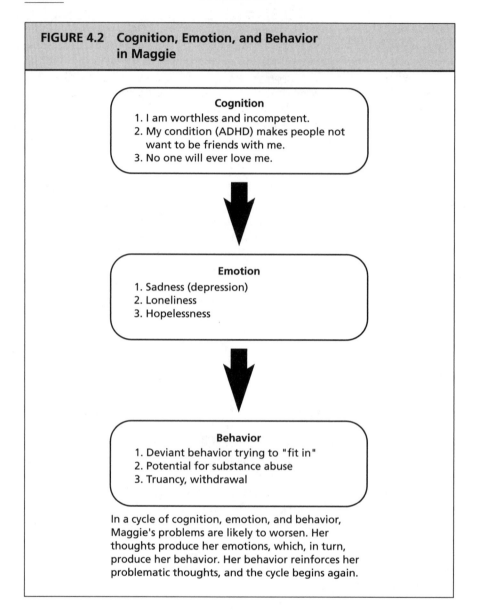

FIGURE 4.2   Cognition, Emotion, and Behavior in Maggie

Cognition
1. I am worthless and incompetent.
2. My condition (ADHD) makes people not want to be friends with me.
3. No one will ever love me.

Emotion
1. Sadness (depression)
2. Loneliness
3. Hopelessness

Behavior
1. Deviant behavior trying to "fit in"
2. Potential for substance abuse
3. Truancy, withdrawal

In a cycle of cognition, emotion, and behavior, Maggie's problems are likely to worsen. Her thoughts produce her emotions, which, in turn, produce her behavior. Her behavior reinforces her problematic thoughts, and the cycle begins again.

(ADHD) makes people not want to be friends with me," or "Nobody will ever love me."

Negative thoughts like the ones described above would produce strong emotions, or feelings. Those feelings might include sadness, loneliness, and hopelessness, all symptoms of Maggie's depression. In an attempt to fit in with her current or other friendship groups, Maggie might smoke marijuana, shoplift, or skip school. Alternatively, she might withdraw altogether, completely isolating herself from any source of social support. These behaviors would probably reinforce Maggie's problematic thoughts, resulting in intensified

**Table 4.2 Examples of Problem Cognitions, Emotions,
and Behavior among Delinquents**

COGNITION	EMOTION	BEHAVIOR
1. Everyone is out to get whatever they can, and will take what is mine. I'd better defend it.	Anger	Violence
2. I'll never make it in school, or in a job. I need to get by. I'll do it however I can.	Frustration	Theft
3. Nobody's ever done anything for me. Why should I care about anyone else?	Isolation	Robbery
4. I need a little something to help me get through the day. I can't get by without it.	Anxiety	Substance abuse
5. Why should I work a minimum wage job. I can make $2,000 a week on the street.	Frustration	Selling drugs
6. Nobody respects me. I've got to prove I deserve respect. Nobody is going to disrespect me.	Anger	Gang fighting

This list is by no means complete; nor do the emotions and behaviors included here always follow the thoughts described in the first column. These are examples that might occur. Juveniles often have many other thoughts and variations of these patterns.

emotion and further problem behavior. For an illustration of this process, see figure 4.2.

The therapist might chose one of several ways to intervene in Maggie's destructive cycle. Typically, he might select either cognitive or behavioral techniques, or both. For example, he might challenge Maggie's thought that no one will ever love her by pointing out people in her life that do love her. He might challenge Maggie's thoughts about her incompetence by showing her how many things she can actually do very well.

Using behavioral techniques, the therapist might teach Maggie specific social skills to make or improve friendships. He would then send her out to try those skills in "personal experiments," providing support and guidance in each session. If these "experiments" produced positive results, they would be used to challenge Maggie's problem cognitions. Although this example has used thoughts related to depression to illustrate problematic cognitions, many other difficulties may exist. Table 4.2 contains examples of other problem thoughts often held by delinquents.

The use of cognitive-behavioral interventions is consistent with the conclusions of other meta-analyses that interventions based on *social learning theory* are particularly effective (Lösel, 1996). Social learning theory asserts that behavior is learned through several processes, including modeling, *imitation,* and differential reinforcement (Bandura, 1979). In *modeling,* a child observes an adult engaging in a behavior. If the child sees that the adult experiences positive consequences, he is likely to imitate the behavior. For example, a child may see his father strike someone in anger, then hear his friends congratulate him on his bravery and strength.

If the child then strikes another child with whom he is angry, and experiences positive consequences (like the child crying and going away, while he himself receives the respect of others), he is likely to repeat that behavior in the future. Over time, if he experiences positive consequences for violence and experiences or observes negative consequences for nonviolence, he may become more consistently aggressive. He is also likely to associate with people who encourage his violent behavior (*differential reinforcement*). Eventually, he develops ideas (cognitions) that support violence. For example, he might tell himself, "The world is a violent place. You have to hit or be hit." Cognitions that support specific behaviors are known as "*definitions*" (Akers, 1985). Definitions justify those behaviors by explaining why they are useful, necessary, or merited. Definitions, then, could be seen as one form of the problematic cognitions that the therapist needs to address.

Cognitive-behavioral therapists use social learning theory both to understand why juveniles commit offenses and to treat them. By examining the connection between the youth's environment, her behaviors, and her thoughts, the therapist begins to understand the changes that must be made for the youth to improve. He can then plan an intervention that supports different behaviors and can challenge problematic definitions. For example, if working with the aggressive juvenile described above, the therapist could model and reinforce appropriate assertiveness while challenging dysfunctional definitions. He could use role play to demonstrate appropriate expression of anger. He might challenge the belief that it is necessary to hit others by asking the youth to think of examples of people who do not hit. The therapist might also recommend some sort of intervention for the family. The father might need anger management (social skills) training. Social skills training will be discussed in chapter 5. Family counseling will be discussed in the next section of this chapter.

Practitioners can use the knowledge of cognitive-behavioral therapy's effectiveness in several ways. Case managers may or may not provide therapeutic services depending on the service delivery model that is used. Case managers who do provide direct therapy to individual clients should become skilled in a form of cognitive-behavioral therapy and use that model. Case managers who do not provide direct therapy should identify community resources where practitioners utilize cognitive-behavioral techniques. According to several meta-analyses, the degree of treatment integrity, that is, the degree to which the therapist is faithful to the therapeutic model, is vital. Practitioners should therefore adhere closely to the cognitive-behavioral model they have chosen when they work with their clients. Case managers should insist that those to whom they refer their clients are equally consistent in their methods.

Practitioners whose primary role is individual counseling should develop skill in cognitive-behavioral methods and techniques. They should then use them to address dysfunctional cognitions and behavior patterns related both to the primary presenting problem (problem behavior) and any related problems or disorders (e.g., depression or impulsivity).

Administrators, advocates, and advisors should familiarize themselves with the literature about cognitive-behavioral methods. They should then use their influence to see that these methods are employed in the agencies they serve. Researchers should then be utilized to monitor the integrity and effectiveness of these interventions.

Cognitive-behavioral therapies have specific protocols that should be followed very strictly. As mentioned early, treatment integrity is very important in ensuring that intervention is effective. Practitioners who have not been trained in these techniques should receive training before attempting to use them. Trained practitioners should resist the temptation to become eclectic.

Several resources are available as treatment manuals for cognitive-behavioral therapists. One of the better resources is *Cognitive-Behavioral Assessment and Therapy* by Janet M. Zarb (1992). For an example of how cognitive-behavioral techniques were used with one client and his family, see boxes 4.1 and 4.2.

Individual therapy can be an important component of intervention when it is indicated in the assessment. A review of recent studies and meta-analyses has provided important guidelines for individual therapy. From those guidelines, it is possible to make several observations about effective therapy. The observations are summarized in table 4.3.

Behavioral Contracting

Behavioral contracting is an important part of both case management and individual counseling. In behavioral contracting a written agreement is prepared between the client and the practitioner. Often, family members or other persons significant to the client also participate. The *behavioral contract* specifies both goals and behaviors. Goals may include activities such as successful completion of a vocational program or 100% negative results on drug tests. Behaviors may include both activities to be completed and activities to be avoided. An example of activities to be completed would be specific household chores to be performed. An example of behaviors to be avoided would be contact with specific peers. Restitution and community service activities would also be included in the behavioral contract.

A good behavioral contract also includes a clear specification of rewards and consequences. Rewards, as used here, refer to both positive reinforcers and other types of incentives. Consequences refer to negative sanctions that may be used to punish inappropriate behaviors. Rewards might be provided after several consecutive weeks of compliance or after several specific tasks have been performed. Rewards should be things that are appealing to both youth and family, and should be provided as quickly as possible after they are earned. Sanctions punish behaviors (loss of privileges), constrict the mobility of the youth (electronic monitoring), or both. Sanctions should also be applied promptly and, when possible, should be clearly related to the juvenile's misbehavior. The youth should also be provided with a clear explanation as to why sanctions are being administered. An example of a behavioral contract for Ricky, the youth discussed in box 1.2 (see chapter 1), is provided in figure 4.3.

Institutional Settings

Depending on the frequency and severity of his offenses, a juvenile may be disposed into one of several levels of institutional care. These levels of care include foster care, *therapeutic foster care* (or special services foster care), day treatment,

Box 4.1 Life Story: Treatment of Lee
As Told to One of the Authors

Lee was a 14-year-old Asian-American male who lived in a major metropolitan area. He was referred for counseling by the state youth authority because he had broken into a home and stolen a substantial amount of jewelry and cash.

Lee lived with both his parents and his older sister in a middle-class neighborhood. His family life appeared to be good, but his parents expressed intense shame at Lee's arrest, stating that he had dishonored their family. Beyond this statement, they would say little other than that they could deal with Lee and did not need the help of a therapist.

All the sessions with Lee were in my office. Family sessions (described in box 4.2) were held in the family's home. Normally during the first session I would do a little rapport-building, reach an agreement as to the problem, describe how the sessions would proceed, and give a little bit of homework for the next week. In the case of Lee, a young Asian-American man from what the case manager reported was a very traditional home, I concentrated on the rapport-building. We devoted only a small amount of time to problem definition and description of future sessions. As an experiment I suggested that Lee refine the problem definition for the following week. "We know what problem brought you here," I told him. "You were arrested for burglary. But I've found that when kids commit crimes, there is usually some problem underlying their crime. You're a very bright young man, from a very strong family that loves you very much. I think you either know or can figure out what that underlying problem is. Why don't you think about that this week, talk it over with your family if you need to, and tell me what you've come up with next week."

The following week, Lee surprised me not only with a strong definition, but with a pretty good idea of what had led to the problem. "My problem is that I want to fit in with the other kids. I feel that I don't belong because I am Oriental and because my parents don't speak English very fluently. The kids at school all wear designer clothing. Mine is all from discount stores. I thought that by stealing money, I might be able to buy some clothes that would help me fit in better."

We immediately moved to identifying Lee's problematic cognitions. "Think of a time you felt rejected by the kids at school," I told Lee. "How did you feel? What were you thinking?" We gradually uncovered an "awfulizing" statement. "It's terrible that I don't fit in with everyone. I have some friends, but I must be friends with everyone."

We worked on Lee's "terrible" and "must" for several weeks. Through challenging these thoughts in sessions and in homework, Lee realized that it was unrealistic to expect to be friends with everyone and that this was not terrible, it was normal. We also worked on his perception of value, that it was valuable enough in his mind to be popular with everyone that he would risk arrest. We discovered that, to Lee, the dishonor of arrest was less than the dishonor of unpopularity. Over the next 14 weeks we worked on changing Lee's problematic thoughts.

During the 16th week Lee returned to court for a status hearing. The case manager submitted his report, which indicated that Lee was doing well in all areas. He also submitted my report, which stated that Lee had made sufficient progress to discontinue therapy. The judge concurred, and permitted three more sessions for termination. I understand that Lee has committed no more crimes, and now is a very successful and popular high school student.

Box 4.2   Life Story: Treatment of Lee's Family

As Told to One of the Authors

The story of the treatment of an Asian-American client, Lee, was reported in box 4.1. As a part of his treatment, I also worked as the therapist for his family. I traveled to their home once each week for 16 weeks. I found the experience rewarding, but very difficult, primarily because of language barriers and an unwillingness of the family to be very open in therapy.

Lee's family was very concerned with the concept of honor. They felt that they had been dishonored by Lee's actions, and that they were further dishonored by the presence of a therapist. I felt that it would be impossible to change their concept of honor, so I concentrated on mobilizing them to help Lee through his problem.

Lee's younger sister, Sue, served as translator for most of the sessions. Once, when she could not be present, a cousin came to translate. The family was very polite, but not very open or disclosing. They would listen respectfully to my comments and give short answers to my questions.

Therapy with Lee's family focused on helping the parents understand the difficulties juveniles often experience in adapting to the culture of a different country. I used none of my former clients' names, but I told them stories of a few other Asian-American youths with whom I had worked. They were very interested in these stories and grad-

ually began to understand Lee's problem.

My therapeutic technique varied from the standard cognitive-behavioral therapy format because of cultural and language issues. Normally sessions are very structured, and I use a lot of questioning to form a hypothesis about the problem, then further questioning to lead the family into dealing with the problem. With Lee's family I was less structured, and made assumptions about their views and cognitions with fewer questions than I normally would use. Once I was able to develop a hypothesis about their needs, I began to teach them about American culture and the adaptation process for Asian youth through storytelling and a few questions directed toward Lee. Whenever I questioned Lee, his sister translated, but Lee responded in their native language. I thought this would show greater respect for their language and customs than having him respond in English.

Eventually, Lee's parents came to understand Lee's problem with acceptance. His sister suggested that they buy him some designer clothing, and they agreed. (Perhaps her motives were not totally unselfish. She got some designer clothing as well.) They also allowed Lee to join some after-school clubs that he had not previously been allowed to join. This gave him an opportunity to make new friends. The story of Lee's termination from treatment is told in box 4.1.

---

or residential treatment. Youths who have special behavioral, substance abuse, or psychiatric issues may be disposed into institutions that deal primarily with those issues.

It is important to note that custodial settings should be used only as a last resort, or on occasions when concerns for community safety outweigh the treatment priority. Several meta-analyses have shown community-based treatment to be more effective than confinement for many juveniles (Lösel, 1996). Treatment in the home and community has been very successful, but only

Table 4.3 General Observations about Counseling Modalities

1. Some modalities appear to be more effective than others. Cognitive-behavioral therapies have been the most supported in empirical studies.
2. Some modalities appear to be ineffective or counterproductive. Nondirective, psychodynamic, and psychoanalytical therapies may have a negative effect.
3. The effectiveness of individual counseling appears to be enhanced when combined with other intervention components. Intensive case management programs using cognitive-behavioral interventions for individuals and families have shown great promise.

when it includes several specific intervention components. These components will be discussed in greater detail at the end of chapter 5.

Youths whose offenses have been infrequent or of low severity and who have serious home problems (e.g., abuse, neglect, or abandonment) may be disposed to foster care. *Foster care* refers to the groups of substitute homes that have been established by dependency systems in each state. Foster parents supervise juveniles in their own homes through a contractual arrangement with the state. Parents agree to care for these children as they would for their own.

In theory, the foster system sounds like a wonderful idea. In practice, it has many serious problems. Although many excellent homes are operated by dedicated parents, many other homes are overcrowded and undersupervised. In some homes children experience abuse at the hands of foster parents and other foster children. Practitioners must be aware of the possibility that foster homes are being mismanaged. Mistreatment of children in foster homes can exacerbate behavioral problems. Problems in those homes should be reported immediately to the agency overseeing the homes and to the court.

Many children who engage in status offenses live in homes that require special assistance but where conditions are not sufficiently severe to require removal of the children. These children and families are referred to by different names in different jurisdictions, but they are often called something like "children in need of services" (CINS) or "families in need of services" (FINS). When practitioners are assigned these juveniles, they should be aware that the home conditions and the child's behavior may worsen. Prevention-based activities can be very useful in these cases.

Day treatment and residential care have already been discussed in some detail in earlier chapters. Both typically provide structured environments in which therapeutic and educational services are provided regularly. The case manager should ensure that her clients are receiving cognitive-behavioral individual and group therapy. She should also see that any special needs such as need for medication, history of substance abuse, and abuse issues are being adequately addressed.

Certain clients with special needs may require specific treatment characteristics. For example, Ellis, O'Hara, and Sowers (1999) discovered important characteristics of troubled female adolescents that were relevant for treatment. The results of their study are discussed in chapter 7.

Institutional facilities often use token economies to help to control and structure their environments. In a token economy juveniles gain or lose privileges by accumulating "points" or some other form of token currency. When

FIGURE 4.3 Sample Behavioral Contract for Ricky

Behavioral Contract for: *Ricky*

Date: *June 1, 2001*

Responsibilities:

I, *Ricky* _____, agree to do the following:

1. Follow the schedule prepared with my case manager
2. Go to counseling once per week at the scheduled time
3. Avoid any delinquent activity
4. Meet with Roy twice each week
5. Attend school regularly
6. Attend after-school computer program regularly

Privileges:

If I meet my responsibilities, I will be able to:

1. Participate in youth league baseball
2. See my girlfriend on Friday nights
3. Go out to eat at McDonald's every Friday

Bonuses:

If I meet all my responsibilities for at least four weeks, I will be able to:

1. Go to a major league baseball game
2. Accumulate 25 points toward a computer system

Sanctions:

If I do not meet my responsibilities, I will:

1. Lose all the privileges listed above for one week
2. Possibly have to go back to court (serious offenses)
3. Possibly be put in a treatment program (serious offenses)

Monitoring:

My case manager and family will check to be sure that I am meeting my responsibilities by:

1. Scheduled visits by my case manager
2. Surprise visits by my case manager
3. Telephone calls and conferences by my case manager

Signed: _____
Juvenile

_____
Case Manager

Table 4.4 Guidelines for Appropriate Seclusion and Restraint (S & R)

1. S & R should be used only when other intervention options have been exhausted.
2. S & R may be used to prevent harm to self or others, to avoid serious disruption to the treatment environment, or to avert serious damage to the treatment facility.
3. S & R should never be used as punishment, to compensate for inadequate staffing patterns or training, or "for the convenience of staff."
4. Prevention of situations that may require S & R should begin at intake. Staff should clearly explain why the client is there, what he will be experiencing, how he is expected to behave, and what consequences he will experience if he fails to behave appropriately.
5. Rules, consequences, and acceptable behaviors should be described verbally, in writing, and (for children) in pictures.
6. Assessment should include an identification of those situations that are likely to trigger inappropriate behavior.
7. Social skills and anger management training should be a part of the client's treatment.
8. Staffing patterns and staff training should be adequate at all times.
9. Restraint techniques should be safe and should be practiced by staff on other staff as a part of training.
10. Decisions to use S & R should be made by a licensed physician or someone to whom a physician has delegated that responsibility.
11. Any client in S & R should be constantly monitored by staff.
12. Clients who have experienced S & R should be returned to the normal treatment environment as quickly as possible.
13. Clients who have required S & R should be assessed as soon as possible after the incident and their treatment plan adapted as needed.
14. All S & R incidents should be reviewed by a multidisciplinary team.

SOURCE: Abstracted from Testimony by Sandra Sexson, MD, American Academy of Child and Adolescent Psychology (Sexson, 1999)

---

the youths behave appropriately they receive points or credits. When they behave inappropriately, they lose points. Specified numbers of accumulated points allow them to advance to higher "levels" or stages of treatment. Higher levels often include greater freedom, some degree of responsibility in working with other youth, and greater privacy.

Sometimes institutional staff finds it necessary to restrain youths whose behavior has become a danger to themselves or others. Appropriate restraint can be difficult to achieve, since it is important that the staff minimize injury to themselves and to others. Some guidelines for appropriate restraint are offered in table 4.4.

On other occasions a youth may be restrained by being ordered to go to a "time-out" room or a seclusion room. In time-out the youth is asked to think through his attitude and to use specific skills for improving that attitude. At the end of a specified time the youth emerges from the room and discusses his conclusions with a staff member. If his conclusions are appropriate, and better behavior seems likely, the youth is allowed to return to regular daily activities. In more difficult cases, additional intervention may be necessary before the juvenile can be returned to the treatment environment. Some states provide guidelines for the use of seclusion in their statutes or administrative codes. The guidelines for the state of Utah are included in table 4.5.

Table 4.5 Utah State Code Regarding Seclusion of Youth

1. Detailed policy and procedures shall be developed and adopted by each facility as to the use of temporary lock-up or secure observation for detained residents. Temporary lock-up or secure observation may not be used to punish residents. Less restrictive measures should be used whenever possible. Any youth subject to lock-up or secure observation pursuant to this subsection shall have a right to have such lock-up or secure observation reviewed by staff designated by the facility director within a reasonable time following confinement. The youth shall be informed of his right to review at the time of lock-up or secure observation.

   a. During waking/program hours, involuntary lock-up or secure observation of a youth may be authorized for a period not to exceed three hours where a resident violates a facility rule and such lock-up or secure observation is necessary to preserve order or maintain security within a unit or facility. Residents shall have a review after the first hour to determine whether continued lock-up is necessary and justified. At the end of any three hour lock-up period, continued lock-up shall be subject to review and approval by staff designated by the facility director to review and approve continued lock-up.

   b. Involuntary temporary lock-up or secure observation of a youth may be authorized for a period of up to 24 hours if evidence clearly demonstrates that: (ACA 8336 and 8340)

      i. The youth presents an immediate threat of physical harm to him/herself or another person;

      ii. The youth presents an immediate threat of escape; or

      iii. The youth is involved in repetitious acts of misconduct which cannot be controlled in any other manner and which requires his removal for the protection of him/herself or another person.

   Residents who are subject to lock-up or secure observation (up to 24 hours) shall have a review after the first hour to determine whether or not continued lock-up is justified and under what conditions. When a decision is made to continue the lock-up status, a review shall then be conducted by staff designated by the facility director at least every eight waking hours or at the beginning of each change of work shift, whichever comes first, to assess the condition of the youth and determine whether continued lock-up is justified.

   c. Policy and procedure specifies that, behavior permitting, youth placed in secure observation are afforded living conditions and privileges approximating those available to the general resident population; exceptions are justified by clear and substantial evidence. (ACA 8338, Also 8175)

   d. Youth placed in secure observation must have constant visual and audio supervision by staff. In addition, youths shall be checked frequently, at least every 60 minutes, either by direct visual contact or direct communication and visited at least twice each day during waking hours by facility or administrative personnel. A visit does not include routine visual checks. (ACA 8339)

   e. When residents are placed in secure observation, the following procedure shall be followed: potentially dangerous articles shall be removed from the resident. This includes articles of clothing, such as belts, if there are reasonable grounds to believe such clothing constitutes a substantial threat to the health or safety of the resident. In no case shall all clothing be removed.

   f. A central record of all lock-ups or secure observation pursuant to this subsection must be maintained, which shall include the date and period of lock-up or secure observation and who initiated the confinement and reason.

SOURCE: Utah Administrative Code R547-4-17(10), 1999

When attitude or behavior problems become severe, a youth may be sent to an isolation room. These rooms often have protected or padded walls, very little furniture, and may or may not be locked, depending on the jurisdiction. When the rooms do contain furniture, it is often fastened to the floor so that it cannot be used to cause harm. As with time-out, youths may remain in an isolation room until they are able to appropriately manage their behavior.

Youths with psychiatric problems may require medication. This, of course, is a decision to be made by a medical doctor, but may require a judge's approval. Depending on the jurisdiction, medication may be administered by a staff member, a nurse, or a medical doctor. Guidelines for effective management of medication are provided in the OJJDP's *Desktop Guide to Good Juvenile Detention Practice* (OJJDP, 1996). If it becomes clear that a youth requires a higher level of care or a more specialized type of care, she may be transferred to a different facility.

When a juvenile has made sufficient progress in an institution, he graduates, or is released from that institution. At this point a new assessment is often needed. Based on that assessment, the youth may be released into the community or may be "stepped down" into a lower level of care. One example of a step-down would be moving a youth from a secure residential facility to a day treatment program. Another would be releasing the youth to community supervision in the custody of her parents.

Service Delivery Systems

Although the type of counseling received by a youth is critical, any form of counseling alone is likely to be insufficient (Henggeler, 1993). Instead, counseling must be a part of an overall package of services that address multiple needs in multiple social environments (Lösel, 1996). Scott Henggeler (1993) and his associates have experienced excellent results with such a program, multisystemic therapy (MST). MST and similar programs will be discussed in chapter 8.

SANCTIONS, MONITORING, AND SUPERVISION

A second important aspect of intervention for individuals is the imposition of sanctions, including the process of monitoring and supervision. Counseling focuses on the first intervention priority of juvenile justice: the rehabilitation of the offender. Sanctions, monitoring, and supervision are useful for rehabilitation, but also focus on the second priority: public safety.

Schedules of Sanctions

Sanctions are corrective actions. They normally punish the offender by taking away some sort of privilege, such as restricting his actions or movements. Since they restrict the offender's mobility, they also enhance community safety. Sanctions may be administered by the case manager or therapist for minor infractions, or by the court for more severe or frequent problems. When specific kinds of sanctions are listed along with the types of infractions for which they should be imposed, the resulting document is known as a "schedule of sanctioning."

Table 4.6 Sample Schedule of Sanctioning

CATEGORY 1 VIOLATIONS	CATEGORY 2 VIOLATIONS	CATEGORY 3 VIOLATIONS
Curfew hours	Chronic repetition of Category 1 violations	Conviction on multiple misdemeanors
AWOL < 24 hours	AWOL > 24 hours	Conviction on felony
Truancy	Abuse of alcohol or drugs	Beyond control of program staff
Failure to report	Fired from job	Active participation in gang activities
Incomplete chores	Refuse to attend court-ordered program	Chronic repetition of Category 2 violations
Associate w/negative peer	Abusive behavior or assault in program	
In off-limits area	Carry weapon	
Fail to pay restitution	New arrest for misdemeanor or felony	
Other	Other	
CATEGORY 1 SANCTIONS	**CATEGORY 2 SANCTIONS**	**CATEGORY 3 SANCTIONS**
Reprimand	Category 1 sanction and/or:	Cat. 1,2 sanctions and/or:
Stricter curfew	Extended house arrest	7-day detention
Loss of privilege(s)	Increased urinalysis	Electronic surveillance
Loss of days	Admin. review hearing	Return to phase 1
Increased surveillance	Weekend detention	Revoke to inpatient
Short-term house arrest	Court review/admonish	Revoke to institution
Add community service hrs.	Return to earlier phase	
Other proportional	Other proportional	

SOURCE: Krisberg, Neuenfeldt, Wiebush, & Rodriguez, 1994, p. 42

Administering Sanctions

Sanctions usually vary according to the severity of the offense. For lesser offenses, the sanction is usually less severe. Greater offenses prompt stronger sanctions. For example, a juvenile who violated curfew for the first time might receive a verbal warning. A youth who consorted with known delinquents might be assigned to house arrest. A youth who repeatedly smoked marijuana might be assigned to a residential substance abuse treatment program.

It can be difficult to identify a sanction that is sufficiently severe yet not so harsh as to discourage the youth. In order to guide workers, some agencies produce guidelines for sanctioning, often called schedules of sanctioning. A sample schedule, offered by the OJJDP (Krisberg, Neuenfeldt, Wiebush, & Rodriguez, 1994), is included in table 4.6.

When sanctions are administered, they should be put in place as quickly as possible. The practitioner should explain why the sanction is being applied, what is expected of the youth to meet the terms of the sanction, and what the consequences will be if the terms are not met. The conditions under which the sanction will be lifted should also be specified. Any significant others who will participate in the sanction should be informed of their role. For example, if a youth is assigned community service, the person supervising the community activities should be made aware of the assigned hours and instructed how to report failure to comply.

Court Involvement in Sanctions

Although sanctions for minor offenses are sometimes administered by practitioners, the court is often involved. The frequency of judicial involvement in the sanctioning process depends on several factors that vary depending on the jurisdiction and the judge. Some judges are very involved in cases and expect to be informed of even the most minor infractions. Others allow the practitioner greater latitude. It is very important that the practitioner learn the preferences of each judge and make every effort to comply with those preferences. Judges must evaluate the competence of individual workers based on a limited amount of courtroom exposure. When a judge expects to be informed of minor infractions and the practitioner fails to do so, the judge may lose confidence in an otherwise competent worker. On the other hand, a judge who is burdened with a particularly heavy caseload may not want to be involved in every detail of a case. If a juvenile has committed an infraction that requires the court's attention, the practitioner may arrange a status hearing. In this hearing the infraction is reported to the judge and the judge may impose sanctions. Often, the worker is asked to suggest appropriate sanctions, and the judge may accept those suggestions.

Monitoring

Monitoring activities actually begin when a youth is disposed into the care of the state youth authority. Monitoring refers to activities by the case manager to ensure that the terms of the youth's disposition are met. These activities are often intensified when a juvenile is sanctioned for violating probation.

Practitioners use various techniques to monitor their clients. Some monitoring is done through personal visits to the home, school, or workplace or through telephone calls. In many cases, members of the community, such as parents or teachers, are asked to participate. Sometimes electronic monitoring and drug testing are also employed.

Monitoring through Visits and Telephone Calls A great deal of offender monitoring is done through visits to the home, school, or workplace. These visits may be scheduled or unannounced. They are often supplemented through telephone calls. During the visit the practitioner has several goals. The most obvious goal is to determine whether the youth is where he is scheduled to be and to determine whether other terms of the disposition are being observed. In addition, the worker may talk to the youth and his family about school, family relationships, vocational issues, or other topics. Schedules are frequently reviewed, and goals for future progress may be set. If the worker is providing counseling to the juvenile or his family, a session may be conducted during the visit.

Telephone contact is another important monitoring tool. Since heavy caseloads often make it difficult for the practitioner to have frequent personal contact, she may call the juvenile's home, school, or workplace. In these contacts her goals may include (1) ensuring that the youth is where he is supposed to be, (2) ascertaining whether the youth is experiencing any problems, (3) reminding the youth that she is both monitoring and available for assistance, and (4) scheduling a future visit in person.

Monitoring through Community Involvement The balanced and restorative approach (BARA) emphasizes community involvement in the monitoring process. By including family members, neighbors, teachers, employers, recreation workers, and others, the practitioner can accomplish multiple goals. First, she can access many other eyes to observe the offender at times when she cannot be present. Second, she can enhance community competence. Third, promoting a positive, concerned attitude on the part of the monitors, she can develop a supportive bond between youth and community.

Family members are involved in monitoring by being asked to note the times the juveniles leave home and return, and to ensure that youths do not leave the home during curfew periods. They may also provide transportation to and participate in some of the activities specified in the youth's disposition.

Neighbors may be asked to observe the times that the juveniles come and go from their homes. They may also be asked to supervise a youth during times that parents are unavailable, or to serve as mentors. Often strong friendships can be developed with older, prosocial neighbors that serve as a strong protection against future problem behavior (Grossman & Garry, 1997).

Teachers can report truancy, classroom problems, and academic process. They can sometimes be encouraged to provide special support to a youth who is returning to class after time in the juvenile justice system. They may also be able to offer information about sources of tutoring or other academic support.

Employers can report on the offender's attendance, timeliness, and job performance. They may also be useful mentors and may provide important insights to the youth's vocational or professional interests. A portion of the wages earned by a juvenile may be used to pay restitution to his victim.

Workers at parks and recreation programs have a unique opportunity to observe youths in a relatively unstructured social environment. These professionals can provide insight on social and behavioral problems that are not obvious in other settings. Often, recreational workers can also be good mentors for troubled youth.

Electronic Monitoring Electronic monitoring involves wearing a device that transmits an electronic signal to a centralized monitoring station when its wearer exceeds a specific boundary. It is most frequently used for house arrest, that is, when a juvenile is required to remain within his home. The device is set to send an alarm if he moves more than a specified distance from the home. Workers then respond with a telephone call or a personal visit. Electronic monitoring devices are normally used only with more severe offenders. Their use is also somewhat controversial, and many question whether their use is appropriate for juveniles.

Drug Testing Drug testing is an important part of monitoring for many offenders. Periodic tests are often ordered for juveniles who have a history of use. The most frequently used form of testing is urinalysis, in which the juvenile's urine is tested for traces of several illicit substances. Tests may be conducted both on a schedule and randomly throughout the monitoring period.

Supervision

In this text, supervision refers to the process of overseeing the youth's rehabilitation. It involves developing a plan for improvement, then ensuring that the plan is followed and, when necessary, adjusted. Supervision is one of the activities performed by a case manager. Two of its aspects, administering rewards and sanctions and monitoring, were discussed in the section above.

A third aspect of supervision is cooperative planning. In many cases it may be beneficial to actually plan the youth's daily schedule, specifying times to get out of bed, when to be at school, when homework will be completed, and when he will go to bed. This is best done with both the juvenile and his family, so that everyone is in agreement with and aware of the plan. Once the plan is in place, the practitioner can monitor the youth's compliance through random checks. Cooperative planning should also be done in the development of the treatment plan and the behavioral contract as well as when rewards or sanctions are administered.

Cooperative planning can be a powerful tool. By involving the youth and family in the planning process, the worker shows them both courtesy and respect. By demonstrating the way in which planning is done, the practitioner can model good planning and problem-solving skills for the juvenile. Also, when the youth has participated in planning, she may be more willing to comply, and to accept sanctions when she does not.

Victim-Offender Mediation

Victim-offender mediation (VOM) is a relatively new and very promising intervention. In VOM, offending juveniles participate in a series of meetings with their victim and a court-appointed mediator. An agreement is negotiated between the offender and the victim in which the offender agrees to make restitution for whatever damages he caused the victim. A contract is developed, and the mediator then monitors the offender's performance to ensure that the terms of the contract are met (Umbreit, 1993). VOM will be discussed in greater detail in chapter 6. A brief discussion of an agency that offers VOM services is provided in box 4.3.

Box 4.3   Mediation Services of Putnam County

Linda Mix, Executive Director

Mediation Services of Putnam County (MSPC) is a community-based, nonprofit agency located in Cookeville, Tennessee. The agency's goals are to reduce violence and the number of cases in the court systems by promoting a peaceful community through education and mediation-based service provision.

MSPC began as a satellite office of Community Mediation Center/VORP in Crossville, Tennessee, in 1993. Mediation Services was organized and chartered as a separate, free-standing agency in July of 1997.

The core of our services is mediation, the involvement of a neutral or trusted third party assisting people to peacefully resolve their conflicts. The mediation process provides a peaceful alternative to taking out a warrant and going through the judicial process or letting conflicts escalate in community settings. District Attorney Bill Gibson describes mediation as "a valuable service to the community" and says it gives his staff more time to focus on the more serious offenses in the community. He also believes mediation "provides an important service to the victims of crime who are most often overlooked."

Participation in mediation is voluntary and confidential. Participants are empowered to resolve their situations themselves, helped by trained volunteer mediators. The resulting agreements are contracts that emphasize responsibility, accountability, restoring balance, future choices, and healing. John Hudson, general sessions and juvenile court judge, states that "successful mediation addresses problems before they become serious, and gives participants the skills to deal with such situations in the future."

MSPC also provides a shoplifting intervention course for youth, mediation training for volunteers, and conflict resolution classes for youths and their parents, adults, and parents with younger children. With parent/guardian involvement in all youth services, services also promote family support, communication, and guidance. Our services presently include court- and community-referred mediation, a shoplifting intervention course, and conflict resolution classes.

Judge Hudson believes that mediation is especially appropriate for many of the situations seen in juvenile court. "The parties are almost always schoolmates and may often be classmates and ride the same bus. Because of this forced interaction/exposure to each other, the traditional restraining order utilized with adults is often not appropriate."

Mediation services also "enables the juvenile court to reduce the volume of cases heard in the court by offering an alternative resource that encourages reconciliation of the opposing parties with a mutual agreement rather than by a court order," says Greg Bowman, Putnam County Youth Services officer. The mediation process gives them the opportunity to learn and practice their skills, determine the options that will resolve the situation, and be responsible for carrying out the agreement reached. Mediation "allows the victim and defendant to meet with each other in person to discuss what happened, why it happened, and to work out any restitution agreement. This, in turn, not only benefits both parties involved, but the court and community as well."

The shoplifting intervention course serves first-time offenders through juvenile court referral. Juveniles participate in meetings with staff, indirect mediation, and a professionally designed course. Through this process they learn the facts about shoplifting and its impact on themselves, their families, and their communities. They are held responsible for their actions, including paying for the course materials, and develop a personal plan to stay out of trouble, including how to make better decisions for themselves in the future.

Conflict resolution classes are offered to youth and to their parents. Classes are also available to parents with younger children who want to learn how to teach these skills to their children while they are young. Through discussion and "homework" assignments, participants identify their own patterns of behavior, including dealing with feelings, identifying what "triggers" their anger and aggressive behavior, and problems/consequences from these patterns. They then make a plan of action addressing what changes they need to make in these areas.

(continued)

Box 4.3 Mediation Services of Putnam County (*continued*)

Initial evaluation results look very promising. The shoplifting program evaluation results indicate that about 90% of youths who successfully complete services do not re-offend. Evaluation of mediation services shows that about 90% of mediations result in an agreement and that about 93% of these contracts are completed successfully. A year after involvement in mediation, youths show lower recidivism rates than youths who did not participate. If youths do re-offend, there is usually a reduction in the seriousness of their crimes.

FAMILY COUNSELING

Family counseling is the second major component of successful intervention for juvenile offenders. In this section we'll discuss some modalities that appear to be more effective than others. We'll also take a look at two techniques of family therapy that have been particularly effective. Finally, we'll look at special needs that families sometimes have. These needs often must be addressed in order for the overall intervention to be effective.

Effective Modalities

There are many different family therapy modalities. These include behavioral, cognitive-behavioral, strategic, structural, psychoanalytic, and others. Despite the presence of so many different modalities, a large group of outcome studies on their effectiveness, and several reviews or meta-analyses examining effectiveness, we still are not able to say with certainty which is best. This is because the quality of many of the studies has been poor, preventing us from being certain that the results were accurate.

The outcome research does offer some guidelines, however. Recent meta-analyses have identified several characteristics of effective therapy: (1) they are based on strong theories of delinquent behavior; (2) they are structured; (3) they use cognitive-behavioral techniques; and (4) they are multi-modal (Lösel, 1996).

Effective interventions are based on what we understand about problem behavior. What we know about why juveniles commit delinquent acts is used to design treatment that addresses those issues. For example, we know that multiple factors within the family and the community contribute to the development of behavioral problems. Effective interventions address several or all of those problems. We also know that juveniles learn by imitating others and receiving reinforcement for that behavior. Effective intervention rewards for prosocial behavior and uses sanctions for antisocial behavior. In family therapy this means looking at the many factors within the family that may produce problems and addressing each of those factors. It also means using modeling, role play, positive reinforcement, and sanctions to produce desired behaviors within the family.

Effective treatment is also structured. This means that the treatment uses distinct processes such as specifically scheduled sessions, homework, daily scheduling, and similar activities. Juveniles know what to expect and what they are expected to do. Typically, the family is involved in treatment as much as possible, so they not only attend sessions but participate in planning and monitoring. They may even share in the rewards and sanctions, depending on the nature of the problem and the intervention.

Cognitive-behavioral techniques were introduced in the section on individual therapy above. In a family setting, dysfunctional cognitions about other members of the family, the world, and other people are addressed using these same techniques. Behavioral techniques such as role play, positive reinforcement, and sanctioning are also employed.

Multi-modal means using multiple techniques to address multiple areas of life, or social systems. The family cannot be regarded as a closed system, that is, not influenced by outside forces. Even if the family were closed, this in itself would be a problem. Effective family intervention looks at the influence of other groups, such as peers or the community, on the family, and tries to make those influences positive. To address these issues, different modes, or approaches, are often used. For example, therapists might meet with the family weekly for traditional therapy sessions, and biweekly for social skills training. Certain characteristics of therapy have also been recognized as counterproductive. In many cases juveniles with whom these techniques are employed actually appear to get worse (Lösel, 1996). These counterproductive characteristics will be discussed in chapter 6.

Techniques of Effective Intervention

Three techniques of family therapy have been identified as particularly effective: behavioral contracting, communication enhancement programs, and combined interventions (Serna, Sherman, & Sheldon, 1996). These techniques can be incorporated into any intervention.

Behavioral contracting was discussed in the section above. It involves establishing a written agreement between the juvenile and the practitioner in which each agrees to specific behaviors and tasks. In family therapy, the contract is broadened to include other members of the nuclear and extended families. Contracts normally contain five sections: (1) the responsibilities of each family member, (2) the privileges of each member, (3) any bonuses that will be received for long-term contract compliance, (4) sanctions that will be imposed for failure to comply, and (5) agreement as to how the contract will be monitored. The steps for developing a family contract are included in table 4.7. A sample family contract for Ricky, the hypothetical client in box 1.2 (see chapter 1), is included in figure 4.4.

Communication training is intended to enhance the communication between family members. Communication skills include the capacities necessary for problem-solving, negotiation, and affectionate behavior. Several researchers have concluded that improving these capacities improves family functioning. This, in turn, diminishes the probability of problem behavior for adolescents in

Table 4.7 Steps in Behavioral Contracting

1. Select and define the behaviors that will be the subject of the contract.
2. Specify the rewards (and sanctions) to be received for compliance.
3. Prepare a clear written agreement.
4. Monitor the contract and collecting data about the behaviors and the rewards and sanctions.
5. Change the contract where the data or other information appear to make it necessary.
6. Continue monitoring and revision processes.
7. Identify additional behaviors to be changed.
8. Get all family members involved in planning and signing the contract.

SOURCE: Compiled by Serna, Sherman, & Sheldon, 1996

the families. Many of the skills taught in communication training are also a part of the social skills training programs described above.

Earlier we discussed the value of multi-modal intervention. The strength of this approach is demonstrated by a number of studies in which behavioral contracting was combined with other modes. A summary of these studies and their results is provided by Serna, Sherman, and Sheldon (1996). Overall, the studies report very impressive results.

Specific Family Problems

Regardless of the modality used, several specific problems are likely to arise with some families. Many require either special attention or referral to specialized resources. Others require that intervention be directed to family members other than the juvenile being supervised. We cannot discuss all the special needs that exist in families in a single chapter, but we will address several here. The special needs we'll talk about include (1) when parents must work multiple, low-paying jobs; (2) when parents are substance abusers; (3) when parents are involved in criminal activity; (4) when the problem-solving and decision-making skills of the youths exceed those of the parents; (5) when parents manage the family poorly; (6) when parents are mentally ill; (7) when there is little parental involvement; and (8) when siblings are deviant.

Parents Who Work Multiple Jobs Parental involvement can be difficult to obtain when the parents are forced to work multiple, low-paying jobs. Practitioners who work with such families can take one or more of several approaches in their interventions. One alternative is to help the family members develop better job skills or locate better employment. Another option is to help additional family members find sources of employment. A third approach is to develop alternative sources of youth supervision. A fourth alternative is to help the parents develop parenting skills that optimize positive influence with whatever time they have available.

Family members can be helped to develop better job skills. Practitioners can refer them for basic training in interviewing skills, help them complete applications, and prepare them to approach prospective employers by telephone. In

FIGURE 4.4   Sample Family Contract

Family Contract for: *Ricky*

Date: *June 1, 2001*

Responsibilities:
We agree to do the following:

1. Father—Attend anger management classes
2. Mother—Seek drug treatment at XYZ agency
3. Parents—Attend parent training classes
4. Parents—Monitor Ricky's activities for compliance
5. Parents—Report noncompliance to case manager

Privileges:
If we meet our responsibilities, we will be able to:

1. Receive gift certificates for clothing
2. Be treated to a family meal at McDonald's

Bonuses:
If we meet all our responsibilities for at least four weeks, we will be able to:

1. Attend a major league baseball game as a family

Sanctions:
If we do not meet our responsibilities, we will:

1. Lose all family privileges
2. Ricky will lose his privileges
3. Mother may be court mandated to drug treatment
4. Dad may be court mandated to anger management
5. Parents may be court mandated to parent training

Monitoring:
We agree to the following monitoring activities:

1. Scheduled visits by the case manager
2. Surprise visits by the case manager
3. Telephone calls and conferences by the case manager with the family and with agencies

Signed: _____

Juvenile

_____

Family Members

_____

Case Manager

some jurisdictions, practitioners may be able to provide access to funds for suitable clothing. When job skills are lacking, practitioners may provide referral and advocacy to adult education and vocational programs.

Practitioners may also be able to help other family members find employment. This might include a nonworking spouse or significant other, an extended family member who lives in the home, siblings, or the juveniles themselves. Interventions for other family members are the same as those mentioned above. It might be important, however, to require the additional family member to sign a behavioral contract agreeing to contribute a portion of his or her earnings to the family. This would be particularly important when the youth or siblings are the additional sources of income. When juveniles do find work, the practitioner must be certain that it does not interfere with their education or vocational training.

In some families it may be necessary to find alternative sources for daily supervision of the juvenile. Potential sources of supervision include extended family members, willing neighbors, and professional child care services. In some cases it may be possible to supervise the juvenile through a highly structured schedule of activities and house arrest. Activities can be arranged with social service programs that supply both supervision and enjoyable activity. Examples of such programs include recreation programs, after-school programs, and organizations such as the Boys & Girls Club or Police Athletic League.

Parental Substance Abuse When a juvenile's parents are substance abusers, several steps must be taken:

1. Every attempt should be made to encourage the parent to seek voluntary treatment. If the parent agrees to receive treatment, the practitioner should refer him or her to an appropriate treatment service and, if necessary, help make temporary alternative living arrangements for the juvenile.

2. If the parent refuses to seek treatment, it may be possible to mandate treatment through the jurisdiction's legal system. Many states have statutes that allow substance abusers to be forced into treatment. When necessary, practitioners can facilitate this process by providing the necessary documentation to authorities. Alternative arrangements must be made for the family during the treatment.

3. If a clear need for treatment exists, yet the parent is unwilling to voluntarily seek treatment and there is no way to compel treatment, alternative living arrangement may be sought. Sometimes this can be arranged voluntarily, and the juvenile can live with a willing relative. At other times it may be necessary to remove the child under the state's dependency statutes.

Parental Criminal Activity When parents are involved in criminal activity, practitioners must report that activity. They must also ensure that the juvenile and her siblings have alternative living arrangements, and that they have adequate transportation to school and other services. These juveniles may also need referrals for specialized counseling to deal with the incarceration of their parents.

Problem-solving and Decision-making Skills Some juveniles have better problem-solving and decision-making skills than their parents. This often produces conflict and family management problems. Interventions for these situations have three components: (1) teach the youth appropriate skills for voicing his opinion, (2) teach the parent appropriate skills for receiving and considering the youth's opinion, and (3) arrange a forum in which these communications can take place.

It is important that a juvenile with strong problem-solving skills learn to communicate his ideas to his parents in a nonthreatening manner. Parents may be threatened by the youth's ideas, and the youth may feel offended by the parent's rejection. Communication techniques taught in many social skills training programs can be used to improve the youth's skills. A list of resources for social skills training is included at the end of this chapter.

Sometimes a parent is both willing and able to learn problem-solving skills. When this is the case, the parent should be referred to a program that can enhance those skills. Sometimes the parent can learn with some assistance from the case manager or family counselor. The social skills training programs described below can be used for both parents and juveniles. When the parents are unwilling or unable to learn effective problem-solving, they must be taught to receive ideas from the youth without feeling threatened. Parents can be taught these skills through a good parent training program. Alternatives for parent training are described in the section below.

When youths can effectively communicate their ideas and parents can receive them, practitioners should recommend a weekly forum in which ideas can be discussed. This can be accomplished through a scheduled family meeting. Training on arranging and conducting family meetings is described in many of the parent training programs described below.

Poor Family Management Poor family management is sometimes the result of other problems described in this chapter. At other times parents simply lack the ability or the skills to manage the family properly. Parental knowledge and skills can be improved through parent training.

Mental Illness of the Parent When a parent is mentally ill, family stress is often increased and family management is undermined. When the parent's condition is successfully controlled through medication or other treatment, little intervention will be necessary. Two other conditions will require intervention: (1) when the parent's condition is untreated, and (2) when the parent's current treatment is inadequate to stabilize his condition.

When parental mental illness is untreated, the first stage of intervention is to attempt to obtain treatment. This involves preparatory counseling, referral to an appropriate social service agency, facilitating transportation, and ensuring that the utilization of services is maintained through careful planning and monitoring. Where the parent is unwilling to comply, it may be possible to mandate treatment through the court.

The second stage of intervention is minimizing stress in the home. Since many mental conditions are worsened by stress, establishing greater equilibrium can help stabilize the parent's condition. Interventions include stress management techniques, social skills training, and referral to sources for financial and other concrete aid. Practitioners also might want to locate a volunteer to assist with household chores and child management responsibilities. Where the parent's condition cannot be adequately stabilized and other sources of support cannot be identified, alternative custodial arrangements may need to be sought.

Poor Family Involvement Often the families of delinquent youth not only lack the skills and knowledge to provide prosocial support, but are also unwilling to provide that support. Sometimes this unwillingness is due to the parents' substance abuse, criminal activity, or mental illness. Interventions for these conditions are described in other sections of this chapter.

When parents are unwilling to support a youth's treatment for reasons other than those discussed above, three steps should be taken. First, the practitioner should try to learn the reasons the parents are unwilling. Second, he should address this unwillingness through referral to individual counseling. Third, if the parent remains uncooperative, the practitioner may be able to mandate participation through the court. Some jurisdictions permit prosecution of parents who do not support their children's treatment. Although this should certainly be a last resort for practitioners, it does provide an option when other efforts have failed.

Deviant Siblings Many youths are from homes where their siblings are actively involved in problem behavior or are consorting with delinquent peers. Their influence can be very difficult for the practitioner to overcome. Intervention for deviant siblings and friends has five components: (1) identification of problem siblings and friends, (2) attempts to change the problem behaviors, (3) attempts to address problem behaviors through police agencies, (4) attempts to remove the sibling from the home (when he is over age 18), and (5) additional support to the client to insulate her against the sibling's influences. The intervention components should not necessarily be performed in the order listed. Depending on individual circumstances, only component 5 or only components 1 and 2 may be practical or useful.

Importance of Extended Family and Mentors

Extended family members can have a strong influence on juveniles. Uncles, aunts, cousins, and grandparents can all impact a youth's progress, either for better or for worse. Other people, not related by blood, but regarded by the family as members, can also be very significant. The influence of extended family members is often particularly important for juveniles of various minority groups (see chapter 9).

When the influence of the nuclear family is questionable, practitioners should maximize the influence of prosocial members of the extended family. When a family friend or relative can be located who is willing to be a mentor to the juvenile, weekly get-togethers and outings should be scheduled. When no positive extended family member can be found, practitioners should try to locate someone who is willing to mentor the youth.

Social Skills Training for the Family

Social skills training can be just as important for the family as it is for the juvenile. Often the youth's skills are deficient because he or she has not seen skills modeled in the home. Teaching parents and siblings appropriate social skills can enhance the effectiveness of the intervention. Many of the social skills training programs currently available can be used with both juveniles and adults. Practitioners should encourage families to participate along with juveniles whenever this option is available.

PARENT TRAINING

Parent training refers to a group of programs designed to help parents learn communication and family management techniques. They focus on skill-building, also providing information on child development. Several different programs exist, each designed on its own philosophy. Several are designed to deal with specific life situations. Since this text is about juvenile justice, it will focus on only those programs that are based on philosophies or issues likely to be beneficial to juvenile justice clients. Readers who are interested in other programs are referred to *Parent Training Today* (Alvy, 1994) for a more comprehensive listing.

Four programs meet these criteria: Confident Parenting (CP), Behavioral Parent Training (BPT), Preparing for the Drug-Free Years (PFDY), and the Nurturing series (NS). Confident Parenting and Behavioral Parent Training are both general parent training programs based on philosophies that have been identified as particularly important for dealing with problem behavior. Preparing for the Drug-Free Years and the Nurturing series both deal with specific issues related to problem behavior.

Confident Parenting complies with all four of the standards mentioned earlier for successful intervention. It is based on social learning theory, which effectively explains a substantial amount of delinquent behavior. It is structured, using class sessions and homework with scheduled class sessions over a specified period at time. It uses cognitive-behavioral techniques, and its approach is multi-modal, using lecture, discussion, video, and homework.

Confident Parenting is designed primarily for use with children rather than teens, but it has specialized units for teaching them to prepare for their teenage years. These units deal with drugs, sex, gangs, and acquired immune deficiency syndrome (AIDS). Because of the age group it targets, CP may be most useful as a prevention tool for preschool and school-aged children. Several studies (Alvy, 1994) have concluded that CP is effective in improving parenting skills and children's behaviors.

Behavioral Parent Training is one of several behavioral parent training programs that have shown good results with troubled children and families. Behavioral Parent Training also meets all four criteria for successful intervention. Further, it actually targets one of the groups that is of greatest concern to juvenile justice practitioners, at-risk children whom the program authors term "pre-delinquent."

Behavioral Parent Training includes seven basic sessions, with additional sessions for particularly recalcitrant or special needs families. The program has been very successful in reducing child problem behavior and in sustaining the improvements over time. Behavioral Parent Training was designed by the Oregon Social Learning Center. We'll talk more about this intervention and others like it in chapter 8.

Preparing for the Drug-Free Years is a risk-based parent training program designed to help parents prevent children from initiating substance abuse. It is intended for parents of high-risk pre- and early adolescent children. Preparing for the Drug-Free Years is produced by Developmental Research Programs.

The Nurturing series is another specialized group of parent training programs. It is designed for families where parents have been abusive. There is a specialized curriculum for families of young children, school-aged children, teenagers, and children with special learning needs.

Several parent training programs either designed or adapted for minorities are currently available. These include programs for African-American, Hispanic, and American Indian families. Some of these programs will be discussed in chapter 7.

SUMMARY

In this chapter we have looked at several components, or modalities, of successful intervention. Each of these modalities focused on either the youth or his family. For the individual, we considered individual counseling, rewards and sanctions, monitoring and surveillance, and victim-offender mediation. For the family, we discussed counseling modalities and three specific counseling techniques, and proposed solutions to several specific family problems. In chapter 5 we will learn about modalities that address problems in the juvenile's social systems outside the family.

ACTIVITIES FOR LEARNING

1. Working in a small group, prepare a behavioral contract for Lee and one for his family. What responsibilities will each contract have? What privileges and bonuses? What sanctions will be applied? In what ways do the two contracts depend on each other?

2. Look at the behavioral contract prepared for Ricky, displayed in figure 4.3. What might you have done differently? What parts do you like? Why? In a small group, present and discuss your ideas.

3. Think about Ricky's family. What special problems do you see? Which interventions discussed in chapter 4 might help with those special problems? Prepare your thoughts in a written recommendation as though it were for a juvenile justice supervisor.

4. Think about Elena's (box 1.3, see chapter 1) family. What special problems do you see? Which interventions discussed in chapter 4 might help with those special problems? Prepare your thoughts in a written recommendation as though it were for a juvenile justice supervisor.

QUESTIONS FOR DISCUSSION

1. Review the case of Lee, presented in box 4.1. Cognitive-behavioral therapy was used very successfully in this case. What other individual interventions might have been used? Why might these interventions have been better than CBT? Why might they have been less effective?
2. Review the case of Elena, presented in box 1.3. What individual interventions might be used? What problematic cognitions might a therapist expect to encounter? What kinds of special problems might her family present?
3. Ricky (box 1.2) has some family problems. Pretend that you are his case manager. What kinds of interventions might you use for his family? What kinds of problems might you encounter with the family contract?
4. Andrew, described in box 3.3, has both individual and family issues. What kinds of interventions might you recommend for him? What kinds of interventions might you use for his family? What kinds of problems might you encounter?
5. Review the case of Maggie, presented in box 3.4. What kinds of responsibilities, privileges, bonuses, and sanctions might you put in her behavioral contract? Would you also contract with her family? What provisions would her contract contain?

KEY TERMS AND DEFINITIONS

Behavioral contract A written agreement between the practitioner and client (either juvenile or family) that specifies responsibilities, privileges, bonuses, and sanctions.

Cognitions Thoughts; in treatment, they usually refer to thoughts that lead to problem behaviors.

Definitions Errant cognitions used to excuse problem behavior.

Differential reinforcement The social learning process by which juveniles acquire behaviors through differing kinds of reinforcement from different groups of people.

Dysfunctional The condition of a person or family that cannot function in an effective, prosocial manner.

Empirically supported Concepts, ideas, theories, or interventions that have been supported through scientific research.

Foster care Temporary or long-term care arrangements for children whose parents have abused, neglected, or abandoned them.

Imitation Copying the behavior of another.

Meta-analysis A scientific technique of comparing the results of several research studies.

Modeling Demonstrating a behavior or series of behaviors for another to emulate.

Restitution Repaying a crime victim for the damages done.

Restorative justice A legal philosophy that attempts to control crime by restoring what has been lost to the victim, providing safety to the community, and helping the offender achieve social competence.

Retributive justice A legal philosophy based on controlling crime by punishing the offender.

Social learning theory An explanation of why people behave the way they do based on modeling, imitation, and reinforcement.

Therapeutic foster care Alternative living arrangements for abused, neglected, and abandoned children in which specialized services are provided to children with special needs.

REFERENCES

Akers, R. L. (1985). *Deviant behavior: A social learning approach.* Belmont, CA: Wadsworth.

Alvy, K. T. (1994). *Parent training today: A social necessity.* Studio City, CA: Center for the Improvement of Child Caring.

Andrews, D. A., Zinger, I., Hoge, R. D., Bonta, J., Gendreau, P., & Cullen, F. T. (1990). Does correctional treatment work? A clinically relevant and psychologically informed meta-analysis. *Criminology, 28,* 369–404.

Bandura, A. (1979). *Social learning theory.* Englewood Cliffs, NJ: Prentice Hall.

Bazemore, G., & Day, S. E. (1996). Restoring the balance: Juvenile and community justice. *Juvenile Justice, 3*(1), 3–14.

Del Carmen, R. V., Parker, M., & Reddington, F. P. (1998). *Briefs of leading cases in juvenile justice.* Cincinnati: Anderson.

Ellis, R. A. (1997). *Community reintegration through environmental assessment, treatment, and evaluation.* Ft. Lauderdale, FL: Broward Sheriff's Office.

Ellis, R. A., O'Hara, M., & Sowers, K. (1999). Treatment profiles of troubled female adolescents: Implications for judicial disposition. *Juvenile and Family Court Journal, 50*(3), 25–40.

Galaway, B., & Hudson, J. (1996). Restorative justice through mediation: The impact of programs in four Canadian provinces. In B. Galaway & J. Hudson (Eds.), *Restorative justice: International perspectives* (pp. 373–385). Monsey, NY: Willow Tree Press.

Grossman, J. B., & Garry, E. M. (1997, April). Mentoring—A proven delinquency strategy. *Juvenile Justice Bulletin.* Washington, DC: Office of Juvenile Justice and Delinquency Prevention.

Henggeler, S. W. (1989). *Delinquency in adolescence.* Thousand Oaks, CA: Sage.

Henggeler, S. W. (1993). Multisystemic treatment of serious juvenile offenders: Implications for the treatment of substance-abusing youth. *National Institute on Drug Abuse Research Monograph 137* (DHHS Pub. No. [ADM]88-1523). Washington, DC: U.S. Government Printing Office.

Krisberg, B., Neuenfeldt, D., Wiebush, R., & Rodriguez, O. (1994). *Juvenile intensive supervision: Planning guide.* Washington, DC: Office of Juvenile Justice and Delinquency Prevention.

Lösel, F. (1996). Working with young offenders: The impact of meta-analyses. In C. R. Hollin & K. Howells (Eds.), *Clinical approaches to working with young offenders.* New York: Wiley.

Office of Juvenile Justice and Delinquency Prevention. (1996). *Desktop guide to good juvenile detention practice.* Washington, DC: Author.

Patterson, G. R., Reid, J. B., & Dishion, T. J. (1992). *Antisocial boys.* Eugene, OR: Castalia.

Ross, R. R., & Fabiano, E. A. (1985). *Time to think: A cognitive model of delinquency prevention and offender rehabilitation.* Johnson City, TN: Institute of Social Sciences and Arts.

Serna, L. A., Sherman, J. A., & Sheldon, J. B. (1996). Empirically based behavior treatment programs for families with adolescents who are at risk for failure. In C. R. Hollin & K. Howells (Eds.), *Clinical approaches to working with young offenders.* New York: Wiley.

Sexson, S. (1999, April 6). Testimony representing the American Academy of Child and Adolescent Psychiatry. Testimony before the Joint Commission on Accreditation of Healthcare Organizations, Restraint Use Task Force [On-line]. Available: http://www.aacp.org/legislation/s&r.htm.

Torbet, P., & Szymanski, L. (1998, November). State legislative responses to violent juvenile crime: 1996–97 update. *Juvenile Justice Bulletin.* Washington, DC: Office of Juvenile Justice and Delinquency Prevention.

Umbreit, M. S. (1993). Crime victims and offenders in mediation: An emerging area of social work practice. *Social Work, 38,* 69–73.

Utah Administrative Code R547-4-17(10). (1999). Rules, discipline, secure observation, use of restraints [On-line]. Available: http://www.rules.state.ut.us/publicat/code/r547/r547-004.htm.

Zarb, J. M. (1992). *Cognitive-behavioral assessment and therapy with adolescents.* New York: Brunner/Mazel.

Chapter 5

◆

Interventions for Social Systems

CHAPTER OUTLINE

In the first section of chapter 4 we discussed the balanced and restorative approach to juvenile justice (BARA). We noted that the approach is very strong, and that interventions that use its philosophy have been very promising. We also suggested, however, that it might be improved by adding a fourth goal: systemic competence. That is, interventions should also focus on improving the competence of the juvenile's social systems to support prosocial behavior. For example, a youth who enters the juvenile justice system with a group of delinquent friends should emerge either with those friends behaving differently or with a different set of friends. Other examples of improvement are better school relationships and functioning and more involvement in positive community activities.

You as a direct practitioner can have a part in helping the juveniles you supervise or treat develop community competence. Administrators and advocates can work to ensure that the appropriate resources are in place. Researchers can advise those programs and can evaluate their effectiveness and guide their adaptation once they are in place.

Chapter 5 provides insight as to how practitioners can help youths transform their social systems. It covers five systems: school, peers, employment, community, and youth gangs. For each system, we will first discuss the ways in which some characteristics of those systems may affect problem behavior. Next, we'll review techniques that direct practitioners can use for special situations within each social system. Third, we'll take a look at a few model programs that some communities use for those systems. This information may be useful for administrators and advocates who want to create effective programs. Finally, we will discuss some things advocates and researchers can do to help juveniles in each of those systems.

INTERVENTIONS FOR THE SCHOOL SOCIAL SYSTEM

The first system we'll discuss will be the school. As we'll see a juvenile's school and the friends he has can have an important influence on his behavior. As we'll also see, some problems can be identified and addressed through specific intervention techniques.

Characteristics That Contribute to Problem Behavior

The school environment is very important for many reasons. It serves as a primary source of socialization. It is one of the earliest sources of information for the youth about herself, her world, and her future. In addition to its academic benefits, school is an important foundation for future social success or failure.

School is a primary source of socialization for the developing child. After the age of 5 or 6 (earlier for children who are enrolled in day care or kindergarten), children spend more waking hours of each day during the school year in school than they do in any other setting. Many of their friends are made at school. As they grow older, the influence of those friends often becomes greater. When children are successful in school and form friendships with others who are successful, they tend to associate with more prosocial groups and less frequently engage in problem behavior. When children are unsuccessful and do not fit in, they often associate with antisocial peer groups and more frequently develop problem behavior (Hawkins, Catalano, & Miller, 1992; Dryfoos, 1990).

The ways in which children interact with teachers and administrators are also very important. Children who receive positive reinforcement and support from educational personnel are more likely to be successful than those who do not. Children whose grades are poor, who fall behind in school, and who do not relate well with school personnel are likely to perform poorly academically, develop behavioral problems, and eventually drop out of school.

School also provides the youth with an ongoing source of information about herself, the world, and the future. Chapter 4 described the way in which one's perceptions of these three dimensions of life affect one's emotions and behavior. Those who experience success at school often come to see themselves as successful, building their sense of self-efficacy. These students are likely to view the world and the future much more positively, since they believe themselves capable of succeeding. Students who do not experience academic success often come to view themselves, the future, and the world much more negatively. Poor self-esteem, low expectations for future success, and a strong external locus of control (feeling that one is controlled almost completely by outside forces) are important risk factors for problem behavior (Hawkins, Catalano, & Miller, 1992; Dryfoos, 1990).

Table 5.1 School-related Problems by Category

Individual	Peer	Administration
Behind in classroom work	Delinquent peers	Poorly managed school
Learning disability	Unsuccessful peers	Oversized school
Poor grades	Inappropriate peer influence	Adverse labeling
Fighting		
Substance abuse		
Truancy		

School not only helps shape a youth's perception of the future, it also provides foundational knowledge and skills for future success. A high school graduate is much more likely to obtain desirable employment than a nongraduate (Dryfoos, 1990; Dupper, 1993). College graduates are more likely to become employed than are high-school graduates. Those who drop out or do poorly in school often find it very difficult to be successful in the adult world.

Clearly, school is an important social system for the adolescent offender. Several kinds of problems can interfere with a youth's academic success. These problems can be separated into three general categories: (1) problems related to the individual, (2) problems related to peers, and (3) problems related to the administration. Examples of the problems included within each category are offered in table 5.1.

Intervention Techniques for Specific Problems

Direct practitioners often work with juveniles who experience a broad range of problems within the school environment. The intervention techniques described in this section will not address all those problems, but do offer insight as to how to approach many situations. Remember, school success is critical to the success of many juveniles.

Individual Many of the problems that occur in the school environment are problems that can be categorized as "individual." Although each is directly impacted by the environment, interventions for these problems normally focus primarily on the individual and secondarily on systemic factors. The problems we will categorize as individual include academic problems, learning disabilities, disciplinary problems, lack of commitment to school, and truancy.

Youths who experience academic problems such as poor grades are at great risk for behavioral problems, truancy, and school dropout. Often, even when they manage to stay in school, they are unable to find satisfactory employment after graduation. Academic problems can be addressed using a three-step intervention: (1) evaluation, (2) provision of appropriate services, and (3) intervention for related problems.

Many different factors can contribute to a juvenile's problems in school. These factors may be as simple as a need to catch up on the lessons missed during suspension. They may be as complex as a child with a learning disability whose parents do not believe in education and who constantly move from school district to school district. They may also be as simple as a youth who needs tutoring. Because of the diversity of problems, it is important that practitioners both obtain educational evaluations and analyze the juvenile's functioning in all social systems when planning and implementing interventions.

Basic interventions for academic problems typically include tutoring, after-school programs, scheduled homework sessions, and summer school. When special needs such as learning disabilities are present, juveniles are referred to educational specialists. Other problems, however, can also affect academic performance. Influences within the family, peer group, and the school itself are often the most important.

Families often take one of two damaging positions regarding their child's education. Either their expectations are higher than the youth can achieve without substantial additional support, or they are not concerned about the youth's academic success.

When parental expectations are too high, practitioners can use cognitive-behavioral techniques to help parents understand what is realistic and fair for their child. In many cases they will also need to be taught how to encourage their child to succeed at his own level, rather than at the unrealistic level they did expect. Cognitive restructuring may also be needed for the juvenile. His confidence may have been diminished by the parent's high expectations. The techniques described in chapter 4 can be used to help the youth improve his confidence.

When parents are unconcerned about their child's success, the intervention may involve one or all of the following elements: (1) cognitive restructuring for the parents, (2) cognitive restructuring for the youth, (3) development of a system of rewards and sanctions, (4) tutoring or after-school programs, and (5) introduction of a *mentor* who can provide encouragement and educational coaching. Parents must be convinced of the importance of education for their child. The juvenile must also be convinced that education is important, and that he is capable of succeeding academically. As awareness of the importance of education grows, parent training programs can be used to teach parents to utilize behavioral techniques. Practitioners should also identify additional resources such as school-based tutoring programs or volunteer mentors. Sometimes local colleges or universities have volunteer organizations that provide tutoring as a community service. Churches or other religious organizations can also be a good source of mentors or tutors.

Some juveniles experience difficulties in school because of learning disabilities. Many of these conditions are fairly complex and some can be very difficult to diagnose. Whenever it appears that a juvenile has a learning disability, she should be referred for evaluation. Practitioners can familiarize themselves with learning disabilities by reading *Exceptional Children: An Introduction to Special Education* (Heward, 1996).

Many juveniles who experience academic problems also experience disciplinary problems. Youths who repeatedly misbehave in school should be referred to counseling so that any unrecognized issues can be addressed. Good conduct should also be required in the behavioral contract.

Truancy is recognized as one of the early warning signs of problem behavior. It can also be a sign that a juvenile in supervision is in danger of re-offending. School attendance should be a part of the behavioral contract. It should be monitored closely and all necessary incentives and sanctions used to ensure compliance.

In addition to the measures described above, several intervention modalities are appropriate for the majority of school problems. They may be used individually, or in combination. These modalities include tutoring, scheduled homework periods, enrollment in after-school programs, and referral for educational, psychological, or medical testing.

Tutoring can be used for juveniles with several different needs. For example, it can help those who have fallen behind in either classroom work or grade level to reach the appropriate level. It can be used to help those with learning disabilities. It can also be used for those who do well in many academic areas, but who struggle with specific areas like math or science.

Juveniles with academic problems should also have mandatory scheduled times for homework and study skills training. These sessions should be planned in family meetings and should be a part of the behavioral contracts. Incentives and sanctions should be used to ensure regular participation. The practitioner will also need to actively monitor these sessions.

Some schools offer after-school programs for youths with academic problems. Practitioners should become familiar with any such programs in their areas and should learn the criteria for acceptance into each program. Juveniles should be scheduled to attend the selected programs, and their attendance should be monitored.

Sadly, many older youth experience educational problems because they have learning disabilities, psychological problems, or medical problems that have remained undiagnosed. When such problems are uncovered during the assessment process, these juveniles should be referred to professionals for evaluation and assistance. Practitioners should be aware of all such resources in their community and should constantly seek information about new resources.

Peer The influence of a juvenile's friends can be very strong. Delinquent peers, peers who are unsuccessful in school, and peers who exert an inappropriately strong influence can all have a powerful negative impact on a youth in supervision. When problems within the peer group inhibit the juvenile's academic success, two options are available. The first is to change the peer group to make it more prosocial. The other is to help the youth develop a new group of peers. The former option, making the peer group more prosocial, is unlikely to be successful. It is usually more practical to use the latter option. The steps involved in helping a juvenile develop new friends are discussed in the section on interventions for peer groups later in this chapter.

Administration Sometimes teachers or school administrators are reluctant to allow juveniles to return to the school or school system they attended prior to their arrest. In some cases their reasons are good, such as concern for the youth or the other youths in their school. In other cases they simply are unwilling to deal with the problems they believe he will create. Obviously, it is vital that a juvenile receive a proper education. When it appears that it will be difficult to enroll a child, the practitioner should review his records to identify any problems that might arise. He should also speak with the juvenile's parents and former teachers or administrators. In some cases, vocational testing or counseling is needed. In some cases, the practitioner needs to advocate with administrators on behalf of the youth, or ask an administrator in her own organization to advocate. When the child is re-enrolled, it should be under a strict behavioral contract with privileges and sanctions clearly specified. The case manager should closely monitor the youth to ensure that both he and the school officials comply.

One of four alternatives is usually available for educating the juvenile. First, the youth might be re-enrolled in the school she last attended. If this option does not appear to be possible, the youth might be enrolled at a more suitable academic site, such as an *alternative school*. A third possibility is enrolling the juvenile in a vocational program. A fourth alternative is to give him employability training, assistance in locating a job, and support in obtaining a GED.

Two other risk factors for school problems may affect the practitioner's decision regarding school placement: when the school is poorly managed and when the school is very large and overcrowded. When either of these conditions exists, it is often best to try to place the juvenile in some other school. It may also be beneficial to make juvenile justice administrators aware of the situation so that they advocate with school system leaders for changes at that school.

Model Programs

Many innovative programs have been designed to enhance the success of at-risk and delinquent youths. Four of those programs will be described here. Many others are in operation around the country and can be identified using the techniques described in the last part of chapter 6.

One promising program is Parent and Community Teams for School Success (PACT). Participants in the PACT program form teams that provide support, education, and intervention for parents of juveniles who share common problems, a common geographical area, or are a part of a common organization. In addition to the team parents, groups also include a team sponsor (often a social service agency or local business) who provides fund-raising and incentive materials, a team facilitator or leader, a group of team parents, and one or more team associates (volunteers who aid the group).

The teams meet on a regular basis. Their meetings include guest speakers, videos, discussion of resource documents, or supportive discussion about specific needs. Topics for these group sessions usually include techniques for improving the juvenile's academic performance, enhancing family management and disciplinary tactics, and accessing community resources. Similar groups are often formed for the juveniles whose parents are PACT members.

PACT is not simply an arena in which experts communicate their knowledge to parents. In PACT, parents are seen as experts, each with important information and insight regarding the success of their children. Although PACT primarily targets educational success, it recognizes the link between academic failure and developing problem behavior. It therefore addresses needs in other social systems as well. A manual for developing a PACT program is available from the Educational Resources Information Center (ERIC) (Larson & Rumberger, 1995).

Full-service schools are another type of intervention that has improved not only school performance but other aspects of many juveniles' lives. In full-service schools, a comprehensive array of social services is offered on school grounds. In addition to standard educational programs, health, mental health, family support, recreation, tutoring, drop-out prevention, delinquency prevention, substance abuse awareness, and other programs are offered on site. Schools that offer these services are often open well beyond their usual operating hours to accommodate the needs of working families and to allow for maximum utilization of space. Services are coordinated between agencies by teams composed of teachers, administrators, mental health and medical personnel, and others. These schools often serve not just the student body and their families but other members of the community.

The concept of the full-service school is very relevant when the importance of and relationship between a juvenile's social systems are considered. It allows a juvenile's problems in many areas to be recognized and dealt with very early, perhaps even before problem behavior begins. Unfortunately, funding cuts and turf issues have caused many full-service schools to fall on hard times. Joy Dryfoos (1994) has written an excellent book describing full-service schools and their implementation.

Several different kinds of programs have been implemented in various schools to control school violence. School violence has many negative effects. It may result in injury or death, may produce suspension or expulsion for its participants, and may cause many students to stay out of school due to fear of injury. High levels of violence in schools have the potential to increase levels of antisocial behavior. Hunter and Elias (1998) divide programs to address school violence into four general categories: those that change the physical structure of the school, those that use conflict resolution or mediation, those that teach anger management and other social skills, and those that target organizational change within the school. These categories are summarized in table 5.2.

One interesting and effective intervention for the school system is the assignment of a law enforcement officer to individual schools. These officers, known as SROs (school resource officers) have offices on campus and, in addition to traditional police activities, provide counseling and support to students. Interviews with two SROs and their chief are included in box 5.1.

The school-based family resource center (SFRC) is another intervention that has been used successfully in many areas. SFRCs are located in schools and staffed by parents and local social service providers. The center's staff links children and families with community resources to meet a full range of needs. Providers work collaboratively to deliver comprehensive services to their clients. Dupper and Poertner (1997) have identified five exemplary SFRC programs. Two of these programs are briefly described in box 5.2.

Table 5.2 Categories of Programs for School Violence

Type of Program	Goal of Program
Changes to physical	Make schools safer with structure of school, metal detectors, mirrored halls, increased monitoring
Conflict resolution	Teach conflict resolution skills and offer format for conducting resolutions
Social skills training	Teach interactional, moral, and cognitive skills
Organizational change	Change school atmosphere through changing administration

SOURCE: Hunter & Elias, 1998

Box 5.1 Life Story: School Resource Officers
Shane Dixon

School resource officers (SROs) are law enforcement officers who are stationed in schools. Although they have and may use their powers of arrest, this is only one of their functions. They try to relate to students in a positive, supportive way, and to help solve problems in the schools before those problems develop.

Wilson County, Tennessee, has had its SRO program in place for four years. During that four-year period, officers have had occasion to intervene in problem situations on several occasions, but report that no "major incidents" have occurred. In order to better understand the role of SROs and how they relate to school safety, I interviewed several of the Wilson County officers.

Lt. Larry Pugh, the officer in charge, emphasizes the importance of giving kids time and attention. He states, "You just need to be there for the kids, to talk to them and to recognize that they are there and that they are somebody." He reported that an SRO has three major responsibilities in a school. First an officer is a law enforcement officer. Second, he serves as a counselor or advisor to students. Third, he functions as a teacher to help the students to think before they commit an act that they will regret in the future.

When Deputy Tony Neal entered the SRO program, he was assigned to a middle school. During his first year there were 39 fights at the school. Two years later, there were only 14 fights, with only 2 actually escalating to physical violence. Both the school and the sheriff's department believe that this success is due largely to the presence of a trained officer. Deputy Neal comments, "The main reason that the fight count is so low, now that officers are in the school, is that we are trying to get the students to come to us before the fight even begins. Parents will call me to ask me to talk to their kids in order to help prevent them from getting into any trouble."

"When we first began the SRO program," reports Chief Larry Bowman, head of the Wilson County Sheriff's Department, "parents were complaining about how they didn't want their kids to be in armed camps when they went to school. Now after all that has happened nationally, and all the rumors that seem to pop up out of nowhere, these same parents are asking us to put more officers in the schools. We have seen a complete turnaround of how people feel about officers in the schools, and it has become a turn for the better."

Box 5.2   Exemplary School-based Family Resource Centers
(Dupper & Poertner, 1997)

WALBRIDGE CARING COMMUNITIES (WCC), ST. LOUIS, MISSOURI

Walbridge Caring Communities (WCC) uses the facilities of an inner city school and a church. It provides links to crisis intervention, substance abuse treatment, tutoring, and recreational activities. The program is overseen by an advisory panel and an interagency team that coordinates the distribution of resources and manages operations. School facilitators help families locate, access, and coordinate services from various providers. Teachers identify youths in need of services and refer their families to the resource center.

"COZI" SCHOOLS (COZI), BOWLING GREEN, KENTUCKY

The COZI program is located in several communities, but one of its most successful is in Bowling Green, Kentucky. School representatives visit the homes of their families and ask what their needs are. The school district then attempts to meet those needs. School staff members also "adopt" students whose parents have died or gone to prison or who are neglectful. COZI reports improved test scores and a 97% attendance rate among its program successes.

Many school-based programs address specific needs or issues of children who are at risk or already displaying problem behavior. One example of such an effort is the alternative-to-suspension program School Survival (Dupper, 1998), discussed in box 5.3. Another excellent example is Sister Soldiers, a project funded by the Broward County Commission on Substance Abuse, which targets at-risk black juvenile girls in southeast Florida. Girls are referred to the program through school administrators. They meet for one hour during the school day for group social skills training, racial pride development, and other positive activities. Counselors refer the juveniles and their families to community resources according to their needs. They also provide tutoring, study skills training, and recreational and educational field trips. Although program staff does refer juveniles for many services, staff members often adopt a quasi-parental role with the children. By becoming a member of the youth's extended family, the staff member enhances her influence on both the juvenile and her extended family.

One interesting aspect of at least two of the successful school-based programs is the degree to which staff become involved in the lives of children. In those two programs staff are described as "quasi-parents" to the children with whom they work. One of the authors of this text has heard this practice challenged by individuals asserting that this constitutes an inappropriate relationship between professionals and clients. Given the initial findings of the potential effectiveness of this approach, perhaps programs should consider using both professional and paraprofessional staff in this kind of role.

Box 5.3   School Survival—An Alternative-to-Suspension Program (Dupper, 1998)

The School Survival intervention was adapted by Dupper (1998) from *Positive Alternatives to Student Suspensions* (Grice, 1986). The program focuses on changing problematic ideas (cognitions) the students have about school and their behavior in the school environment. They also learn alternative ways of responding to various situations in school, and the kinds of consequences that are likely to result from those responses. They learn to think through those and similar situations before responding to them.

The program consists of 10 highly structured group sessions. The 40- to 50-minute sessions include a didactic component, group discussion, modeling, and role play. Those who attend the program consistently are rewarded with a pizza party at completion.

Suspension of a student involves several issues. One issue is that the behavioral problems associated with the suspension are often not really addressed by being excluded from school. A second issue is the loss of classroom learning that many juveniles experience while suspended. The School Survival intervention addresses the behavioral issue. Additional components might be included to address the educational issue.

It is also noteworthy that at least one of these programs is for black juveniles. Since (as we will see in chapter 7) the extended family is particularly important to many minority groups, a practitioner as extended family may be particularly important to those groups. It is important that we not allow white, middle-class values to unduly influence the interventions we develop.

Work for Advocates and Researchers

Advocates and researchers can have an important part in changing conditions in schools that promote problem behavior. Advocates should familiarize themselves with the programs mentioned above and others like them. They should then encourage local administrators to adopt, implement, and evaluate the programs. Researchers can continue to explore the factors that promote problem behavior in school, can work with direct practitioners and administrators to develop programs, and can evaluate those programs for effectiveness.

INTERVENTIONS FOR THE PEER SOCIAL SYSTEM

Friends are a powerful influence in developing problem behavior. Often juveniles are unable to find friends among groups that support prosocial behavior. They sometimes turn to delinquent peer groups to develop friendships.

In this section we'll look at several factors related to the juvenile's peer social system. We'll use the same process we did for the school social system. First we'll look at factors among peers that contribute to problem behavior. Next we'll look at some specific intervention techniques for special situations involving peers. Third, we'll discuss several model programs. Finally, we'll talk about what advocates and researchers can do to improve the system of services for peer-related problems.

Characteristics That Contribute to Problem Behavior

Researchers have found several conditions within friendship groups that increase the probability that juveniles will begin or continue problem behavior. These conditions include associating with deviant peers, observing peers modeling problem behavior, and youths for whom the peer influence exceeds family influence. Other conditions, such as prosocial attitudes among peers and having friends who are close to their parents, tend to decrease the probability that juveniles will become delinquent.

Juveniles begin to associate with deviant peers for several reasons. Many of these have to do with acceptance, degree of success in school, and similarity of norms and values learned from parents. Children and adolescents who lack the social skills to make friends in mainstream groups often become involved with groups that are more antisocial. Others, unsuccessful in school and feeling alienated from teachers and more successful students, align themselves with other juveniles with similar problems. Still others have become accustomed to criminal values because their parents are involved in criminal activities. Youths can be influenced by these conditions in various combinations.

Some juveniles find it easy to develop prosocial friendships, and others manage to do so by persistently working at it. Others have close relationships with their families, or relationships that can be enhanced through family intervention. Either of these conditions is a powerful influence in avoiding problem behavior.

Practitioners can develop interventions that affect these conditions so that the peer group is a positive rather than negative influence.

Intervention Techniques for Specific Problems

Several specific intervention techniques are available to the practitioner. The use of techniques should be guided by three strategies. These strategies include (1) teaching the youth skills to interact with prosocial peer groups, (2) enhancing the youth's desire and opportunity to associate with prosocial peers, and (3) diminishing the youth's desire and opportunity to associate with antisocial peers.

The first strategy is teaching the youth skills to interact with prosocial peer groups. Several programs are available to help in this process; two good examples are EQUIP (Gibbs, Potter, & Goldstein, 1995) and the PREPARE Curriculum (Goldstein, 1990). The PREPARE Curriculum and one of its components, Aggression Replacement Training (ART), are described in greater detail in chapter 8.

Social skills training programs are based on two premises. Researchers have noted that many youths who become delinquent are deficient in certain social skills and capacities compared to nondelinquent youth. The first premise is that those skills and capacities can be improved through training and that improvement will reduce the probability that the youth will be delinquent. The second is that when a youth's social skills have been improved, he can form prosocial friendships using those skills.

Social skills training includes much more than conversational skills. It also develops situational perception, anger management, moral reasoning, empathy, and stress management capacities. These skills will be discussed in greater detail in chapter 8. The sessions programs use social learning techniques, such as modeling, role play, and verbal reinforcement. They are usually conducted in groups so that partners are readily available for these activities. Sometimes separate sessions are also held for parents, since skills deficiencies are often developed from family interactions. Practitioners should consider involving juveniles who have deviant peer groups in social skills training whenever possible.

The second guiding strategy is enhancing the youth's desire to associate with prosocial peer groups. This strategy has three components: (1) individual counseling to change the juvenile's belief system about peers, (2) identifying existing or new sources of prosocial friendship groups available to the youth, and (3) including scheduled association with these groups along with related incentives and sanctions in the behavioral contract.

The juvenile's beliefs about the importance and value of peer groups can be affected through cognitive-behavioral therapy. If the practitioner is a case manager who is not directly providing therapy, she should ensure that the youth's therapist understands this need. If the practitioner is a therapist, she should devote a portion of her efforts to addressing those beliefs.

Prosocial peer groups may already exist within the juvenile's social systems. In other cases, the practitioner may need to identify prosocial sources of friends in the youth's school or community. Pre-existing prosocial groups should be identified during assessment. New groups can be identified by locating clubs, recreational programs, vocational training, or other activities that correspond to the juvenile's interests and abilities.

The behavioral contract should specify times and places when the juvenile will meet with these prosocial groups. Incentives and sanctions should also be clearly written and explained. The practitioner should then monitor these activities both to ensure compliance and to provide support when the youth needs it.

The third strategy of peer-related intervention is decreasing the juvenile's desire to associate with deviant peers. This strategy also has three components: (1) individual counseling to change a youth's cognitions about peers, (2) identification of deviant peers and peer groups within the youth's social systems, and (3) inclusion of peer-related provisions in the behavioral contract.

Individual counseling for the first component should use cognitive-behavioral techniques to change the juvenile's ideas about the value of delinquent behavior and of having delinquent friends. The second component, identifying deviant peers, should be performed during the assessment process. Practitioners should interview the youth, family, teachers, and other significant individuals as a part of this process. Personal visits to the youth's neighborhood and school may also be helpful. Individuals, groups, and places to be avoided should be specified in the behavioral contract. Practitioners should monitor this portion of the contract closely and may need to use family members or other significant persons to help with the monitoring.

Under extreme circumstances it may be necessary to help the family move to a different community. For example, a juvenile who has been active in a local gang may not be able to return to his neighborhood and avoid participation with the gang. In such cases the practitioner should help the family access the resources needed to relocate.

Youths whose peers have greater influence over them than their parents are also at substantial risk for developing or maintaining problem behavior. Although the natural developmental process for adolescence requires that the influence of the family decrease and the influence of the peer group increase, the influence of peers should not be excessive. When peer influence exceeds parental influence, the following steps should be taken: (1) ensure the presence of a prosocial family group, (2) use cognitive-behavioral individual and family counseling, (3) refer to resources for parent training, and (4) encourage positive experiences for the family.

Step one is addressed by using the family therapy and parent training interventions described in chapter 4. Obviously, the practitioner would not want to optimize the influence of an antisocial family group. Therefore, efforts must be made to ensure prosocial support from parents and siblings.

Cognitive-behavioral therapy should be used for both the individual and the family. Juveniles may have several inaccurate perceptions, including beliefs about the value of their friend's influence and perceptions of their parent's willingness to listen. Where parents really are unwilling to listen, or where they lack the necessary skills, the families should be referred for counseling and parent training.

The third step involves referring the parents for training. Parents may need communication skills, behavioral management skills, or other important abilities. Juveniles must perceive their parents as open, willing, and competent before they will trust their guidance and instruction.

One of the ways to improve family relationships is by encouraging positive experiences for youth and parents. When possible, practitioners should provide opportunities for family outings and activities. These can be offered as incentives in the behavioral or family contracts. Although many youth agencies lack the funds to pay for family outings, private businesses are often willing to provide free tickets, meals, or other opportunities.

Model Programs

Many types of programs are available for peer intervention. Some of the programs focus on helping juveniles develop the social skills they need. Others are intended to provide opportunities for positive activities and prosocial interaction with friends.

Most of the programs designed to help juveniles develop social skills are either conflict resolution training (such as the ones described under school interventions) or more general social skills training. One example of an effective social skills training is Aggression Replacement Training (ART), designed by Arnold Goldstein and published by Research Press.

ART uses a core group of four techniques to teach fifty specific skills to aggressive children and adolescents. The techniques are cognitive-behavioral in nature and include modeling, role playing, performance feedback, and transfer training (Goldstein & Glick, 1998). Juveniles receive the training in small groups led by a professional or a professional and a peer with training in ART.

Many communities have social and recreational programs for at-risk and troubled youth. Examples include sporting activities and programs sponsored by the Boys & Girls Clubs, YMCA, or YWCA. Some organizations offer late-night sports activities such as midnight basketball. County or city recreation programs, Boy Scouts or Girl Scouts, and similar programs are also excellent alternatives.

Many schools offer after-school sports, arts, or drama activities. These can usually be accessed either through the school's administrative offices or through their social workers or guidance counselors. Arts and recreational programs are also sometimes offered by local social service agencies. Church and other religious organizations often have activities for at-risk youth. Many in the faith community are also developing intervention programs, funded partially with government dollars and partially by members.

Mentoring programs have been very successful in helping juveniles avoid delinquent behavior. Although these programs are not designed to affect only the peer group, mentors can have a significant influence in directing the juveniles with whom they work away from deviant peers and in helping them develop new friends. A mentor can be like a member of the extended family, or like an older, wiser peer who can provide insight and support to the juvenile.

Mentoring programs typically attempt to match juveniles and mentors using a prespecified set of criteria. Mentors then arrange regular get-togethers with the juveniles for conversation, recreational activities, field trips, and other activities. One example of a successful, long-term mentoring program is Big Brothers/Big Sisters of America (BB/BS)(Grossman & Garry, 1997). The results of an outcome evaluation of BB/BS are reported in table 5.3.

Recently the OJJDP funded mentoring programs at pilot sites in several states. The Juvenile Mentoring Program (JUMP) has provided funding guidance and technical support to the pilot programs. Two of the programs are described in box 5.4.

Practitioners should also remember that many conventional programs can have a very positive effect on the children who become involved in them. The Girl/Boy Scouts of America, Little League baseball, community recreation programs, and other such initiatives have helped many juveniles improve their self-esteem and develop positive relationships. Box 5.5 includes an article from the *Miami Herald,* published in 1997. That article, written by a then high school sophomore, describes the positive impact participation in the Girl Scouts of America had on her life.

Work for Administrators, Advocates, and Researchers

Administrators, advocates, and researchers have important work to do in the area of peer intervention. Although many communities have social opportunities for juveniles, many others do not. Administrators and advocates can work

Table 5.3 Outcome Evaluation of Big Brothers/Big Sisters

OUTCOME	CHANGE
Antisocial Activities	
Initiating Drug Use	−45.8%
Initiating Alcohol Use	−27.4%
Number of Times Hit Someone	−31.7%
Academic Outcomes	
Grades	3.0%
Scholastic Competence	4.3%
Skipped Class	−36.7%
Skipped Day of School	−52.2%
Family Relationships	
Summary Measure of Quality of the Relationship	2.1%
Trust	2.7%
Lying to Parent	−36.6%
Peer Relationships	
Emotional Support	2.3%

Note: All impacts in this table are statistically significant at least at a 90% level of confidence.

SOURCE: Grossman & Garry, 1997, p. 3

Box 5.4   Model Mentoring Programs
(Grossman & Garry, 1997, p. 5)

SOUTHWEST IDAHO

The Big Brothers/Big Sisters of south-west Idaho have made 41 matches of at-risk youth and mentors in this JUMP project. According to parents and teachers familiar with the program, 30% of the youth who participated in the program showed improvement in their school attendance, 30% showed academic improvement, 35% showed improvement in their general behavior, and 48% increased the frequency of appropriate interactions with their peers. For example, a female being raised by her father was matched to a female volunteer and, after the match, scored higher in measures of grades, self-esteem, positive attitude toward others, and pride in appearance.

CINCINNATI, OHIO

The Cincinnati Youth Collaborative in Ohio matched 136 youths and volunteers in its first year in JUMP. Mentors include doctors, dentists, lawyers, teachers, chemists, police officers, nurses, waiters, postal clerks, travel agents, and college students. Some special activities were a trip to New York City, visits to college campuses, a community bowl-a-thon, job-shadowing, and participation in a school beautification project. The project reports that 99 of the 136 young people have improved academically and 102 have improved socially.

Box 5.5   Story of a Female Adolescent
"Girl Scouts: More Than Good Cookies"
Wendy Moore (*Miami Herald,* 28 May 1994. © 2000 by the Miami Herald. Reprinted with permission.)

Wendy Moore was a sophomore at Taravella High School in Coral Springs, Florida, when she wrote this article for the op-ed page of the Miami Herald. *She is now a recent college graduate planning a successful career. Wendy had a wonderful mother who was a powerful influence in helping her make positive decisions about her life's direction. But Wendy also faced some important risk factors, as she discusses in her article. Wendy also discusses the positive effects she experienced from her involvement in a popular youth organization, Girl Scouts of America.*

When you say "Girl Scouts," most people think of cookies or little girls in uniform.

Today, Girl Scouts is more than campfires and selling cookies. It's more than workshops on preventing teenage pregnancy or learning first aid.

Girl Scouts has taken the lead in programs that serve all races, religions, origins, and, like me, abilities. Their program has given me tools and the experience to determine my future.

My Girl Scout experience began in the Brownies. Laura Scannell, my leader, gave me confidence in myself, and began to feel that I could try and do new things. Over the following 11 years, each of my leaders showed me ways that one person can make a difference.

For example, my junior and Cadette troops adopted West Lake park as our wetland while earning ecology badges. The first year we planted mangroves, and the fun part was playing in all that mud. The next year we were shocked to find that the mangroves were as tall as we were. Plants, fish, and birds had returned.

The third year our seedlings had grown into a forest. We had fun teaching Brownies about the wetlands and helped them play in the mud—oops, I mean plant mangroves.

Along the way I met Jeanne Mills. She might have been a Coral Springs city commissioner, but she got dirtier than I did digging at a Plant Rescue project. She taught me leadership that I hope to emulate some day. I saw her stand up for values and principles that she believed in.

I decided that public service was a good career, that being in public office is a very direct way to make a difference.

I had one problem. While Girl Scouts had been giving me opportunities and building up my self-confidence, my school counselor and learning disabilities teacher were telling me that kids with learning disabilities couldn't go to college and certainly shouldn't consider law school or politics.

My mom and Girl Scouts came to the rescue. I took what I had learned from scouting and developed a plan.

First, I did research to figure out who was right. (Sorry, Mom, but I had to be sure.) Then I did research on colleges that have programs for kids with learning disabilities.

Next year I will be out of all my specific learning disabilities classes. I will be mainstreamed with little assistance.

I have been working on projects outside school so that I can have other references and ways to demonstrate my abilities.

This past legislative session I spent a week in Tallahassee working in the majority office. I learned a great deal, and I met people such as Mandy Dawson, another great role model.

Girl Scouting encourages me to be active in my school and my community. I play alto saxophone. To improve my writing, I applied to and was accepted by the school newspaper. I played sports until I hurt my knee.

Girl Scouts has given me a way to dream, to plan, to work toward a better future. It has taught me to respect myself and others around me and to help where I am needed.

Girl Scout laws are values for everyday living. I share those values with my family and my sister scouts everywhere. I hope that you will remember that Girl Scouts today is a lot more than good cookies.

---

to found such programs, or to develop other alternatives where there are few choices. Another weakness that administrators and advocates should address is the absence of social skills training and conflict mediation training in their communities. Administrators should be certain that staff are appropriately trained in these areas and that the latest, most effective programs are used within their agencies.

Advocates and researchers can also work to increase the number of persons willing to become volunteer mentors in their communities. Public speaking engagements, public service announcements, and newspaper interviews are all possible avenues for involving the public. The OJJDP lists lack of willing volunteers as one of the two greatest problems in developing a mentoring program (Grossman & Garry, 1997). Making the public aware of the need for volunteers is one way to increase availability.

Researchers should help practitioners develop new and even more effective interventions for peer group problems. One particularly important area is helping families where the parent's influence has decreased relative to that of peer groups. Culturally sensitive alternatives should also be developed and evaluated.

INTERVENTIONS FOR THE EMPLOYMENT SOCIAL SYSTEM

In this section we will discuss the effect of employment or vocational choice for the juvenile. The employment system affects the youth for many reasons. If she is employed, that system may contain either positive or negative influences. Whether or not she is employed, expectations for future employment and success are very important. Interventions that include a vocational component can be very effective, particularly for middle and older adolescents.

Characteristics That Contribute to Problem Behavior

Sometimes an adolescent's co-workers can be very positive influences. At other times they can be very negative. For example, one of the authors once had a client who made deliveries for a fast-food restaurant. The juvenile had an arrangement with the assistant manager in which he delivered illegal drugs to small-time suppliers while en route to food deliveries. Interestingly, the assistant manager's role in the youth's problems was not discovered during the juvenile's arrest and processing. When the involvement of the assistant manager was reported to the practitioner, the intervention included both a new job for the worker and the arrest of the assistant manager.

Intervention alternatives for youths who face antisocial influences in the workplace are relatively simple. Practitioners must facilitate either removal of the juvenile, removal of the influences, or a combination of the two. Juveniles should not remain in a workplace where they are constantly exposed to the influence of delinquent or criminal influences.

Sometimes a youth can be helped to develop a career interest through part-time employment. This may be even more effective if it is implemented through a restitution agreement or if it helps to support his family. Many troubled juveniles have little hope for the future because they believe their educational and employment opportunities to be very limited. These teens can often be helped through part-time employment or vocational testing and training.

Intervention Techniques for Specific Problems

Juveniles who can benefit from part-time employment should be given assistance in interviewing skills and appropriate dress for interviewing. When the family has insufficient resources to purchase appropriate clothing, the teen should be referred to community agencies that can help with funding. Practitioners can also help with scheduling and planning interviews.

When juveniles have made a clear decision that they will not pursue a standard education, they can be referred to GED or vocational programs. GED programs provide specialized training to allow persons who have not completed high school to receive a general education degree (GED). That serves as the equivalent of a high school degree for many employers. At the end of the training, participants are tested and, if they pass the test, receive their GEDs.

Vocational training may be more appropriate for some teens. In these programs youths are tested to determine where their interests and abilities lie. They are then trained in such careers as auto repair, heating and air conditioning service, and computer technologies. Practitioners should be familiar with vocational programs in their area and should refer appropriate youths to those programs. They should also be aware of community resources that can provide tuition money or other educational assistance when it is needed.

Model Programs

Employment-related programs for juveniles often include four stages: employability training, job training, interviewing support, and aftercare. During employability training the youths are taught to dress appropriately for interviews and what kinds of things to say and kinds of questions to ask during interviews. During job training they are taught the knowledge and skills to perform certain jobs. Interviewing support assists them with reviewing classified advertisements, preparing lists to call, and making telephone calls to secure appointments. Aftercare provides ongoing support to juveniles who have found positions, helping them adjust to the demands and expectations of their new employers. Some programs also have placement services or operate small businesses in which the juveniles can participate.

Work for Administrators, Advocates, and Researchers

Administrators and advocates should ensure that educational and vocational alternatives are available in their communities. They should also develop funding for juveniles who cannot afford tuition and other fees. They should also ensure that employability training and funding are available for those who will

seek work. Researchers can advise practitioners who are developir
programs and can evaluate those programs.

INTERVENTIONS FOR THE COMMUNITY SOCIAL SYSTEM

Many characteristics of communities are known to affect the behavior of children. In communities where the residents are relatively stable, the community
is reasonably organized, and community members model prosocial behavior,
children are unlikely to become delinquent. When communities are very transient, are crowded and disorganized, and have many residents who engage in
criminal behavior, the probability that its children will become delinquent is
increased.

Characteristics That Contribute to Problem Behavior

Children learn from the behaviors they see modeled and the ideas they hear expressed by their family and their neighbors. Children who grow up watching
drug deals on the corner and fights on Friday nights come to believe that this
is the appropriate way to live. Many children adopt the norms and values of
their community. When many people in that community believe that theft, assault, and other crimes are an acceptable way to behave, children often adopt
those attitudes. This provides a foundation for a belief system that supports deviant behavior.

These problems are worsened by community crowding, transience, and
disorganization. Crowded neighborhoods often include crowded housing, with
too many people living in a single dwelling. Stress levels can be very high, resulting in short tempers and fighting. Crowded communities often mean limited economic opportunity, leading some residents to engage in illegal activities such as prostitution or drug sales to make money. Others turn to alcohol
and other substances to help alleviate the pressures they experience. Transience
adds to the problem. Neighbors do not know one another; so commitment to
the community is low. Many residents do not know whom they can trust or to
whom they can turn for help with a problem. Community organizations, such
as block clubs or community councils, can help to solve these problems, but
where they do not exist or are ineffective, few controls exist to solve neighborhood problems.

Neighborhoods where some or all of these conditions exist often have a
higher percentage of juveniles who engage in problem behavior. Practitioners
at every level can help to make positive changes in these neighborhoods, and
can thereby help the youths who live in them.

Intervention Techniques for Specific Problems

Community problems can be addressed on an individual or a community level.
Individual interventions attempt to either diminish the effects of negative influences on a youth or enhance the effects of positive conditions. Community
interventions try to change conditions within the community itself.

Many of the techniques described in the section for intervening with peer
groups also apply to individual community interventions. In order to minimize

a client's contact with deviant peers, the practitioner may want to draw a map of the youth's community, highlighting areas where most criminal activity occurs. For example, the back of a convenience store might be a hangout for drug dealers. An abandoned building might be a meeting place for gang members. The practitioner could label these zones as "no-entry" and other areas as "safe." The maps could then be coordinated with the behavioral contract so that the juvenile agrees to stay out of "no-entry" zones. Positive areas or organizations could also be identified on the maps. When a youth is pursued by criminal influences, practitioners may need to enlist the aid of law enforcement. In particularly difficult cases, practitioners may need to expedite the relocation of the youth and/or family.

A juvenile's commitment to the community can sometimes be enhanced through involvement in community-based programs and projects. By working to improve their community, they often begin to feel more a part of it, and develop a sense of wanting to care for their neighborhood. Practitioners may also be able to help families with crowded homes find other living arrangements.

Community-level interventions include provider consortia, coordinating councils, block clubs, community councils, and similar programs. Many such programs exist in different forms in various parts of the country. Practitioners in every role in the juvenile justice system can and should be involved with these programs.

Model Programs

Many communities have established organizations known as coordinating councils. These councils are usually composed of the chief executive officers of the major human services agencies for a given area. They are usually concerned with juvenile justice issues along with other human service issues. The council has several purposes, the most comprehensive being to facilitate the provision of effective services to the community. Many also are involved in community organization activities, targeting specific communities for program development and funding.

Coordinating councils can be very useful to practitioners. The organizations represented on these councils have the potential to direct substantial resources into needy neighborhoods and can set up agencies where no services exist. Practitioners should become aware of and establish communication with any coordinating council that exists in their areas.

Some communities form block clubs or block watch organizations. These groups share in various kinds of responsibilities. Some are strictly observers, monitoring the streets and calling police at the first sign of any trouble. Others provide "safe houses" for children in need. Still others conduct regular resource meetings in which ideas for community improvement, public safety, and the well-being of children are shared.

Many communities have community councils, or groups of citizens that meet to discuss issues, handle neighborhood business, and form a collective voice for the individuals in that neighborhood. These organizations are usually smaller than coordinating councils, represent smaller geographical areas, and are composed of community residents. They can be very active in developing block watches, youth safe houses, and other programs.

Sometimes local service providers form groups called consortia. Usually these groups are composed of agencies with a common purpose, such as juvenile diversion or aftercare. Often they share the broader purposes of prevention and treatment of problem behavior. Although these organizations are not usually able to organize the communities themselves, they are able to organize and coordinate services to these communities more effectively. Often they can also seek funding that will target a certain neighborhood or community in need of specific services.

Practitioners should be aware of and should interact with these types of organizations in the communities in which their clients live. Direct service workers are often aware what services are lacking and of the places they are most needed. They can also use safe houses and block watch programs on behalf of their clients. Administrators can bring the resources of their agencies to communities through these organizations. This will allow them to enhance service delivery by empowering communities to participate in their own decision-making processes.

Some interventions have components that address the needs of juveniles and their families, but address the needs of the community simultaneously. These interventions are attempts at the type of comprehensive treatment we discussed in this and previous chapters. One example of such an intervention is discussed in box 5.6.

Work for Administrators, Advocates, Advisors, and Researchers

Administrators, advocates, advisors, and researchers have very important work to do in community intervention. A primary task they share is to ensure that a sufficient number and variety of effective programs are in place within their service areas. They can enhance their efforts by participating in coordinating councils and community councils in their areas. They can further improve their effectiveness by involving people from neighborhood organizations in their planning and program development process.

Workers who do not practice directly in communities must also find a way to be in contact with the members of those communities. They must understand the changing needs of those communities and must plan service delivery accordingly. This communication also helps community members to feel that they are a part of the government process for their neighborhood. Leaders should also make every effort to ensure that once their organization has begun to participate in a community, it stays active there as long as it is needed. One of the authors was involved in the development of a community project in a major metropolitan area. The three major complaints of the people of the community were (1) "Social service organizations don't understand us and try to tell us what we need anyway"; (2) "Your program won't work anyway"; and (3) "People like you just come in, make a lot of promises, then go away."

Box 5.6 Comprehensive Intervention
The Family Network Partnership
Michael Forster, PhD

The Family Network Partnership (FNP) is a community-based project of the School of Social Work of the University of Southern Mississippi in Hattiesburg, with offices in the Robertson Place Apartments, a public housing complex located in the city's highest crime district. The Partnership is directed by social work faculty members Michael Forster and Tim Rehner.

The Partnership uses three general strategies to reduce and prevent juvenile crime in Robertson Place and the immediate surrounding community.

1. *Intervene early with youth already involved with the county youth court.* Referrals of first- and second-time offenders are made to FNP by the county youth court. Following an ecological assessment of individual, family, and systemic factors, Partnership staff and student interns engage the youth's family and other relevant community agents—schoolteachers, police, employers, health and mental health providers, churches, and neighborhood organizations—to address immediate needs and improve coping capacities.

Time-limited individualized case plans are used to organize and evaluate planned intervention. The range of possible interventions is extensive and inclusive, from direct counseling and skill instruction to some form of systems advocacy and referral for one or another type of specialized service. In cases where the risk of re-offense is high, involvement of the community policing team figures prominently into case plans.

2. *Develop positive skills and capacities in youth before they engage in delinquent behaviors.* FNP builds competencies in the community's young people through tutoring, recreational activities, cultural events, an arts program, a gardening project, community service opportunities, and peer-oriented skill development (for teens). The power of the peer group can be effectively tapped to build a culture of positive values and learning among high-risk youth. In addition, the Partnership operates a lending library of children's books, runs a popular "token store" that provides earned rewards for youth who demonstrate pro-social behaviors, and maintains a schedule of "drop-in" hours at the office.

3. *Reduce environmental risk factors through community capacity building.* Robertson Place is an impoverished and relatively isolated community characterized by limited internal "youth friendly" resources—recreational, cultural, spiritual, age-appropriate work, community service, and the like. Moreover, numerous financial, transportation, and social barriers severely restrict the ability of youth and families to access resources external to the immediate community. Perhaps worst of all, many if not most residents feel powerless to effect substantial change in their life circumstances.

The Partnership addresses these issues through a range of resident/community empowerment activities. In the first place, the agency has literally joined the community, with offices adjoining the apartments' community center. Second, FNP engages the community in program development, collaborating with indigenous community agents, such as local churches, to enhance their own services and opportunities for families and youth. Third, FNP supports residents' efforts to take more control over their lives. The Partnership offers consultation and training to parents on working with their children and on advocating for their own interests with public service providers. Staff participate in the planning and execution of community residents' meetings. The agency led one voter registration drive and intends more in the future.

Principal funding for the Family Network Partnership is provided by the Mississippi Division of Public Safety

Planning and the Mississippi Arts Commission.

Michael Forster and Tim Rehner are associate professor and assistant professor, respectively, of social work at The University of Southern Mississippi. They can be reached at 601-266-4163, Box 5114, Hattiesburg, MS 39460.

INTERVENTIONS FOR GANG INVOLVEMENT

Although relatively few juveniles are involved in gangs, many law enforcement personnel believe that the number is growing (Battin-Pearson, Thornberry, Hawkins, & Krohn, 1998). They also report that gangs influence schools, communities, and individual youth in very powerful ways. In this section we will speak briefly about intervention for gang members.

Characteristics That Contribute to Problem Behavior

Youth gangs create a new and different world for their members. The rules are different from those of the rest of the world. Their members value aggression, theft, drug sales, violence, and other delinquent acts. These conditions create a separate culture in which members receive positive reinforcement for criminal acts and are sanctioned for some prosocial behaviors.

Gangs can be very attractive to troubled youths. They often provide a sense of acceptance and belonging that has been lacking in the youth's home. They may also provide a way to make large sums of money relatively quickly through drug sales or other illegal activities. Sometimes juveniles join simply for protection: gangs have become so prominent in their neighborhood that they need allies to protect them against other gang members.

Whatever the reason juveniles join a gang, it can be very difficult to get them to leave their gang. Many groups require an oath of life membership, and will allow only one way out: a beating from all the other members. Many juveniles who try to leave their gangs are harassed, assaulted, or killed by other members. These forces—a sense of love and belonging, financial opportunities, and fear of reprisal—can make work with gang members very challenging.

Intervention Techniques for Specific Problems

Successful work with gang members may require intervention on many levels. The juvenile's desire to associate with other members may need to be diminished. Family conditions may need to be improved. Although the youth will probably have no way to replace income lost by leaving a gang, it may be necessary to locate a source of employment so that the loss is not too severe. It may even be necessary to arrange some sort of protection by law enforcement or to help the family relocate in order to avoid reprisals from other gang members.

The juvenile's desire to be a gang member may be reduced through cognitive-behavioral therapy. Participation in an antisocial culture will have caused the youth to develop definitions (cognitions) that make him believe that gang membership is good and beneficial. These definitions can be changed using the techniques discussed in chapter 4.

Not all gang members come from troubled families, but many do. When the family is a factor in gang membership, the practitioner should refer the family for counseling and parent training. She may also want to consider social skills training.

Not all gang members make a lot of money through their gangs, but many do. One of the authors was told, "I have $1,000 in my pocket, a beeper, a gun, a car, nice clothes, and three girlfriends. If I leave the gang, and flip burgers, I won't have any of that. Tell me again why I would want to get out." This gang member, not at all unusual in his situation, was willing to exchange long-term risk (incarceration) for short-term gain (money).

Obviously, juveniles who have made large amounts of money from gang activity are unlikely to be able to replace it from part-time, entry-level work. They must be shown that the long-term risks of gang membership outweigh the potential for financial reward, and may need to be helped to replace some of their lost income. When this is the case, interventions discussed above for the employment should be used.

Some gangs are not very organized or active. Others are very strong, serious, and dangerous criminal organizations whose members will not hesitate to harm those who try to withdraw from membership. When gangs are not very organized and powerful, juveniles can sometimes withdraw simply by avoiding meetings and other gang activities. When the gangs are strong, members may not allow this withdrawal. In these cases, involvement by law enforcement or physical relocation may be necessary.

Model Programs

A number of programs have been used to target gang members in various parts of the country. Some focus on the individual, using prevention and treatment technologies. Others are intended to make the environment less conducive to gang activity.

Gang Resistance Education and Training (GREAT) is a school-based education program designed to make juveniles aware of the dangers presented by gangs and gang membership. It is usually taught by police officers and focuses on pre-adolescent children. Designed as a prevention program, GREAT has been evaluated several times. The results have been encouraging (Esbensen & Osgood, 1997).

Some communities have instituted parent education programs. In these programs experts from law enforcement, schools, and local universities teach parents to recognize signs of gang involvement in their children or their children's friends. They also learn techniques for helping their children avoid further involvement.

Aggression Replacement Training (ART) is a social skills training program that we discussed in a section above. ART has been used with gang members and other aggressive youth in several studies. Most of those studies have show... marked reductions in recidivism among program graduates. In a New York study that included only gang members, most of the participants left their gangs and took conventional jobs in various fields (Goldstein & Glick, 1998). Aggression Replacement Training and other social skills interventions will be discussed in greater detail in chapter 8.

Some schools have developed policies aimed at reducing gang activity. Examples of school policies include the use of uniforms (prevents members from wearing *gang colors* or symbols), zero tolerance rules (expulsion for gang-related activities), and installation of metal detectors (to detect weapons). Some of the anti-gang measures adopted by schools are summarized in chapter 7 of *The Gang Intervention Handbook* (Stephens, 1993).

Some jurisdictions have passed laws that allow or require juveniles who are arrested for gang-related crimes to be prosecuted as adults. These laws are intended to serve as deterrents to gang membership and to ensure that active gang members are removed from the streets. A summary of similar legislation is provided in *Prosecuting Gangs: A National Assessment* (Johnson, Webster, & Conners, 1995).

Many cities and schools where gangs are active have started *graffiti* removal programs. In these programs groups are designated as graffiti spotters. In cities it may be citizens' groups or social service agencies. In schools, it may be club members or faculty. Graffiti spotters are responsible for patrolling designated areas of the community or school and noting the presence of any gang-related graffiti. Spotters report its presence to appropriate authorities, who then ensure that it is removed. Graffiti removal serves many purposes. One of these is to prevent escalating tensions between rival gangs.

Work for Administrators, Advocates, Advisors, and Researchers

As with the other social systems described in this chapter, there is important work for every practitioner in gang-related intervention. Administrators can ensure that programs for individuals are available within their agencies, and can participate in community-level anti-gang programs. Advocates can work to see that such programs are in place, and can encourage evaluation to ensure that effective measures are implemented. Advisors should familiarize themselves with effective programs (see chapter 6) and should be certain that decision-makers are aware of those programs. Researchers can help design and evaluate effective programs.

SUMMARY

In this chapter we have reviewed interventions for several specific social systems, including the school, peer group, employment, and community systems. We also looked at a special case, the youth who has added a youth gang as an additional social system. We've spent the last two chapters looking at things that work: interventions that have been effective in some of our communities. In the next chapter we'll talk about some things that don't work, and some ways to make sure you avoid those kinds of interventions.

ACTIVITIES FOR LEARNING

ram in your community
ned to deliver school-
vention for delinquents.
ices does the program offer?
they offered? Does the
laim to be successful? How
does in determine its level of success?

2. Identify a community-based program in your area and follow the same steps as in activity 1.

3. Does your community have a gang problem? What kinds of evidence might you look for to determine whether or not a gang problem exists?

If a problem does exist, what interventions are being used? What others should be introduced?

4. Working in a small group, identify resources from which mentors could be drawn in your community. How would you reach potential volunteers? How would you approach them? How would you screen them for appropriateness and match them with appropriate juveniles? If necessary, contact Big Brothers/Big Sisters of America and ask them about their selection and matching criteria.

QUESTIONS FOR DISCUSSION

1. What do you think are the most important factors in the school environment that contribute to the development of delinquent behavior? How would you design an intervention to counteract those factors? What are the factors for the peer group? For the community? How would you counteract those factors?

2. Assume that you have discovered that one of your clients has a learning disability, but has never received any

treatment, counseling, or assistance for coping with that disability. What steps would you take to help your client?

3. Imagine that your client lives in a community that is high in crime and has several areas in which drugs are sold and used. How would you design an intervention to help him cope with that problem? What resources might he have that would be helpful? What would you do if the influences in the community were too strong?

KEY TERMS AND DEFINITIONS

Alternative school A school for children who have experienced problems in conventional school settings. Often these problems have been behavioral.

Gang colors The colors gangs use to identify themselves, such as red, black, or blue. Clothing the members wear is often selected because of these colors.

Graffiti Marks or messages left on the wall to symbolize the gang. Graffitied

names of members or gangs are sometimes referred to as tags.

Mentor An adult who develops a one-on-one helping relationship with a juvenile. The two meet regularly for recreational, social, and instructional activities. The mentor attempts to provide general help and support to the youth.

REFERENCES

Battin-Pearson, S. R., Thornberry, T. P., Hawkins, J. D., & Krohn, M. D. (1998, October). Gang membership, delinquent peers, and delinquent behavior. *Juvenile Justice Bulletin.* Washington, DC: Office of Juvenile Justice and Delinquency Prevention.

Dryfoos, J. G. (1990). *Adolescents at risk: Prevalence and prevention.* New York: Oxford University Press.

Dryfoos, J. G. (1994). *Full-service schools: A revolution in health and social services for children, youth, and families.* San Francisco: Jossey-Bass.

Dupper, D. R. (1993). Preventing school dropouts: Guidelines for school social work practice. *Social Work in Education, 15*(3), 141–149.

Dupper, D. R. (1998). An alternative to suspension for middle school youth with behavior problems: Findings from a "school survival" group. *Research on Social Work Practice, 8,* 354–366.

Dupper, D. R., & Poertner, J. (1997). Public schools and the revitalization of impoverished communities: School-linked, family resource centers. *Social Work, 42,* 415–422.

Esbensen, F., & Osgood, D. W. (1997, November). National evaluation of G.R.E.A.T. *Research in Brief.* Washington, DC: National Institute of Justice.

Gibbs, J. C., Potter, G. B., & Goldstein, A. P. (1995). *The EQUIP program.* Champaign, IL: Research Press.

Goldstein, A. P. (1990). *The PREPARE curriculum.* Champaign, IL: Research Press.

Goldstein, A. P., & Glick, B. (1998). Aggression replacement training: Development, procedures, and efficiency evaluations. In A. R. Roberts (Ed.), *Juvenile justice: Policies, programs, and services* (2nd ed.). Chicago: Nelson-Hall.

Grice, M. (1986). *Positive alternatives to school suspensions (P.A.S.S.), 1985–1986.* Portland Public Schools: Evaluation Report. Portland, OR: Portland Public Schools Research and Evaluation Department. (ERIC Document Reproduction Service No. ED 276 794)

Grossman, J. B., & Garry, E. M. (1997, April). Mentoring—A proven delinquency strategy. *Juvenile Justice Bulletin.* Washington, DC: Office of Juvenile Justice and Delinquency Prevention.

Hawkins, J. D., Catalano, R. F., & Miller, J. Y. (1992). Risk and protective factors for alcohol and other drug problems in adolescence and early adulthood: Implications for substance abuse prevention. *Psychological Bulletin, 11*(1), 64–105.

Heward, W. L. (1996). *Exceptional children: An introduction to special education* (5th ed.). Englewood Cliffs, NJ: Prentice Hall.

Hunter, L., & Elias, M. (1998). School violence: Prevalence, policies, and prevention. In A. R. Roberts (Ed.), *Juvenile justice: Policies, programs, and services* (2nd ed.). Chicago: Nelson-Hall.

Johnson, C., Webster, B., & Conners, E. (1995, February). Prosecuting gangs: A national assessment. *Research in Brief.* Washington, DC: National Institute of Justice.

Larson, K., & Rumberger, R. (1995). *PACT manual: Parent and community teams for school success.* Minneapolis: Institute on Community Integration, University of Minnesota.

Stephens, R. D. (1993). School-based interventions: Safety and security. In A. P. Goldstein & C. R. Huff (Eds.), *The gang intervention handbook.* Champaign, IL: Research Press.

Chapter 6

◆

Interventions to Avoid

CHAPTER OUTLINE

The History of Ineffective Intervention
Characteristics of Ineffective Intervention
Counterproductive Interventions
How to Find Interventions That Work
Summary

Practitioners need to know what interventions work so that they can use them with their clients. It is equally important, however, that they know which ones *do not* work so that they can choose other alternatives. Practitioners of various types have been struggling with juvenile justice issues for many years. They have worked hard, but often futilely. Their work has left a legacy of knowledge of what is effective and what is not. This is extremely useful information to today's practitioner. It is also the subject of this chapter.

In chapter 6 we'll talk about ineffective intervention. First we'll review some of the history of intervention with troubled youth and will see what lessons can be learned from that history. Next, we'll take a look at the characteristics of ineffective programs and talk about ways practitioners can avoid these pitfalls. Then, we'll discuss interventions that appear to do more harm than good. Practitioners will certainly want to avoid these. We'll close the chapter with a section that describes techniques for identifying and finding effective interventions. This will allow practitioners to do their own research to find out how to best help their clients.

THE HISTORY OF INEFFECTIVE INTERVENTION

The juvenile justice system has developed as the result of a number of different philosophies and influences. Originally, it was intended to intervene in the lives of troubled children and families to try to divert the delinquent youth from future criminal behavior. It was based on philosophies borrowed from British law, primarily a doctrine called *parens patriae*. *Parens patriae* refers to the right of the state to act as a parent on behalf of those who are unable to care for themselves. In the case of delinquent juveniles, this meant that the court system would assume responsibility for their development and training if it found that either the child or his family was not able to do this adequately. The founders of the system believed that the court would serve as a good and faithful parent. They also believed that, given the right support and attention, children could be diverted from a life of crime.

As the system has developed over the years, it has continued to be influenced by various sources. State laws originally created the court, and it has changed in various jurisdictions through revisions to its statutes. *Case law* has also affected the court, as emphasis has gradually shifted from absolute power of the court to more emphasis on the rights of the juveniles. Public opinion has also shaped the course of the system, in large part by insisting on changes to state statutes. For example, the public has mandated the recent tough stance that states have taken toward some categories of crime.

Programs and interventions have changed over the years as well. The original treatment programs were residential institutions. Through the years an array of programs has been tried, with very little success until recently. In this section we'll review a few of the interventions that have been attempted and talk about what we know about why they did not work.

Adult Prisons: The Earliest Interventions

The earliest interventions for juveniles were adult prisons. These existed well before the juvenile court was founded. As recently as the early 1800s, juveniles were incarcerated in the same cells with adults. They received no treatment, education, or vocational training. These early prisons were thought to be beneficial because it was believed that the punishment inmates received would deter them from future criminal activity. Prisons also served a social control function by keeping offenders off the streets.

Obviously, these prisons were not particularly effective in turning youths to a prosocial lifestyle. Juveniles in adult prison were closely associated with hardened criminals who taught them more about criminal behavior. Youths left the prisons as better criminals rather than better citizens. Prisons were actually early evidence of the ineffectiveness of punishment as a deterrent to future crime. We have since learned that the possibility of arrest, incarceration, or even death does little to avert many from committing crimes.

Juveniles who were imprisoned were also exposed to abuse and neglect at the hands of their fellow prisoners. Many may have developed a greater level of anger and toughness in response to this abuse. Others may have become depressed and hopeless, certain that a prosocial life would never be an option for them. A primary lesson to be learned from the early imprisonment of juveniles is that incarceration alone is not sufficient to prevent or treat delinquency. A second important lesson is that more severe and chronic offenders (such as adults) should not be imprisoned with lesser offenders.

Despite their many limitations, early institutions formed the basis for many of our modern programs. Through the years, institutions gradually became more humane and eventually began to provide training and treatment. Among the first recorded efforts to educate juveniles in institutions in the United States was a group of facilities modeled after the Bridewell House in England. Troubled youths were removed from their homes or the streets and placed in confined settings where they were taught a trade. Although these programs may have helped some juveniles, they did not turn a great number of their residents away from lives of crime (Krisberg & Austin, 1978). The failures of these early institutions provide important insight to today's practitioner. One such lesson is that incarceration and vocational training alone are not adequate treatment for many youth.

Houses of Refuge

Houses of Refuge were a treatment of choice during the early 1800s. These institutions were intended to reform deviant youth by providing juveniles with education, vocational skills, religious training, and a strong disciplinary environment. They were intended to provide a positive family environment to counteract what their founders saw as the negative effects of poverty and criminal behavior in the youths' biological families.

The houses were secure buildings, sometimes surrounded by brick walls (Rothman, 1971). Incarcerated juveniles wore uniforms and had their hair cut at a standard length. Inmates followed a strict schedule, beginning with a 6:00 A.M. wake-up bell and ending with classes and prayers in the evening. Youths were punished for infractions in various ways. Severity of punishment varied from a bread and water diet to whipping or chaining (Rothman, 1971).

Although many of the philosophies that guided the Houses of Refuge were sound, many others (e.g., dietary and corporal punishments) were not. In addition, the institutions became overcrowded, were not run effectively, and eventually became little more than prisons for juveniles (Piscotta, 1979; Rothman, 1971). One of the lessons of the Houses of Refuge is that good ideas, if implemented incorrectly, may be no better than bad ideas. Quality implementation is necessary to ensure an effective program.

Cottage Reformatories

Some experts in the middle 1800s felt that a different physical structure could make the philosophies of the Houses of Refuge work. They proposed that youths be housed in cottages overseen by adults who were compensated for their supervisory activities. The cottages would be in rural settings, away from the negative influences of city life. Juveniles would also receive training similar to that intended in the Houses of Refuge. Apprenticeships would be offered to facilitate the juvenile's training.

Despite the promise of these cottage reformatories, they quickly encountered difficulties similar to those of the Houses of Refuge. They became overcrowded, forcing staff to focus on custodial issues rather than treatment. Discipline was harsh, and living quarters were cramped and uncomfortable. Conditions at many of the apprenticeships were brutal, and juveniles ran away from both apprenticeships and cottages in droves. These problems were complicated by violence, fire-starting, and sexual acting out among some of the inmates (Piscotta, 1979). As the Houses of Refuge had failed, so did cottage reformatories. The problems experienced by cottage reformatories underscored the lessons of their predecessor: a good idea, poorly implemented, will not work. It also warned of a problem that has persisted until today: inadequate resources produce program failure.

The failure of the cottage reformatories led to the development of other institutions, such as the Elmira Reformatory. These institutions were more secure than the cottages, but housed adults and juveniles in the same facility, replicating many of the problems of the early prisons. Deviant youths were also housed with dependent children with no previous history of delinquency. Again, the facilities were crowded, discipline was harsh, and little education or treatment was available (Platt, 1969).

The First Juvenile Court

Reformers argued that change was needed at the judicial level. A new court should be formed, they argued. This new court would process juveniles separately from adults. Using *parens patriae* as a guiding philosophy, it would act in the best interests of the juveniles, focusing on rehabilitation rather than punishment. It would be a nonadversarial system in which all parties would seek to see that the offender received help. In response, the first juvenile court was established in Cook County, Illinois, at the turn of the century. Other states soon followed (del Carmen, Parker, & Reddington, 1998).

Unfortunately, the new court faced several problems. First, despite its new approach to litigation, it had no new intervention strategies available other than the types used in previous programs. There were also philosophical differences as to the rights of juveniles under the law. These problems, along with other issues such as underfunding of the agencies intended to implement the programs, compounded the difficulties of the court. Over the next 70 to 80 years, new interventions would be developed and tested. Many of those interventions would fail. Some would succeed. All would provide valuable insight to us, the practitioners at the turn of the next century. As the court and practitioners have slowly developed a knowledge base about effective intervention, however, the public has grown increasingly impatient. One of the results of this impatience has been the current movement toward punishment of offenders rather than treatment.

Psychotherapy and Psychotropic Medication

One of the early additions to the juvenile court's treatment repertoire was psychotherapy. Sigmund Freud's work in the early 1900s became the basis for generations of psychiatric and psychological treatment of offenders. Counselors treated what they called unconscious forces and repressed drives that compelled juveniles to be deviant. They strove to strengthen the egos of their clients and to resolve their *Oedipus* or *Electra complex*. If the juvenile's ego could be strengthened sufficiently, and the youth could gain control over his unconscious sexual and aggressive drives, he would then abstain from criminal behavior.

The court began to order counseling and evaluation for many of the youths whose cases it heard. Psychiatrists and psychologists eventually made important discoveries that helped some of the juveniles. Some could be stabilized through *antidepressant* or *psychotropic medications*. These discoveries were major breakthroughs in the treatment of some juveniles.

The majority of the delinquent youth that came before the court, however, were probably not in need of psychotropic medication. Nor did the psychoanalysis they received from court-appointed professionals help reduce their deviant behavior in many cases. In fact, as we will see later in this chapter, psychoanalytical and psychodynamic interventions actually may have worsened the condition of some clients. As other professionals built on the work of Freud, more successful treatment modalities eventually emerged. These processes, often referred to as cognitive-behavioral therapies, were discussed in greater detail in chapter 4.

Decades after Freud a new type of therapy emerged. The original psychotherapy had focused on the individual. The new therapy treated the family unit, and was therefore known as family therapy. Various practitioners addressed various characteristics of troubled families: communication patterns, inappropriate alliances, intergenerational behavioral patterns, and others. Some of the techniques were based on the previous training their founders had received for treating individuals. Others moved off in bold new directions.

Several different approaches to family therapy have been used to treat the families of delinquent youth. Although some programs have shown some positive results, the overall effect has not been great without other supportive intervention (Henggeler, 1989). Family therapy is often used in combination with other intervention components such as day or residential treatment. It is also a part of many comprehensive prevention and treatment programs for various levels of at-risk and delinquent youth. From the family therapists we have learned much about the importance of the family in helping juveniles. We have also learned that family therapy, alone, is not usually enough to change a juvenile's antisocial patterns.

Despite the development of psychotherapeutic techniques during the early 1900s, the setting in which the intervention took place remained relatively unchanged. Most interventions took place in a practitioner's office or in an institution. During the 1940s, reformers developed new programs that moved offenders in treatment from institutions to open settings. One example of these programs was the forestry camps established by the state of California.

Treatment in Open Settings

Forestry camps provided educational, vocational, and environmental training to troubled youth in a wilderness atmosphere. The facilities were not secure; there were no walls or locks. They excluded severe and chronic offenders, the mentally ill, and youths whose level of intelligence was particularly low (Kogon, 1958). Juveniles were taught the basics of nursery work, fire-fighting skills, reforestation techniques, and forestry-related construction and maintenance skills. They also received basic educational training in the evenings (Kamm, Hunt, & Fleming, 1968).

Younger juveniles (ages 13 through 15) were sent to junior probation camps. These were similar to the forestry camps, but put greater emphasis on education, including up to four hours of classroom training each day. Juveniles in the junior probation camps did the same kind of forestry-related work as the older youths, but for only two hours daily. Both types of camps included a counseling component (Kamm et al., 1968).

The forestry camp model provided helpful experiences to some juveniles. Graduates have distinguished themselves in military service and other areas (Bremner, 1974). Program participants also played important roles in fire fighting while enrolled in the program (Kogon, 1958). The lack of methodologically sound evaluations of these programs makes it impossible to fully evaluate their effectiveness, but Weber (1960) stated that the counseling component of the intervention was probably weak, and that enhanced counseling might have improved program outcomes. Several different versions of these types of programs have been tried in various jurisdictions since the forestry camps were founded in the 1940s.

Other kinds of wilderness programs have also been developed. The Outward Bound model, developed in Wales during the 1940s, has been used in several forms. Associate Marine Institutes (AMI) offers intensive treatment and training in a program built around ocean-related activities. VisionQuest, a Tucson, Arizona, organization, provides Wagon Train, a traveling wilderness intervention that replicates many of the experiences of the wagon trains of pioneer America. The OJJDP is currently sponsoring six pilot wilderness programs in three states (Roberts, 1998).

Wilderness programs have experienced varying degrees of success. Published outcome studies have reported recidivism rates as low as 19% within 12 months (Jack and Ruth Eckerd Foundation, 1997) and as high as 43% (Greenwood, Lipson, Abrahamse, & Zimring, 1983). Unfortunately, different standards were used for recidivism in many of these studies; so the results are difficult to compare. There are very few published studies on wilderness programs. A review of those that do exist led the authors to conclude that the most effective programs delivered consistently high-quality services that addressed a comprehensive set of needs.

From the forestry camps and other wilderness programs we have learned the value of integrated treatment, education, and vocational training. We can also see the importance of providing quality services in each of these areas. It is also clear that while these components address important areas of need for many juveniles, they fail to address other equally important needs. Programs that are more comprehensive, we have learned, have a greater probability of being effective.

In recent years several types of programs have been introduced to try to use the lessons learned from previous efforts. These newer programs include day treatment, halfway houses, community-based intervention, shock interventions, boot camps, psychoeducational programs, prevention programs, and diversionary programs. Most of these programs make an effort to deliver multiple services that address multiple needs. Many try to provide the services in an environment that is more like the juvenile's natural environment.

Day Treatment

The first day treatment programs for children were developed in 1943 (Westman, 1979), but were not frequently used until recently. For example, in 1963 the National Institute of Mental Health (NIMH) listed only 10 such programs in the United States. Today there are hundreds of day treatment programs in mental health programs, substance abuse facilities, and other locations across the country (Sayegh & Grizenko, 1991).

Day treatment programs were discussed in some detail in earlier chapters. Juveniles attend these programs during daytime hours for treatment, education, recreation, and other services. The youths are returned to their homes at night. This format allows comprehensive services to be provided without completely separating the youth from his natural environment. This is important because he can be helped through the process of learning to use his new prosocial skills and attitudes in the community with the help of workers and the support of others in his group (Zimet, 1985).

Day treatment is most often used for those who have mental health or substance abuse issues. Many of these programs have shown some success. Others appear to have helped very little (Sayegh & Grizenko, 1991). These varying outcomes may be due in part to the wide variation in their components. Those who choose effective intervention components and deliver them well are likely to be successful.

Community-based Intervention

Community-based interventions have been employed with some success. In many of the meta-analyses mentioned in chapters 4 and 5, in-home and in-community intervention were mentioned as particularly successful as compared to in-office or institutional intervention. Like day treatment programs, community-based interventions vary widely in their components. As we will see in the next section, this can greatly impact their effectiveness.

"Shock" Programs

Shock programs have also been used for juveniles. Programs such as "Scared Straight" and "shock incarceration" have been employed in some jurisdictions. The former program and others like it take at-risk juveniles into prisons to see and talk to inmates who try to frighten them sufficiently to divert them from further offenses. Shock incarceration programs place sentenced juveniles into higher-level settings for ostensibly extended periods of time before returning them to a lower level of incarceration. There is little evidence that either is very effective (Sherman et al., 1998).

Boot camps are a special case of shock incarceration. Juveniles are selected by prosecutors or courts for diversion into these programs. Typically, youths are offered a shorter term (three to six months) in a boot camp program rather than a longer period of incarceration. Groups of juveniles enter the program and are treated as cohorts, usually by police personnel who were formerly involved in the military. Programs follow a military schedule and use military discipline on offenders. Educational and counseling components are sometimes included. Boot camps have been very controversial, and, although many programs claim high levels of success, professional evaluations have not been encouraging (MacKenzie & Souryal, 1994). Some have suggested that intensive aftercare for graduates might improve results.

Psychoeducation

Psychoeducational intervention involves providing the juvenile with information about the negative effects of specific behaviors such as substance abuse or sexual promiscuity. Weekly training sessions are often used to communicate this information. Judging from evaluations, it appears that psychoeducational programs are effective only when paired with other intervention components.

Prevention programs were introduced in earlier chapters. Practitioners target youths who are believed to be at risk of developing problem behavior. They try to diminish the effects of factors that may contribute to problem behavior and enhance the effects of those factors that prevent it. Prevention programs have had mixed success (Ellis, 1998). It appears that in order to be successful, programs must address multiple risk factors in multiple systems of the juvenile's environment (Sherman et al., 1998).

Diversion Programs

Many diversion programs were developed during the late 1960s and early 1970s following the report of the President's Commission on Law Enforcement and Crime. However, funding has been inadequate, and many communities never actually developed the kinds of programs appropriate for successful diversion (Legler et al., 1996). Diversion programs divert juveniles from the court and from adjudication. Youths may be referred by law enforcement, prosecutors, or the courts. Juveniles typically agree to complete these programs successfully, or to return to the court for alternative sentencing.

The results of outcome studies of diversionary programs are inconclusive, partially because there are so many different approaches to diversion. Even when programs have been evaluated, many of the studies have been seriously flawed. Two components of successful diversionary programs have been identified as particularly important by Legler and associates (1996): (1) number of hours of intervention received by the juvenile (more is better) and (2) location of the intervention (in the home or community is preferable).

Consistent problems in both institutional and open settings have been apparent throughout the history of juvenile justice intervention. In institutional settings juveniles have been subjected to crowded living conditions, inhumane disciplinary measures, ineffective treatment modalities, and unrealistic living situations that failed to prepare them for reentry into the real world. In open settings, they have experienced cookie-cutter approaches that failed to meet individual needs. Many of the problems of past interventions can be traced to inadequate funding. Other interventions have suffered from inaccurate theoretical foundations, poor implementation, insufficient comprehensiveness, and the inclusion of ineffective modalities.

This brief review of the history of juvenile justice makes at least two things very clear. First, many different types of interventions have been attempted to help troubled youths, including imprisonment, counseling, and vocational training. Second, many of those interventions have simply been recycled versions of earlier programs. We have tried different versions of incarceration, different types of counseling, and different kinds of training. Some interventions have shown promise. Others have resulted in failure.

One result of the inadequacies of historical juvenile justice programming has been the current movement toward punishment of offenders. Until recently, we have not understood why the excellent philosophy of the juvenile courts has not spawned successful juveniles. A series of outcome evaluations of juvenile programs led many experts as recently as the early 1980s to conclude that "nothing works" (Lösel, 1996). Recently, however, a series of encouraging outcome studies and meta-analyses have caused experts to rethink the issue of effectiveness. Experts have reviewed the history of intervention and have evaluated current programs. As a result, they have recognized that intervention success is often the result of specific components and characteristics of interventions. Thus, one residential intervention might have been successful because it included these characteristics. Another might have failed because it did not.

CHARACTERISTICS OF INEFFECTIVE INTERVENTION

As we reviewed the history of ineffective intervention in the section above, it became clear that many of the basic philosophies and settings of intervention from the past are still in use today. Yet we also observed that many of today's interventions are showing promise where past efforts had failed. Why would today's programs be more successful than similar programs offered 25 years ago?

A partial answer to this question is provided by looking at past programs and the meta-analyses described in earlier chapters. From these sources we have learned that certain characteristics of modern interventions help make them successful. Other characteristics may actually have a negative effect. In this section, we'll look at some factors that contribute to making interventions ineffective. These factors include lack of comprehensiveness, the use of ineffective program components, the inclusion of untrained or unskilled workers, the inability of families to participate in treatment, inconsistent service delivery, inadequate follow-up with program graduates, insufficient availability of placement alternatives, and inadequate funding for programs.

Some interventions have failed because they were insufficiently comprehensive. In reviewing the programs discussed in the section above, it is clear that many practitioners have focused on only one aspect or problem in the life of a troubled youth. For example, early programs removed juveniles from environments that contributed to their problems, but did not help them learn the skills needed to live in those environments when they returned. Another example was the forestry camps. Despite excellent vocational programming, the counseling component was weak. The programs were not as strong as they might have been because of this deficiency.

Other interventions have failed because they have used ineffective components to address specific problem areas. For example, some programs have provided educational and vocational training, but have delivered their services in environments that were harsh and punitive. Other programs have used ineffective counseling modalities.

Programs have also suffered from a lack of trained, professional workers. Many of the early programs were plagued by high staff turnover, a problem that persists today. High turnover negatively impacts morale, generates large caseloads, and diminishes the quality of service an agency can deliver. Another problem related to workers is educational background. State agencies often hire persons whose training is in areas other than juvenile justice. When these new workers have a background in a related field, such as counseling or criminal justice, the transition is often quick and easy. When it is in some unrelated area, the transition to effective practitioner can be both long and difficult. Untrained workers often lack the basic knowledge and skills needed to help juveniles succeed. They often do not understand the multiple factors that contribute to delinquency and, as a result, may fail to address many. They may also lack knowledge of the principles of effective intervention and may not have the skills to acquire that knowledge. Although experience and in-service training may eventually provide the worker with sufficient knowledge and skills to assist juveniles, the high turnover among these employees means they often leave the agency before they develop sufficient competence.

Another problem that has contributed to the failure of juvenile programming is the unavailability or unwillingness of the family to participate in treatment. Many early programs took youths away from their homes to remote locations difficult for families to reach. Where families could be included in the programs, some were unwilling to participate. Either situation meant that problems in the family often could not be adequately addressed.

Even today there is often little sensitivity to the need for family involvement. Some juveniles are sent to institutions with higher levels of security that are often geographically remote from their parents. Even when youths are placed in facilities within their own cities, transportation and access can be a problem, particularly for low-income families. As we saw in earlier chapters, the participation of the family can be critical to the intervention's success. When the family cannot see the juvenile or participate actively in her treatment, the chances of success may be substantially decreased.

The unwillingness of families to participate in treatment is a difficult and persistent problem. Sometimes cognitive-behavioral intervention can change a family's perspective on the importance of participation. Some jurisdictions have experimented with mandating parental participation. Regardless of the barriers that exist, family participation in the treatment process should be encouraged whenever possible.

Quality of service delivery has been a frequent issue for juvenile justice programs. For example, both Houses of Refuge and cottage reformatories failed to deliver the programs they promised. In both cases the institutions became overwhelmed by sheer numbers of youths. Overburdened staff were not able to consistently deliver quality service and eventually gave up. The result was another prison, not at all what the founders envisioned. Today this problem is frequently referred to as "treatment integrity." Practitioners may find it difficult to consistently provide the service they are trained to provide for many reasons. Sometimes it is because of a high caseload. At other times it may be because a few clients need an inordinate amount of attention. In other cases it is because they deliberately choose to stray from the principles of effective intervention they have been taught. Whatever the reason, the failure to adhere to a theoretically and empirically sound treatment plan caused many early programs to fail. It also diminished the effectiveness of programs today.

Failure to provide adequate follow-up to treatment has also contributed to program failure. Early programs had little support available to program completers. Even today many juveniles complete intervention activities, graduate, and are released into a world that is hostile to their new attitudes and skills. It is important to remember that youths who are in treatment receive those services in an unreal world. Those who are placed in residential or day treatment programs have little contact with old friends and environmental conditions. Those who are treated in the community have more contact with negative influences, but have an unrealistic level of support. When the intervention is terminated, the juvenile must stand alone in his environment. This is a difficult task, and may contribute to the recidivism of many former offenders.

Many successful programs gradually reduce the amount of support their clients receive. In the case of residential programs, the youth may be referred to a halfway house or an intensive aftercare program upon graduation. For open programs, the case manager may involve the youth in community activities, and may enlist the aid of a mentor to monitor the juvenile's activities after services have been terminated.

A lack of adequate placement alternatives has been a persistent problem throughout the history of delinquency treatment. Sometimes the problem has been a lack of beds or slots in facilities. In other cases treatment slots have been available, but the services offered by those programs were not appropriate for the juvenile in need of treatment. Early institutions, such as the Houses of Refuge and the cottage reformatories, were overcrowded, preventing practitioners from delivering effective interventions. Practitioners today often find that no programs are available to meet the juvenile's needs in specific areas, or that the programs that are available are filled to capacity.

Insufficient funding has been a persistent problem for juvenile justice practitioners. This has been true since the days of the overcrowded and understaffed Houses of Refuge. A lack of funding may result in higher caseloads, unqualified workers, and deficient interventions. It inhibits the activities of program developers and evaluation researchers. Clearly, inadequate resources contribute to many of the other problems experienced by practitioners and programs, both historically and in the present.

As we have seen, a number of factors have inhibited the success of juvenile justice programs throughout history. Unfortunately, some factors have not only prevented interventions from working but actually made things worse for juveniles. In the next section we'll talk about two counterproductive interventions. Then, in the final section of this chapter, we'll look at some ways you can find out the most current information on what does work.

COUNTERPRODUCTIVE INTERVENTIONS

Some experts have argued that participation in juvenile justice programs has actually increased the level of delinquency (Bullington et al., 1990). Certainly this seems like a reasonable possibility given the abusive conditions, contact with adult criminals, and history of ineffective intervention that juveniles in custody have experienced. Some of these conditions are obviously counterproductive. For example, few experts would argue that a 10-year-old shoplifter should be incarcerated with adult sexual offenders. Other conditions, however, are far less obvious.

Meta-analyses mentioned earlier in this book have uncovered some conditions that negatively impact a broad range of juveniles. Other research has suggested that specific subgroups of delinquents may be adversely affected by some conditions. Ethnic minorities, girls, and juveniles who experience developmental delays may be harmed by conditions that help juveniles who are not a part of those groups. Some conditions that may harm specific subgroups of youths are described in chapter 7. We'll talk about the conditions that negatively affect broad groups of juveniles in this section. These conditions include use of interventions that are not strongly founded in supported scientific theory, interventions that are weakly structured, counseling modalities that are not clearly defined, nondirective counseling modalities, psychodynamic counseling modalities, and deterrence-based intervention (Lösel, 1996).

Interventions that are not strongly supported by scientific theory have, at times, been counterproductive for juveniles. Programs that have relied on punishment, for example, do not draw from any scientific understanding of the causes or cures of delinquency. Juveniles who have been subjected to harsh, punitive environments have often emerged from their incarcerations more likely to offend than when they entered treatment. Those who experience severe punishment may see it as a continuation of the abusive conditions in their own homes or neighborhoods. The presence of abusive conditions in a program intended to help them can lead to greater distrust, alienation, and despair. This is not to say that behavioral techniques should not include sanctions, but sanctions, administered properly, are very different from punishment. It is also important that we be clear that punishment is not the only kind of unsupported intervention that can be harmful to juveniles. The safest way to pick an intervention is to use those that have been developed based on theory and that have been tried successfully in other places. Techniques for finding such interventions will be discussed in the last section of this chapter.

Other interventions have been detrimental to juveniles because the interventions were weakly structured. Juveniles who come into state custody are often from environments where structure is terribly lacking. There are no rules for behavior, or the rules that do exist are inconsistently enforced. Often there is no real schedule, and a prosocial work ethic is not modeled or required. These juveniles need to learn to structure their lives, and cannot do so when the professionals model disorder in treatment settings.

Structure in an institution is relatively easy to obtain. A preset schedule is rigorously followed. The rules are clearly stated and both positive reinforcers and sanctions are swiftly and consistently employed. Structure can be somewhat more difficult to obtain in an open environment, but it can be achieved by carefully scheduling and monitoring activities as described in chapter 4. Clarity and consistency are key issues in this very critical aspect of successful intervention.

Inconsistent, unspecified counseling modalities have also been harmful to juveniles in treatment. Effective therapy requires knowledge, skill, and experience. Professional training in a specific modality is a must. Although many effective practitioners use techniques from several modalities, most have extensive training in at least one modality. Since the scientific literature indicates that cognitive-behavioral therapy is most effective for delinquent juveniles, this should be the modality of choice for practitioners. Unspecified counseling, that is, counseling approaches with no specific theoretical basis or set of treatment techniques, should not be used. Practitioners who deliver counseling services directly should develop competence in one of the cognitive-behavioral therapies. Case managers should ensure that the practitioners to whom they refer their clients use these techniques.

Nondirective counseling has also exacerbated problems in some studies of adolescent treatment. Nondirective modalities begin with the philosophy that all clients intrinsically know the answers to their problems. The role of the therapist is to provide an atmosphere in which the juvenile can discover those answers. Although some studies have supported the effectiveness of nondirective techniques for other populations, it appears that this approach actually worsens the problems of many adolescents.

We know that many troubled juveniles lack adequate problem-solving and decision-making skills as well as normal levels of empathy and situational perception. Because these skills are logical prerequisites for successfully identifying solutions to one's problems, it is clear that they do not represent favorable alternatives for treating delinquents. Many juveniles need these skills to be able to solve their own problems. They can be taught these skills through cognitive-behavioral counseling.

Psychodynamic interventions may also be of limited value or counterproductive for many juveniles (Lösel, 1996). Psychodynamic therapists attempt to uncover hidden inner conflicts and emotions in their clients. They believe that such hidden emotions as anger, frustration, and fear cause juveniles to act inappropriately. They believe that by uncovering and dealing with these emotions, the youths can change their behavior. Regardless of whether repressed emotions exist, and whether they so strongly direct human behavior, psychodynamic interventions are not supported by the current literature for use with juvenile justice clients.

Deterrence-based programming focuses on consequences for inappropriate actions. Punishment, incarceration, and similar techniques are used in an at-

Table 6.1 Lessons from the History of Intervention

1. Incarceration is not a sufficient deterrent.
2. Lesser offenders should not be housed with more serious offenders.
3. Juveniles should not be housed with adults.
4. Incarceration and vocational training are not sufficient to be effective.
5. Inadequate funding can cause even the best ideas to fail.
6. Good ideas can be ruined by poor implementation.
7. Psychotherapy alone is insufficient for many juveniles.
8. Some psychotherapeutic treatment modalities can actually be harmful to juveniles.
9. Psychotropic medications can be helpful when used responsibly.
10. The family is important to successful intervention.
11. Family intervention alone is usually not sufficient.
12. Wilderness programs may be helpful if they provide quality, comprehensive services.
13. Day treatment may be helpful if it provides quality, comprehensive services.
14. Shock programs and shock incarceration are not effective.
15. Boot camps are generally not effective.
16. Psychoeducation may be useful in combination with other interventions, but is ineffective alone.
17. Diversionary programs are more successful when greater numbers of service hours are provided to juveniles.
18. Diversionary programs are often more successful when services are delivered in the community.
19. Programs must be comprehensive to be effective.
20. Otherwise good interventions can be ruined by the inclusion of ineffective or counterproductive components.
21. Workers must be trained and skilled for programs to be effective.
22. Service delivery must be consistent for interventions to work.
23. Programs must have sufficient follow-up to be optimally effective.
24. Practitioners must have sufficient placements and program slots available for clients who need them.

tempt to deter or discourage troubled juveniles from further criminal action. Although good behavioral interventions have been very effective for youths, deterrence-based programs have actually worsened the behavior of some juveniles. Practitioners should avoid programs and interventions that use these techniques as primary intervention strategies.

As we've seen in this chapter, what you do with your clients, and what the agencies to which they are referred do, is critical. Many mistakes have been made throughout the history of juvenile justice programming, yet we have learned from the mistakes, as well as from the things that have been done well. It is clearly important for the practitioner to be informed about which interventions work and which do not. To help, a summary of the characteristics of ineffective intervention discussed in this chapter is included in table 6.1. But how can today's practitioner stay current on effective intervention and avoid the mistakes of the past? Some of the techniques for finding effective intervention alternatives are discussed in the section below.

HOW TO FIND INTERVENTIONS
THAT WORK

This book has summarized much of what is currently known about interventions that work for troubled juveniles. There are many other programs that could not be included because of a lack of space. Also, current interventions are continually being evaluated and new interventions are constantly being developed. This means that a great deal may have been learned about successful treatment of juveniles between the time these words were written and the moment that you are reading them. There are, however, techniques that you as a practitioner can learn to help you stay abreast of recent developments in intervention technologies. In the next several pages we'll examine some of those techniques, including (1) accessing information from national experts directly, (2) using the Internet to gain new information, and (3) using library research procedures.

Accessing Information from National Experts

There are several national sources of information about effective intervention for juveniles, including both federal agencies and privately funded organizations. Four such organizations will be described here, along with information on how to reach them. Those organizations are the Office of Juvenile Justice and Delinquency Prevention (OJJDP), the Office of Justice Programs (OJP), the National Criminal Justice Association (NCJA), and RAND.

The OJJDP is an agency of the federal Department of Justice. It was created by the Juvenile Justice and Delinquency Prevention Act of 1974 and has been further shaped by subsequent amendments to that act. It is a part of the Office of Justice Programs (OJP), which is within the federal Department of Justice. The legislation that established the OJJDP had several goals, including funding innovative programs and effective research for delinquency treatment and prevention, to develop national standards for juvenile justice programs, to provide assistance to state and local government in their attempts to deal with delinquency, and to disseminate information about effective practice to individuals and organizations across the country. The full text of the purpose and policy of the Juvenile Justice Delinquency and Prevention Act is included in table 6.2.

To accomplish its goal of disseminating information nationally, the OJJDP provides publications on several different types of juvenile justice issues. Recent publications (1999) include such issues as school safety, gang intervention, violence prevention, court and legal problems, and employment training for court-involved youth. Past publications have described effective programs, the effects of OJJDP-sponsored research, and other relevant information.

The OJJDP can be reached on the *World Wide Web* (WWW) at *http://ojjdp .ncjrs.org/*. It can be reached by mail or telephone at 810 Seventh Street, NW, Washington, DC 20531, 202-307-5911. Its fax number is 202-307-2093. Practitioners can request a catalogue and can ask to be included on the office's mailing list. Most OJJDP publications are available at no charge or for a nominal fee.

Table 6.2 Text of the Legislation Establishing the OJJDP

(1) It is the purpose of this chapter—

  (1) to provide for the thorough and ongoing evaluation of all federally assisted juvenile justice and delinquency prevention programs;

  (2) to provide technical assistance to public and private nonprofit juvenile justice and delinquency prevention programs;

  (3) to establish training programs for persons, including professionals, paraprofessionals, and volunteers, who work with delinquents or potential delinquents or whose work or activities relate to juvenile delinquency programs;

  (4) to establish a centralized research effort on the problems of juvenile delinquency, including the dissemination of the findings of such research and all data related to juvenile delinquency;

  (5) to develop and encourage the implementation of national standards for the administration of juvenile justice, including recommendations for administrative, budgetary, and legislative action at the Federal, State, and local level to facilitate the adoption of such standards;

  (6) to assist States and local communities with resources to develop and implement programs to keep students in elementary and secondary schools and to prevent unwarranted and arbitrary suspensions and expulsions;

  (7) to establish a Federal assistance program to deal with the problems of runaway and homeless youth;

  (8) to strengthen families in which juvenile delinquency has been a problem;

  (9) to assist state and local governments in removing juveniles from jails and lockups for adults;

  (10) to assist State and local governments in improving the administration of justice and services for juveniles who enter the system; and

  (11) to assist States and local communities to prevent youth from entering the justice system to begin with.

(2) It is therefore the further declared policy of Congress to provide the necessary resources, leadership, and coordination

  (1) to develop and implement effective methods of preventing and reducing juvenile delinquency, including methods with a special focus on preserving and strengthening families so that juveniles may be retained in their homes;

  (2) to develop and conduct effective programs to prevent delinquency, to divert juveniles from the traditional juvenile justice system and to provide critically needed alternatives to institutionalization;

  (3) to improve the quality of juvenile justice in the United States;

  (4) to increase the capacity of State and local governments and public and private agencies to conduct effective juvenile justice and delinquency prevention and rehabilitation programs and to provide research, evaluation, and training services in the field of juvenile delinquency prevention;

  (5) to encourage parental involvement in treatment and alternative disposition programs; and

  (6) to provide for coordination of services between state, local, and community-based agencies and to promote interagency cooperation in providing such services.

SOURCE: Juvenile Justice and Delinquency Prevention (JJDP) Act of 1974 (Pub. L. 93-415, 42 U.S.C. 5601 et seq.)

Another organization that provides information on treatment of juveniles is the Office of Justice Programs (OJP). The OJP, the parent agency of the OJJDP, addresses crime involving offenders of all ages. The OJP is directed by the assistant attorney general and coordinates the activities of several subordinate agencies, including the Bureau of Justice Assistance, the Bureau of Justice Statistics, the National Institute of Justice, the OJJDP, and the Office for Victims of Crime. It offers funding opportunities and disseminates information in addition to those offered by its agencies. The OJP's description of its activities is included in table 6.3.

The OJP offers informative publications on interventions, federal crime statistics, and research grant opportunities. Many of their publications are available either free or at a very low cost. Recent publications available through the OJP that might be of interest to practitioners include *Early Warning, Timely Response: A Guide to Safe Schools* (U.S. Department of Education, 1999) and *Compendium of OJP-Sponsored Projects Related to Sex Offenders* (OJP, 1999). The OJP can be reached at Office of Justice Programs, 810 Seventh Street, NW, Washington, DC 20531. Its telephone number is 202-307-0703. Its Web page can be accessed at *http://www.ojp.usdoj.gov/.*

The National Criminal Justice Association (NCJA) is a Washington, DC, special interest group concerned with juvenile and criminal justice issues. It is a political group that attempts to influence policy regarding justice issues. The NCJA requires an annual fee to become a member, but provides free or low-cost access to many publications to nonmembers. One of its publications that may be useful to practitioners is its journal *Policy and Practice,* available to members at no cost and to nonmembers for $7. The organization also refers practitioners to relevant publications by other organizations. A recent example is *Juvenile Justice Reform in the States: 1994–1996* (OJJDP, 1997). The NCJA can be reached at 444 N. Capitol Street, NW, Suite 618, Washington, DC 20001. Its telephone number is 202-624-1440, and its World Wide Web address is *http://www.sso.org/ncja/.*

RAND is a not-for-profit organization that conducts research and disseminates information on several topics, including national defense, health care, education, juvenile or criminal justice, and others. Recent publications of interest to juvenile justice practitioners include *Diverting Children from a Life of Crime: Measuring Costs and Benefits* (Greenwood et al., 1998) and *Investing in Our Children: What We Know and Don't Know about the Costs and Benefits of Early Childhood Interventions* (Karoly et al., 1998). These and other publications are available free or at a minimal cost. RAND can be reached at 1700 Main Street, P.O. Box 2138, Santa Monica, California 90407-2138. Its telephone number is 310-393-0411, and its World Wide Web address is *http://www.rand.org/.*

There are many other organizations, both national and local, that are concerned with juvenile justice issues and that can be helpful to practitioners. In the past, those organizations have sometimes been difficult to access. Internet technologies have made this task much easier. In the next section we'll talk about how to find some of those resources on the Web. We'll also talk about developing searches for documents on specific topics, and how to use the results to plan interventions.

Table 6.3 Office of Justice Programs' Description of Its Function, Structure, and Purpose

Since 1984 the Office of Justice Programs has provided federal leadership in developing the nation's capacity to prevent and control crime, improve the criminal and juvenile justice systems, increase knowledge about crime and related issues, and assist crime victims. OJP's senior management team—comprised of the Assistant Attorney General (AAG), the Deputy Assistant Attorney General (DAAG), and the five bureau heads—works together with dedicated managers and line staff to carry out this mission.

The Assistant Attorney General is responsible for overall management and oversight of OJP. The AAG sets policy, ensures that OJP policies and programs reflect the priorities of the President, the Attorney General, and the Congress. The AAG promotes coordination among the bureaus and offices within OJP. The bureaus are the Bureau of Justice Assistance, the Bureau of Justice Statistics, the National Institute of Justice, the Office of Juvenile Justice and Delinquency Prevention, and the Office for Victims of Crime.

The OJP also includes the Violence Against Women Office, the Executive Office for Weed and Seed, the Corrections Program Office, the Drug Courts Program Office, the Office for State and Local Domestic Preparedness Support, the Office of the Police Corps and Law Enforcement Education. OJP's American Indian and Alaska Native (AI/AN) Affairs Office coordinates AI/AN-related programmatic activity across the bureaus and program offices and serves as an information resource center for American Indian and Alaskan Native criminal justice interests.

Seven other offices within OJP provide agency-wide support. They are the Office of Congressional and Public Affairs, the Office of Administration, the Equal Employment Opportunity Office, the Office for Civil Rights, the Office of Budget and Management Services, the Office of the Comptroller, and the Office of General Counsel. The General Counsel's office is playing a lead role in the work of OJP's Executive Council (Information Technology), which is developing a coordinated grant funding strategy to enable state and local governments to implement compatible technologies that serve the collective needs of many criminal justice components without duplication or unintended system overlap. Additionally, the National Criminal Justice Reference Service (NCJRS) provides information services in support of the bureaus and program offices.

Through the programs developed and funded by its bureaus and offices, OJP works to form partnerships among federal, state, and local government officials to control drug abuse and trafficking; reduce and prevent crime; rehabilitate neighborhoods; improve the administration of justice in America; meet the needs of crime victims; and address problems such as gang violence, prison crowding, juvenile crime, and white-collar crime.

The functions of each bureau or program office are interrelated. For example, the statistics generated by the Bureau of Justice Statistics may drive the research that is conducted through the National Institute of Justice and the Office of Juvenile Justice and Delinquency Prevention. Research results, in turn, generate new programs that receive support from the Bureau of Justice Assistance and the Office of Juvenile Justice and Delinquency Prevention.

Although some research and technical assistance is provided directly by OJP's bureaus and offices, most of the work is accomplished through federal financial assistance to scholars, practitioners, experts, and state and local governments and agencies.

Many of the program bureaus and offices award formula grants to state agencies, which, in turn, subgrant funds to units of state and local government. Formula grant programs in such areas as drug control and system improvement, juvenile justice, victims compensation, and victims assistance, are administered by state agencies designated by each state's governor. Discretionary grant funds are announced in the *Federal Register* or through program solicitations that can also be found through bureau and OJP Web sites. Grant applications are made directly to the sponsoring OJP bureau or program office.

SOURCE: Office of Justice Programs, *http://ojp.usdoj.gov/about.htm*

Using the Internet to Gain New Information

The *Internet* provides an excellent opportunity for practitioners to obtain up-to-date information on juvenile crime and effective intervention. Many of the national, state, and local agencies offer Web pages where information can be obtained and documents can be ordered or downloaded. For example, as the authors were writing this chapter, we downloaded several documents that helped us prepare this book. All of the organizations described in the preceding section have Web pages. Other groups can be located using a few simple steps. When organizations that may be helpful have been located, other simple procedures will allow practitioners to access relevant information.

Locating Organizations on the Web

Basic computer training for Internet access is often available from public library or college library research librarians. Those same libraries often have computers with Web capability for use by their patrons. Practitioners may also have access at their offices or may use their home computer through a modem connection.

The steps for accessing the Web are relatively simple. First a software package known as a Web browser (most often Netscape or Internet Explorer) is opened on the computer's screen. The word "File" on the menu bar at the top of the screen is clicked, and then "Open Page" is clicked. A box then opens on the screen, the address is entered into that box, and the "Open" button is clicked. The computer then connects to the computer that hosts that organization's page and displays the page on the screen. From the home page, other pages that contain documents and other resources can be accessed.

Some organizations have additional pages that include links. Links are images (often in the form of words or pictures) that will respond to a click. When the image is clicked, the computer automatically accesses a Web page for a new organization. For example, at the Web page hosted by the OJJDP at *http://ojjdp.ncjrs.org/resources/resources.html* you will find links to state, national, and international resources for juvenile justice issues. Another example would be the "Other Sites" image on the NCJA Web page. If you click this icon, you will find images leading to the pages of its member agencies.

Many documents are available for downloading onto your computer. This means that you can copy the file from an organization's Web site onto your own computer. The file might be a graphic illustration of statistics, a description of an outcome study, or a review of court procedures in several jurisdictions. After you have displayed these documents, you can print them or save them to a disk.

Obtaining Useful Documents

When you have learned the mechanics of accessing remote Web sites, you are ready to obtain documents. A series of steps can make your search more effective and efficient. These steps include (1) identifying potential sources of documents and preparing a checklist of potential publication sources, (2) preparing a list of descriptor words, (3) developing a publication tracking form (PTF), and (4) planning and executing research paths to the desired documents.

The first step in obtaining documents is to prepare a checklist of potential sources. One way to prepare your checklist is to visit the Web sites listed in the

---

FIGURE 6.1   Checklist of Publication Sources

Substance Abuse Prevention
___ Public library
___ University library
___ PSYCHLIT
___ *Social Work Abstracts*
___ SOCIOFILE
___ ERIC
___ National Institute on Drug Abuse (NIDA)

SOURCE: Adapted from Sowers, Ellis, & Meyer-Adams, in press

---

section above and review the pages that contain links. Record for future refer-ence the links that appear to be relevant on the checklist. Add other links as you discover them on other Web pages. A sample checklist of potential resources is included in figure 6.1.

The second step in obtaining documents that will help you develop inter-ventions is to prepare a list of descriptor words. Some Web sites simply list the titles of their publications. When this is the case you can simply review those lists and download or order the documents you want. Other organizations pro-vide search engines, which are computer programs that will look through all the documents on their Web site for publications that contain a key word (de-scriptor) you select. Some of the engines will also search other, related sites.

It is wise to prepare a checklist of possible descriptor words before begin-ning an actual search. Using a list and checking off the words that have been tried can be very helpful. For example, one of the authors once searched for several hours using the words "substance abuse" and different combinations of such words as "treatment," "intervention," "counseling," "adolescent," and "teenagers." He was frustrated and ready to give up when a student sitting next to him suggested, "Try drug abuse instead of substance abuse." He did, and was rewarded with a long list of articles. For sample descriptors for intervention for delinquents, see figure 6.2.

The third step is the preparation of the publication tracking form (PTF) (Sowers, Ellis, & Meyer-Adams, in press). The PTF is a worksheet that helps the practitioner track which publications have been ordered and which have been received. It can help to ensure that no duplicate orders are placed and all documents ordered are received. A sample PTF is included in figure 6.3.

The fourth step is the planning of research paths. A research path is the ac-tual method by which documents will be obtained. A research path contains three stages: identify, locate, and obtain.

In the identification stage the practitioner finds out what documents exist that may be helpful to her and her clients. This can be accomplished through a review of the list of available documents on each organization's Web page. When the organization lists its publications alphabetically or in some other or-der, the process is easy but rather time consuming. The practitioner simply reads down the list and selects those documents that appear to be of interest.

FIGURE 6.2   Checklist of Descriptor Words

Assessment of the Propensity toward Violence
___ Delinquency
___ Assessment
___ Adolescent(s)
___ Violence
___ Dangerous behavior

SOURCE: Adapted from Sowers, Ellis, & Meyer-Adams, in press

FIGURE 6.3   Publication Tracking Form

Author/Date	Title	Publication	Source date	Order date	Receive

SOURCE: Adapted from Sowers, Ellis, & Meyer-Adams, in press

When the site is set up to be scanned using a search engine, the practitioner must use descriptor words.

Search engines are usually activated by entering a descriptor word in a window and pressing a button that is labeled "Search." A practitioner looking for information about mentoring might type "mentor and adolescents" or "mentors and children" and click the Search button. If the organization whose archives are being searched has documents containing those words, the titles, and perhaps an abstract or summary of the article, are displayed on the screen.

The second stage of the research path is locate. Usually the organization whose Web page you have visited will possess the documents you have identified on its page. When this is the case, the second stage is already complete. In some instances, however, the organization will not possess the document, but may refer you to another resource, such as another federal agency. When this occurs, the practitioner should note the article and its source on the PTF so that she can obtain it later.

The final stage of the research path is obtain. This will usually involve downloading the document to a disk, ordering the document through the Internet, or recording the necessary information and ordering by telephone or mail. All ordering information should be recorded on the PTF.

Each of the organizations discussed in the section on accessing information from national experts has a Web page and can be reached through that page. Other sources of information such as on-line journals, articles, and library catalogues can be found by visiting pages of links such as *http://www.cde.ca.gov/spbranch/safety/crjusticelinks.html* or by using search engines such as the one at *http://www.usdoj.gov/*.

Using Library Research Procedures

Another source of information regarding effective treatment is public or university libraries. The easiest way to use these facilities is to ask a research librarian for assistance. Those who have a basic familiarity with computer systems and library databases can follow the same steps outlined in the section above.

Libraries offer at least two options in addition to those available on the Internet: professional journals not published on the Web and books. Both these resources can be identified through the library's catalogue and through *CD-ROM databases*. Different libraries use different computer programs to access their cataloguing systems. These differences make it impossible to discuss the search process for library catalogues in this book. Research librarians are the best option for those who need assistance with the catalogues. CD-ROM databases, however, have many similarities regardless of what library houses them. For this reason we will briefly discuss finding documents using these databases.

CD-ROM databases are warehouses of information stored on compact discs similar to the ones used to record music. For libraries, they are used to record information about books and professional journal articles. They include titles, abstracts, and other brief information about publications from various fields. CD-ROM databases that are particularly relevant to juvenile justice practitioners include PSYCHLIT, Sociofile, Social Work Abstracts, and Medline.

CD-ROM databases can be searched using the same procedures described above for the Internet. A checklist of potential resources should be prepared including the relevant databases, a list of descriptor words should be developed, and a PTF should be created. The practitioner could then use a computer terminal to access the databases and to begin to develop a research path.

A practitioner looking for information about prevention programs might type the descriptors "adolescent problem behavior and prevention" into the PSYCHLIT database. This would initiate the "identify" stage of the research path. If the practitioner were an administrator interested in model programs, he might be interested in an article by Ellis (1998) entitled "Bridging the Prevention Gap: Multi-factor, Multi-system, Multi-level Prevention." He would not be able to obtain the entire article from PSYCHLIT, but he could read the abstract and find out where he could get the article. In this case, he would find that the article was published in the fall 1998 issue of *Journal of Primary Prevention*. The practitioner would carefully record this information on the PTF before proceeding to the next step.

In order to complete stage two, locate, the practitioner needs to find a library that owns *Journal of Primary Prevention*. He would first search the catalogue of the library he was using to determine whether it is owned there. If so, he can simply borrow the correct edition of the journal from the periodical section. If not, he can use a library service known as interlibrary loan. Borrowing the journal from the periodical section or sending for it through interlibrary loan actually constitutes the third stage, obtain. In either case, the results of each stage should be included on the PTF.

As you can see, the procedures for obtaining information about effective intervention are not difficult. There are many potential sources of information, and most of those sources are very interested in helping practitioners. Several exercises for contacting these resources are listed in "Activities for Learning" at the end of this chapter. Using these exercises should help you hone your research skills.

SUMMARY

In this chapter we have discussed ineffective intervention. We took a look at the history of juvenile justice treatment and the many interventions that have failed to help youth. We also reviewed the important characteristics of ineffective intervention and talked about some treatments that may be counterproductive. Additionally, we reviewed some ways to avoid being ineffective by studying methods for learning about what has worked for other practitioners. Finally, we discussed methods of staying current on what interventions are effective.

ACTIVITIES FOR LEARNING

1. Using a computer with Internet access, go to the Web page of the Office of Juvenile Justice and Delinquency Prevention. Find a recent OJJDP publication reporting on an evaluation of a program for delinquent juveniles. Download the evaluation. Use it to prepare a report on the evaluation for your class.

2. Using a computer with Internet access, go to the PREVLINE (Prevention Online) Web page. Search the links for information on funding for new programs. What kinds of funding opportunities are listed there for programs that would be beneficial to your community? Report your results to the class.

3. Using a computer with a connection to the Internet, find the Justice for Kids page on the U.S. Department of Justice server. Click one of the icons on the page and read the information provided there. Follow the links to other information available there. Imagine that you are starting a program for youth in your community. How will you use this page and the information on it?

4. Go to your local or university library. Find the section that allows patrons to access PSYCHLIT or other CD-ROM databases. Choose one of your areas of interest in juvenile justice practice and make up a list of descriptor words that are likely to help you find articles on

that topic. Search the database and read the abstracts of the articles that appear to be relevant. Pick an article, then find out whether your library has it. If so, make a copy. If not, use inter-library loan to obtain a copy.

5. Working in a small group, identify a local juvenile justice program that has a good reputation for success with ju-

veniles. Think about the characteristics of successful and unsuccessful programs we have reviewed in chapters 4, 5, and 6. Which of these characteristics does the successful local program have? Which does it lack? How could this information be used to make the programs better?

QUESTIONS FOR DISCUSSION

1. Review the programs discussed in chapters 4 and 5. What characteristics do they have (or not have) that are likely to affect their success? How might they be changed to include more characteristics?

2. In a small group, discuss some of the differences between early programs such as the Houses of Refuge or the cottage reformatories and the interventions of today. What changes do you see? How have those changes made juvenile programs better? What changes still need to be made?

3. How can you use the discussion in this chapter on accessing information about successful programs to improve your practice?

4. Incarceration of juveniles does not appear to lower their rates of recidivism, yet public safety issues sometimes require that offenders be kept in secure facilities. Given the necessity of incarceration, how might you design a program that would both house juveniles and provide effective treatment?

KEY TERMS AND DEFINITIONS

Antidepressant medication Medication that helps its user overcome feelings of depression.

Case law The law as it has been interpreted in individual cases in court.

CD-ROM databases Sources of information about subjects related to various professions and disciplines. Information is saved onto a compact disc like those used to record and play music.

Electra complex A condition that psychoanalysts believe girls experience during the phallic stage of development. Girls develop a sexual desire for their fathers and feelings of antagonism and rivalry with their mothers.

Internet An interconnected system of computers around the world. Information

on the Internet can be obtained from any number of different sources, including many libraries and home computers with modem connections.

Oedipus complex A condition that psychoanalysts believe boys experience during the phallic stage of development. Boys develop a sexual desire for their mothers and feelings of antagonism and rivalry with their fathers.

Psychotropic medication Medication that helps patients who have various psychological problems.

World Wide Web Consists of millions of pages of information, arranged in sites, connected by hyperlinks, and navigated and viewed with a browser.

REFERENCES

Bremner, R. H. (Ed.). (1974). *Children and youth in America: A documentary history* (Vol. 3, pts. 5–7). Cambridge, MA: Harvard University Press.

Bullington, B., Sprowls, J., Katkin, D., & Phillips, M. (1990). A critique of diversionary juvenile justice. In R. A. Weischeit & R. G. Culbertson (Eds.), *Juvenile delin-*

quency: A justice perspective (pp. 117–130). Prospect Heights, IL: Waveland Press.

Del Carmen, R. V., Parker, M., & Reddington, F. P. (1998). *Briefs of leading cases in juvenile justice.* Cincinnati: Anderson.

Ellis, R. A. (1998). Filling the prevention gap: Multi-factor, multi-system, multi-level intervention. *Journal of Primary Prevention, 19*(1), 57–71.

Greenwood, P. W., Lipson, A. J., Abrahamse, A., & Zimring, F. E. (1983). *Youth crime and juvenile justice in California: A report to the legislature.* Santa Monica, CA: RAND.

Greenwood, P. W., Model, K. E., Rydell, C. P., & Chiesa, J. (1998). *Diverting children from a life of crime: Measuring costs and benefits.* Santa Monica, CA: RAND.

Henggeler, S. W. (1989). *Delinquency in adolescence.* Newbury Park, CA: Sage.

Jack and Ruth Eckerd Foundation. (1997). *Annual descriptive summary 1997.* Clearwater, FL: Author.

Kamm, E. R., Hunt, D., & Fleming, J. (1968). *Juvenile law and procedure in California.* Beverly Hills, CA: Glencoe Press.

Karoly, L. A., Greenwood, P. W., Everingham, S. S., Houbé, J., Kilburn, M. R., Rydell, C. P., Sanders, M., and Chiesa, J. (1998). *Investing in our children: What we know and don't know about the costs and benefits of early childhood interventions.* Santa Monica, CA: RAND.

Kogon, B. (1958). Probation camps. *Federal Probation, 22*(3), 35–36.

Krisberg, B., & Austin, J. (1978). *The children of Ishmael.* Palo Alto, CA: Mayfield.

Legler, R. E., Schillo, B. A., Speth, T. W., and Davidson II, W. S. (1996). In C. R. Hollin & K. Howells (Eds.), *Clinical approaches to working with young offenders.* New York: Wiley.

Lösel, F. (1996). Working with young offenders: The impact of meta-analyses. In C. R. Hollin & K. Howells (Eds.), *Clinical approaches to working with young offenders.* New York: Wiley.

MacKenzie, D. L., & Souryal, C. (1994). Multi-site evaluation of shock incarceration. *National Institute of Justice Research Report.* Washington, DC: National Institute of Justice.

Office of Justice Programs. (1999). *Compendium of OJP-sponsored projects related to sex offenders* [On-line]. Available: http://www.ojp.usdoj.gov/pubs.htm.

Office of Juvenile Justice and Delinquency Prevention. (1997). *Juvenile justice reform initiatives in the states: 1994–1996.* Washington, DC: Author.

Piscotta, A. W. (1979). *The theory and practice of the New York Houses of Refuge.* Unpublished doctoral dissertation, Florida State University.

Platt, M. (1969). *The child savers.* Chicago: University of Chicago Press.

Roberts, A. R. (1998). Wilderness experiences: Camps and outdoor programs. In A. R. Roberts (Ed.), *Juvenile justice: Programs, policies, and services* (2nd ed.). Chicago: Nelson-Hall.

Rothman, D. J. (1971). *The discovery of the asylum: Social order and disorder in the new republic.* Boston: Little, Brown.

Sayegh, L., & Grizenko, N. (1991). Studies of the effectiveness of day treatment programs for children. *Canadian Journal of Psychiatry, 36,* 246–253.

Sherman, L. W., Gottfredson, D. C., MacKenzie, D. L., Eck, J., Reuter, P., & Bushway, S. D. (1998, July). Preventing crime: What works, what doesn't, what's promising. *Research in Brief.* Washington, DC: Department of Justice.

Sowers, K., Ellis, R. A., & Meyer-Adams, N. (in press). Reviews of the literature. In B. Thyer (Ed.), *Handbook of research methods in social work.* Newbury Park, CA: Sage.

U.S. Department of Education. (1999). Early warning, timely response: A guide to safe schools [On-line]. Available: http://www.ojp.usdoj.gov/pubs.htm.

Weber, G. H. (1960). *Camps for delinquent boys: A guide to planning* (Children's Bureau Publication No. 385). Washington, DC: U.S. Government Printing Office.

Westman, J. C. (1979). Psychiatric day treatment. In J. D. Noshpitz (Ed.), *Basic handbook of child psychiatry* (Vol. 3). New York: Basic Books.

Zimet, S. G. (1985). Review article: Day treatment for children in the United States. *Journal of the American Academy of Child Psychiatry 24*(6), 732–738.

Chapter 7

♦

Intervention with Different Populations

CHAPTER OUTLINE

Sensitivity to Racial and Ethnic Differences
Gender Differences and Intervention
Intervention and the Developmental Stages
Summary

In the earlier chapters of this book we discuss some interventions that work and many that do not work. Many of the interventions that do work begin with a basic assumption, that different kinds of youths are different in many ways, and that some of those differences can affect the outcome of interventions. Those interventions that have been unsuccessful have failed for many reasons. One of those reasons has been their failure to account for differences between sub-groups of adolescents.

As we saw in chapter 6, early efforts at intervention were directed toward white males. Many of today's treatment approaches have grown out of those efforts. Because little effort has been made to understand and accommodate groups other than white males, many interventions are still philosophically directed to that group. This means that interventions are often designed and implemented using several basic assumptions: (1) that youths of different races can be treated successfully using the same techniques as for white males; (2) that youths of different ethnic backgrounds can be treated successfully using the same techniques as for white males; (3) that youths of both sexes can be treated successfully using the same techniques as for white males; and (4) that youths at different developmental stages can all be treated using similar techniques.

Recent research into effective intervention has shown that these assumptions are not correct. In fact, race, ethnicity, gender, and developmental stage all make important differences in how juveniles view the world. These differences have important implications for treatment (Atkinson & Hackett, 1998; Atkinson, Morten, & Wing Sue, 1998; Ellis, O'Hara, & Sowers, 1999). This

169

chapter discusses some of those differences, and some of the ways practitioners can use that information to enhance the effectiveness of their interventions.

No single chapter (or book) can adequately describe all the differences between groups. In fact, there are many subgroups within the general groups we'll discuss here. For example, American Indians from different tribes have many similarities, but also many differences. It is important not to assume that a Hopi looks at the world in exactly the same way as a Cherokee. This chapter is intended to give you a start—a foundation for beginning to understand differences. It will also provide a listing of other resources to help you broaden your understanding. Ultimately, the thing that will most help you understand the differences discussed here is open-minded, nonjudgmental contact with juveniles from each group.

SENSITIVITY TO RACIAL AND ETHNIC DIFFERENCES

There are many important differences between racial and ethnic groups. In many areas of the country four groups are particularly important because they represent either a large or growing portion of the population. These groups include blacks, Hispanics, Asian Americans, and American Indians.

Blacks

As with all the groups discussed in this chapter, there are many similarities between subgroups of blacks, but also many differences. This is one of the reasons the authors chose to use the word "black" to describe this group rather than the more politically correct term "African American." In fact, although many of the groups thought of as "black" are descended from Africans, different tribal groups in the country of origin had different ideas and customs. Their views of the world have diverged even more since leaving Africa, depending on their experiences. For example, families who have lived in the United States for several generations after being brought here as slaves are very different in many ways from others whose families have lived in the Caribbean Islands. Both groups are very different from an African family that has moved to this country recently and of its own volition.

Despite the significant differences between subgroups, there are often many similarities. This chapter will focus on those similarities. Practitioners should approach a family with an awareness of these characteristics, but should never assume that they exist. This section, as well as this book, is not, therefore, an exhaustive summary of important treatment characteristics for every person of African descent. Rather, it is a general discussion that provides specific guidelines that may be used as a basis for assessment and intervention planning. It may also be used as a foundation for developing a greater understanding of the diversity among African-American people.

Despite the differences between subgroups, many characteristics of persons of African heritage have been maintained in family relationships and social interactions. Sensitivity to these characteristics can be very important to effective intervention with youth and their families. Atkinson, Morten, and Wing Sue

(1998) have summarized these characteristics in four general categories: the historical perspectives of the families, social support systems, social values, and communication barriers. Based on these categories, they make several specific suggestions regarding strategies for intervention.

Historical Perspectives of Families   The family is particularly important for many black youths. Blacks have experienced years of oppression and discrimination in many cultures over many years. In response to these pressures, family members and extended family members have become a central source of support. Atkinson, Morten, and Wing Sue (1998) identify the family as a primary source from which many youths of African descent derive their sense of self. Gary, Beatty, and Price (1983) also found that black Americans see the family as their most important source of satisfaction. Clearly, when working with black clients, family relationships may be particularly important.

The importance of the family to many black youth underscores the importance of effective intervention for the family. Professionals who provide individual and family counseling should direct at least some of their energies toward maintaining or restoring positive family relationships. Where there is no family or where families are resistant to treatment, the counselor should try to build positive relationships with members of the extended family.

The family history of many blacks also raises important issues not often considered in traditional interventions. Many therapists use family history extensively. Some encourage the family to develop comprehensive charts, known as genograms, that display family history. By discussing these charts with the family, therapists look for harmful patterns of interaction that have been passed from generation to generation.

However, genograms may not be practical for some black families (Atkinson et al., 1998). Using therapeutic techniques that emphasize information gathering, genograms, and ancestral family patterns may even be counterproductive. Often, generations of slavery and transience have all but eliminated any family records. In these situations asking families to produce elaborate diagrams may produce feelings of discomfort or inadequacy. Where family records do exist, a genogram may be a source of pride, and it may strengthen family relationships. Practitioners should have a good sense of how aware a family is of their history before insisting on genograms and similar devices. When histories are not available, working with recent family structure and patterns may enhance intervention effectiveness (Atkinson et al., 1998).

The fact that a therapist may choose not to pursue the development of extensive family trees does not mean that she should not emphasize African-American heritage. Developing a strong sense of racial identity can be very important to black youth (Helms, 1995). Some communities have programs that encourage participants to develop a knowledge of and pride in their racial heritage. Where no such programs exist, practitioners can encourage these characteristics in monitoring meetings and within the family. A model for developing pride in racial heritage and identity is discussed at the end of this chapter.

Social Support Systems As we discussed in chapter 3, social support can be very important in helping prevent delinquent behavior from developing. Among minority groups, where prejudice and discrimination increase stress, social support is often a crucial component of effective coping (Lyles & Carter, 1982). For juveniles, this coping may be the key to avoiding delinquent behavior.

In addition to the family, two sources of social support may be important for black youth: the *kinship group* and religious groups. Practitioners should emphasize the development of relationships between the youths and persons from both these sources. Outings and get-togethers with those persons should be a planned part of the youth's schedule. The practitioner should particularly emphasize mentors who are either within walking distance of the youth's home or who are willing to travel to be with the youth.

Social Values Because most interventions have evolved through the treatment of white males, the norms and values of other groups have often been ignored. For example, whites often emphasize individuality, achievement, accumulating wealth, planning for the future, the value of youth, and the acquisition of power. Blacks more frequently value sharing, obedience to authority, spiritual development, respect for the aged, and respect for heritage (Pinderhughes, 1982). Treatment has often focused on teaching white values, while denigrating or de-emphasizing black values.

Practitioners should not try to change the cultural values of black clients. Rather, they should regard those values as strengths to be used in developing an intervention. For example, the sense of empathy engendered through the process of sharing, an important value to many blacks, might be transferred to empathy for the victim of the juvenile's offenses. If the juvenile can begin to feel a greater empathy for crime victims, he may be less likely to harm those victims.

Communication Barriers Several problems have contributed to ineffective intervention with minority groups by white counselors. Many of these barriers are particularly relevant to working with blacks. We'll discuss four of those problems here: (1) distrust of the dominant group, (2) failure to recognize intraracial differences, (3) excessive reliance on intrapsychic treatment, (4) conflicting values between counselor and client, and (5) problematic verbal and nonverbal communication.

Distrust of the Dominant Group Slavery, oppression, prejudice, discrimination, blocked opportunities, institutional racism, and poorly conceived or implemented policies have all taken their toll on the trust of many blacks in America. Terrell and Terrell (1981) found that blacks often mistrust whites in the educational, political and legal, workplace, and interpersonal arenas. Several researchers have concluded that this mistrust also affects counseling and social service intervention (Nickerson, Helms, & Terrell, 1994; Terrell & Terrell, 1984).

White counselors may face a long period of rapport-building when working with some black (and other minority) clients. They may need to demonstrate honesty, openness, and a nonbiased attitude toward their clients over an extended period in order to gain their client's trust. In some cases, when the barrier appears to be great, it may be important to assign a black counselor to black clients or families.

Failure to Recognize Intraracial Differences Another frequent problem is failure by practitioners to recognize differences between subgroups of blacks, that is, blacks from different countries, those from different geographical areas of this country, and those with differing family, economic, and social experiences. Juveniles and families from different backgrounds have been affected by different variables. Some have experienced little discrimination and prejudice. Others experienced little until they came to this country. Some have experienced severe economic hardship. Others have lived relatively comfortable middle- or upper-class lives. Practitioners cannot assume that "All black people are the same." Even if well intentioned, this attitude can have a severe negative impact on their relationships with their clients. An open, accepting attitude that seeks to understand rather than stereotype is most likely to enhance professional relationships.

Excessive Reliance on Intrapsychic Model of Treatment Minorities can experience psychopathology just as some nonminorities do. Many of the problems experienced by minority groups, however, are the result of the environmental factors discussed above. Even when psychopathology is present, it may be necessary to help clients improve their physical circumstances before intrapsychic change can be made. A mother whose children are hungry is likely to remain depressed and immobilized until her children are fed. Case managers should ensure that multiple needs in multiple systems are addressed, and should ensure that counselors who receive their referrals are sensitive to these needs (Atkinson et al., 1998).

Conflicting Values between Counselor and Client White practitioners may not be aware or accepting of many values that are important to minority groups. One example is the emphasis on extended family. Many black families consider some non-biologically related individuals to be part of their family. Making any decision without including that person is unthinkable. Practitioners who try to develop treatment plans without including those persons might either totally alienate the family or undermine the treatment plan. Practitioners must consider the value system of blacks and other minorities when planning interventions.

It is also important to remember that families can be very forgiving. Practitioners should be very careful not do anything to damage their rapport with a family. If, however, they do make a mistake, a simple apology and an expression of a willingness to learn more about a family can go a long way toward healing the relationship. Ignorance will often be forgiven. Prejudice may permanently destroy a professional relationship.

Conflicting Verbal and Nonverbal Communication Patterns Some black families will be very aware of a practitioner's behavior. They will look at her dress, skin color, language, social class, and, more important, her genuineness, sincerity, warmth, level of respect, openness, and other interpersonal factors. If the practitioner's verbal or nonverbal expressions denote a judgmental attitude, prejudice, ethnocentrism, or other negative attitudes, her relationship with the client or family may be negatively affected.

Specific Strategies for Intervention Atkinson and associates (1998, pp. 123–124) recommend several strategies for working with black clients:

1. Become aware of the historical and current experience of being Black in America.

2. Consider value and cultural differences between Blacks and other ethnic groups and how your own personal values influence the way you conduct therapy.

3. Consider the way your own personal values influence both the way you view the presenting problem and the goals for therapy.

4. Include the value-system of the client in the goal-setting process. Be sensitive to spiritual values and the value of the family and the church.

5. Be sensitive to Black family norms due to normal adaptations to stress, and be flexible enough to accept these variations.

6. Be aware of how ineffective verbal and non-verbal communication due to cultural variation in communication can lead to premature termination of therapy. Become familiar with non-standard Black English, and accept its use by clients.

7. Consider the client's problems in the large context. Include the extended family, other significant individuals, and larger systems in your thinking, if not in the therapy session.

8. Be aware of your client's racial identification, and do not feel threatened by your client's cultural identification with his or her own race.

9. Learn to acknowledge and be comfortable with your client's cultural differences.

10. Consider the appropriateness of specific therapeutic models or interventions to specific Black families. Do not apply interventions without considering the unique aspects of each family.

11. Consider each Black family and each Black family member you treat as unique. Do not generalize the findings of any study or group of studies on Black families to all Black clients. Use the studies to help you find your way, not to categorize individuals.

These categories provide a general summary of the kinds of characteristics of blacks studied by researchers. As was mentioned earlier, not all black youth and families display these characteristics. Furthermore, there may be many other characteristics that are important for treatment but have not yet been identified by scientists. Additional resources for learning about working with blacks are listed at the end of this chapter. As more research becomes available, practitioners should familiarize themselves with that material. New research can be located using the techniques described in the last section of chapter 6.

Skills for Intervention with Black Juveniles Knowing distinctive characteristics shared by many black youths and families is a step toward successful intervention. To capitalize on that knowledge, however, the practitioner must learn to use it in everyday interactions with clients. She must also learn to adapt interventions accordingly.

The ability to interact with clients in a culturally sensitive manner can be learned through the accumulation of knowledge about the client's group, interaction with members of the client's group, and the use of educational exercises. The basic skills gained by using these methods can be enhanced and developed through actual interaction with minority clients.

Accumulation of Knowledge Knowledge about the client group can be accumulated by reading research articles as recommended above. Although important, this approach has its limitations. Research articles summarize many life experiences in a few words or sentences. Since many of us learn well through example, the most valuable content of the research is sometimes lost.

Box 7.1 contains a story written by a black person. The authors asked him to write about some experience that would help people of other races understand what it is like to be black in the United States. Reading books or watching movies about black experiences may also be helpful.

Interaction with Blacks Another excellent way to gain understanding of the black culture is by developing relationships with persons of that culture. Practitioners who make friends with members of other races and groups can learn about those groups through actual participation in their lives. Hearing about their experiences and listening to the ways they make everyday decisions can be very beneficial in developing cultural sensitivity. Some examples of such experiences are included in box 7.1.

Educational Exercises In addition, a series of exercises for developing sensitivity to the black culture is included in "Activities for Learning" at the end of this chapter. Other activities can be found in resources such as *Counseling American Minorities* by Atkinson, Morten, and Wing Sue (1998).

Hispanics

Just as blacks are originally from a single area of the world, Africa, Hispanics originate from a single country, Spain. However, just as many persons of African descent have ancestors who lived in other countries, today's Hispanics are descended from people who lived in the Caribbean and South and Central America. Hispanic is a word chosen by the United States government to represent people whose families originally came from Spain, but who have lived in one of these areas. Some people prefer the term Latino. A single word to identify this group is useful because it recognizes some of the ancestral commonalities unique to this group. Several of these commonalities are discussed in this chapter. No one term, however, is adequate to describe the diversity that has developed among Hispanics through their experiences in various countries in the New World. Thus, as with other racial and ethnic groups, Hispanics are

Box 7.1   Life Story: A Black Person's Story

Stan L. Bowie, PhD, is an African-American assistant professor at the College of Social Work, University of Tennessee, Knoxville. He was asked to respond with stories that would illustrate the experience of growing up as an African American in this country. He responded with the following article.

It is difficult to decide where to begin in addressing the issue of what it's like to be an African American living in the United States. Some of the famous authors of days gone by have referred to the "Invisible Man" syndrome (Ellison) or the "Marginal Man" situation described by DuBois, where black people have to live in dual worlds. My view of the situation is that it's a crazy scenario that has to be addressed every single day. On the one hand, the United States is the greatest country on earth and a true land of opportunity. It has enabled me to seize opportunities, scratch and claw, and work to transcend the ghettos of Pittsburgh to become a professor at one of the most prestigious universities in the country. On the other hand, the road to success has been a continuous litany of incidents, personal insults, and obstacles in place to inhibit my success because of my skin color. From the time when I first became cognizant of the word "nigger" and what it meant to me and my people until today when I see and understand the motives of sincere people, this socially induced duality has been a part of my life. I occasionally let my "guard" down, only to face unexpected racism in the strangest situations. When I choose to keep my guard up, I may find that good-hearted people come into my life that do not deserve the shield to be placed in front of them. It's really a crazy situation. It would be funny if it wasn't so sad.

What come to mind are pictures of incidents that typify the racism I have experienced:

- My brother and some friends were excitedly filling out applications for summer jobs at a major department store. As we are exiting the store, my brother glances back and observes the white personnel clerk tossing our paperwork into the wastebasket.

- My brothers and I, ranging in age from 7 to 10 years old, are walking to the movie theater on Easter Sunday in our nice holiday clothes. We notice a white man in a car following us. When we try to evade him down a one-way street and he screeches behind us into the street, we are terrified. Fortunately, our friend lives on the street. We knock on his door. His mother answers and confronts the man, who tells her someone stole copper pipes from his home and he thought we were the culprits. She sent him on his way.

- As an adult in Miami, Florida, I'm present when a white man attempts to steal several items from a department store. I assist the employees in foiling the crime and keeping the criminal at bay. When the police arrived, they immediately rushed to arrest me until the employee shouted that the other guy committed the crime.

- As a PhD student, my professor returns my well-written term paper, and in his critique writes "This is a very good job. Much better than I expected." Another faculty member makes me cite the paper number for *every single reference* in the draft of my dissertation (hundreds). After he checks it out, he allows me to remove them and says, "I just wanted to make sure; I thought someone else wrote it for you."

- As a researcher for the police foundation, I have access to the Miami-

Dade Police Department in Miami. The desk sergeant repeatedly checks my driver's license through the computer because it indicates I have never been arrested. He says to me, "Well, I guess you just never been arrested," smiles and returns my license.

As an African American in a predominantly white society, you have to keep it all in perspective for it to make sense. You can't be totally happy with your success because so many of your friends, relatives, and others in the black community are suffering. On the other hand, your success positions you to help change the situation. I guess the bottom line is that God placed me here for a reason, and I will fulfill that mission as others have in the past. I understand now that racism is a universal phenomenon. I understand that many people died, were maimed, or suffered so that I would have an opportunity to maximize my potential in America. I understand my historical connection to all people in the African diaspora over time from Africa to Brazil to Australia to North America, and I am tuned to our historical suffering as a people. I understand now that evil feelings of superiority over another culture can even occur among those of the same color. I understand now that black on white racism is as bad as white on black racism, even if it is "the hate that hate produced." I have it (racism in America) in perspective now, and I fully understand my mission in life with respect to it.

---

characterized by both similarity and diversity. These similarities and diversities must both be considered when developing culturally sensitive interventions.

The Hispanic Americans are from several countries, including Cuba, Puerto Rico, Santo Domingo, Mexico, the countries of Central and South America, and the West Indies and other Caribbean Islands (U.S. Office of Management and Budget, 1987). They share many cultural characteristics, language, and some religious beliefs. One of the most distinctive cultural characteristics is the Hispanic emphasis on the family.

The family is a key source of social support for many Hispanic youths. Families are often very close, and their members often believe that all problems should be handled within the family. This closeness can be a source of great strength to juveniles, but can also inhibit the intervention. Activities by outsiders, such as counselors and case managers, may be seen as intrusions, and may be either quietly resented or openly opposed (Falicov, 1999). An early challenge for the practitioner, then, is to overcome any family resistance to his presence, and to establish a collaborative relationship with the family.

Another challenge is to ensure that the cultural norms and values of the family are respected. Practitioners need to find a way to promote the development of healthy relationships without imposing their own norms and values. For example, many Hispanic families see the father as the leader, who is to be respected and obeyed. Practitioners of European descent might tend to view this pattern as dysfunctional. It is not, however, dysfunctional for that culture. Attempts to restructure the lines of power to lessen the father's authority are likely to be resisted.

The closeness of the family can also be a weakness, however. Hispanic families can become enmeshed, totally insulated against outside influences that might help them. Other potential problems include dependence among the wife and children, excessive submission to the father, and over-involvement by the mother on behalf of the children (Falicov, 1999). Minuchin (1974) identified the enmeshed pattern of family interaction as a significant contributor to the problems of families and disturbed youth. Practitioners must be aware of the presence of dysfunctional patterns while maintaining sensitivity to cultural patterns and preferences.

Practitioners should make every effort to include the entire family in the intervention. This also includes *extended family* members such as grandparents, aunts and uncles, cousins, and, in some cases, family friends. Among some Hispanics, individuals may join families through a process known as *compadrazgo* (Altaribba & Bauer, 1998). *Compadrazgo* is a ritual process that transforms outsiders into family members or draws distant relatives more closely into the family. The new relative becomes a participant in all aspects of family life and is known as a companion parent, or *compadre.*

Another distinctive characteristic shared by many Hispanics is their very distinct gender roles. As we mentioned earlier, men are often dominant in the family. This dominance often extends to broader society. Males are often more independent and have greater expectations than do females (Falicov, 1999). Specific cultural identities are often developed. Males must display courage and manliness, or machismo (Altaribba & Bauer, 1998). Females are expected to be feminine, engaging in home-related activities such as parenting and housekeeping. Sometimes females are forbidden to socialize with males without a family member present. Practitioners should be careful not to offend a family by insisting on solitary visits with a member of the other sex.

Some Hispanic males are reluctant to accept case management or therapeutic services. This reluctance is sometimes due to a perceived threat to their self-esteem. The machismo male must be self-reliant and capable. To acknowledge that he needs assistance may threaten the Hispanic male's self-esteem. Practitioners can often avoid resistance by avoiding such words as "therapy" or "treatment." Instead, words like "visit" or "planning" can be used to describe activities with clients.

Machismo is a cultural characteristic that should be respected by the practitioner. Excessive machismo is undesirable, however, and may be evidence of other problems, such as poor self-esteem or a developing personality disorder (Falicov, 1999). These conditions may require psychological or psychiatric intervention. Clients whose machismo appears to be excessive should be referred for psychological evaluation and treatment.

Although machismo is most often a characteristic of males, it is also seen among some adolescent females. Some Hispanic females, particularly those who join youth gangs, can be very aggressive and violent. When females display machismo and aggression, interventions should incorporate anger management and situational perception as they do among males. Females should not necessarily be encouraged to return to traditional patterns of interaction, however. Rather, they might be encouraged to express their newfound independence in a positive, prosocial manner. More will be discussed about intervention for females later in this chapter.

Language is a third common characteristic shared by many Hispanics. As with the first two characteristics, an awareness of language similarities and differences can be very important for intervention. The ability to speak Spanish is often vital for communication between juveniles and their families. Many first-generation immigrants do not speak English, or speak it only in a very limited way. Practitioners sometimes resort to interpreters, but this should be avoided if possible. The most difficult scenario arises when the family of a juvenile in state supervision does not speak English but the juvenile does. A non-Spanish speaking practitioner may have to use the juvenile as an interpreter, an extremely unreliable source of information (Sue et al., 1990)!

Even when the practitioner speaks Spanish, differences in country of origin may affect communication. Many people from Spain speak Spanish with a different accent and different words than do people whose families have lived in other countries. One example is "Spanglish," a mixture of English and Spanish spoken in some parts of the United States. Families from South America might have difficulty understanding a person of Hispanic origin born in the United States because of differences in word usage.

At least two other common characteristics of many Hispanics should be considered here: (1) religious affiliation, and (2) immigration status. Many Hispanics are Catholics, and rely heavily on the church for guidance and social support. Others have adopted indigenous religions from the countries in which their ancestors have lived. Those who have adopted these other religions may seek the assistance of a *santero* or *curandero* when dealing with their problems. The juvenile justice practitioner should make every effort to learn about and be sensitive to the faiths of these juveniles.

Immigration status can affect an intervention in several ways. For example, immigration status may affect a family's eligibility for certain social services and benefits. Other families may include members who are in the country illegally, and fear that the practitioner will discover and report them. Again, an awareness of these issues can be critical to successful intervention.

As with other minorities, Hispanics have many experiences that are different from those of other groups. Being familiar with some of these experiences can help practitioners be more sensitive to the needs of their clients.

American Indians

American Indians also have many commonalities and differences that are important to intervention. Some of the similarities are derived from ancient tribal approaches and philosophies. Some of the differences are due to dissimilar tribal practices and varying degrees of acculturation to the mainstream white culture.

One major factor in shaping American Indian culture has been the extreme level of prejudice and oppression experienced at the hands of the American government. During the 1800s the American government waged a war of genocide and ethnic cleansing on the Indian people. Decimated by disease, forced relocation, and inadequate provisions and living conditions, the approximately 1,000 tribes that existed before the arrival of Columbus have diminished to only about 300 today. The survivors are often extremely poor and lack most of the social and economic opportunities available to mainstream society (LaFromboise, 1998). Many are understandably hostile toward the American government. Many also have a distinct need to develop a positive racial identity.

One important characteristic shared by many Indians is the importance of the tribe. Many actually see themselves more as extensions of their tribes than as individuals. Their values, therefore, often center on the good of the tribe as a whole, sometimes referred to as "the people." This emphasis on the tribe is seen in many American Indian customs and ceremonies, including the "give-away" and the Sun Dance, practiced by some tribes. In the give-away, an individual gives away many or all of his possessions to other members of the tribe. This is often done in memory of a loved one or to celebrate some important occasion. In the Sun Dance, individuals pierce their chests and dance for several days around a central pole. This painful and demanding practice is a spiritual ritual, performed for the good of all the people.

Historically, many whites, particularly the government, have misunderstood these native practices. Most of them were actually outlawed for many years. Much of the prejudice, ignorance, and bias that produced these bans has diminished, but it is vital that white practitioners who have learned such biases through their own culture do not allow those biases to affect their interaction with American Indians.

Tribes also serve as government organizations and interact with the federal government to distribute benefits to individual tribal members. One example of these benefits is therapeutic services offered through the Indian Health Service and the Bureau of Indian Affairs (BIA). Practitioners can often use these services for Indian clients. Tribal governments also have a judicial process and often a police department to handle tribal problems and controversies (LaFromboise, 1998). This sometimes leads to involvement with juvenile justice practitioners.

The tribe is also an extended family to many Indians. Its members are known as grandfather, grandmother, aunt, uncle, brother, sister, or cousin. These extended family members provide emotional, mental, parental, and financial support to one another. The Indian extended family may regard outside assistance, such as treatment or therapy, as unnecessary and undesirable. Practitioners often must do considerable rapport-building before initiating an intervention for Indian youth.

In other cases, Indian families may be receptive to help, but may also believe in the efficacy of naturalistic and holistic medical and psychological treatment (Garrett & Walkingstick-Garrett, 1998). They may wish to include the assistance of the medicine person or shaman. At the center of these beliefs and practices is a worldview that emphasizes wholeness and the unity of all things. The Indian who has emotional or psychological problems may be thought to be out-of-balance mentally, physically, psychologically, or spiritually. It is the role of the shaman to help restore that balance (Garrett & Walkingstick-Garrett, 1998). Important American Indian values also include wisdom, respect for elders, and responsibility for and protection of all life forms (Trimble, 1981).

Garrett and Walkingstick-Garrett (1998) have identified several characteristics of culturally sensitive intervention with American Indians. These characteristics are (1) ascertaining individual level of cultural commitment, (2) supporting the Indian view of illness, (3) accepting the juvenile and family, (4) demonstrating trustworthiness and respect, (5) learning Indian communication, and (6) using humor. Practitioners who learn and apply these characteristics are more likely to be successful.

Ascertaining the individual level of cultural commitment means determining the degree to which the juvenile and her family are committed to traditional Indian culture. The levels of commitment to the tribal structure and spiritual customs are particularly important. It is also important to remember that members of a family may differ greatly in this regard. Some may be staunch traditionalists. Others may have fully adopted the "white man's way."

For traditionalists, the Indian view of illness must be supported by and incorporated into the intervention. This often requires the participation of the medicine person or treatment with various herbal formulas. In using the Indian view of illness, the practitioner becomes a support system who listens to and works with the client to identify the problem. He then works with the medicine person and family to help restore environmental harmony and bring healing.

Accepting the juvenile and family and being accepted by them are critical factors in intervention. Years of persecution and neglect have left many Indians skeptical about the government. As a practitioner (particularly if you work for a state or federal agency), you may need a substantial amount of time to be accepted. Even after you are, the acceptance is likely to extend only to you, not to the agency you represent.

Trustworthiness and respect are fundamental Indian values. If a worker is to be effective, he must demonstrate trustworthiness and earn respect. Remember that cultural values may cause clients to regard different things as respectful or disrespectful. For example, Indians often joke about Indian time, meaning that they often disregard clocks and are often late for meetings. This does not show disrespect, just a different cultural orientation toward time.

Native American communication can be learned and used. Specific techniques include minimized eye contact, careful listening, and deliberate, soft speech patterns. The practitioner who learns to speak "in the Indian way" has taken a major step toward acceptance.

Humor is vital to American Indian communication. Appropriate teasing, practical joking, and humorous stories can be used to strengthen rapport. Receiving a humorous nickname or being the butt of a joke may actually show that the worker is on his way to acceptance.

In addition, Garrett and Walkingstick-Garrett (1998) recommend that any type of intervention for Indians should rely heavily on activities. It should also focus on the present, since this is consistent with the American Indian view of the universe (Trimble, 1981). They also advise the use of social learning-based treatment to take advantage of the numerous learning activities available in the tribal extended family.

Indians live in many different settings, yet many of their experiences are similar. Box 7.2 relates the story of an interview conducted by a white practitioner. She talked with several Indian teenagers, with very interesting results.

Asian Americans

Like other ethnic groups, Asians often place a high value on family and family relationships. Family structure is traditionally patriarchal: the father is revered, and is the disciplinarian and the leader of the family (Sue, 1998). Males are more highly valued as children and in the culture generally.

Loyalty to the family is also an important value in Asian homes. Parents come first, particularly to male children, even when children have married and have started their own families. This conflicts with typical American values that emphasize the importance of the new family created by marriage and children. Practitioners may find it difficult to intervene with family problems without violating this norm (Sue, 1998).

Some aspects of Asian gender roles are similar to those of the Hispanic culture. Men are leaders and providers. Women conduct domestic and child-rearing activities. A primary obligation of the members of this cultural group is to honor and respect the family. To fail to do so dishonors both the individual and the family (Fong, 1994). Because of these values, obtaining assistance outside the family is considered shameful. This is likely to present a substantial

---

Box 7.2   Life Story: An Interview with American Indian Youths
Gail Horten, MSW

Tim is a surprisingly mature and thoughtful 14-year-old. He is also a full-blooded Chippewa from Red Lake, Minnesota. I interviewed Tim as he sat on the floor of a richly decorated banquet hall at the Breakers in Palm Beach, Florida. Tim had come to Florida with five of his friends and North Dakota state's attorney Bud Meyers. The group was at the Breakers as a part of an initiative developed by Meyers. The six Indian teens were learning photographic skills at the Palm Beach Photographic Center, as well as getting a look at life away from their school and families and a boost to their self-esteem. With Tim were Heather (an Assiniboine-Sioux from the Fort Peck Reservation), Jaime (a Menominee from Keshena, Wisconsin), Marcus (a Ute/Sioux from Mesa, Arizona), Chanel (also a Ute/Sioux from Mesa), and Toni (a Northern Ute from the Fort Duchesne Reservation).

The kids appeared oblivious to the richness around them, and were interested only in the fact that pizza was about to be delivered to a nearby group.

"You know, a lot of kids on the rez, they don't know what they want to do," Tim reported. "They don't have a dream, 'cause, how can they? There's nothin' there. There's no work. There's nothin' for them to do." Although silent, the other teens nodded their agreement.

These Indian youths were only 13 or 14 years old, and they could be silly at times, just like other kids their age. But they were very serious about some things. When asked about the differences between Indians and other races, they looked puzzled momentarily, then all started talking at once. "There's nothin' different. We're all the same. There's just differences in the color of our skin. That's all." They wriggled and murmured among themselves a bit self-consciously for a few moments. Then Heather told a story. She spoke quietly about how her family went into a restaurant once, placed an order for food, then had to wait while a white family who had come in after them was served first. This seemed to free the others to speak, and some told of how they are followed around in stores by shopkeepers when white kids are allowed to walk by themselves.

They also spoke about how it is on the reservation. They talked about poverty, despair, and alienation from the outside world. One said, "Everybody drinks or uses drugs on the rez." They reported that very few adults there don't use drugs and that some use many drugs. Two of the girls admitted that they started smoking cigarettes in the second grade. One started using marijuana about that same time, and has gone on to use cocaine, tranquilizers, and whatever else she could find. Comments from others suggested that they were familiar with drugs, but were unwilling to share with me, a stranger.

When one of the teens spoke of an adult who didn't use drugs, she did so with pride. Other group members then spoke of those they knew who did not use drugs. When asked why anyone who lives on the rez wouldn't use drugs when everyone else does, Heather said, "Well, to break the cycle, is one good reason." Jaime answered, "So you can maybe stay alive longer." Tim responded, "So you can get off the rez, man!"

What's the difference between Indians and other races? Marcus said that the families he knows that aren't Indian are stricter than Indian families. Others agreed with him, and talked about how they mostly go their own way. They all said that they had stopped going to church. Three of the girls counted off on her fingers the number of years since they last went to church: 5, 10, and 12 years. All the teens became very ani-mated, however, when they began to speak about their traditional ceremonies and religious practices. Their eyes sparkled, there was new energy in their voices, and they squared their shoulders and sat straight and tall. The slouching, relaxed teens became proud and excited. Every one of them said that they preferred the old ways to those brought by the whites.

When asked about their dreams, only Tim knew instantly what he wanted to be, "A politician," he said. He mentioned Ben Nighthorse Campbell, and how he thinks he could one day be like him. He wasn't clear, though, about what specifically he could do to help his people.

Chanel said she wanted to work for National Geographic. Marcus wanted to play basketball.

When asked what the federal governments could do to help the Indians, Marcus replied, "Give them jobs." Toni mentioned that the government already gives tribes money. She isn't sure this is such a great thing for Indians, however. "It sort of makes us dependent on the government, don't you think?"

As we were leaving, Tim stopped and spoke. "You know," he said, "I one time knew a boy on the rez who wanted to get a job. He went to this place and that place and filled out applications. He went to maybe 8, 10 different places. That boy, he never did get a job, you know? I think it was because he was an Indian. That's not fair."

These kids knew a lot about what is fair and what is unfair. They all had dreams, although some were not yet well formed. They all had pride in their race and culture. They had all experienced prejudice, loss, and brutality. They were resilient and street-smart. They all had a chance to better their place in the world because Bud Meyers had turned his attention toward them. Who knows, maybe Tim will be our first Indian president!

barrier to successful intervention. Unlike with many other ethnic groups, the extended family is not as important to many Asians as are biological parents and siblings.

Practitioners can use the family to strengthen the intervention process. The family should be encouraged to use its own strengths and become more effective in dealing with the problems of its members. When the practitioner is able to empower the family to solve its own problems, the family can maintain its sense of sufficiency. This transforms a potentially dishonorable situation, seeking help, to the act of fulfilling the family's obligation to care for its own (Sue, 1998).

Cultural values also stress the restraint of strong feelings and emotions (Nishio & Blimes, 1998). This may result in *somatization* of emotional and mental problems. Somatization occurs when psychological problems and stresses are expressed through the body rather than through outward actions. A common example of somatization is developing an ulcer in response to anxiety or fear. Because of the Asian tendency to internalize problems, practitioners should obtain as much information as possible about the psychosocial and medical histories of the juvenile. Assessments should give particular attention to physical ailments as signs of stress or psychological turmoil. An Asian American tells his story in box 7.3.

Adapting Interventions for Cultural Differences

Knowledge of cultural differences is useful in helping practitioners communicate more effectively with minority clients, but that knowledge can also be used to enhance interventions. In this section we'll offer a few ideas on how to develop culturally sensitive intervention. Other ideas can be developed from reviewing the professional and scientific literature, as is described in chapter 6.

Individual and Family Counseling Case managers should be careful to select therapists and agencies that are sensitive to and successful with minority groups. Sometimes it can help if the therapist is of the same group as the client. A racial or cultural match between therapist and client is by no means necessary for effective intervention, however.

Practitioners should encourage the juvenile and her family to develop a sense of pride in their heritage. Youths should learn their family and racial history when it is possible. They should also learn to recognize the unique strengths they have developed as a result of that history.

Professionals can often use success stories of others from the juvenile's group. This is particularly effective when a successful person can become the youth's mentor. Extended family members are often good sources of mentors.

Parent Training There are several culturally sensitive parent training programs or modules. Many of those programs have been tested and have been successful with members of the minority for which they were designed.

Case Management Case managers must not only practice in a culturally sensitive manner, they must try to ensure that the resources to whom they refer are also culturally competent. At times this may require that they use their mediation skills to explain the perspective of both client and professional. At times

Box 7.3 Life Story: An Asian American's Story

Hisashi Hirayama, PhD, is an Asian-American professor at the College of Social Work, University of Tennessee, Knoxville. He was asked to respond with stories that would illustrate the experience of living as an Asian American in this country. He responded with the following article.

I am a first-generation Japanese American who came to this country in 1955 as an exchange student at a small college in Oklahoma. After arriving in Seattle by a freighter, I boarded a Greyhound bus for a 48-hour trip to a small city in Oklahoma. The journey was long and weary, but it was also immensely enjoyable. In most of my waking hours, my eyes were glued to ever-changing majestic views of the Wyoming and Colorado mountains and the vast prairie of Kansas. After many hours, our bus crossed the Kansas-Oklahoma state line and stopped at a small rural town in Oklahoma for a rest stop. I got off the bus with other weary passengers. When I walked into a shabby bus depot, first I noticed a set of two water fountains; one said "Colored" and the other "White." Inside the depot, I also saw two sets of the four toilets; one set said "Colored men and women," and the other said "White men and women." With a little hesitation, I walked into the toilet that said white men because it appeared much larger and cleaner than the one designated for the colored men. A few white men glanced at me in the toilet, but said nothing. Nonetheless, I felt profound uneasiness, apprehension, and, most of all, confusion. I am neither black nor white, but an Asian. Which toilet or water fountain to use, or be allowed to use, colored or white? As a yellow-skinned person, is it not more appropriate to share the facilities designated for the colored?

After arriving at the college, I learned from an Asian student that in the South, "colored" was meant for African Americans, not Asians. Therefore, he said all Asians would be allowed to share all facilities reserved for white people. Was I relieved to hear his comment? Certainly, but not entirely happy with the answer. Because I also thought that by accepting the racially segregated arrangement and accepting the subservient position and role of blacks in the segregated society, I not only became a collaborator to the oppressors, but also a betrayer to the oppressed. Furthermore, under the system of biracial segregation in Oklahoma, Asians, a race between black and white, were mostly invisible and in isolation. After four years of an unsettling experience in Oklahoma, I left for a more multiracial and multiethnic environment.

they must be advocates for the youth. They may also need to be able to provide translators or referrals to agencies operated by members of the juvenile's ethnic group.

Developing Racial and Ethnic Identity

The book by Atkinson, Morten, and Wing Sue (1998), *Counseling American Minorities,* represents an excellent summary of recent research into culturally sensitive intervention. It also includes many valuable exercises to facilitate the development of these skills. In addition, it describes an overall model for understanding the process minority individuals must complete to develop a positive racial identity. It can also be used as a guideline to help juveniles through this important developmental process. This model, known as the Minority Identity

Table 7.1 Summary of the Minority Identity Development Model (MIDM)

Stages of Minority Development Model	Attitudes toward Self	Attitude toward Others of the Same Minority	Attitude toward Others of Different Minority	Attitude toward Dominant Group
Stage 1— Conformity	Self-depreciating	Group-depreciating	Discriminatory	Group-appreciating
Stage 2— Dissonance	Conflict between self-depreciating and self-appreciating	Conflict between group-depreciating and group-appreciating	Conflict between dominant-held views of minority hierarchy and feelings of shared experience	Conflict between group-appreciating and group-depreciating
Stage 3— Resistance and Immersion	Self-appreciating	Group-appreciating	Conflict between feelings of empathy for other minority experiences and feelings of culturocentrism	Group-depreciating
Stage 4— Introspection	Concern with basis of self-appreciation	Concern with nature of unequivocal appreciation	Concern with ethnocentric basis for judging others	Concern with the basis of group-depreciation
Stage 5— Synergetic Articulation and Awareness	Self-appreciating	Group-appreciating	Group-appreciating	Selective appreciation

SOURCE: Atkinson, Morten, & Wing Sue, 1998, p. 35

Development Model (MIDM) (Atkinson et al., 1998), is further detailed in table 7.1. The MIDM identifies five stages often experienced by minorities as they develop racial and ethnic identities: conformity, dissonance, resistance and immersion, introspection, and synergetic articulation and awareness. The process culminates in a healthy concept of self and of the individual's race.

GENDER DIFFERENCES AND INTERVENTION

Several recent studies have found that important differences exist between boys and girls. Although that might seem like an obvious finding, these differences had not previously been considered important for treatment. Most current treatment methods were developed for boys. However, girls are engaging in more problem behaviors with greater regularity. These factors make it critical to be aware of gender differences.

Ellis, O'Hara, and Sowers (1998) conducted a research project to identify characteristics of troubled females that were likely to be both different from males and important for treatment. The researchers discovered two distinct profiles composed of psychosocial problems and problem behaviors. One profile was composed predominantly of females, the other primarily of males. The researchers then returned to the literature to identify treatment modalities and approaches that might be important for the female profile.

The study by Ellis and associates (1998) was conducted in a South Florida residential treatment facility. It examined gender differences on specific psychological, social, and behavioral problems in a group of adolescent substance abusers. The sample included 137 (f = 65, 47.5%; m = 72, 52.5%) adolescents who were treated over the period of one year. Although the primary presenting problem was substance abuse, every youth had displayed other antisocial behaviors including multiple status offenses and, in many cases, serious property crime or even violent crime.

A cluster analysis revealed two distinct treatment profiles: one predominantly female, the other predominantly male. The predominantly female group was characterized as abused, self-harmful, and social, and the male group was identified as aggressive, destructive, low achieving, and asocial. The females displayed high levels of the problems that were low for the males and low levels of problems that were high for the males. The results of the cluster analysis are presented in graphical form in figure 7.1.

The characteristics found in the profile of the adolescent females suggest that current treatment strategies for troubled adolescents may not be addressing the needs of the adolescent females. A review of the treatment literature found several important implications for treating females.

First, treatment needs to be comprehensive. That is, it should not focus on only one problem behavior (such as truancy or substance abuse), but should view the presenting problem as one in a continuum of problem behaviors. Second, the profile suggests that the young women often have a different set of problems to be addressed during treatment. For example, among girls, the incidence of sexual abuse was much greater. This resulted in more internalized or self-directed harmful behaviors such as depression, self-mutilation, and suicidal ideation. These are different from the externally aggressive behaviors of the male group. Girls may need a stronger focus on eliminating feelings of guilt, shame, anxiety, and other conditions related to their abuse history. They also need treatment to focus on appropriate coping skills to redirect their self-injurious behavior. Conversely, boys may require a focus on anger management and other social skills.

A third finding of the literature review was that girls need a more supportive, less confrontational treatment environment than they currently experience. Punitive, confrontational environments may be counterproductive for females, re-creating the frightening milieu generated by their abuser. Further, women who do not disclose or address their sexual abuse history are more likely to recidivate (Wadsworth, Spampneto, & Halbrook, 1995). A more supportive environment may make it safer for girls to disclose their experiences, and more likely to respond to treatment.

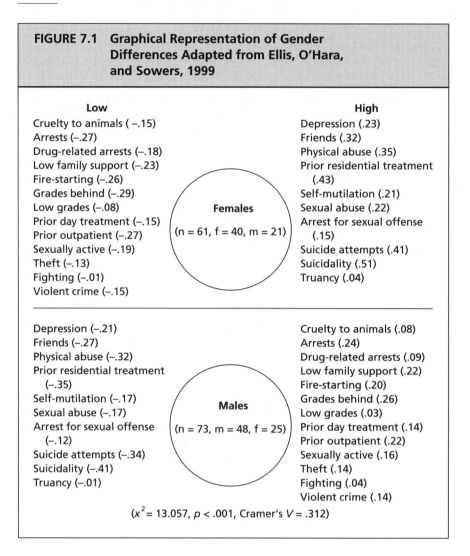

FIGURE 7.1 Graphical Representation of Gender Differences Adapted from Ellis, O'Hara, and Sowers, 1999

Low	High
Cruelty to animals (–.15)	Depression (.23)
Arrests (–.27)	Friends (.32)
Drug-related arrests (–.18)	Physical abuse (.35)
Low family support (–.23)	Prior residential treatment (.43)
Fire-starting (–.26)	Self-mutilation (.21)
Grades behind (–.29)	Sexual abuse (.22)
Low grades (–.08)	Arrest for sexual offense (.15)
Prior day treatment (–.15)	Suicide attempts (.41)
Prior outpatient (–.27)	Suicidality (.51)
Sexually active (–.19)	Truancy (.04)
Theft (–.13)	
Fighting (–.01)	
Violent crime (–.15)	

Females (n = 61, f = 40, m = 21)

Low	High
Depression (–.21)	Cruelty to animals (.08)
Friends (–.27)	Arrests (.24)
Physical abuse (–.32)	Drug-related arrests (.09)
Prior residential treatment (–.35)	Low family support (.22)
Self-mutilation (–.17)	Fire-starting (.20)
Sexual abuse (–.17)	Grades behind (.26)
Arrest for sexual offense (–.12)	Low grades (.03)
Suicide attempts (–.34)	Prior day treatment (.14)
Suicidality (–.41)	Prior outpatient (.22)
Truancy (–.01)	Sexually active (.16)
	Theft (.14)
	Fighting (.04)
	Violent crime (.14)

Males (n = 73, m = 48, f = 25)

$(x^2 = 13.057, p < .001, \text{Cramer's } V = .312)$

The importance of social support for females suggests a fourth factor: that interventions should focus on positive relationships with peers, family, counselors, and other community agencies. Interventions should provide support and training to help girls develop social skills as well as linkage to sources of prosocial support.

Treatment should be noncompetitive, emphasizing teamwork and mutual support. Every effort should be made to enhance the girl's learning and to promote positive school experiences. Practitioners must also ensure that girls are protected from past and future abuse, and from unwanted contact with prior perpetrators.

In summary, gender-sensitive treatment for adolescent females must target multiple factors, be individualized, and exist within the framework of a safe environment that emphasizes mutual support, caring, and empowerment. Treatment staff should use a balanced approach that promotes individuality and connectedness by being attuned to and supportive of the girls while simultaneously providing supervision, discipline, and high expectations for mature behavior. Rewards and sanctions should be implemented supportively rather than punitively, and should include cognitive components to enhance the clients' perceptions of the positive ways in which they can control themselves and their environments. Also, whenever possible, female-only group therapy and activities should be used to develop a sense of bonding to other prosocial females. Such groups should provide support and encouragement to the girls as they develop new skills and identities. Involving family members and school personnel will help the girls find additional support for their prosocial attitudes and behaviors.

Adapting Interventions for Gender Differences

Many of the adaptations needed for interventions for girls were discussed in the summary of the study above. This section will deal only with adaptations for four specific interventions: counseling, parent training, case management, and psychoeducational groups. Also, although the study described above provides a nice summary of the current knowledge of treatment-related gender differences, many other resources are available to further enhance your understanding of this important area.

Individual, Group, and Family Counseling Cognitive-behavioral therapy has been found to be particularly effective for depressed or suicidal clients. Because girls show such a high incidence of these problems, cognitive-behavioral interventions should be the treatment of choice for individual girls. Although the treatment environment should be supportive of the disclosure of a history of abuse, girls should not be coerced into such revelations.

Therapy groups should probably include only girls, at least in the initial stages of treatment. There are several reasons for this approach. First, boys are often more competitive, talkative, and participatory. Their presence may intimidate girls who would otherwise participate more actively. Second, it may be more difficult for girls to discuss abusive experiences in the presence of boys. Third, because boys are often inappropriately aggressive, it will be easier for staff to use and teach appropriate assertiveness when negative modeling is not present. Once some of these issues have been resolved by individual girls, mixed-gender groups may be appropriate. This is a matter for further research.

Family counseling should focus on reestablishing damaged relationships and restoring appropriate family functioning. Sexual abuse perpetrators should be removed from the home. Girls who have been abused with the nonabusive parent's knowledge may have significant issues regarding that parent's failure to protect them. Parents who fail to protect should receive cognitive-behavioral interventions focused on their responsibility to protect and designed to develop the skills necessary to protect.

Parent Training Parent training should include instruction on helping the juvenile deal with depression and anxiety. Parents should be taught skills to enhance communication and provide emotional support. In cases where social skills training is needed for the juvenile, it may be needed by the parents as well.

Case Management Girls should be referred to programs where group activities are emphasized. Schools should be encouraged to cultivate participation by females. Female case managers might consider themselves role models, and should identify female mentors who can help girls enhance self-esteem and prosocial attitudes.

Psychoeducational Groups Psychoeducational intervention in groups may be very useful for girls. Given the types of problems found in the female profile, several kinds of topics may be needed. Appropriate topics may include substance abuse education, assertiveness training, problem-solving and decision-making skills, stress management training, development of positive coping skills, and development of positive self-esteem.

Summary of Gender-related Intervention

Clearly, important differences exist between the genders that affect the selection and planning of intervention. Those differences can be very subtle and, as with the differences between racial minorities discussed above, they may be best understood through stories. Box 7.4 includes the story of Amy, an adolescent female. As you read the story of Amy, think about the ways in which a boy might have reacted to the stressors that Amy experienced. In what ways might he have reacted differently? In what ways might he have reacted similarly? What kind of intervention would be appropriate for Amy? What would be appropriate for the boy you envisioned?

Box 7.4   Life Story: Amy's Story

Social forces can be very powerful in shaping children. Some of what we are is determined by genetics. Much of what we become, however, is shaped by our experiences. The way we act, the way we think, even the things we hope for, are often very much a product of our interactions with others. This is the story of Amy, a 17-year-old girl known to one of the authors. Amy's story should help to illustrate that girls often have important issues in treatment that are very different from those of boys.

I first met Amy when she entered a counseling program for troubled teens. Some of her problems were obvious when we did her psychosocial at intake. Others did not become clear until I had gotten to know her much better.

Amy was obviously depressed. Her affect was flat (therapist lingo for unresponsive). She answered my questions in one- or two-word sentences. She

wore rumpled clothing, and her glasses needed cleaning so badly that I could see the smears of dirt from across the room. Consistent with her appearance, she reported that she was depressed. She had been arrested for prostitution, and also reported frequent use of alcohol, marijuana, and cocaine.

Amy didn't talk much in our first three sessions. I was concerned that I might not be a good choice as a therapist for her, and was considering asking if she would rather talk with a woman. Then, for reasons I still do not understand, Amy came to the fourth session, sat down, and began to talk. She talked about her childhood, about her father's death, about how she used to love school, about how she now hated school and everything else. Her story was tragic: a story of loss, betrayal, sexual abuse, and of cries for help gone unanswered. Amy continued to talk through many future sessions, and I came to understand much of why she had some of her current problems. We also found the keys to helping her solve some of those problems.

Amy's life had looked pretty promising in her early years. Her parents were both loving and supportive, and she could recall long afternoons spent happily in the nice house they owned in an upper-middle-class neighborhood. Amy's parents encouraged her to play with dolls, her mother started to teach her to cook and clean the house. They directed her away from "boy things" like sports and toy trucks. They taught her that good girls never hit, and that they are always polite and friendly. Amy was one of the best students in her first and second grade classes. She was bright, interacted well with the teachers, and particularly loved math and science.

When Amy was in the third grade, tragedy struck. Her father, whom she adored, was killed in an automobile accident. Amy can't recall much about the funeral, but remembers that they could not open his casket because "they said he looked too bad." Amy took her dad's death very hard, and was not ready for the stepfather who rapidly came into her life.

Amy's mother remarried within a year of her husband's death. Her new husband was very different from Amy's father: loud, often harsh, a believer in corporal punishment, and a man who either could not or would not control his sexual urges. Within a few months he was fondling Amy at night. Within two years, his abuse had progressed even further. When Amy was 13 she tried to tell her mother about her stepfather's behavior, but her mother refused to listen. She ignored the problem even after she walked in during one of her husband's abusive sessions.

Amy's grades dropped in school. She began to notice that her teachers paid more attention to boys, actually encouraging them to speak out in class more often. She still loved math, but her teachers pushed her toward other fields that were "more suitable for girls." She believed somehow that her father's death was her fault, and that she deserved the treatment she was receiving from her stepfather and her teachers.

At age 14, Amy began to cut herself. At age 15 she attempted suicide. When her stepfather moved out, she was happy for a while, but, lacking hope and social support, she rapidly sank back into a depression. She fantasized about watching her stepfather die, but never could imagine herself as the killer. Instead, she cut herself, and took more and more drugs.

Amy was like many teenage girls. She had been taught to deal with her issues "the way girls should." As a result, she directed her anger toward herself, rather than toward those who had wronged her. Teachers had squelched her interest in math, and had caused her to hate the educational process she once had loved. Her stepfather had abused her, and her mother had betrayed her by failing to deal with the situation. She dealt with life as best she could, with self-mutilation, depression, suicide, and drugs.

Amy's story had a happy ending. She is currently attending a major university and majoring in mathematics. She has dealt with many of her issues regarding her stepfather's abuse and her mother's betrayal. She has been alcohol and drug free for several years.

Many stories do not end this happily. Many treatment programs ignore the special needs of the girls they treat. Practitioners must learn more about what the girls in their care need to get better. They then must use that knowledge in their practice.

INTERVENTION AND THE
DEVELOPMENTAL STAGES

One of the distinctive features of adolescence is its many important developmental stages (Steinberg, 1993). Cognitive capabilities, social skills, and emotional capacities all develop, but do so at different rates for different youths. Adolescents also experience extreme physical changes, producing a variety of reactions from pride to stress and anxiety.

The changes of adolescence have important implications for practitioners with preteen or teenaged clients. Understanding these changes can help the professional understand many of a child's behaviors and actions. Recognition of a juvenile's developmental level can help the practitioner choose appropriate interventions.

Cognitive Development

Many of the most important changes of adolescence have to do with thought processes and capabilities, and are therefore referred to as cognitive. Preteens are usually concrete thinkers who live in the present with very little understanding of the opportunities or consequences of tomorrow. As they progress through adolescence, they are able to think abstractly and can consider future alternatives and consequences. These are important capacities for teens to develop, and they are crucial to becoming a fully functional adult. Some teens move through the stages very slowly, lagging far behind their peers. Others have their development arrested at early stages, never gaining the capacity for adult reasoning. Those who progress very slowly through the cognitive development process, and those whose development is arrested altogether, are at higher risk for delinquency and other problem behaviors.

At least five specific cognitive capacities develop during adolescence (Keating, 1980):

1. the capacity to think through hypotheses,
2. the ability to consider possibilities,
3. the ability to plan ahead,
4. the capacity to think about their own thoughts, and
5. the ability to think beyond old limits.

Each is crucial for full adult functioning, and each plays a key role in avoiding the development of problem behaviors.

Most youths begin the adolescent stages of cognitive development at about age 11 or 12. More advanced skills, such as abstract and moral reasoning, tend to develop at age 14 or 15 (Forehand & Wierson, 1993). Where specific capacities or skills are lacking, intervention may strengthen those skills, increasing the probability that youths will refrain from problem behavior. In other cases, where the teen is unable to develop the capacities, professionals can teach coping mechanisms that diminish the probability of delinquent behavior.

Thinking through Hypotheses At some point during early to middle adolescence most teens develop the capacity for deductive reasoning. Deductive reasoning refers to the ability to develop hypotheses about how things are likely to be in the world based on information one already has. One example of deductive reasoning can be seen in the case of Demetria, a 14-year-old female. Demetria was approached after school by an older boy, Germaine, who invited her to a party the following weekend. Demetria was very excited because she had seen Germaine several times and found him very attractive. He had smiled at her several times, always spoke to her, and had learned her name by asking her best friend about her.

Demetria told several of her friends about the invitation, but was surprised when they were cautious. "Be careful, girl," one of them warned. "That boy and his friends love to party. There'll be drugs at that party for sure." At first, Demetria thought her friends were just jealous, but after several had warned her, she began to wonder whether their warnings were true.

Demetria decided to test the hypothesis that Germaine and his friends would have drugs at the party. She thought of several ways to find out, but finally decided to ask Germaine. She realized that if he said, "No," she might still need to do some checking to find out whether he was being honest. If he said, "Yes," however, she would then know that she should not go to the party.

Demetria approached Germaine after school the next day and asked him simply, "Will there be drugs at your party?" Germaine responded, "Sure, a little reefer and a little blow. That won't hurt anyone." Demetria then thanked Germaine again for his invitation, but told him that she would not be able to attend the party.

Demetria used deductive reasoning to make her decision. She employed all five of the steps of the deductive reasoning process:

1. Identifying the problem (Demetria realized that being at a party where drugs were being used might present a temptation for her and might cause other problems if the police found out.)

2. Developing a hypothesis about the problem (She decided that there might indeed be drugs at the party.)

3. Imagining what will confirm and disconfirm the hypothesis (She thought through several alternative ways of testing her hypothesis such as asking friends or asking Germaine himself.)

4. Testing the hypothesis (She chose to ask Germaine, then did so.)

5. Evaluating the results (Based on the information she received, she decided not to go to the party.)

The deductive reasoning process sounds simple to many adults, but it is very complex to those whose cognitive capacities have not developed sufficiently to allow them to reason in this manner. The process is central to effective problem-solving, and teens who are unable to perform these steps often cannot understand the kinds of difficulties that might develop from specific problem behaviors.

Evelyn is an example of a teen who cannot reason hypothetically. Evelyn has a group of friends who shoplift frequently. When her friends ask her to help them steal from a store, Evelyn says "no." However, when they ask her to hold the stolen merchandise from one store for them while they go to a second store, she agrees. She does not understand that by holding the merchandise she is an accomplice. She is not able to reason that police officers might find her with stolen goods and arrest her for the crime. She is not able to perform the first or second steps of hypothetical reasoning. She cannot identify the problem or develop a hypothesis about that problem.

Juveniles who have not developed hypothetical thinking can often be helped by social skills training techniques described in earlier chapters. One potentially effective intervention might be the problem-solving curriculum in the EQUIP program (Gibbs, Potter, & Goldstein, 1995). If a teen like Evelyn cannot be taught hypothetical reasoning, behavioral techniques might be used to teach coping skills to keep her away from problem friendship groups and situations.

Thinking about Possibilities Children are able to think only about the concrete and real. As a result, they often lack the ability to think about what may happen, or to consider what others may think or want. Adolescents and adults who have gained this capacity can examine the motives of others and can draw conclusions about an individual's guilt or innocence based on these motives (Steinberg, 1993). Children, for example, are simply warned to stay away from strangers, without any discussion of what the stranger's motives might be. An early adolescent, however, might be able to understand the stranger's desire to kidnap or harm. Youths whose capacity for thinking about possibilities has not yet developed may misjudge the intentions of others. For instance, a friend might say, "Here, try this marijuana. It's good for you. It will help you relax." The juvenile might not understand that the other youth's motivation is to sell drugs, and choose to try the marijuana.

Another example of misunderstood motivations occurs when a juvenile has observed only a limited range of behavior and has learned to interpret the world accordingly. One example would be when her mother has shown only two emotions, angry and happy. This youth might be inclined to react to her peers as though they experience only these two emotions. She might therefore mistake frustration, anxiety, or annoyance for anger. Anticipating violent behavior, she might then act violently toward other teens.

Deficiencies in thinking about possibilities can be addressed using the situational perception training described in the EQUIP curriculum (Gibbs, Potter, & Goldstein, 1995) or similar interventions. When the capacity for thinking about possibilities is lacking, coping skills should be developed. For example, the practitioner might help the violent youth above develop anger management skills.

Thinking Ahead Hypothetical thinking skills form the basis for another important skill, considering multiple possibilities. This skill allows the youth to plan ahead, inventing many possible courses of action and examining their consequences. It also allows him to predict the consequences of a series of events. For instance, a youth with a good capacity for thinking ahead might reason, "If I do not develop vocational skills, I will not be able to find a good job. If I cannot find a good job, I will not have enough money. If I do not have enough money, I will be tempted to commit criminal acts as an adult to survive. If I commit criminal acts, I will go to jail." A youth lacking the capacity to reason in this manner is unlikely to understand the long-term consequences of problem behavior and is therefore more likely to engage in that behavior.

Practitioners can help many juveniles develop these skills through social skills training programs. Often, offering real-life cases or examples from the movies can also be beneficial. Juveniles who lack the capacity for thinking ahead can be taught many specific things to which they should simply say no, and when to seek advice about what to do in other cases.

Thinking about Thoughts During adolescence, the youth becomes aware of his own process of learning and thinking. Instead of just thinking, the teen is able to think about thinking; that is, he is able to evaluate his own thinking processes. This capacity is known as *metacognition* and should begin to occur somewhere in the middle stages of adolescence.

One important way in which juveniles can use metacognition is through introspection. Through the process of introspection he evaluates his actions and motivations, as well as the actions and motivations of others. It is often important, for example, for a youth to understand why he has become angry or why he has chosen to run away from home. By thinking about his thoughts, and understanding why he has become angry, the juvenile can determine what thoughts he needs to change in order to more effectively control his temper.

Metacognition is one of the more complex cognitive skills developed during adolescence. It is somewhat dependent on other skills, such as abstraction, which must be developed first. Cognitive interventions for those who lack metacognition skills require that the therapist be more active in helping the youth identify his problem thoughts. Initial interventions to develop metacognition should focus on developing the foundational skills (such as abstraction), then proceeding to more complex skills after the foundational aspects have been mastered.

Thinking beyond Old Limits As cognitive capacities increase, juveniles begin to move beyond old limits in thinking. As children, they were able to see the world from their own perspective. As they grow older, they usually gain the ability to understand the points of view of others, and of society in general. At this point they are able to begin to understand whether their own views of problem behavior agree or conflict with society's views.

When youth are not able to grasp the importance of their own ideas relative to those of society, perspective-taking skills, such as those taught in social skills training programs can be very important. Juveniles can then be shown that while their friends may have certain beliefs about the value of substance abuse, this perspective is inaccurate. Instead, they can be taught the importance of sharing society's perspective, that the abuse of substances is physically damaging, harmful to their futures, and may result in arrest.

Cognitive development also allows youths to perform the important process of *moral reasoning*. Moral reasoning refers to a juvenile's ability to recognize and respond to right and wrong. Kohlberg (1969) identified three levels of moral reasoning, each level containing two stages.

The first two levels of reasoning include development typical of childhood and early adolescence. In stage 1 of the first level, a child makes decisions about right and wrong based on reward and punishment. In level 2 such decisions are based on the expectations of others. A third level of moral reasoning should develop somewhere between middle adolescence and early adulthood. In this stage, decisions about right and wrong are based on an individual's own beliefs and values. The standards of others are examined and may be adopted, modified, or rejected as the youth develops his own moral code. Youths who are able to reach level 3 can reject the values of their peers and adopt more prosocial patterns of thinking and behaving. Those who do not reach level 3 may be susceptible to the influence of problematic peer groups.

Social skills training can help some youths whose capacity for moral reasoning has not developed to level 3. Since the ability to perform advanced moral reasoning may be dependent on other cognitive development, it may be necessary to begin with more basic skills before progressing to the more difficult. Where juveniles are unable to achieve level 3, a behavioral system of rewards and punishments may be effective.

This chapter has provided only a brief overview of adolescent developmental stages. Practitioners should use the resources discussed in this chapter to gain further knowledge. Additionally, some of the material presented here does not consider gender differences. For instance, Gilligan and Attanucci (1988) argued that moral development for females differs from that process among males. Those who work with girls should familiarize themselves with that work. It also seems likely that some aspects of the process may vary between racial or ethnic groups due to cultural differences in norms and values, although the authors are not familiar with any research in this area. Practitioners should be aware that such differences may exist, and should modify their interventions accordingly.

Adapting Effective Interventions for Cognitive Skill

As has been noted above, some youths lack the capacity for complete cognitive development. In these cases, interventions may require special components in addition to social skills training. These components include referral for psychological testing, development of coping strategies, and use of monitoring and sanction techniques.

Referral for Psychological Testing Cognitive development may be arrested by psychological or physiological factors. When a juvenile does not respond to intervention, practitioners may wish to refer him to a community mental health center or a similar facility for testing and treatment. The professionals at these facilities should also rule out any physiological problems impeding the juvenile's development.

Development of Coping Skills and Strategies When youths cannot reason about right and wrong, practitioners can teach them to recognize problem situations and provide them with a repertoire of appropriate behaviors. Many social skills training packages include some basic coping skills. One example is the refusal skills techniques included in the EQUIP program.

Use of Monitoring and Sanctions When youths are delayed in their cognitive capacities, planning, monitoring, and sanctioning become very important. Since youths who function at lower levels of moral reasoning may respond best to rewards and sanctions, interventions for these youth should be highly structured. Interventions for these juveniles will require detailed planning, frequent contacts, and swift and concrete rewards and punishments.

SUMMARY

In this chapter we discussed some of the important differences between different groups of juveniles that you might be required to supervise or treat during your juvenile justice career. We reviewed differences between racial and ethnic groups, genders, and developmental stages. We also discussed how you might adapt your intervention for members of each group. Although we have made these warnings several times throughout the chapter, we feel that is important to repeat them here. Remember that no two persons of any group are exactly alike; so it is important not to stereotype either people or interventions. Remember that we have provided only an overview of the differences, so use the resources referenced within this chapter to enhance your knowledge. Remember that what we know about these groups changes almost daily. Become a student of the characteristics and needs of your clients. It will make you a much more effective practitioner.

ACTIVITIES FOR LEARNING

1. Review the case study of Ricky, the African-American youth described in box 1.2 (see chapter 1). What special factors relevant to many blacks might you want to consider in Ricky's assessment? In his intervention?

2. Imagine that you are assigned an American Indian client, Mary. Mary is not very talkative, seldom looks you in the eyes, and is silent for long periods of time. She displays very little change in her facial expression. You are perplexed as to the reason for Mary's behavior. It might be depression, for which you would need to refer her to treatment. But your juvenile justice practice course has taught you to consider other possibilities with American Indians. What things other than depression might explain Mary's behavior?

3. You are assigned Elena, a Hispanic juvenile. Elena speaks English fluently, but her parents do not, having recently immigrated to the United States from Central America. Elena is rapidly learning American ways, but her parents oppose these changes. She was recently arrested for stealing a popular compact disc from a music store. When her parents searched her room following her arrest, they found several stolen discs. Elena's parents were very angry, not only because she had stolen the discs, but also because her father had forbidden her to buy them. What special considerations will need to be made for Elena? How will you approach her family? It is likely that Elena will simply rebel more if she is not given the freedom to integrate into American culture, yet her parent's values insist that she obey. How will you help her without alienating her parents?

4. Phillip is an Asian-American teenager who was arrested for assault on a white boy his own age. At his dispositional hearing the judge assigned him to your care, telling his family, "This is an excellent worker. She will give you a lot of help." What barriers exist to effective intervention? What will your strategy be to overcome those barriers? How will you implement your strategy?

5. Read one of the books about a racial group that has been referenced in this chapter. Make a presentation to your classmates about what you learned from that book. Tell them how the things you've learned will affect your future work. Ask them to describe their reactions. How will what you've presented affect their future work?

6. Claudia is a 16-year-old with a history of amphetamine and alcohol abuse. She was referred to you because of an arrest for possession of amphetamines. Claudia has a history of depression and suicidal ideation. She also has several marks on her arms that look like scars. What factors will you need to consider as you develop an intervention for Claudia?

7. Jimmy is a 15-year-old adolescent who was arrested for stealing his neighbor's car. Jimmy has trouble thinking abstractly and reports that he sees no wrong in what he did because he was "planning to bring it back." What factors might you want to have tested in Jimmy's assessment? What do you think you might need to do in the intervention?

8. Read *Reviving Ophelia* (Pipher, 1994). What are your impressions of the book? If you are female, can you relate to anything the author says? How? If you are male, can you think of any friends who had these kinds of experiences? What happened to them?

QUESTIONS FOR DISCUSSION

1. Why is it important to be sensitive to cultural differences? Why not just make a family of immigrants think and act like Americans?

2. Imagine that you are a member of a minority group other than your own. What would it be like to be a member of that group? What effects would prejudice and discrimination have on you?

3. As a practitioner with girls on your caseload, what could you do to make their school environment more positive for them?

4. How could you help a client of Asian ancestry develop a positive cultural identity? An American Indian client? A black client?

5. What resources are available in your community for youth with delays in cognitive development? Where can they go for social skills training. If you don't know, find out. If there are no resources, what could you do to help create some?

KEY TERMS AND DEFINITIONS

Curandero A shaman or healer among some Central American groups.

Extended family A group of people that are important enough to members of a nuclear family to be regarded as part of that family.

Kinship group A group of people related by blood, usually including aunts, uncles, and close cousins.

Metacognition The ability to think about the thinking process.

Moral reasoning The process by which one decides what is right and wrong.

Santero A priest of an Afro-Caribbean religion, Santeria.

REFERENCES

Altarriba, J., & Bauer, L. M. (1998). Counseling Cuban Americans. In D. R. Atkinson, G. Morten, & D. Wing Sue (Eds.), *Counseling American minorities.* Boston: McGraw-Hill.

Atkinson, D. R., & Hackett, G. (1998). *Counseling diverse populations* (2nd ed.). Boston: McGraw-Hill.

Atkinson, D. R., Morten, G., & Wing Sue, D. (1998). *Counseling American minorities.* Boston: McGraw-Hill.

Ellis, R. A., O'Hara, M., & Sowers, K. (1999). Treatment profiles of troubled female adolescents: Implications for judicial disposition. *Juvenile and Family Court Journal, 50*(3), 25–40.

Falicov, C. J. (1999). The Latino family life cycle. In B. Carter & M. McGoldrick (Eds.), *The expanded family life cycle: Individual, family and social perspectives* (3rd ed., pp. 141–152). Boston: Allyn & Bacon.

Fong, R. (1994). Family preservation: Making it work for Asians. *Child Welfare, 73,* 331–333.

Forehand, R., & Wierson, M. (1993). The role of developmental factors in planning behavior interventions for children: Disruptive behavior as an example. *Behavior Therapy, 24,* 117–141.

Garrett, J. T., & Walkingstick-Garrett, M. (1998). The path of good medicine: Understanding and counseling Native American Indians. In D. R. Atkinson, G. Morten, & D. Wing Sue (Eds.), *Counseling American minorities.* Boston: McGraw-Hill.

Gary, L., Beatty, L., & Price, M. (1983). *Stable black families: Final report.* Washington, DC: Institute for Urban Affairs and Research, Howard University.

Gibbs, J. C., Potter, G. B., & Goldstein, A. P. (1995). *The EQUIP program.* Champaign, IL: Research Press.

Gilligan, C., and Attanucci, J. (1998). Two moral orientations. In C. Gilligan, J. V. Ward, J. M. Taylor, and B. Bardidge (Eds.), *Mapping the moral domain.* Cambridge, MA: Harvard University Press.

Helms, J. E. (1995). An update of Helm's white and people of color racial identity models. In J. G. Pontero, J. M. Casas, L. A. Suzuki, & C. M. Alexander (Eds.), *Handbook of multicultural counseling* (pp. 181–198). Thousand Oaks, CA: Sage.

Keating, D. (1980). Thinking processes in adolescence. In J. Adelson (Ed.), *Handbook of adolescent psychology.* New York: Wiley.

Kohlberg, L. (1969). *Stages in the development of moral thoughts and action.* New York: Holt, Rinehart & Winston.

LaFromboise, T. (1998). American Indian mental health policy. In D. R. Atkinson, G. Morten, & D. Wing Sue (Eds.), *Counseling American minorities.* Boston: McGraw-Hill.

Lyles, M., & Carter, J. (1982). Myths and strengths of the black family: A historical and sociological contribution to family therapy. *Journal of the National Medical Association, 74*(11), 1119–1123.

Minuchin, S. (1974). *Families and family therapy.* Cambridge, MA: Harvard University Press.

Nickerson, K. J., Helms, J. E., & Terrell, F. (1994). Cultural mistrust, opinions about mental illness, and black students' attitudes toward seeking psychological help from white counselors. *Journal of Counseling Psychology, 41,* 378–385.

Nishio, K., & Blimes, M. (1998). Psychotherapy with Southeast Asian American clients. In D. R. Atkinson, G. Morten, & D. Wing Sue (Eds.), *Counseling American minorities.* Boston: McGraw-Hill.

Pinderhughes, E. (1982). Afro-American families and the victim system. In M. McGoldrick, J. K. Pearce, & J. Giordano (Eds.), *Ethnicity and family therapy* (pp. 109–122). New York: Guilford Press.

Pipher, M. (1994). *Reviving Ophelia: Saving the selves of adolescent girls.* New York: Putnam.

Sue, D. (1998). The interplay of sociocultural factors on the psychological development of Asians in American. In D. R. Atkinson, G. Morten, & D. Wing Sue (1998). *Counseling American minorities.* Boston: McGraw-Hill.

Steinberg, L. (1993). *Adolescence* (3rd ed.). Boston: McGraw-Hill.

Terrell, F., & Terrell, S. (1981). An inventory to measure cultural mistrust among blacks. *Western Journal of Black Studies, 5,* 180–184.

Terrell, F., & Terrell, S. (1984). Race of the counselor, client sex, cultural mistrust level, and premature termination from counseling among black clients. *Journal of Counseling Psychology, 31,* 371–375.

Trimble, J. E. (1981). Value differentials and their importance in counseling American Indians. In P. Pedersen, J. Draguns, W. Lonner, & J. Trimble (Eds.), *Counseling across cultures* (2nd ed., pp. 203–226). Honolulu: University Press of Hawaii.

U.S. Office of Management and Budget. (1987, May 4). Directive 15: Race and ethnic standards for federal statistics and administrative reporting. *Federal Register, 43,* 19269.

Wadsworth, R., Spampneto, A. M., & Halbrook, B. M. (1995). The role of sexual trauma in the treatment of chemically dependent women: Addressing the relapse issue. *Journal of Counseling and Development, 73,* 401.

Chapter 8

◆

Best Practices in Juvenile Justice

CHAPTER OUTLINE

Multisystemic Therapy
Victim-Offender Mediation
Families and Schools Together
The PREPARE Curriculum
Family Intervention Project
Intensive Aftercare Program
Summary

Several current interventions have been either empirically tested or are based on empirical evidence and are currently being tested. In this chapter we will review some of these interventions: those that have been successfully tested or appear likely to be effective based on what we have learned about successful work with juveniles. We will discuss multisystemic therapy, victim-offender mediation, the PREPARE Curriculum, Families and Schools Together (FAST), and the Family Intervention Project (FIP). We'll also take a look at a model for aftercare developed by the OJJDP (intensive case management) and provide a list of resources from which you can obtain descriptions of other interventions.

For each of the programs we discuss in this chapter, we'll talk about three important areas. First, we'll describe the intervention and offer a hypothetical case study to show how it might work for a juvenile. Next, we'll discuss the ways in which the intervention meets (or fails to meet) some of the criteria for effectiveness identified in chapter 6. Finally, we will review the outcome literature regarding that intervention.

MULTISYSTEMIC THERAPY

Multisystemic therapy (MST) is an intervention that uses intensive case management to target multiple problems both in a juvenile and in his environment. In MST, a therapist/case manager, assisted by a team of other professionals, is assigned to individual juveniles. Although some services may be brokered, the team is the primary source of all services and is available to the family on a 24-hour-per-day, seven-day-per-week basis. Caseloads are kept small, to allow intensive, personalized work with the families. The team identifies and addresses multiple problems in the juvenile and throughout his social systems. Specific interventions are used for specific situations, including cognitive-behavioral counseling for the individual and family, and other pre-identified strategies for the school, peer, and community systems. It also provides concrete services by helping families access sources of money to meet needs for clothing, food, housing, and medical services. The case management team has frequent contact with the family throughout the early stages of the intervention, gradually reducing the number of contact hours as prosocial competence grows (Henggeler & Borduin, 1990).

The multisystemic approach can be illustrated with the case of Ken, an imaginary 16-year-old who was arrested for possession of marijuana. John, the case manager, initiates the intervention with a visit to Ken's home, where he visits with Ken, his parents, and his two siblings. Although he knows the reason for Ken's referral, the case manager opens the session by asking, "What do you see as the reason that I am here today?" He asks this question of the parents first, then of Ken, then of each of the siblings.

John has at least three goals for this first session. He wants to make it clear that he recognizes and respects the authority of the parents while getting everyone's opinion as to the nature of the problem. He also hopes to begin to develop an understanding of the problem that Ken is experiencing and how it is affected by conditions in the family, the school, Ken's peer group, and the neighborhood. His third goal is to reach a consensus with the family as to the nature of the problem and to develop a plan for addressing it. John is able to accomplish all three goals in the first session. He and the family agree on several intervention steps.

Ken clearly has some personal issues that need attention. He appears to be depressed. He looks sad, spends long hours alone in his room, and never seems to enjoy anything. He says he would like to get involved in neighborhood sports programs at the local park, but has no money for the enrollment fee or for equipment. Ken's grades in school are marginal, having dropped from a solid B average in the last school year to Cs and Ds on his last report card. He reports he has few friends and the ones he has don't attend school regularly. Ken reports that he doesn't want to go to school any more and plans to drop out as soon as he can legally do so.

Ken's personal problems are complicated by conditions within his family. His father is an authoritarian disciplinarian, who is extremely critical of Ken and frequently uses severe corporal punishment. He often becomes enraged at Ken's behavior, yelling at him, threatening him, and ordering him to spend days in his room for the slightest infraction of family rules.

Ken's mother is not very involved with Ken. She protects his younger siblings by siding against the father, but says nothing in defense of him. She reports that he is a troublemaker and has been since he was a young child. Ken's siblings are distant from him, apparently afraid that they will suffer the wrath of their father if they appear to be too close to him.

Ken reports that he once enjoyed school, but that he no longer sees its use-fulness. He was a member of the football and basketball teams until two years earlier, when his father forced him to quit because Ken stayed out one night after curfew. He is frequently truant.

Ken's friends are all two or more years older than he is. They are all frequently truant, and two have officially dropped out of school. Ken gets together with them on the few weekends during which his father has not grounded him. He reports that they "just talk and smoke reefer."

John initiates the intervention by referring Ken to a psychologist to be evaluated for depression. He also uses some of his agency's discretionary funds to get Ken enrolled in a football program at a local park. He calls Ken's school to arrange for after-school tutoring three days per week.

Although John feels that Ken's issues are very important, he recognizes that they are exacerbated by other conditions in his family and social systems. He believes that the parents' family management style is poor and that this contributes to Ken's problems. He refers the parents to a local parent training program.

John schedules weekly meetings with Ken and his family to talk about ways to improve their interactions. Using a cognitive-behavioral approach, he begins to work on some of the father's errant beliefs about discipline and the mother's ideas about the kind of relationships she should have with her children.

Ken is a bright young man, and John feels certain that the tutoring will improve his grades rapidly. He thinks, however, that Ken may have some special interests that might help him do even better. In Ken's room, John notices an aquarium full of fish, a bird in a cage, and several posters of various kinds of dogs, cats, horses, and other animals. When asked about the animals, Ken responds that he loves animals, and had once hoped to be a veterinarian. John recognizes this as a strength that can be used to help Ken. He begins to build on Ken's love of animals, suggesting that he do his school projects and reports on topics related to the care of animals. He arranges trips to the zoo as family outings and helps Ken obtain a volunteer position at the Humane Society.

John also addresses the problems in Ken's peer group. Ken agrees to stay away from his current friends, but he clearly needs a group for social support. John believes that he will be able to develop friends through football and through his work at the Humane Society. They pick an after-school club in which Ken can become involved. Ken is shy about meeting new people; so John provides some tips on conversation. They also role-play situations in which these tips can be used to help Ken develop his skills.

Ken is scheduled for a 16-week intervention. After 6 weeks his grades have improved substantially and he is very involved in both football and Humane Society activities. He sees a therapist once each week for counseling regarding his depression, and seems to be doing much better. His parents have been attending training courses, but have made little progress in changing their management style. It appears, however, that the additional support Ken is receiving is enough to counteract the negative influence of his parents' communication and disciplinary style.

After 12 weeks the parents have made some progress. John has convinced them to experiment with alternative techniques of family management and they have found that their children respond well to those techniques. The family has had several outings that all have reported enjoying, and their weekly family meetings have been very beneficial to their communication.

By the 16th week, Ken's grades have improved to nearly all As. He participates in sports and other school and community activities. His parents have seen his improvement and have responded by offering him some financial assistance for these programs. The family relationships are much improved and Ken no longer has contact with his former friends. He says that he has not smoked any cannabis since the first week of the intervention. This has been confirmed through regular, court-ordered urinalysis. John terminates a successful intervention with a report to the court.

Characteristics of Successful Intervention

This description of multisystemic therapy is brief and greatly simplified. It also may include some components of intervention that would not be the first choice of a therapist trained in that modality, since neither of the authors received training from Dr. Henggeler's organization. The description is based, however, on a book by Henggeler and Borduin (1990), *Family Therapy and Beyond,* that was the first treatment manual. Practitioners who want to learn more about MST should read this book.

As we will see in a later section, MST has been very successful in several outcome studies. There are many reasons for this success. Among these is the fact that it meets so many of the criteria for successful intervention. We'll look at a few of those criteria, including theoretical basis, level of comprehensiveness, structure, and use of effective components.

Theoretical Basis Multisystemic therapy is solidly founded in well-supported theory. This means that it carefully uses a great deal of what we know about why juveniles commit delinquent acts. As we saw in chapters 4, 5, and 6, this is very important for developing and delivering successful interventions.

Much of the assessment and intervention approach of MST is based on systems theory (Henggeler & Borduin, 1990). Systems theory envisions individuals as integral parts of several different but overlapping social systems. The behavior of those individuals affects the systems with which they interact and the behavior of the systems affects the individual. When a juvenile develops a behavioral problem, it is in part because of choices the juvenile has made and in part because of the way he has been influenced by his environment. Because of the influence of various social systems, intervention cannot focus only on the juvenile. Rather, as the youth changes, his social systems must change. For the most effective and lasting results, change should occur in as many systems as possible.

The use of systems theory in MST is clearly demonstrated in the case of Ken discussed in the section above. When John assessed Ken's situation, he looked at individual issues such as depression and school problems, but he also considered the effects of such things as family management style and the nature of Ken's friends. John then developed an intervention to address the totality of the environment, rather than just Ken's substance abuse or his depression. By facilitating change throughout the juvenile's system, John was able to produce change quickly and effectively. Also, by changing the social systems, he was able to improve the probability that the change would last because it would be supported by those systems.

Structure Multisystemic therapy is highly structured, using intensive planning and scheduling activities with the juveniles and their families, as well as frequent visitation. A great deal of structure is provided initially, until the clients are able to develop the skills to structure their own lives. Support is gradually withdrawn as prosocial knowledge and skills are developed.

Structure includes planning such activities as school, homework, household chores, community service, and similar projects. It may also, however, include recreational activities such as scheduled free time or family outings. Monitoring for these activities may be done by parents, neighbors, teachers, siblings, or professionals in community programs.

Comprehensiveness Multisystemic therapy is very comprehensive. It does not view the problems that juveniles experience as isolated problems of clusters of behavior, such as substance abuse. Rather, its practitioners look at multiple factors in multiple systems to try to understand how they affect one another. Intervention is then designed to address all those factors rather than one or a few.

Multisystemic therapy has experienced continual revision and improvement since its conception. A new treatment manual, *Multisystemic Treatment of Antisocial Behavior in Children and Adolescents* (Henggeler, Schoenwald, Borduin, Rowland, & Cunningham, 1998), has recently become available. Despite recent revisions, MST is still based on the original primary principles of MST listed in a National Institute on Drug Abuse monograph (Henggeler, 1993). These principles are included in table 8.1.

Outcome Evaluations

Several outcome evaluations have examined the effectiveness of MST. It has been used with delinquents in Missouri and South Carolina, with sexual offenders, with substance abusers, with abusive and neglectful families, and with a group of inner-city offenders. All the studies have shown positive results when MST was compared with conventional forms of treatment. We'll briefly discuss the results of two of those studies here.

In a study reported in 1992 by Henggeler, Melton, and Smith, MST was used to treat serious juvenile offenders in South Carolina. Outcomes for youths treated with MST were compared to those for juveniles who received the usual services offered by the Department of Youth Services. At the post-test the group that received MST had committed significantly fewer new offenses than the other group. At a 59-week follow-up, MST participants had fewer re-arrests and had spent an average of 73 fewer days incarcerated.

In the Missouri evaluation, MST participants showed significant improvement over the group that received standard services. After four years the MST group had a 22% recidivism rate as compared to 71% for the other group. Those juveniles who did re-offend committed crimes that were significantly

Table 8.1 Principles of Multisystemic Therapy

1. The primary purpose of assessment is to understand the fit between identified problems and their broader systemic context.
2. Interventions should be present-focused and action-oriented, targeting specific and well-defined problems.
3. Interventions should target sequences of behavior within or between systems.
4. Interventions should be developmentally appropriate and should fit the developmental needs of the youth.
5. Interventions should be designed to require daily or weekly effort by family members.
6. Intervention efficacy is evaluated continuously from multiple perspectives.
7. Interventions should be designed to promote treatment generalization and long-term maintenance of therapeutic change.
8. Therapeutic contacts should emphasize the positive, and interventions should use systemic strengths as levers for change.
9. Interventions should be designed to promote responsible behavior and to decrease irresponsible behavior among family members.

SOURCE: Henggeler, 1993

less serious than those of their counterparts in the standard treatment group (Henggeler, 1993).

VICTIM-OFFENDER MEDIATION

Victim–offender mediation (VOM), a relatively new and particularly encouraging approach to juvenile justice, was introduced in chapter 4. VOM programs typically involve the victims and perpetrators of property offenses and minor assaults. However, in response to the expressed needs of many crime victims, there have been efforts to broaden the scope of VOM to include violent crimes, such as rape and murder (Flaten, 1996; Umbreit, 1994). A recent survey showed that there are more than 300 VOM programs in the United States, and more than 900 in Europe (Umbreit & Greenwood, 1998).

There are a number of ways in which VOM is conducted, though all are based on the philosophy of restorative justice. The heart of VOM is a face-to-face mediation session between the victim (or victims) and the offender under the supervision of a trained VOM mediator. The goal of this meeting is to provide a safe environment in which the involved parties can engage in a genuine dialogue so that emotional and informational needs can be met and so that a plan for the offender to "make things right" can be developed. Most, though not all, VOM sessions include restitution agreement between victim and offender.

In a very important sense, VOM programs are for victims. The victim is given the opportunity to express her feelings about the incident, as well as have the offender answer important questions she may have about the event. Common questions asked are, "How did you pick me?" and "Were you stalking me?" Having these questions answered frequently reduces the victim's fear of repeat victimization. However, VOM programs are also for offenders. These programs offer offenders the opportunity to be accountable for their behavior in ways not possible in the retributive justice model. Meeting the victim in a very real sense "puts a face" on the victim in the offender's mind. This makes it more difficult for the offender to stereotype the victim. Some researchers have speculated that this meeting may trigger whatever empathy skills the offender has and thereby reduce subsequent delinquent behavior (Nugent, Umbreit, Wiinamaki, & Paddock, in press).

Umbreit (1993) describes four phases in the mediation process. These phases include intake, preparation, mediation, and follow-up. In the intake phase the court refers the offender to the program. The referral may occur after a formal confession of guilt or as a part of a diversionary process. During preparation, the mediator meets separately with offender and victim. At these meetings, the mediator listens to each party's description of the circumstances surrounding the crime, explains the nature of the program, and encourages both parties to participate. Voluntary participation on the part of both victims and offenders is critical to the success of VOM.

The third phase, mediation, typically includes the offender, the victim, and the mediator. The mediator explains her role in the discussion, the rules under which the process will operate, and the agenda for the meeting. The initial part of the mediation session allows each party to explain the circumstances and their feelings regarding the crime. The discussion then moves to the nature of the victim's loss and the development of a plan for restitution. Finally, a plan is negotiated, requiring the agreement of each party. The plan is put into the form of a contract that is signed by both parties and witnessed by the mediator.

The final phase of the VOM process is follow-up. The mediator monitors the progress of the youth in complying with the terms of the agreement. Regular phone calls, occasional visits, and joint meetings with offender and victim are used as needed. Problems in offender compliance may result in the juvenile being returned to court. However, it is noteworthy that 90% of restitution agreements agreed to in VOM are completed within one year. This compares with a one-year completion rate of 20–30% in court-ordered restitution programs (Umbreit & Greenwood, 1998).

The process of VOM can be illustrated by the example of Arthur, an imaginary 14-year-old who was arrested for burglarizing a home. Arthur was a first-time offender who had no history of problems other than occasional truancy from school. At intake, Arthur was assigned a juvenile justice worker, who arranged that he be diverted into the VOM program.

The mediator scheduled a meeting with the victim. At this meeting she described the mediation process, got the victim's consent to participate, and talked with the victim about her feelings and experiences related to the offense. At the conclusion of the meeting she obtained three possible times when the victim could be available to meet with her and the offender.

The mediator's second meeting was with Arthur. During this meeting they discussed the situation surrounding the burglary, including Arthur's motivation for his crime. Arthur reported that he was from a poor family that could not afford to purchase new clothing for him to wear to school. He felt embarrassed by his attire, and was subjected to ridicule by his classmates who dressed better. Arthur reported that he wanted to go to school and make his life better than that of his parents, but that he could no longer deal with the scorn of his peers. He expressed regret at the burglary, but reported that he felt that he had no other alternative at the time. The mediator discussed other options Arthur might have taken, including seeking part-time employment. Arthur agreed that one of these other options would have been preferable, and agreed to enter into a contract to make restitution to his victim. Using the three dates provided by a victim, the mediator scheduled a meeting including herself, the victim, and Arthur.

At the third meeting, the mediator stated the purpose and agenda, then asked the victim to relate her feelings and experiences related to the burglary. She spoke of her physical losses, but spoke even more vividly of the emotional losses she had suffered, including her fear and anxiety. She reported being unable to sleep at night and being afraid to return home after having been away.

When the victim had finished her story, Arthur was asked to relate his. He described the ridicule he had experienced at school and his reluctance to return to classes in his old, tattered clothing. He spoke of the anxiety he had experienced before the break-in and of the remorse he had felt afterward. He apologized to the victim, and offered to find a part-time job to repay her losses.

At this point the victim revealed an additional concern. She was afraid that the burglary had been the result of gang activity, and that she would be targeted in the future. Arthur assured her that he had acted alone, and that he had chosen her house only because "it looked like she had nice stuff." The victim replied that she did have some nice things, but that this was only the result of long years of hard work and careful savings. She was relieved that Arthur was not a part of a gang and that she was not likely to be a future target for other youths.

The victim was a retired teacher, and as Arthur spoke, she thought of other children like him that had been in her classes over the years. She thought of those who had finished school and those who had not. She remembered reading of the later arrests of some of those students that had dropped out. She felt compassion for Arthur, and wanted to help him. She suggested some resources that might help him, and offered to call a friend who might provide him with part-time work.

The three participants developed a contract in which Arthur agreed to find a part-time job and make scheduled restitution payments. The victim requested that he be allowed to keep a portion of his earnings to purchase clothing and school supplies. All parties agreed. The contract was written and signed by both victim and offender. The mediator witnessed the agreement.

Arthur found employment with the friend mentioned by the victim. He made his payments and purchased new designer clothing to wear to school. Once he stopped by the program office to display his new outfit. He committed no further delinquent acts.

Characteristics of Successful Intervention

VOM meets several of the criteria for successful intervention. In this section we'll talk about two of the criteria it meets, theoretical foundation and structure. We'll also look at one of the criteria it does not meet, and talk about some of the reasons this may not be important when VOM is used.

Theoretical Basis VOM uses portions of several theories of delinquency. Developmental theories suggest that troubled juveniles often lag behind in specific skills, including empathy, decision-making, and problem-solving skills. Exposure to the victims of their crimes may help them understand the physical and emotional losses experienced by victims and may help activate empathy skills. The process of meetings, discussion of alternatives, and development of a plan provide modeling and reinforcement for positive decision-making and problem-solving. This is consistent with social learning theory. Strain theory suggests that those who feel deprived of opportunities available to others may react with criminal behavior. In cases such as Arthur's, recognizing that his victim had struggled to create her own opportunities might help the offender understand that he could do the same.

Structure Victim-offender mediation is highly structured as an intervention. It does not structure the lives of its clients as completely as an intervention such as MST. It is, however, very specific regarding its expectations and its schedule of repayment. Payments must be made on a regular basis. This activity is monitored by the mediator. Sanctions for failure to comply are clearly specified.

Sometimes juveniles who receive VOM are also assigned a case manager. The case manager may provide additional services such as referral to resources or monitoring and surveillance. In these cases structure is added by the presence and actions of the case manager.

Comprehensiveness At first glance, VOM may not appear to be comprehensive. It does, however, incorporate processes that address several areas of the juvenile's life. The negotiation provides problem-solving and decision-making training as well as an opportunity for light counseling by the mediator. A behavioral contract is used, providing yet another component of successful intervention. If the juvenile is employed to enable him to make restitution payments, this limits the amount of time that can be spent with antisocial peers and increases the time likely to be spent with prosocial influences.

When VOM is used as a component of an intervention by a case manager, the case manager may make referrals to other agencies. These other agencies would provide services for other areas of need. Services by other agencies increase the intervention's comprehensiveness. A summary of the benefits of VOM combined with effective case management is included in table 8.2.

Outcome Evaluations

Several researchers have studied the effectiveness of VOM in reducing recidivism among specific categories of juvenile offenders. VOM is normally used for property crime and minor assault, but some have begun to explore its use with violent crime (Flaten, 1996; Price, 1998).

Four published studies have reported the results of outcome evaluations. Two of those studies have reported positive results for VOM. Also, at least one doctoral dissertation has reported the results of an evaluation of VOM. The results of that study were positive. These three positive outcome evaluations will be discussed.

Table 8.2 Benefits of Comprehensive Intervention Using the Balanced and Restorative Justice Model

INTERVENTION	ACCOUNTABILITY BENEFITS	COMPETENCY DEVELOPMENT BENEFITS	COMMUNITY SAFETY BENEFITS
Community Service	Makes amends to the community	Develops skills, including work skills (experiential)	Structures time, involves community in supervision
Victim-Offender Mediation	Answers personally to the one harmed and makes amends	Develops communication and conflict resolution skills and empathy	Reduces victim fear in most cases and increases understanding of crime
Small or Large Group Conferencing (Family Group Conferencing)	Makes amends to all impacted by the offense	Develops communication and conflict resolution skills and empathy	Reduces victim fear in most cases and increases understanding of crime.
Monitored School Attendance		Builds skills	Structures time, community supervises
Victim Empathy Classes	Increases understanding of impact of own behavior	Increases interpersonal skills	Structures time
Residential Placement		May address some skills	Provides high degree of supervision
Electronic Monitoring			Restricts movement to reduce opportunities to offend
Secure Detention			Removes youth from opportunity to offend
Drug Testing			Reduces likelihood of behavior associated with substance abuse
Work Experience	Generates revenue to pay restituion	Teaches work and social skills	Structures time under adult supervision
Cognitive Skills Classes	Increases understanding of responsibility for behavior and the impact of behavior	Improves decision-making and critical thinking skills	Structures youth's time

SOURCE: OJJDP, 1995

Umbreit (1994) examined the results for program participants from four states. After one year VOM participants had an 18.1% re-offense rate compared with 26.9% for nonparticipants. Nugent and Paddock (1996) found that VOM participants had re-offended at a 37.5% lower rate than nonparticipants after one year. They also noted that participants who re-offended committed less severe offenses than those who did not participate in VOM. Wiinamaki (1997) replicated the Nugent and Paddock study. She found that VOM participants committed 54% fewer minor offenses and 16% fewer property and violent offenses than did their counterparts.

Two other published studies (Niemeyer & Schichor, 1996; Roy, 1993) found no differences in outcomes for VOM participants when compared to nonparticipants. Recently, however, Nugent and associates (in press) demonstrated that the results of the Umbreit (1994), Nugent and Paddock (1996), Niemeyer and Schichor (1996), and Wiinamaki (1997) studies were homogeneous and may constitute a successful replication series. This finding argues very strongly for the effectiveness of VOM. Two things seem clear: VOM is a cost-effective method of treating some categories of juvenile offenders. However, further study is needed to determine what factors contribute to or detract from its success.

FAMILIES AND SCHOOLS TOGETHER

Families and Schools Together (FAST) is a *school-based intervention* that uses various resources in the community to address the multiple needs and risk factors of at-risk juveniles and their families (McDonald, 1997; McDonald & Sayger, 1998). Parents who are already program participants invite families of identified children to join the program. Participation is voluntary; so families may elect not to participate. Children from families that participate are evaluated using the Revised Behavior Problem Checklist (RBPC) (Quay & Peterson, 1987) both before and after the intervention.

The intervention begins with eight clinical family sessions. Between 10 and 15 families participate in the sessions. Families engage in empirically supported activities designed to enhance cohesion and family identity, improve a sense of community between families, and develop positive family management and communication skills. Following successful completion of the sessions, the families graduate in a ceremony at the school that hosts FAST.

After the eight initial sessions, families continue to meet twice monthly for two years in the FASTWORKS portion of the program. The meetings are run by parents who follow a preset agenda. Parents can also receive leadership training and can join FASTPAC, a parent advisory council that meets with other FAST groups to coordinate events and deal with budgetary issues. The monthly meetings provide ongoing support from other parents and an opportunity for mutual assistance and problem-solving. FAST practitioners withdraw from the FASTWORKS groups after two years, but the groups often continue to meet. FAST staff remain available to such groups for telephone communication in the event of emergencies.

When special needs arise during the program, participants may be referred to community resources. Examples include a child who needs a psychiatric evaluation or a parent in need of substance abuse treatment. Other issues may be dealt with by parents or by FAST staff.

The FAST intervention can be illustrated with the story of Alicia, an Asian-American teenager. Alicia was struggling in school, frequently truant and getting poor grades. Her parents, the Tans, were approached by Mrs. Watts, a parent involved in the FAST program meeting at Alicia's school. The Tans were embarrassed by Alicia's problems and were reluctant to get involved in the FAST program. Mrs. Watts shared how helpful the program had been to her own family and the Tans were convinced.

Alicia was evaluated using the RBPC before the first meeting. She reported more problems than anyone had been aware of, admitting that she occasionally smoked marijuana and had been involved in minor shoplifting. She also reported that she could not relate to her parents and they made no attempt to understand.

The family attended its first meeting on a Wednesday evening in a large meeting room at Alicia's school. Eleven other families attended. Each was seated at its own family table, and a FAST staff member led introductions and explained the agenda for the next eight weeks. Each family was given the task of developing a flag to identify its table in subsequent sessions.

During their eight weekly sessions the families took turns preparing dinner for the meetings, sang with one another, and engaged in therapeutic games. Favorite games included "scribbles," in which positive communication is encouraged, and feelings charades, in which gestures are used to communicate feelings to other family members. There were also special times for the children to be together without the adults and for the adults to be alone without the children. Each session provided fifteen minutes for parent-child communication. During the eight sessions, Alicia's attitude toward her parents improved considerably and her parents reported feeling more comfortable in their communications with their daughter. During the third week of the program Alicia was referred to a tutoring program, and her grades have improved since then.

After the eight weeks of clinical sessions, the families participated in a graduation ceremony. Each member wore a graduation cap and marched in to graduation music. Each received a certificate of completion from the principal of the school and was applauded by the friends and extended family members who had been invited to attend.

After graduation the families continued to meet twice each month at the school. At those meetings they discussed individual and family problems, issues with the school, and problems in the community. They also chose to take training available in grassroots leadership, designed to facilitate positive change in the community. Alicia's parents developed friendships with some of the parents in the group and Alicia found friends there as well. Alicia's grades continued to improve, and she reported that she had stopped smoking marijuana and shoplifting.

Characteristics of Successful Intervention

FAST has many of the characteristics of effective intervention. Two of those characteristics will be discussed here. The first is its sound theoretical basis. The second is its comprehensiveness.

Theoretical Basis FAST is based on two theories of human behavior: family stress theory (Hill, 1958) and social ecology (Bronfenbrenner, 1979). *Family stress theory* uses an A, B, C model to explain how stressors impact family functioning and juvenile behavior. "A" refers to a stressor event, which might be poverty, violence, victimization, or similar acute or chronic problems. "B" represents family resources, both internal and external. Families may have multiple resources, including such characteristics as money, emotional support, and strong linkage to social services. "C" is the shared ideas and perceptions of the family regarding its capacity to deal with the stressor, "A," using resources, "B." If a family's resources are good and if it believes it is competent to deal with stressors using those resources, the impact of the stressors is reduced and the likelihood of the children developing behavioral problems is reduced. FAST works on all three components of the ABC model. Stressors may be diminished by the introduction of new resources. A family's beliefs about its

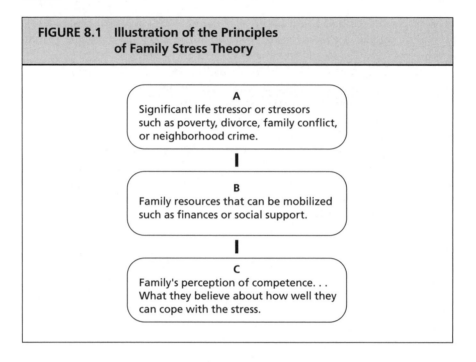

FIGURE 8.1 Illustration of the Principles of Family Stress Theory

A
Significant life stressor or stressors such as poverty, divorce, family conflict, or neighborhood crime.

B
Family resources that can be mobilized such as finances or social support.

C
Family's perception of competence. . . What they believe about how well they can cope with the stress.

capacity to deal with stressors can be improved through the introduction of new resources and through changing its cognitions about its capacity. The relationship between A, B, and C is illustrated in figure 8.1.

Social ecology theory is another basis for FAST. Social ecology has similarities to systems theory in that it views the individual and her environment as interrelated and interdependent. For the individual to change, her social environment must change as well.

FAST tries to induce change in the individual, family, school, peer, and community social systems.

Comprehensiveness FAST is comprehensive in that it addresses multiple risk and protective factors for the juveniles and families involved in the program. Children are identified by teachers and parents as being at risk for problem behavior. Such factors as early substance use, family substance use, poor family management, high family conflict, poor family communication and support, school problems, neighborhood influences, and peer group problems are addressed.

Protective factors are also considered. The program attempts to develop family cohesion, structured family lifestyle and activities, positive family and peer social networks, school atmosphere, and community relationships.

Outcome Evaluations

FAST has been evaluated, and its effectiveness has been supported in several areas. In one sample it increased family cohesion and decreased family conflict, negative and aggressive behaviors, attention problems, and motor excesses. Children who had exhibited conduct disorder decreased their undesirable behaviors, and the frequency and severity of problem behavior across the group also decreased (McDonald & Sayger, 1998).

THE PREPARE CURRICULUM

The PREPARE Curriculum is one of several social skills training programs available for treating troubled juveniles and their families. The curriculum is composed of a group of modules that can be taught collectively or individually. The modules include problem-solving training, interpersonal skills training, situational perception training, anger control training, moral reasoning training, stress management training, and empathy training. The modules are summarized in table 8.3. In at least one case a group of modules has been grouped and tested for use with violent youth, including gang members. This package of modules, known as Aggression Replacement Training (ART), was discussed briefly in chapter 5. It will be used here in a case study. The PREPARE Curriculum (Goldstein, 1990) is available from Research Press.

The PREPARE Curriculum uses cognitive-behavioral techniques to teach skills and to help *skill transfer* and *skill maintenance*. The text explains how to use those techniques and offers suggestions for recruiting volunteers to participate in training. Both videotapes and audiotapes are also available. The PREPARE intervention techniques are organized into a system referred to as skillstreaming. Skillstreaming consists of teaching and modeling appropriate behavior, role play in which the client practices appropriate behavior, positive reinforcement for exhibiting positive behavior, and support for the use of the learned behaviors in the real world.

PREPARE modules are usually offered as weekly or biweekly group sessions. Professionals or paraprofessionals often lead the sessions, assisted by peer or adult volunteers. Sessions may be at neighborhood centers, schools, parks, or in a professional's office.

Since there are several modules in PREPARE, one variation of its curriculum will be illustrated here as a case study. The imaginary client, Josie, is a 14-year-old African-American female who has a significant anger management problem. She has expressed her anger by fighting with classmates several times in the past. She was committed to state custody and referred to the treatment program because she assaulted a teacher.

Josie is referred to Anger Management for Angry Youth (AMAY), an imaginary program serving a large metropolitan area. Her case manager meets with Andrea, the director of AMAY, and two of her trainers, Jennifer and Steve, to discuss the case before Josie begins. The four professionals select a starting date for the following Thursday. The case manager informs Josie of the beginning date and the following schedule, and makes sure that she has transportation available. Josie is told that she will attend training one time each week for about 1½ hours each session. She will be working in a group with other adolescents who also have problems managing their anger.

Josie shows up for the first meeting to find seven other juveniles present for training. After a brief introduction and summary of the activities of the next

Table 8.3 Summary of the Modules of the PREPARE Curriculum

Module	Function
Problem-solving training	Teaches a series of defined steps and techniques for solving problems and making decisions; important as a foundation for other modules.
Interpersonal skills training	Teaches skills relevant to personal interaction with others, including such skills as listening, having a conversation, asking for help, and knowing your feelings.
Situational perception training	Students learn to use the right skill in the right place. Helps them properly understand and interpret situations so that they can respond appropriately.
Anger control training	Helps juveniles develop alternative skills to de-escalate and manage their anger.
Moral reasoning training	Teaches skills to develop appropriate values, apply those values, and how to deal with conflicting values.
Stress management training	Helps students learn to decrease the symptoms and effects of stress.
Empathy training	Enhances the levels of empathy of the student.
Cooperation training	Teaches students skills to collaborate effectively.

10 weeks, Jennifer, the professional in charge of this group, introduces Jackie, a 17-year-old former gang member who took this training three years earlier and has been very successful in managing his anger (and other prosocial activities) since that time. Jennifer tells the group that Jackie will help her lead the group.

Jackie and Jennifer lead their group through a prescribed set of activities over the next 10 weeks. These activities use the skillstreaming techniques described above to teach two modules of PREPARE, Moral Reasoning and Anger Control. These two components constitute the basic modules of ART. The group learns specific techniques of relaxation, thought-stopping, and various self-control techniques to help manage their anger. They use a number of case studies and vignettes to develop their capacity for moral reasoning. Josie finds that she always handled her anger the way she had seen her mother handle hers, by lashing out. She also finds that many of her thoughts about what is morally correct behavior are not correct. Gradually, the group activities help her correct those thoughts.

Jackie and Jennifer also help their clients work on transferring their skills to the world outside the group. They explain to their clients that the first step is learning how to act appropriately and doing it successfully in the group. The second step, which takes a little more work, is learning to use those skills in real life. The practitioners use a specific approach described in PREPARE to help the juveniles learn to transfer their new skills.

At the end of the 10-week period Josie receives a graduation certificate and the congratulations of her case manager. The case manager reports to the court that Josie has done well and presents a revised plan for ongoing monitoring and supervision. With the court's approval, the case manager arranges weekly contact with Josie, her mother, and school officials. The case manager continues to monitor Josie's activities for several months. Six months later, when the judge orders the case closed, none of the case manager's contacts have reported any aggressive behavior from Josie.

Characteristics of Successful Intervention

As with the other successful interventions described in this chapter, PREPARE and ART meet several of the criteria for effective intervention. They were developed using a solid theoretical foundation, they are both structured and provide their participants with structure, and they are done as much as possible in the juvenile's environment with emphasis on success in the juvenile's natural environment.

Theoretical Basis PREPARE is based on a central theory of antisocial behavior: social learning theory. This theory was discussed in earlier chapters. The PREPARE Curriculum assumes that delinquent attitudes and behavior were learned through interactions with parents and other social systems and can be replaced with prosocial attitudes and behavior through carefully planned interactions with other individuals and social systems. In fact, the group environment actually creates a small social system in which intensive learning can take place.

Structure PREPARE does not structure the juvenile's environment, but it structures many of her reactions to it. Systematic techniques of self-control are taught as a form of self-structure. Scheduled meetings and homework assignments also provide some structure.

Emphasizes Success in Natural Environment The importance of emphasizing success in the juvenile's natural environment is demonstrated by the success of many community-based interventions and aftercare programs. It also addresses the issue of transferring attitudes and skills from the office or classroom into the youth's real world. The exercise and activities used in ART appear to have been particularly effective in facilitating transfer. Goldstein and Glick (1994) report a 45–50% skill transfer rate using skillstreaming. This compares with 15–20% using other forms of treatment (Goldstein & Kanfer, 1979; Karoly & Steffen, 1980).

Outcome Evaluations

Because there are many components in the PREPARE Curriculum, our discussion of its outcome evaluations will focus on one cluster of its components, Aggression Replacement Training (ART). ART has been evaluated on at least eight occasions, seven with positive results. We'll consider four of those studies here: one conducted by Goldstein and his colleagues at a New York State Division for Youth facility in Annsville, New York; the second a community-based evaluation, also by Goldstein and his associates; the third a Gang Intervention Project also conducted by Goldstein and his colleagues in Brooklyn,

New York; and the fourth by Gibbs and his co-workers at the Ohio Department of Youth Services.

The first study of ART was conducted at the Annsville Youth Center, a limited-security facility in central New York. Most of the residents of Annsville had been incarcerated for burglary, robbery (unarmed), and drug offenses. Members of the treatment group acquired 4 of the 10 ART skills and improved in acting-out behavior while in custody. After release from Annsville, the ART group was significantly better in four of six of the areas tested than the control group. These areas included home and family, peer, legal, and overall. There were no differences between the groups in the areas of school or work (Goldstein, Glick, Reiner, Zimmerman, & Coultry, 1986).

ART has also been evaluated in a community-based setting. In this project the intervention was delivered in a post-release setting (the community) to both the offender and former family members. The researchers wanted to know whether the skills of ART could be learned outside an institutional setting and whether teaching family members those skills would enhance the program's effectiveness by providing a prosocial environment for the youth at home. The researchers noted that the recidivism among juveniles whose parents also received ART was lower than for juveniles who were trained without their families and those who received no training (Goldstein, Glick, Irwin, McCartney, & Rubama, 1989).

Goldstein and colleagues also evaluated an ART intervention as a part of the Gang Intervention Project in Brooklyn, New York. The researchers used this project to determine whether the prosocial environment created in the family might be duplicated in a peer group. The group chosen was the youth gang. Members of 12 different New York City gangs received ART. Only 13% of those who received ART were re-arrested during follow-up. This compared to 52% of those who received other services (Goldstein & Glick, 1998).

A fourth evaluation of ART was conducted at the Buckeye Youth Center. Juveniles in the custody of the Ohio Department of Youth Services received a combination of ART and an approach known as Positive Peer Culture (PPC). Recidivism rates were significantly lower for the ART/PPC group than for the no-treatment group (Leeman, Gibbs, Fuller, & Potter, 1991).

FAMILY INTERVENTION PROJECT

The Family Intervention Project (FIP) is a program designed to target gang members and their families. It was developed in Denver, Colorado, in response to a dramatic increase in youth gang activity. Finally, after a series of consultations with experts, authorities decided to develop an intervention that would address key issues of gang-affiliated youths through their biological families. Authorities believed that the family's central role in the socialization of children had laid the foundation for many individual gang members' problems. Consequently, they also believed that the family could be the central factor in correcting those problems (Branch, 1997).

The FIP program begins with a letter to the family of a juvenile inviting them to attend a program meeting. The entire family is invited and is expected

Table 8.4 Agenda for Family Intervention Project Meeting

Time	Activity
8:30–9:00 A.M.	Registration
9:00–10:00	Orientation by facilitator
10:00–10:15	Break
10:15–10:45	Individual work with "Black Delinquent Gang Youth Values"
10:45–11:30	Group work with "Black Delinquent Gang Youth Values"
11:30–12:00	Debrief morning exercises
12:00–1:15 P.M.	Lunch
1:15–1:30	Review morning activities
1:30–2:00	Threats to effective communication
2:00–2:30	Guidelines for effective communication
2:30–2:45	Break
2:45–3:15	Practice good communication
3:15–4:00	Work sessions for families
4:00–4:30	Summarize afternoon, plan for future

SOURCE: Branch, 1997

to participate. Practitioners use the reaction of the families to the letters, and to a metal-detecting scan at the entrance to the program site as clinical indicators of potential resistance to treatment.

Meetings are held at facilities provided by a sponsoring agency. That agency is well informed as to the goals of FIP, and has specific plans for the ongoing care of the juveniles and families following the meeting. At the meeting, the families participate in a series of structured activities that lead them from a discussion of why they have been invited to participate in the program through an examination of their systems of values, through work sessions on family communication and cooperation. The final session of the day involves planning the next steps the families will follow. In this session the agency sponsoring the FIP lays out strategies for building on gains made during that day's session. A copy of the agenda for the FIP meeting is included in table 8.4.

Follow-up work by the sponsoring agency may focus on continued communication, effective transmittal of values to children, and specific techniques of avoiding further gang involvement. Efforts may also be directed toward meeting the multiple needs of many of these families. It often involves referral to a mental health professional for one or more members.

Derek was a 14-year-old African-American male who had not yet joined a gang, but had engaged in several activities of a branch of the Crips. He freely admitted that he was ready to join the group. Derek and his family were invited to attend the FIP meeting by a local police officer, who suggested this as an alternative to an arrest for Derek. His family reluctantly agreed, denying Derek's gang involvement despite his clear testimony that he wanted to become a member.

When Derek, his parents, and his brother entered the agency hosting the meeting, they were shocked to see parents of children with clear gang tattoos, hairstyles, and attire displaying hostility at having to pass through a metal detector. Seeing the reactions of these parents, Derek's family became more aware of its own denial, and found themselves more receptive to the program by the time the meeting began.

The meeting began with a brief introduction and a "Why Are We Here?" exercise. One parent from another family showed notable difficulties in processing the information and was unable to remember why she was present and what the group hoped to accomplish. Clinicians at the meeting noted this difficulty for future intervention. Another family displayed clear problems of anger and resentment between its members. Again, practitioners noted these issues for future intervention.

A short break after the opening exercise was followed by a discussion and debriefing regarding the values of black delinquent gang members. Despite the fact that some of the families were not black, the exercise helped families understand similarities and differences between their values and those of gang members. It also provided a forum for the discussion of racial issues that were significant to some of the families.

After lunch the group reviewed the morning's activities and received training on good intrafamily communication. Following a mid-afternoon break, they participated in practice and work sessions to develop the skills they had been taught in the early afternoon. The meeting concluded with a summary of the day's activities and a session to plan each family's next steps. Case managers established visitation schedules for each family and began the process of referral to community agencies.

Derek and his family were favorably impressed with the day. They agreed that they had learned new things about one another and about youth gangs. They also felt they had learned new and better ways to communicate. Derek agreed not to join the Crips and to participate in the case management program.

Characteristics of Successful Intervention

The FIP is actually a single component of a larger intervention, yet it is a focused and very important component. As such, it meets some of the criteria for effective intervention mentioned in earlier chapters. When combined with effective follow-up that includes comprehensive service delivery, it can meet even more criteria.

Theoretical Basis FIP uses both family systems and social learning theory. It uses *family systems theory* in that it views the family and the forces that impact its members individually and collectively as primary in shaping and maintaining the behavior of the family's members. It therefore addresses its intervention to the family unit. It uses social learning theory in that it uses modeling, role play, and positive reinforcement in its training sessions.

Structure The activities of the program meeting are highly structured. The degree to which the follow-up is structured depends on the planning and activities of the sponsoring agency. Some structure during follow-up is provided (although not imposed by the program) when families make use of the communication and management techniques they have learned. Follow-up supervision by the case manager can help to provide needed structure.

Comprehensiveness FIP is not, in itself, comprehensive, but when combined with effective case management and aftercare activities it can be. The program meeting focuses only on family issues, and time constraints probably prevent even all those issues from being addressed. Effective aftercare can address individual issues as well as those in other social systems.

Outcome Evaluations

At the time of this writing the authors were able to locate no structured outcome studies of FIP. Anecdotal evidence and several case studies are reported by Branch (1997). He offers four observations made by the agencies who have sponsored FIP meetings. One reports that it helps his agency make an early assessment of which families have the skills and willingness to be involved in intervention. A second feels that the meetings with other parents enhance the therapeutic characteristics of those meetings. The third believes that the mandatory appearance of all family members presents diagnostic and therapeutic opportunities that often do not exist in other settings and systems. The fourth notes that the FIP meeting provides an opportunity for a struggling family to try to be a successful family while showing them that they are not alone in their struggle.

Branch also offers several case studies. In one he describes the clinical benefit the group received from a parent who was unwilling to participate. The mother was so persistent and demonstrative in her resistance that other program participants tried to quiet her and her own children actually moved to another part of the room. Other participants saw their own resistance played out before their eyes, and reported that their own attitude and willingness to participate improved as a result. In another vignette, Branch describes a middle-class family that resists program participation, wanting to hire its own attorney and therapist. Eventually they attend and benefit from seeing other families with problems similar to their own as well as from the discussions of racial and ethnic issues during the meeting.

INTENSIVE AFTERCARE PROGRAM

The Intensive Aftercare Program (IAP) offered by the OJJDP is actually a model from which other programs can be designed. It uses risk-based assessment and intervention, directing its services through intensive case management. It considers multiple risk factors, and, for this reason, also considers many of the social systems in the youth's environment.

The IAP is intended to provide guidelines for juveniles leaving residential programs. With minor modifications, however, it can be adapted for use with delinquent juveniles who have not yet been in a program or those who are at risk. Programs using its guidelines are currently being evaluated by OJJDP-sponsored organizations across the country. Other practitioners have used it to develop programs not sponsored by the OJJDP. For example, one of the authors used the model extensively to develop Community Reintegration through Environmental Assessment, Treatment, and Evaluation (CREATE) (Ellis, 1997), an aftercare program for a juvenile boot camp, and the Truancy Intervention and Prevention Program (TRIPP) (Ellis, 1998).

The IAP was developed through a four-step process supported by the OJJDP and implemented by the Johns Hopkins University Institute for Policy Studies and the Division of Criminal Justice at California State University in Sacramento. It was conceived as four stages: (1) assessing programs in operation, programs being developed, and relevant scientific literature; (2) developing and publishing program models and policies and procedures; (3) preparing materials for training and technical assistance for practitioners to use in developing programs; and (4) testing the model and materials by implementing them in selected areas. Four documents were submitted to the OJJDP. The publications are *Intensive Aftercare for High-Risk Juveniles: An Assessment* (Altschuler & Armstrong, 1990); *Intensive Aftercare for High-Risk Juveniles: A Community Care Model* (Altschuler & Armstrong, 1994a); *Intensive Aftercare for High-Risk Juveniles: Policies and Procedures* (Altschuler & Armstrong, 1994b); and *Intensive Community-based Aftercare Programs: Training Manual for Action Planning Conference* (Altschuler & Armstrong, 1992). At least two of these are currently available from that agency. The discussion in this chapter is based on those documents.

Because IAP is a model, the features of an IAP-based program can vary between jurisdictions. For example, in one area services might be delivered completely by state agencies. In others, the program might be operated by a consortium of providers. The basic characteristics of a program built on the IAP model, however, would be the same. We'll talk about three characteristics here.

The first basic characteristic is community commitment and involvement. The OJJDP recommends the development of a steering committee that includes representatives from juvenile justice, child welfare, and the private providers that work with children in the area to be served by the IAP. To be effective the program needs support that is comprehensive (including a sufficient number of stakeholders) and authoritative (has sufficient support by the decision-makers in each organization).

A second vital characteristic is overarching case management. This means that comprehensive services are delivered, brokered, and managed by a practitioner or team of practitioners. The team actually begins to work with the juvenile during confinement and continues until his release from supervision. It provides not only counseling and other social services, but also monitoring and surveillance.

Overarching case management includes careful use of assessment, classification, and selection. This ensures that the juvenile's strengths and weaknesses are well known and can be considered in intervention planning. It also ensures that only juveniles who are appropriate for this intervention are included in the caseloads. Juveniles with special needs requiring more specialized intervention can be referred elsewhere.

Case managers use individualized case planning that incorporates the family and the community. This means that the juvenile is not viewed or treated as an isolated individual. Rather, she is a part of a family and community where needs exist that can be met and strengths exist that can be utilized.

Overarching case management also uses a mix of intensive surveillance and services. Accountability is ensured through regular visitation, telephone contact, and communication with significant others. Sufficient support is ensured through ready availability of the case manager and accessibility of adequate services.

Case managers employ incentives and consequences that are clearly in response to specific behaviors that are outlined in the terms of the juvenile's supervision. Both incentives and consequences are graduated; that is, they intensify as behavior intensifies. The conditions of the youth's supervision are also clear, so that the expectations for his behavior are clear and realistic.

Some services may be provided directly by the case manager. Others are brokered to community resources. Juveniles are also carefully linked to community social networks where they can make new friends and become involved in prosocial activities.

Aftercare begins when confinement begins. Case managers meet with the youth during his incarceration to begin assessment and identification of community resources. They may also meet with the family, school personnel, and other significant persons. Youths may meet with persons who will be involved in aftercare during furloughs from the institutions in which they are incarcerated.

The third basic characteristic of the model is effective oversight and evaluation. The principles and practices of the model must be employed consistently and continuously. To ensure that case managers and other personnel are doing their jobs properly, a strong management system must be in place. This management system must incorporate effective evaluation to provide input on adjustments to program or personnel as they become necessary.

The IAP is based on five principles of programmatic action. These principles incorporate at least two of the ideas of restorative justice, focusing on offender competence and community safety. The five principles of programmatic action are listed in table 8.5.

An example of a youth in an aftercare program based on IAP is Allen, a 17-year-old white male who was disposed to secure residential placement for his participation in a series of armed robberies. During his orientation on the first day of his placement, Allen was introduced to Terry, his aftercare counselor. Despite the fact that Allen was scheduled to remain in the facility for at least six months, Terry explained that she would meet with him at least twice per week during his confinement. One of those times would be with the placement staff; the other would be with her aftercare team. She described some of the purposes of their meetings, including assessment, planning, and arranging meetings with those who would participate in aftercare. She told Allen that she would also be meeting with his family, teachers, and other persons who were important to him. She gave Allen a chance to ask questions, then told him when they would next meet.

Allen next saw Terry in his first treatment team meeting, three days after he entered the facility. As the team talked with Allen, it was clear that she knew a great deal about him already. When he asked how she knew so many things,

Table 8.5 Five Principles of Programmatic Action

Five principles of programmatic action requisite to the IAP model embody its theoretical assumptions and the empirical evidence regarding the multiple causes of and behavioral changes associated with repeat offenders.

1. Preparing youth for progressively increased responsibility and freedom in the community
2. Facilitating youth-community interaction and involvement
3. Working with both the offender and targeted community support systems (e.g., families, peers, schools, employers) on qualities needed for constructive interaction and the youth's successful community adjustment
4. Developing new resources and supports where needed
5. Monitoring and testing the youth and the community on their ability to deal with each other productively

she responded that she had read his records from school, law enforcement, juvenile justice, and substance abuse and mental health providers. She had also met with his family. She explained that this was only a beginning, and that she was interested in getting to know him through conversations as well.

Terry and Allen met privately the next Monday. Their session lasted a little over an hour, and consisted mostly of light conversation about Allen's role in the robberies and some of his past legal problems. They also talked about some of the things Allen enjoyed doing and about what he hoped to do after graduation from high school. At the end of the meeting Terry explained that in their next private meeting they would begin the assessment process. During this meeting she would ask Allen some questions and would ask him to complete a couple of forms. She explained that these forms would be questionnaires that would help her determine what kind of help he would need to be successful when he returned home.

Over the next six months Terry met regularly with Allen. After several meetings, she introduced the other two members of her treatment team, Bev and Mark. They also met regularly with his family, and initiated both family counseling and parent training. Together, the three began to structure a new world for Allen after graduation. They identified agencies that could help him with his schoolwork and others that would help him arrange employment. They planned recreational programs for him and his family. They visited his neighborhood and his school to determine what areas he should avoid following his release.

Shortly before Allen's release date, the team met with Allen and his family to discuss the plans for his release. They developed a plan including weekly activity scheduling, ongoing individual and family counseling, after-school tutoring, and a series of recreational activities. Everyone agreed to the plan. Terry presented it to the judge, who approved both the plan and Allen's release.

After Allen returned home the team met with the family weekly to plan Allen's schedule and to decide which family member would be available at what times to monitor his activities. They introduced Allen to the staff at the local recreation center and took him to the community service site where he would perform several hours of service. Over the next six months the team continued regular visits and provided ongoing services to Allen and his family.

Several weeks before Allen's supervision was expected to end, Terry met with him to develop a termination plan, a strategy that Allen could use to maintain the progress he had made while in state custody. They presented the plan to the judge, who approved it, and terminated Allen's supervision. Allen and his family received follow-up phone calls at three-, six-, and twelve-month intervals. They reported that Allen had not re-offended, that he had graduated from high school, and was planning to enter college.

Characteristics of Successful Intervention

The IAP has many of the characteristics of successful intervention discussed in chapter 6. As with the other interventions in this chapter, we will focus on three characteristics: theory, structure, and comprehensiveness. As you will see, the IAP meets each of these criteria.

Theoretical Basis The IAP is based on an integration of three theories of delinquency: social control, strain, and social learning theories. *Social control theory* states that weak bonding with conventional structure in the community causes the juvenile to feel a sense of separation and alienation. This alienation leads to delinquent acts on the part of the youth. Strain and social learning theories were both discussed in earlier chapters.

The IAP uses social control theory. It attempts to restructure the offender's world into an environment that will provide positive modeling and appropriate reinforcement for prosocial behaviors. Social learning principles are also used in counseling sessions and in training meetings. It uses *strain theory* in that case managers attempt to create opportunities for their clients to succeed in conventional settings. New opportunities diminish strain and the resulting frustration that contributed to delinquent behavior.

Practitioners try to improve family relationships and develop new relationships with supportive, prosocial community members. This provides the social bonding needed to maintain prosocial behavior.

Structure The IAP is highly structured, using intensive intervention and supervision to ensure that the youth complies with and recognizes the value of scheduling and planning. Daily and weekly activities are planned, including recreational and free time. Various resources, including the family and members of the community, are used to monitor activities.

Comprehensiveness The IAP is clearly comprehensive, since it is designed to meet multiple needs in multiple areas of the juvenile's life. Comprehensive planning begins with thorough and ongoing assessment while the juvenile is incarcerated. It continues as comprehensive intervention as the case manger or service team builds a treatment program that will address all those needs (and use the juvenile's strengths) in the community.

Outcome Evaluations

The OJJDP has not yet published any outcome studies of its IAP programs. Several factors argue for its success, however. These factors include its strong foundation in theory and successful practice and the degree to which it includes the characteristics of successful intervention. You may also have noticed that it has many similarities to MST and other successful interventions based on intensive case management. The model is clearly a useful tool for developing an aftercare program.

SUMMARY

In this chapter we have reviewed several successful or promising programs for juvenile justice clients. We talked about how each program works and gave a hypothetical case study to help illustrate each one. We also discussed some of the characteristics of effective intervention of each program and reviewed some of the published outcome studies.

In the next chapter, we'll take a look at evaluation. We can't make you an expert in professional evaluation in a single chapter, but we provide you with the tools you need to measure the improvement of your clients in a meaningful way. The chapter should also help you understand more of the research articles you find when you use the techniques for locating effective interventions described in chapter 6.

ACTIVITIES FOR LEARNING

1. In a small group, discuss the section of chapter 8 that summarizes MST. The text discusses only its application of system theory, yet it clearly uses other theories of delinquency explained in this book. In your group, identify some of those theories of delinquency. Explain how MST uses those theories in intervention planning and implementation. Present your results to the class.

2. In a small group, discuss the section of chapter 8 that summarizes VOM. As with MST, the text discusses only its use of one theory, yet it may use other theories of delinquency explained in this book. In your group, identify some of those theories. Explain how MST uses those theories in intervention planning and implementation. Do the same for the other programs described in this chapter.

3. Obtain the literature on VOM and the balanced and restorative approach (BARA) offered by the OJJDP. (Hint: the techniques for obtaining this literature are discussed in chapter 6.) Read the literature to answer the following questions. How does VOM fit into the philosophies of the BARA? How

does it fit (and not fit) the philosophies of retributive justice? What advantages does VOM offer over retributive justice? What are its disadvantages?

4. Obtain and read the book *Clinical Interventions with Gang Adolescents and Their Families* (Branch, 1997). The book reviews the FIP. Read chapter 2 on developmental aspects of gang membership. How does the intervention proposed by Branch address these developmental aspects? How might it address them more effectively?

5. Watch newspaper articles about juvenile justice over a period of several weeks. What delinquent acts are reported in the press? What kinds of problems do the youths who commit these acts appear to have? What kind of intervention might be useful for them? Make a scrapbook containing the articles and your response to each.

6. Obtain a copy of your state's statute regarding the treatment of juvenile justice clients. Which of the interventions in this chapter would the statute allow? Which would it not allow? What kinds of changes would need to be made to implement the intervention?

QUESTIONS FOR DISCUSSION

1. Which of the programs discussed in this chapter does your community need the most? Why? Which do you think would work best? Why? If you decided to start the program in your area, how might it be funded?

2. The early chapters of this book discussed prevention technologies. Which interventions in chapter 8 use those technologies? Which do not? How might prevention technologies be incorporated into the interventions that do not use them already?

3. Think of a juvenile you have known who has gotten into trouble. What kinds of social skills, if any, was that youth lacking? What skills did she have? Which units of the PREPARE Curriculum might have been beneficial to the juvenile?

4. What schools in your area might benefit from a FAST program? What agencies could be involved? How would you get the program started?

5. Each of the summaries in this chapter contains a brief discussion of how the program uses the characteristics of effective intervention outlined in chapter 6. The discussions include only two or three of the characteristics for each intervention. Some programs may meet more of the criteria. Look at the list of characteristics provided in chapter 6. Now review each intervention in chapter 8. Which characteristics does each intervention possess? Which does it not possess? How might other intervention modules be added to increase comprehensiveness?

6. Suppose that your community had an effective case management program, but was lacking a social skills training program to which case managers could refer. What steps would you take to start such a program? Where would the meetings be conducted? How would the juveniles who would be included be selected? What juveniles would be excluded, if any? Why? How would you ensure that all the selected juveniles could actually get to the meetings?

KEY TERMS AND DEFINITIONS

Family stress theory Theory of deviant behavior that suggests that families have a series of beliefs about their capacity to deal with stress that are based on their available resources and their actual experienced stressors. Members of families that lack resources and believe themselves incapable of dealing with stressors are more likely to behave in deviant ways.

Family systems theory Theory derived from systems theory that focuses on the family as the central and most important social system in determining the behavior of its members.

School-based intervention Intervention that occurs at school and includes components focused on school-related activities.

Skill maintenance The ability of a juvenile who has gained a set of skills and has learned to use them in the natural environment to continue to use those skills over an extended period of time.

Skill transfer The ability to use new skills learned in a training setting in the "real" world outside that setting.

Social control theory Theory of human behavior that suggests that when an individual's level of bonding with conventional society is low, deviance may result.

Social ecology theory Theory of human behavior that views the individual as an integral part of several layers of interrelated social systems. The behavior of the individual is influenced by the systems, and the behavior of the systems is influenced by the individual.

Strain theory Theory of human behavior that suggests that deviance is a product of the frustration experienced by those whose opportunities to improve themselves and their situations are blocked by inequities in society.

REFERENCES

Altschuler, D. M., & Armstrong, T. L. (1990). *Intensive aftercare for high-risk juveniles: An assessment.* Washington, DC: Office of Juvenile Justice and Delinquency Prevention.

Altschuler, D. M., & Armstrong, T. L. (1992). *Intensive community-based aftercare programs: Training manual for action planning conference.* Washington, DC: Office of Juvenile Justice and Delinquency Prevention.

Altschuler, D. M., & Armstrong, T. L. (1994a). *Intensive aftercare for high-risk juveniles: A community care model.* Washington, DC: Office of Juvenile Justice and Delinquency Prevention.

Altschuler, D. M., & Armstrong, T. L. (1994b). *Intensive aftercare for high-risk juveniles: Policies and procedures.* Washington, DC: Office of Juvenile Justice and Delinquency Prevention.

Branch, C. W. (1997). *Clinical interventions with gang adolescents and their families.* Boulder, CO: Westview Press.

Bronfenbrenner, U. (1979). *The human development: Experiments by nature and design.* Cambridge, MA: Harvard University Press.

Ellis, R. A. (1997). *Community reintegration through environmental assessment, transformation, and evaluation (CREATE).* Ft. Lauderdale, FL: Broward Sheriff's Office.

Ellis, R. A. (1998). *Truancy intervention and prevention program (TRIPP).* Ft. Lauderdale, FL: Broward Sheriff's Office.

Flaten, C. (1996). Victim offender mediation: Application with serious offenses committed by juveniles. In B. Galaway and J. Hudson (Eds.), *Restorative justice: International perspectives* (pp. 387–402). Monsey, NY: Criminal Justice Press.

Goldstein, A. P. (1990). *The PREPARE curriculum.* Champaign, IL: Research Press.

Goldstein, A. P., & Glick, B. (1994). *The prosocial gang: Implementing aggression replacement training.* Thousand Oaks, CA: Sage.

Goldstein, A. P., & Glick, B. (1998). Aggression replacement training: Development, procedures, and efficiency evaluations. In A. R. Roberts (Ed.), *Juvenile justice: Policies, programs, and services* (2nd ed., pp. 312–326). Chicago: Nelson-Hall.

Goldstein, A. P., Glick, B., Irwin, M. J., McCartney, C., & Rubama, I. (1989). *Reducing delinquency: Intervention in the community.* New York: Pergamon Press.

Goldstein, A. P., Glick, B., Reiner, S., Zimmerman, D., & Coultry, T. (1986). *Aggression replacement training.* Champaign, IL: Research Press.

Goldstein, A. P., & Kanfer, F. H. (1979). *Maximizing treatment gains: Transfer enhancement in psychotherapy.* New York: Academic Press.

Henggeler, S. W. (1993). Multisystemic treatment of serious juvenile offenders: Implications for the treatment of substance-abusing youth. *National Institute on Drug Abuse Research Monograph 137* (DHHS Pub. No. [ADM]88-1523). Washington, DC: U.S. Government Printing Office.

Henggeler, S. W., & Borduin, C. M. (1990). *Family therapy and beyond: A multisystemic approach to treating the behavior problems of children and adolescents.* Pacific Grove, CA: Brooks/Cole.

Henggeler, S. W., Melton, G. B., & Smith, L. A. (1992). Family preservation using multisystemic therapy: An alternative to incarcerating serious juvenile offenders. *Journal of Consulting and Clinical Psychology, 60*(6), 953–961.

Henggeler, S. W., Schoenwald, S. K., Borduin, C. M., Rowland, M. D., & Cunningham, P. B. (1998). *Multisystemic treatment of antisocial behavior in children and adolescents.* New York: Guilford Press.

Hill, R. (1958). Social stresses on the family: Generic features of families under stress. *Social Casework, 39,* 139–158.

Karoly, P., & Steffen, J. J. (1980). *Improving the long-range effects of psychotherapy.* New York: Gardner.

Leeman, L. W., Gibbs, J. C., Fuller, D., & Potter, G. (1991). *Evaluation of a multicomponent treatment program for juvenile delinquents.* Department of Psychology, Ohio State University.

McDonald, L. (1997). *Families and schools together: Final report for CSAP Grant #3699* (1991–1996). Madison, WI: Family Service.

McDonald, L., & Sayger, T. V. (1998). Impact of a family and school based prevention program on protective factors for high risk youth. *Drugs and Society, 12*(1/2), 61–85.

Niemeyer, M., & Schichor, D. (1996). A preliminary study of a large victim offender reconciliation program. *Federal Probation, 60*(3), 30–34.

Nugent, W., & Paddock, J. (1996). Evaluating the effects of a victim-offender reconciliation program on re-offense. *Research on Social Work Practice, 6*(2), 155–178.

Nugent, W., Umbreit, M., Wiinamaki, L., & Paddock, J. (in press). Participation in victim-offender mediation and re-offense: Successful replications? *Research on Social Work Practice.*

Office of Juvenile Justice and Delinquency Prevention (OJJDP). (1995). *Guide for implementing the balanced and restorative justice model.* Washington, DC: Author.

Price, M. (1998). *The mediation of a drunk driving death: A case development study* [On-line]. Victim-Offender Reconciliation Program Information and Resource Center. Available: www.vorp.com/articles/art.html.

Quay, H. C., & Peterson, D. R. (1987). *Manual for the revised behavior problem checklist.* Coral Gables, FL: University of Miami, Department of Psychology.

Roy, S. (1993). Two types of juvenile restitution programs in two Midwestern counties: A comparative study. *Federal Probation, 57*(4), 48–53.

Umbreit, M. S. (1993). Crime victims and offenders in mediation: An emerging area of social work practice. *Social Work, 38,* 69–73.

Umbreit, M. S. (1994). *Victim meets offender: The impact of restorative justice and mediation.* Monsey, NY: Criminal Justice Press.

Umbreit, M. S., & Greenwood, J. (1998). *National survey of victim offender mediation programs in the United States.* Washington, DC: Office of Victims of Crime, U.S. Department of Justice.

Wiinamaki, L. A. (1997). *Victim-offender reconciliation programs: Juvenile property offender recidivism and severity of re-offense in three Tennessee counties.* Unpublished doctoral dissertation, University of Tennessee, Knoxville.

Chapter 9

♦

An Evaluation Primer

CHAPTER OUTLINE

Single-Subject Design
Outcome Evaluation
Summary

As we have seen in earlier chapters, it is very important to be able to test the effectiveness of any intervention. Only by carefully examining the results of an intervention can we determine whether a youth is ready for release from custody. Similarly, only when we look at the effects of interventions across large groups can we determine whether that intervention is likely to be effective for other juveniles.

The process of testing interventions for individuals is called single-subject design. The process of testing the effectiveness of interventions for larger groups is known as outcome evaluation. Single-subject designs are relatively simple and easy to use with clients. Some kinds of outcome evaluations, on the other hand, require extensive planning, professional design, and complex statistical analysis. Other kinds do not require this degree of rigor, and can be easily used by any practitioner. This chapter focuses on the evaluations that are relatively easy to use: single-subject designs and outcome evaluations that can be performed by the field practitioner.

The fact that these evaluations can be conducted with relative ease does not mean that they should be conducted carelessly or haphazardly. It is important that practitioners carefully plan how they will measure and track the progress of each client. In this chapter we will learn basic guidelines on how to plan and conduct these two types of evaluations. We'll begin by reviewing the basic principles of single-subject design. We'll include a look at a case study in which an imaginary therapist, Franklin, uses this method to track an imaginary client through an intervention. Next, we'll discuss outcome evaluation, the method used to study the effectiveness of interventions with groups of clients. We'll end the chapter with a case study of a hypothetical outcome evaluation.

The sections at the end of the chapter, particularly the "Activities for Learning," will be helpful in learning to use evaluation techniques. Additional books are mentioned in the text that can help you use these techniques. The book by the United Way, *Measuring Program Outcomes,* will likely be very helpful in learning to do the kind of program evaluation discussed here.

SINGLE-SUBJECT DESIGN

As was indicated above, *single-subject design* is an evaluation method that allows the practitioner to track the progress of individual clients. Since it records results for only one person, it cannot be used to determine what might work for other clients. It can only be used to determine whether specific target behaviors for individual youths have gotten better, gotten worse, or remained the same. These designs are called single subject because there is only one person (the subject) being studied. They are called designs because specific patterns (designs) are followed in their execution.

Single-subject designs are easy to construct and require very little time to execute. They can be used by the practitioner, shared with the client and his family, and used in court to help the judge gauge the youth's progress. They can also provide important clinical insight regarding outside factors that influence the juvenile. Table 9.1 includes a checklist for performing single-subject design.

Using Single-Subject Design

The first step in single-subject design is identifying and defining the problem to be targeted. Identifying refers to picking a *behavior* that can be described in such a way that it is clear to both the juvenile and others exactly what the behavior is. The behavior should have three characteristics: (1) it should be something that will help the youth toward her goal; (2) it should be a behavior that can reasonably be expected to be affected within the period of the youth's supervision; and (3) it should be measurable or definable (Bloom, Fischer, & Orme, 1995; Tripodi, 1994).

"Defining" a behavior refers to the process of describing that behavior so that it cannot be mistaken for any other behavior. When a behavior is adequately defined, it is possible to observe the frequency (how often), intensity (how strongly), and duration (over what period of time) with which it occurs. If frequency, intensity, or duration can be accurately observed, the practitioner can determine whether the identified problem is increasing, decreasing, or staying the same (Bloom et al., 1995).

The process of identification and definition can be illustrated with the example of an overly aggressive youth, Billy. Because it would be desirable to decrease the number of fights in which Billy participates, the identified behavior might be fighting. By properly defining "fight," then observing Billy's behavior, the practitioner could determine whether the frequency of Billy's fights was changing.

Table 9.1 Checklist for Single-Subject Design

_____ Identify the problem to be addressed
_____ Define the problem
_____ Decide how the problem will be measured
_____ Obtain baseline information
_____ Make a daily behavior log
_____ Make a weekly progress graph
_____ Collect data from client on a regular basis
_____ Discuss the implications of your findings with the client

Different people might view the term "fight" in various ways. For example, suppose that the judge in Billy's case thinks that the youth should never have a disagreement with anyone. The judge might consider any disagreement a fight. The case manager, on the other hand, might think that angry disagreements are not fighting, so long as no one raises his voice. To her, if Billy speaks loudly and in a threatening manner to someone, that constitutes a fight. Billy might not consider any confrontation a fight unless punches are traded. Given these very different perspectives on what constitutes a fight, no one is likely to be satisfied with the results. Further, no one would really know whether the frequency of Billy's fighting had decreased.

The problems involved in defining fighting illustrate the factors that must be considered when developing an adequate definition. First, the definition might include frequency, intensity, or duration (Tripodi, 1994). *Frequency,* as we discussed above, refers to how often a behavior occurs—for example, the number of fights each week. *Intensity* refers to the strength with which it occurs—for example, yelling versus pushing or pushing versus hitting. *Duration* is not a measure of the fights themselves, since measuring how long fights lasted might tell more about the development of Billy's brawling skills than about the effectiveness of the intervention. Rather, duration measures the length of time Billy stays angry after having a disagreement with someone. This could tell the practitioner how much improvement Billy is making on his anger management skills.

A second consideration in problem definition lies in making that definition sufficiently specific to exclude other behaviors (Bloom et al., 1995). This issue was discussed above when we compared the judge's definition of fighting to that of the practitioner and the juvenile. This need for clarity is one reason that it is easier to monitor behavioral events rather than perceptions or attitudes. Physical contact is a very clear indicator of aggression. Billy's answers to questions about how close he came to striking someone are likely to be much less clear.

Another issue in the development of a single-subject design is how the behavior will be observed (Bloom et al., 1995). In other words, after the behavior has been identified and defined, the practitioner must decide how she will know when it has occurred. There are three options for observing juvenile behaviors: (1) asking the juvenile whether it occurred (self-report), (2) asking significant others whether it occurred (report by significant other), and (3) reviewing school and police records (official records). Each of these methods has strengths and each has weaknesses.

Self-report is frequently used by juvenile justice practitioners. To use self-report the practitioner simply asks the juvenile how many times the behavior has occurred during a given period (often one week). The results for that week can then be compared to the results for previous weeks.

Self-report has a clear advantage. It accesses the only source of information that would know about every time the behavior occurred, the juvenile. For instance, Billy might fight in any one of several settings: home, school, the park, on the school bus. Only Billy would be present in each of those settings, and only Billy would know whether a fight occurred in each.

The two greatest weaknesses of self-report are that the juvenile might forget instances in which the behavior occurred, or might lie about them. The possibility of forgetting about instances of the behavior can be minimized by providing the juvenile with a daily behavior log (DBL) such as the one illustrated in figure 9.1. The youth is instructed to complete the log at the end of each day. The possibility that a youth will lie can be reduced by occasionally asking other sources, such as parents or teachers, whether their numbers agree with those of the youth.

Report by significant others (i.e., teachers, parents, siblings, social program staff, and others) has the advantages of a greater likelihood of accuracy. This is only true, however, if the reporter has no personal reason to either underreport or overreport instances of the targeted behavior. For example, a parent who wants the youth out of the home might overreport. A sibling who is afraid of retribution might underreport.

Official records usually contain an accurate account of the times behaviors have come to the attention of authorities. Unfortunately, many problem behaviors do not come to the attention of authorities. This often results in underreporting. Observation through official records is often most useful when the behavior being monitored occurs only within a specific setting, such as a classroom.

It is important to remember that single-subject design can also be used to monitor behaviors that need to be maintained or increased. Suppose that a part of Billy's treatment plan is to encourage more responsibility in helping his mother around the house. Instances of taking out the garbage or cutting the grass might be monitored. Similarly, instances of completed homework assignments might be monitored to ensure that he completes his educational plan.

Measuring Attitudes or Emotions

Although behaviors are often easier to observe, it is sometimes important to measure a juvenile's attitude or emotion. For example, consider Tara, a 16-year-old female who was arrested for shoplifting. Tara was referred to a psychologist by the judge, who suspected that she might be suffering from depression. The psychologist, a practitioner providing diagnostic and treatment services for the court, determined that Tara was experiencing moderate depression. The psychologist used the Beck Depression Inventory (BDI), a paper-and-pencil

FIGURE 9.1 Daily Behavior Log					
Days of Week	Week 1	Week 2	Week 3	Week 4	Total
Sunday					
Monday					
Tuesday					
Wednesday					
Thursday					
Friday					
Saturday					
Weekly total:					

instrument to determine how depressed Tara was at the time of the evaluation. He also decided to use the BDI on an ongoing basis to monitor the progress Tara made in therapy.

The BDI is one of many paper-and-pencil instruments available to practitioners. These instruments can be used for many purposes, including identifying severe psychopathology, measuring attitudes toward delinquent behavior, measuring family and peer relations, and assessing risk of specific behaviors (Bloom et al., 1995). Although some instruments can be used only by persons trained in psychometrics, others can be used by any practitioner. Examples of paper-and-pencil instruments were discussed chapter 4.

In order to use a paper-and-pencil instrument, the practitioner identifies an appropriate time and place for the juvenile to answer the questions. He then establishes a schedule during which it will be completed regularly. The instrument should be completed in a place that is as quiet and private as possible. The juvenile should be undisturbed, and should not be in a position to be influenced by anyone else. The first time the instrument is completed, the practitioner carefully explains why it is being used and how it will be used. In most cases, she will share the results with the youth, as will be described below under "Applying the Design Clinically." An example of a paper-and-pencil tool for measuring depression is included in figure 9.2. We need to emphasize that the tool in figure 9.2 has not been scientifically prepared; it is intended as an example only.

Establishing a Baseline

In order to determine whether a behavior has increased, decreased, or has remained the same, the practitioner must establish a baseline. A baseline is a record of the frequency, intensity, or duration of the targeted behavior before

---

**FIGURE 9.2   Sample Paper-and-Pencil Tool
                for Depression**

Please circle the number that best represents your thoughts and feelings.

	Always	Usually	Sometimes	Never
1. I feel very sad.	4	3	2	1
2. I don't eat very well.	4	3	2	1
3. I have problems sleeping.	4	3	2	1
4. I feel as though things will never get better.	4	3	2	1
5. I don't enjoy life.	4	3	2	1
6. I wish I were dead.	4	3	2	1
7. I wish I had never been born.	4	3	2	1
8. I don't have many friends.	4	3	2	1
9. I don't feel like doing much of anything.	4	3	2	1

---

the intervention began. When obtaining a baseline, there are three important factors to keep in mind. First, the practitioner must measure the same characteristic (frequency, intensity, or duration) of the behavior both during and after the baseline. For example, the practitioner would not want to record the frequency of Billy's fights during the baseline and the intensity of his angry thoughts during intervention (Bloom et al., 1995).

The second important factor to remember is that the periods of measurement for the baseline must remain the same during the intervention. In other words, if Billy reports the number of fights he had each week for the baseline, he should also report weekly totals (not daily) for the intervention (Tripodi, 1994).

The third important factor to remember is that behavior may vary over time depending on the circumstances. Billy might have been ill for several days during the previous week and had little opportunity for fighting. It is therefore important to acquire baseline data over a fairly extensive period. Many experts recommend a period of at least three to five weeks (Bloom et al., 1995).

It is sometimes difficult to acquire baseline information. One reason for this is that the practitioner cannot usually say to someone like Billy, "Just go out this week and have the number of fights you would usually have." Instead, she often must begin the intervention immediately. This requires her to acquire information using a technique known as a "retrospective baseline" (Bloom et al., 1995).

In a retrospective baseline, the juvenile is asked to re-create his activities of the last several weeks. For example, Billy might be asked to recall the number of fights he had over the past week, then the week prior, and then the week prior to that. The practitioner would record this information and use it to construct the baseline. If Billy had been incarcerated or in other unusual circumstances during the past week, he would be asked to remember the period prior to his incarceration. When official records are used, the baseline can often be constructed by reviewing records for the last several weeks. Similarly, when a

---

Box 9.1 Jennifer, A Hypothetical Client

Jennifer is a 16-year-old white female who was arrested for smoking marijuana. She has no other arrest record. She resides with both her parents and her younger sister in a middle-class neighborhood in a major metropolitan area.

Jennifer denies using any kind of drugs other than marijuana. Her initial urinalysis after her arrest was positive for cannabis, but negative for every other substance. Jennifer denies selling or transporting any kind of substance. When asked where she obtains the cannabis she smokes, she reports "from friends."

Jennifer reports using marijuana approximately one time per week. She says she smokes it when she feels "nervous and jittery" and gets "all worried about things." She reports that she first smoked cannabis at the age of 13.

Jennifer's parents and sister report that their home life is "good." Jennifer agrees, saying that she feels loved and accepted. Her family agrees, however, that Jennifer sometimes becomes difficult to talk to because she becomes "very nervous."

Jennifer's grades in school are good, and she has a satisfactory attendance record. She is involved in two extracurricular organizations: the Spanish and Drama Clubs. She reports that she likes school, but that she sometimes worries about her grades.

Jennifer has several close friends, none of whom use alcohol or drugs. She is acquainted with a group of girls that her parents refer to as "troublemakers." They believe that these are the teens from whom Jennifer obtains her cannabis.

---

report by a significant other is used, the significant other can be asked to recall the events of the last several weeks.

Jennifer, a hypothetical juvenile justice client, is described in box 9.1. Jennifer manifests many symptoms of anxiety, and it appears that her use of cannabis is due, at least in part, to her attempts to control that anxiety. One of the ways to treat Jennifer's use of cannabis would be by helping her overcome her anxiety. A practitioner, using a cognitive-behavioral intervention, might track both the frequency and intensity of her anxiety attacks during the course of a week. The practitioner might use both self-report (asking Jennifer about her anxiety) and report by significant others (asking her family). He might measure the frequency of Jennifer's anxiety by asking her to use a daily behavior log. He might measure intensity by asking her to rate her anxiety on a scale of 1 to 5.

Recording the Results

When using single-subject design with a client, it is important that the results be recorded clearly, and in a way that can be readily understood by both practitioner and client. This can be accomplished by graphing the results. In order to graph the results, a horizontal and a vertical line are drawn to form an L shape. The horizontal line is labeled according to the time intervals being used, and the vertical is labeled by the instances of the behavior (Bloom et al., 1995; Tripodi, 1994). In the case of Billy, the horizontal line would be broken into weeks. The vertical line would contain numbers representing the instances of

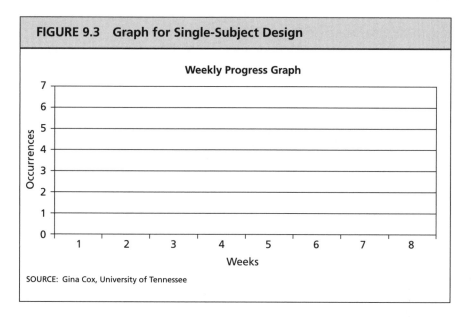

FIGURE 9.3   Graph for Single-Subject Design

Weekly Progress Graph

SOURCE: Gina Cox, University of Tennessee

fighting. The baseline would be separated from the intervention period by drawing a broken line across the horizontal (time) axis. The resulting graphic could be termed a weekly progress graph (WPG). A sample WPG is included in figure 9.3.

After collecting baseline data, the practitioner would mark the graph at the point indicating the number of behaviors for that week. If, for example, Billy had been in five fights three weeks before beginning the intervention, the practitioner would record that number on the graph. If he had four and six fights in the next two weeks respectively, the practitioner would mark those points accordingly. Weekly observation totals for the intervention period would be recorded in the same manner. See figure 9.4 for an example of a graph of Billy's first six weeks of intervention.

Applying the Design Clinically

A single-subject design provides more than a mechanism for determining intervention effectiveness. It can also be used clinically as a motivational and diagnostic tool. It can provide encouragement to the youth who believes she is not doing well and can help to identify collateral problems that affect the intervention (Bloom et al., 1995; Tripodi, 1994).

Single-subject design can be used clinically as a tool for encouragement or motivation. Frequently youths have an exaggerated idea of their performance in treatment, feeling that they are doing better or worse than they actually are. A graph showing their performance can be a reality check, helping them to see their actual progress and becoming the basis for planning revisions and strategies for the next step in intervention.

The graphs can also be used to identify collateral problems. Sometimes a juvenile will appear to be doing well, then will suddenly have a period of exacerbated problem behavior. This will appear on the graph as a sudden increase

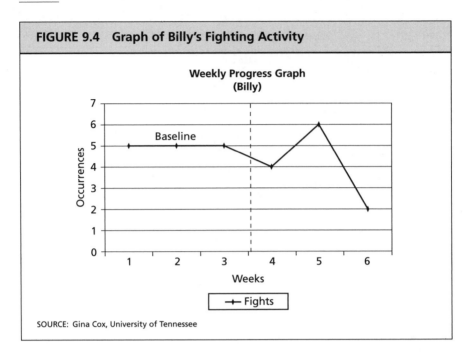

FIGURE 9.4 Graph of Billy's Fighting Activity

Weekly Progress Graph
(Billy)

Baseline

Occurrences

Weeks

Fights

SOURCE: Gina Cox, University of Tennessee

in the undesirable behavior. Alternatively, the youth's behavior might dramatically improve very suddenly.

When the pattern of behavior during an intervention takes a sudden turn for the better or the worse, it is important to find out why. A sudden change in behavior may indicate that something other than the intervention is having an effect. For example, if Billy has reduced his number of fights to one every three weeks, and suddenly has two weeks of very active fighting, there may be other factors involved. For instance, it might be that Billy's mother has a new boyfriend that Billy does not like or that he is having problems with a group of youths at school. Knowing that these problems were affecting Billy's behavior would allow the practitioner to craft an appropriate response.

If Billy's behavior suddenly improved, the practitioner might also suspect outside influences. Perhaps Billy has found an older person whom he respects and who is modeling and encouraging less aggressive behavior. Perhaps he has seen someone experience severe consequences from a fight and has decided that he does not wish to experience those consequences. Whatever the reason for the decrease in Billy's fighting, it may form the foundation for effectively revising the intervention.

Applying the Design Judicially

Single-subject design can also be used in the courtroom. When used properly, it is an excellent mechanism for informing the court of the progress of the juvenile. The graphs can be presented in the courtroom along with verbal and written explanations. When the judge uses a computer in her court, the graphics might also be provided on a diskette.

Communication is very important when single-subject design graphics are used in the courtroom. The judge must be clearly informed about the behavioral definitions that have been used and the meaning of any fluctuations in the data. The limitations of the design should also be described and references made to resources that can further the court's understanding of single-subject design, where needed.

Applying the Design in Interdisciplinary Meetings

Graphic presentations can also be very helpful in interdisciplinary meetings where future interventions for juveniles are planned. This can be important because various disciplines are trained to look at the problems of juveniles in different ways. For example, a psychiatrist may be inclined to look at repression of innate drives as the cause of a behavioral problem. Demonstrating that the problem has been corrected through good behavioral management may avoid many years of costly and unnecessary analysis. Alternatively, professionals from other disciplines may be able to apply your techniques to their own interventions. For example, educators at a committee meeting might be interested in what techniques you used to improve your client's behavior at home. A visual demonstration would provide them with opportunities to ask questions about your techniques of intervention. On the other hand, if your intervention is not working well, discussing the client's weekly progress using the graph as an aid might help another professional make useful suggestions about your next step with a client.

Limitations of Single-Subject Design

Single-subject design does have several limitations that are important for the practitioner to understand. First, although tracking behavioral patterns does allow the practitioner to determine when the client has improved, it does not provide clear answers about why he has improved. Many factors may work together to enhance or create the youth's progress. In single-subject design, it is impossible to control for all those factors. Therefore, the practitioner may be able to say that the client has improved, but never know whether it was her intervention that caused the improvement (Bloom et al., 1995).

A second limitation of single-subject evaluation is its *generalizability*. Generalizability refers to the ability to say that, because the intervention worked for one client, it can be expected to work for others. It is impossible to generalize from single-subject design for two reasons: (1) the practitioner cannot say with certainty that the intervention is what worked for the first client, and (2) it is impossible to know what differences between clients might affect the outcome of the intervention (Bloom et al., 1995).

A third limitation is imposed by the inability to know how accurate the data are. As we saw earlier, self-report, report by significant others, and official records all have limitations. If the information regarding the juvenile's behavior is not accurate, the design will not record changes in behavior; it will record changes in reporting or arrest rate.

Despite these limitations, single-subject design is a valuable tool for the juvenile justice practitioner. It can help to monitor the client's progress, allowing the practitioner to know when the client is doing well and when to revise the intervention. It can be used as a clinical and motivational tool with the juvenile. It can also serve as an effective reporting mechanism in court or at interdisciplinary meetings.

Case Study of a Single-Subject Design

Franklin is a therapist with the Youth Outreach Team (YOT), a program that provides in-home counseling to at-risk juveniles and their families. YOT's clients are referred by a local case management program. They, in turn, receive the referrals as a part of a diversionary effort by the local police department. The juveniles Franklin sees are typically under the age of 13 and have come to the attention of police departments by committing some status offense, usually running away from home or truancy.

Judy, one of Franklin's clients, has been referred to the program for frequent truancy. During the assessment Franklin discovers that Judy's grades have dropped significantly during the past year. She reports that she formerly enjoyed school, but since her grades have dropped she dislikes her classes. Franklin sends Judy for educational testing and discovers that she has a moderately high IQ and no learning disabilities. She is, however, almost two grade levels behind in her reading skills. When Franklin inquires about her study habits, Judy reports that she rarely does her homework. Her parents work in the evenings and her older sister allows her to watch television until bedtime.

Franklin schedules family counseling sessions to address the issue of Judy's homework time. He uses a cognitive-behavioral approach to make everyone more aware of and committed to Judy's need to complete her homework. Working with Judy and her family, he develops a plan in which the teen will devote two hours each day (from 4:00 P.M. to 6:00 P.M.) to school assignments. Her sister and parents agree to monitor her activities to ensure that the work is completed. Franklin also speaks with Judy's case manager about arranging a tutor two times each week.

Franklin believes that his plan will work. He is sure that he has identified a major barrier to school attendance, and has put a system in place that will remove that barrier. He needs to be certain, however, that the plan is followed. He decides to use single-subject design to monitor Judy's homework activities.

Working with Judy, Franklin develops a daily behavior log and a weekly progress graph (see figures 9.5 and 9.6). He establishes a baseline, teaches Judy how to track her daily results, and sets a time each week when they will meet to graph the results. He then arranges for Judy to present the results to her family.

The weekly progress graph shows that Judy had not done homework during any of the weeks prior to developing the plan. During the first three weeks of the plan, she did homework four, three, and four days, respectively. Beginning in the fourth week, she completed her homework every day for the next 10 weeks. Franklin verifies Judy's report with her teacher and finds that it is, in fact, accurate. The results of Judy's activity are reported in a weekly progress graph, shown in figure 9.6.

FIGURE 9.5   Daily Behavior Log for Judy

Days of Week	Week 1	Week 2	Week 3	Week 4	Total
Sunday					
Monday	X		X	X	3
Tuesday	X	X	X	X	4
Wednesday	X	X		X	3
Thursday	X		X	X	3
Friday		X	X	X	3
Saturday					
Weekly total:	4	3	4	5	16

FIGURE 9.6   Weekly Progress Graph for Judy

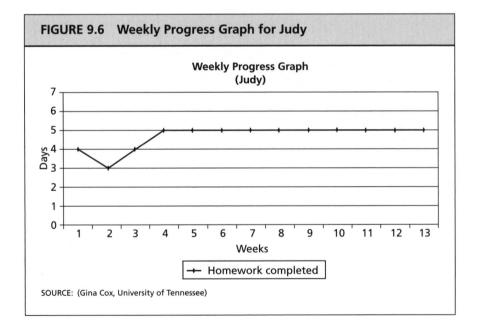

SOURCE: (Gina Cox, University of Tennessee)

The single-subject design has made it clear that Judy is following the plan. But Franklin must also be sure that the plan is having the overall effect of improving her grades. To be sure that Judy's grades are improving, he arranges weekly telephone conferences with her teacher. He discovers that her quiz grades have gone from Ds in the first week to Cs by the 10th week and Bs by the 16th week of intervention. The case manager has also been monitoring Judy's school attendance, and reports that she has not missed any classes since the third week of the intervention.

Franklin chose to monitor completed homework to test his intervention. He might have chosen several other variables to graph, such as attendance, grades, or reading skills. Alternatively, he might have tracked all these factors, providing a very comprehensive picture of the progress of the intervention.

Obviously, single-subject design was very helpful to Franklin and to Judy. At times, however, practitioners will want to look at effectiveness for groups rather than for individuals. As was mentioned earlier, this requires the use of a different method, outcome evaluation.

OUTCOME EVALUATION

Outcome evaluation (also called program evaluation) refers to a method of measuring the success of programs by looking at their effectiveness across groups of people. It is similar to single-subject design in that it uses many of the same techniques. It is different in that it uses larger numbers of subjects and more complex designs to allow the practitioner to make inferences about an intervention's effectiveness for groups of people similar to, but outside, the group being treated.

Some practitioners believe that a program evaluation must be conducted by a trained researcher. Professional expertise can certainly improve an evaluation and may be absolutely necessary at times. However, there are many occasions when, given the proper guidance, a practitioner can conduct his own outcome evaluation. The purpose of this section is to provide guidance in developing a basic program evaluation. First, we will review the ways in which many of the issues discussed in single-subject design apply to the larger process of outcome evaluation. Next, we will examine a step-by-step model of how to conduct an evaluation. Finally, we will review a case study of an evaluation of a hypothetical juvenile justice program. A checklist for outcome evaluation is also available in table 9.2. This may be useful to help remember the steps described in this chapter.

Deciding Whom to Include in the Study

The process of selecting which juveniles to include in the evaluation is known as sampling (Yegidis & Weinbach, 1996; Rubin & Babbie, 1997). It might seem the best alternative to simply include everyone who has been or will go through the program in the study, but this is often impractical. Practitioners often select a group that has been through the program over a pre-specified period of time, such as one year.

Using this sampling technique prevents the practitioner from making certain inferences about the intervention. Other techniques are available that use a process called *random sampling,* but practitioners often do not have control over who enters their program. A second process, *random assignment,* also strengthens a study, but is often impractical because it requires that some clients not receive the program's standard treatment. These two processes are often used by professional researchers to strengthen the results of their studies, but, for the

Table 9.2 Checklist for Successful Program Evaluation

_____ Identify the desired outcome
_____ Decide how the outcome will be measured
_____ Design a tool to use in collecting the data
_____ Design a code sheet for the data you will collect
_____ Collect the data
_____ Enter the data into a matrix
_____ Analyze the data
_____ Write up and report your results

reasons mentioned above, they are not commonly used by practitioners evaluating their own programs (Rubin & Babbie, 1997).

Getting Permission for the Study

State laws vary regarding the need to get the juvenile or parent to consent to be included in a group study. It is important to be aware of what the laws are in your jurisdiction. If permission is required, you should ask the teen or parent to complete an informed consent form. An example of this document is included in figure 9.7. You should discuss the purposes of your study with your client and assure them that the information will be kept confidential (Rubin & Babbie, 1997; Yegidis & Weinbach, 1996).

Confidentiality is an important issue for clients. To ensure that no one other than program staff has access to personal information, you may wish to assign each client an identification number. Both the client's name and identification number would appear in the client's treatment chart, but only the number would appear on the instrument used to collect outcome data. This ensures that any outsiders assisting with the evaluation (for instance, performing statistical analysis) do not know the names of the subjects.

Measuring Success

As with single-subject design, the first step in outcome evaluation is measurement. The practitioner must decide what he will use as a standard for success and how he will determine whether that standard has been met. This requires that the standard be identified and defined, just as in single-subject design. The practitioner must then decide what source he will use for gathering data and how the data will be recorded (Yegidis & Weinbach, 1996).

The identification and definition process is crucial to evaluation. If the desired outcome is not clearly defined, the evaluation is likely to be meaningless. Frequently, the standard for success in juvenile justice is recidivism, that is, instances of re-offense by the juvenile. Recidivism can be defined in many ways. Three of those options are (1) presence of offense or absence of an offense, (2) degree of offense, and (3) frequency of offense.

Presence or absence of offense refers to whether juveniles commit any delinquent acts during or after the intervention. The greatest strength of this definition is its simplicity. A youth either has or has not committed an offense. Its greatest weakness is that it lumps all offenses together. Consider the example

FIGURE 9.7   Sample Informed Consent Form

UNIVERSITY OF TENNESSEE

Office of Research, Compliance Section

SAMPLE INFORMED CONSENT FORM

(Include or exclude the following information as applicable)

INFORMED CONSENT STATEMENT
[List title of project here]

INTRODUCTION

State that participants are invited to participate in a research study. State the purpose/objectives of the study.

INFORMATION ABOUT PARTICIPANTS' INVOLVEMENT IN THE STUDY

List all procedures, preferably in chronological order, that will be employed in the study. Point out any procedures that are considered experimental. Clearly explain technical and medical terminology using nontechnical language. Explain all procedures using language that is appropriate for the expected reading level of your participants.

State the amount of time required of participants per session and for the total duration of study.

If audiotaping, videotaping, or film procedures are going to be used, provide information about the use of these procedures. (If applicable, please review the document entitled Videotape Guidelines.)

If you are plan to include children in your study, please review the document entitled Special Considerations for the Protection of Children Participating in UT-Sponsored Research.

The videotaping/film and child-participant consideration documents can also be obtained from the Compliances Section, 404 Andy Holt Tower.

RISKS

List all reasonably foreseeable risks, if any, of each of the procedures to be used in the study, and any measures that will be used to minimize the risks.

BENEFITS

List the benefits you anticipate will be achieved from this research, either to the participants, others, or the body of knowledge.

CONFIDENTIALITY

State that the information in the study records will be kept confidential. Data will be stored securely and will be made available only to persons conducting the study unless participants specifically give permission in writing to do otherwise. No reference will be made in oral or written reports which could link participants to the study.

_____ Participant's initials (place on the bottom front page of two-sided consent forms)

COMPENSATION (*If applicable to your study, add compensation information here*)

Indicate what participants will receive for their participation in this study. Indicate other ways participants can earn the same amount of credit or compensation. State whether participants will be eligible for compensation if they withdraw from the study prior to its completion. If compensation is pro-rated over the period of the participant's involvement, indicate the points/stages at which compensation changes during the study.

EMERGENCY MEDICAL TREATMENT

The University of Tennessee does not "automatically" reimburse subjects for medical claims or other compensation. If physical injury is suffered in the course of research, or for more information, please notify the investigator in charge (list PI name and phone number).

CONTACT INFORMATION

If you have questions at any time about the study or the procedures, (or you experience adverse effects as a result of participating in this study,) you may contact the researcher, [Name] , at [Office Address], and [Office Phone Number]. If you have questions about your rights as a participant, contact the Compliance Section of the Office of Research at (865) 974-3466.

PARTICIPATION

Your participation in this study is voluntary; you may decline to participate without penalty. If you decide to participate, you may withdraw from the study at anytime without penalty and without loss of benefits to which you are otherwise entitled. If you withdraw from the study before data collection is completed you data will be returned to you or destroyed.

[**Note:** Please delineate the "Consent" section of the Informed Consent Form by drawing a line across the page. This delineation is especially important when your consent form grammar shifts from second person to first person, as shown in this example.]

CONSENT

I have read the above information. I have received a copy of this form. I agree to participate in this study.

Participant's signature _____ Date _____

Investigator's signature _____ Date _____

Additional Notes to Investigators:

1. Researchers are urged by the Committee to use the wording in the checklist and follow the format in the sample, unless researcher supported reasons are provided for alternative wording. Use of alternative working or different format may slow down the review process. All sections of the consent form, except the "Consent Section" should be written in second person ("You are invited..."). Use of first person ("I") can be interpreted as suggestive and coercive.

2. Be sure to follow the directions for preparing the signature lines. Separate forms should be prepared when minors are used; one for the minors and one for the parents.

3. If your form is more than one page, there should be a line at the bottom of each page for the subject's initials, except for the last page where the signature is obtained.

4. Be sure to include any elements of informed consent that are appropriate to your study. If they apply to your study, they must be included. A listing on the basic elements of consent can be also obtained from the Compliances Section Office, 404 Andy Holt Tower (974-3466).

Compliance Section | OR Home | Human Subjects | Research Good News | UT Home Page

---

Comments or suggestions to Sandy Lindsey
at the Office of Research
at the University of Tennessee
Revised October 14, 1998

SOURCE: The University of Tennessee

of a juvenile who is placed in state custody because of an armed robbery. Following his treatment he does not commit any more violent crimes, but is arrested for shoplifting a package of chewing gum. The shoplifting arrest would be considered re-offense, indicating that the program had failed for this youth. In fact, although the juvenile did commit an offense after treatment, shoplifting is much less severe than armed robbery. The youth's treatment might be considered a success since the severity of his offense was reduced.

Another way to define recidivism is to group offenses according to severity. This helps solve the problems generated by the offense/no offense definition. In offense severity definition, status offenses, misdemeanors, felonies, and violent offenses might be grouped separately. Curfew violations would have the same weight as truancy. Robbery would be considered similar to assault. A curfew violation would be treated differently than would rape.

A third option for defining recidivism is by frequency of offense. That is, "How often does the youth commit a crime?" If the juvenile regularly ran away from home prior to treatment and runs away only once in three years after treatment, it would appear that the intervention was effective.

Obviously, measuring recidivism can be either a very simple or a very complex task. The most desirable alternative is to have information about presence of offense, severity of offense, and frequency of offense. However, collecting that amount of data is very complex and time consuming. It is usually more practical for the juvenile justice professional to consider all crimes (except, perhaps, status offenses) as recidivism and to simply count any criminal activity as recidivism.

Once the target problem has been defined, the practitioner must decide from what source he will collect the data. His options are the same as for single-subject design: (1) self-report, (2) report by significant others, and (3) official records. The strengths and weaknesses of each method were discussed in the section above. We will now discuss the kinds of questions that might be used to obtain data when using each method.

When using the self-report method, the juvenile may be interviewed or asked to complete a brief, written form. The types of questions asked would depend on the definition of recidivism being used.

To measure presence or absence of delinquency, the juvenile might be asked, "Have you done anything for which you might have been arrested since you started in this program?" The teen would then answer either "yes" or "no." To measure degree of delinquency, the practitioner might ask, "What kinds of delinquent behavior have you engaged in since you entered this program?" The youth's responses would be grouped into categories such as "none," "status offenses," "misdemeanors," and "felonies." To measure frequency of offense, the juvenile might be asked, "How many times have you shoplifted since you entered this program?" The youth might respond, "none," "once," "twice," "three times," and so on.

The practitioner would need to have some method of recording the juvenile's responses and preparing them for "coding," a process that we will discuss later. Responses are usually recorded on a questionnaire that is either used in an

---

**FIGURE 9.8 Sample Questionnaire for Presence
or Absence of Recidivism**

Identification number: _____

Date: _____

1. How old are you? _____

2. Indicate client's gender: _____ Male _____ Female

3. With which racial or ethnic group do you identify?
   _____ Caucasian
   _____ African American
   _____ Black, non-American
   _____ Hispanic
   _____ American Indian
   _____ Oriental
   _____ Other _____ (specify)

4. What is your family's annual income? _____
   (If the youth does not know this information it can be obtained from the
   client file.)

5. Have you committed any delinquent acts since you entered this program?

---

interview or completed by the youth. An example of an interview questionnaire to measure presence or absence of recidivism in several categories is shown in figure 9.8.

Similar techniques are used when data are collected from significant others. The nature of the questions and the way in which they are asked might vary depending on the source (parent, teacher, sibling). The basic process remains the same.

When collecting data from significant others, the practitioner prepares a questionnaire similar to the one described in the section above. When defining recidivism as presence or absence of offense, the practitioner might ask questions like, "To the best of your knowledge, has your child committed any delinquent acts since starting this program?" To measure degree of offense, he might ask, "What kinds of delinquent offenses has your child committed since beginning this program?" To determine offense frequency, the interviewer might ask, "How many times has your child committed each of the following offenses since entering this program: (1) skipping school, (2) running away from home, (3) other status offenses, (4) misdemeanors, (5) felonies?" A sample questionnaire for use with significant others is shown in figure 9.9.

The third method of collecting data is by reviewing official records. Potential sources of data include police records, juvenile assessment center records, school records, and court records. Official records reviews rarely include interviews. Rather, the practitioner usually prepares a questionnaire that he completes while viewing the youth's record. Questions are written similarly to those provided above, except that they are phrased in the third person. An example of a question used in official records data collection would be, "How

---

**FIGURE 9.9   Sample Questionnaire for Interviewing
                Significant Others (Parents)**

Identification number: _____

Date: _____

1. How old is your child? _____

2. Is your child male or female? _____ Male _____ Female

3. With which racial or ethnic group does your child identify?
   _____ Caucasian
   _____ African American
   _____ Black, non-American
   _____ Hispanic
   _____ American Indian
   _____ Oriental
   _____ Other _____ (specify)

4. What is your family's annual income? _____

5. To the best of your knowledge, has your child committed any delinquent
   acts since entering this program? _____ Yes _____ No

6. How has your child gotten along with the family since entering the program? _____ Better _____ Worse _____ About the same

7. How has your child done in school since entering the program?
   _____ Better _____ Worse _____ About the same

---

many times has the juvenile been arrested for possession of drugs since entering this program?" A sample questionnaire for reviewing official records is
shown in figure 9.10.

The way questions are written and asked is very important regardless of the
source of the data. The questions must be clearly written, concise, and should
be written at a level the interviewee can understand. Questions asked of older
teenagers might need to be rewritten to be used with children. Questions should
be asked in a nonthreatening, nonjudgmental manner to encourage honest
responses.

Other factors must be considered when writing questions for different
kinds of definitions. Questions should be written so that no other responses are
possible. This means that every possible response should be covered by the
question and that it should be possible to answer either "yes" or "no," but never
"maybe."

Collecting the Data

We discussed the concept of a baseline under single-subject design. Although
it is not usually referred to as "baseline," it is equally important to know the
severity of the problem prior to the intervention in outcome evaluation. In
evaluation, the baseline is usually the mean of the group of offenders rather
than an individual number. For example, if the practitioner chose to define recidivism as the number of offenses, the baseline would be the average number
of offenses committed by the group to be studied. These data might be acquired

---

FIGURE 9.10 Sample Questionnaire for Reviewing Official Records

Identification number: _____

Date: _____

1. How old is the subject? _____

2. Indicate client's gender: _____ Male _____ Female

3. With which racial or ethnic group does the subject identify?
   _____ Caucasian
   _____ African American
   _____ Black, non-American
   _____ Hispanic
   _____ American Indian
   _____ Oriental
   _____ Other _____ (specify)

4. What is the annual income of the subject's family? _____

5. How many members are there in the subject's family? _____

6. Has the subject committed any status offenses since entering the program?
   _____ Running away   _____ Truancy
   _____ Drinking   _____ Other
   _____ Violation of probation

7. Has the subject committed any delinquent offenses since entering the
   program? _____ Yes _____ No
   If yes, what offenses? _____

8. Has the subject committed any offenses for which he/she was processed as
   an adult since entering the program? _____ Yes _____ No
   If yes, what offenses? _____

---

through self-report, report of significant others, or review of official records (Rubin & Babbie, 1997; Yegidis & Weinbach, 1996).

Data regarding behavior after beginning the intervention can be acquired by using any of these three techniques. Interviews can be conducted during routine monitoring visits or at specially scheduled meetings. Similarly, questionnaires can be completed at routine or special visits. In each case the interviewee should be as comfortable as possible, free from distractions and influence from other sources.

Coding the Data

After the data have been collected, they must be coded. Coding is the process by which a numerical value is assigned to the answers to each question. This is done so that the number of each type of response can be easily totaled and so that the data can be used in statistical analysis (Rubin & Babbie, 1997).

Coding is usually done by preparing a second copy of the questionnaire, including all the possible responses to each question, then listing a numerical value next to each. For "yes/no" responses, the number 0 is used for "no" and the number 1 is used to represent "yes." For categories such as status offense and misdemeanor, any number other than 0 is often used. Practitioners usually

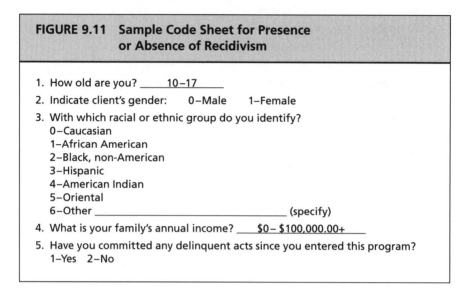

FIGURE 9.11 Sample Code Sheet for Presence or Absence of Recidivism

1. How old are you? _____10–17_____
2. Indicate client's gender: 0–Male   1–Female
3. With which racial or ethnic group do you identify?
   0–Caucasian
   1–African American
   2–Black, non-American
   3–Hispanic
   4–American Indian
   5–Oriental
   6–Other _____ (specify)
4. What is your family's annual income? ___$0–$100,000.00+___
5. Have you committed any delinquent acts since you entered this program?
   1–Yes   2–No

label one category as "1," the next as "2," until all the categories have a number. In this case the values of the numbers have no meaning other than to make a distinction between categories. For numbers that require a numerical response, such as the number of instances of truancy, the actual number is used. An example of a code sheet is shown in figure 9.11.

When the answers have been coded, the results are often recorded into a data matrix (see figure 9.12). The data matrix gives the practitioner a visual summary of the results for each juvenile. If the data are to be analyzed by computer, most statistical packages require that data be entered in matrix form. Columns can then be tallied and analyzed using mathematical and statistical techniques. Although this may sound very challenging, the analysis need not be complex. For example, it is relatively easy to calculate the percentage of youth who do not re-offend by calculating the number of youths for whom a "0" has been recorded and dividing that number by the total number in the study. Alternatively, the results may be compared to behavior during the baseline period. More complex analyses can be performed using computerized statistical programs, if they are desired. If you are not familiar with these programs, you might be able to find a local university student who needs data for a project. You could provide the student with use of the data in return for analyzed results.

Including Demographic Data

So far we have discussed only inferential statistics, that is, statistics that will allow you to determine how successful the program has been for a group of juveniles and to infer how successful it might be for others. It may also be important to include certain demographic information in your study. There are at least two reasons for including demographics. First, knowing some of the characteristics of your treatment group allows you to know more about other groups for whom it may be effective. Second, knowing group characteristics may help you determine what groups the intervention has helped and which

FIGURE 9.12 Sample Data Matrix					
Subject #	**Age**	**Sex**	**Race**	**Number of Offenses before Intervention**	**Number of Offenses after Intervention**
1.					
2.					
3.					
4.					
5.					
6.					
7.					
8.					
9.					
10.					
11.					
12.					

groups it hasn't (Rubin & Babbie, 1997). You might find, for example, that your intervention has worked well for white youth, but has been less effective for blacks. Similarly, you might find that very few males have re-offended following treatment, but a high percentage of females have committed additional crimes.

Some demographic characteristics are particularly important to include in the study. These include age, race, ethnic group, gender, family income, and grade in school. You may find differences in effectiveness between any of these groups.

Demographic information is usually collected first on a questionnaire. This helps to alleviate anxiety before the questions about behavior are asked. Demographic questions are included in the sample questionnaires in figures 9.8 through 9.10.

To determine whether your program is working better for one group than for another, you need to compare the percentage of successful youth from one group with the percentage of successful youth from another. Small differences may not mean very much. Large differences may indicate that your program needs to better consider the needs of that special population (see chapter 7 on differences between groups).

Using Standards for Success Other Than Recidivism

At times you may wish to use measures of program success other than recidivism. Many juvenile justice programs have other goals in addition to protecting society. It is important to measure the success of your program on meeting those goals as well. For example, many programs have a mission of developing productive citizens. To measure success on such goals, you need to look at factors such as educational or vocational achievement, social skill improvement, or housing stability.

You can measure educational or vocational goals by looking at successful participation in or completion of programs. The standards for success could be things like grade point average for successful participation or number of grade levels caught up in school. The average GPA of program participants should increase. Those juveniles who remain in traditional school settings and are behind in school should gradually achieve their appropriate grade level. This can be measured by looking at the average number of semesters caught up for the group. Those who participate in vocational programs should successfully complete those programs. The percentage of those completing programs should be high to indicate success.

Improvements in social skills can be measured in several ways. The juvenile can be asked about his relationships with others, and significant others can be asked about changes they perceive. Several good instruments are available for measuring social skill improvement.

Housing stability is not usually a sign of the youth's success, but can be a measure of the intervention's success. Youths whose home lives are stable are less likely to re-offend than those whose lives are transient. Measuring housing stability might include several items. To determine whether the youth's housing is stable, questions might be asked such as, "Has the youth found permanent, acceptable housing?" or "In how many different homes has the juvenile resided since entering the program?" Another alternative would be to ask, "Does it appear that the youth will be able to remain in her current housing arrangements through her 18th birthday?"

Research Design

Research design refers to the type of strategies that are put in place to strengthen a study against threats to its *validity* and *reliability.* Generally this means that the researcher is trying to be as sure as possible that the intervention is what produced the change and that the same changes would be found in the group no matter how many times they were tested. Complex designs (such as those including a second group that does not receive treatment) tend to offer greater assurance of reliability and validity. Simple designs tend to provide less protection (Rubin & Babbie, 1997; Yegidis, 1996).

Although it is possible to conduct an evaluation using a very complex design, it is beyond the scope of this book to explain the process. If you want to

---

Box 9.2 The Learning Place
A Hypothetical Alternative-to-Suspension Program

The Learning Place (TLP) is an alternative-to-suspension program for middle school students located in a small western city. Youths who are suspended for five or more days can participate in the program during their suspension. Students at TLP receive individualized attention with their lessons, social skills training, and referral to tutoring for further assistance after school hours. The program has been in existence for four years, and has worked with an average of 200 students each year. Program goals include the following: (1) youths who are suspended will keep pace in their lessons with their classmates in regular classes; (2) youths who are suspended and are behind in their classwork will show measurable progress in catching up with their classmates; (3) youths with social skills deficiencies will show measurable improvement in those skills during their participation in the program; and (4) each youth in need of educational testing or tutoring will be referred for those services during their participation in the program.

---

conduct a more complete evaluation, it would be best to involve a professional researcher who is experienced in study design. Box 9.2 describes a program that might need to be evaluated. Read the box and determine whether you would choose to evaluate this program or involve a professional researcher. Many other resources are available to help you understand the basics of program evaluation. The steps we've discussed in this section are summarized in the "Checklist for Successful Program Evaluation" included in table 9.2.

A Case Study in Outcome Evaluation

In this section we'll take a look at a sample outcome evaluation. An imaginary practitioner will evaluate the success of her program. Hopefully, this case study will help you better understand how to apply the techniques we discussed above.

Irene is a program manager for the Youth Action Program (YAP), a case management program for juveniles who have been adjudicated delinquent on minor charges such as status offenses and misdemeanors. She has been supervising five case managers who work with the teens and their families for approximately three years. During that period her program has served over 250 clients. Irene and her staff believe that the program is helping juveniles because they occasionally hear from former clients who are doing well, but Irene wants more evidence. She also believes that their program is more successful for boys than it is for girls. She wants to determine whether or not this is true.

By describing what she wants to know about the youths her program has treated, Irene has identified the outcomes she wants to measure. She is primarily interested in knowing whether the arrest rate for the youths who finish her program is lower than it was before they entered the program. She also wants to know whether gender affects outcome. After talking with her staff, Irene decides that she needs to know three other pieces of information: (1) the average age of the juveniles who enter her program, (2) the representation of racial

---

FIGURE 9.13   **Irene's Evaluation Questionnaire**

Date: _____

Identification number: _____

Date entered program _____ Date completed _____

---

1. Age of the juvenile _____
2. Gender of the juvenile _____
3. Race/ethnicity of the juvenile _____
4. Annual income of the juvenile's family _____
5. Has the juvenile been arrested since entering the program?
   _____ Yes _____ No _____ Don't know
6. If the juvenile has been arrested, for what offense/s? _____
   _____

---

groups among her clients, and (3) the average income of her clients' families. She develops a brief questionnaire that asks questions about these factors. Irene's questions can be found in her questionnaire, illustrated in figure 9.13.

Next, Irene must select a *sample,* that is, the group of juveniles that will be included in the study. One alternative would be to review the records of those youths that have passed through the program in the past. By reviewing their records, Irene could determine how many offenses each had before entering the program, and obtain the relevant demographic data. She could then review the records of local law enforcement to determine how many of them were arrested after treatment. Irene decides that this alternative would be too time consuming, and that some of the information that she wants might not have been collected from some clients. She determines that the best way to accomplish her goal is to study the outcome of all the clients who enter the program within the next year.

Irene decides that she will attach her questionnaire at the end of the intake form that is completed for each youth at his entrance into the program. She will also include an informed consent form. She knows that the past arrest record for each youth is not needed, since it can be assumed that all of them had been arrested before entering her program. After each youth graduates, his subsequent arrest history will be collected from local law enforcement at 6, 12, and 18 months after program completion.

Irene explains her intentions to each case manager at her weekly staff meeting. She instructs her administrative assistant to make copies of the questionnaires and attach one to each intake form. She trains the case managers on how to present the informed consent form and ask the questions on the questionnaire. She explains how the forms will be used, modeling their use through role play. She then has staff practice using the questionnaire on each other. Finally, Irene prepares a "tickler file," a group of index cards filed by date to remind her when juveniles will complete her program and when their police records

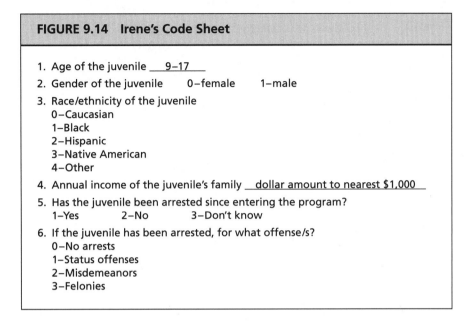

FIGURE 9.14   Irene's Code Sheet

1. Age of the juvenile ___9–17___
2. Gender of the juvenile   0–female   1–male
3. Race/ethnicity of the juvenile
   0–Caucasian
   1–Black
   2–Hispanic
   3–Native American
   4–Other
4. Annual income of the juvenile's family ___dollar amount to nearest $1,000___
5. Has the juvenile been arrested since entering the program?
   1–Yes   2–No   3–Don't know
6. If the juvenile has been arrested, for what offense/s?
   0–No arrests
   1–Status offenses
   2–Misdemeanors
   3–Felonies

should be reviewed. She also purchases a cabinet where completed questionnaires can be filed.

As the months go by, Irene occasionally reviews the questionnaires to ensure that they are being completed accurately. During the year of the study, two of her case managers leave her program and are replaced. She trains each new employee in the data collection process before they actually begin seeing clients. During that year she also develops her code sheet, a matrix on which she can track her results, and a basic form in which her results can be reported.

After one year Irene removes all the questionnaires from her file, codes the data, and enters the information on her matrix. A sample questionnaire, code sheet, and data matrix for Irene are included in figures 9.13, 9.14, and 9.15. Note that in the matrix only the questionnaire data have been recorded. This is because, at this stage of the process, Irene has no record of client re-arrest.

Seven months after the first client graduates, Irene reviews local law enforcement records to determine how many juveniles have been re-arrested over the last six months. She waits one additional month because she knows that, in her local jurisdiction, arrests sometimes do not show in official records for three to four weeks. She also reviews the records of all graduates after 13 months and 19 months. Irene then enters the final numbers on her matrix and proceeds to analyze her data.

Irene begins her analysis by tallying the numbers in each column. For instance, to tally arrests before (arrests before entering the program), Irene totals all the 0s (for those who were not arrested) and all the 1s (representing those who were arrested at least once). She then uses basic mathematical techniques to obtain re-arrest rate, success rate between genders, the percentages of each race within her sample, and the average family income of the study participants. When these figures have been obtained, Irene prepares her final report.

FIGURE 9.15	Irene's Data Matrix Variables					
	Subject #	Age	Sex	Race	Number of Offenses before Intervention	Number of Offenses after Intervention
1.						
2.						
3.						
4.						
5.						
6.						
7.						
8.						
9.						
10.						
11.						
12.						

Irene and her staff discover some very important things about their program. They find that their clients over the past year were 65% Caucasian, 25% African American, 7% Native American, and 3% Other. This is fairly consistent with the percentages of racial groups in the local population, except that African Americans are somewhat overrepresented. They discover a relatively low average income for their families, about $17,500.

Irene and her staff also make two very important discoveries about treatment. They find that their program appears to be very successful overall, since their graduates have a low (15%) re-arrest rate. They also find, however, that they are much more effective in working with males than with females, because the re-arrest rate for females was 18% higher than for males. Knowing that their program needs improvement for girls, Irene is able to use the research techniques described in chapter 6 to find out what interventions are most effective for girls and apply them to her program.

Irene's program evaluation has several limitations. Her sample prevents her from making strong statements about how her intervention might be used with other youth in other places. Since Irene cannot compare her results to those of a group that did not receive her program's intervention, she cannot be certain that other factors did not influence the youths' improvement. Despite these and other problems, Irene has gained valuable information. She has strong evidence that her program is worth continuing, and reason to believe that she and her staff are doing many things right. She also knows, however, that certain areas need improvement (such as treatment of girls) and that other areas, such as success rates between races, may need further examination.

SUMMARY

In this chapter we have reviewed the two basic types of evaluation tools available to practitioners: single-subject design and outcome evaluation. We have discussed the basic principles of each and have examined a case study in which a practitioner used each. Additional materials have been referenced in the text that can help strengthen your evaluation skills. We also recommend that you complete the "Activities for Learning," also listed below. These activities will strengthen your understanding of evaluation.

ACTIVITIES FOR LEARNING

1. Review the case of Jennifer, the juvenile described in box 9.1. Imagine that you chose to measure the intensity of her attacks of anxiety to determine the effectiveness of her intervention. Draw a graph that you could use to record the results.

2. Review the description of The Learning Place, the alternative-to-suspension program described in box 9.2. What outcome would you choose to measure? How would you collect the data?

3. Working in a group, develop a description of a hypothetical client. Determine what problem you want to target and determine how you would measure the results. Develop a daily behavior log and a graph to display the outcome.

4. Working in a group, develop a description of a hypothetical program for delinquents. Identify the program's goals, then decide how it might be evaluated. Who would be your sample? What outcomes would you measure? How would you collect the data?

QUESTIONS FOR DISCUSSION

1. Why is it sometimes difficult to measure problem behavior among juveniles? What are some techniques that can be used to improve accuracy?

2. Why is it important to measure other factors, such as social skills, school achievement, and family functioning? How might a practitioner measure these factors during a program evaluation?

3. What are some of the strengths of single-subject design? What are some of its weaknesses?

4. Look at the case study of Jennifer in box 9.1. Earlier we discussed ways to measure Jennifer's anxiety. What other variables might we want to measure? How might we measure them?

5. What uses might there be for a program evaluation? How might a practitioner use positive outcomes to seek additional program funding?

6. If a practitioner discovers that her program is not meeting its goals, what steps should she take? Explain how she might take those steps.

KEY TERMS AND DEFINITIONS

Behavior Actions, verbalizations, or cognitions on the part of an individual or group.

Duration The length of time that a behavior persists.

Frequency How often a behavior occurs.

Generalizability The degree to which the results of a study can be applied to persons other than those in the study.

Intensity The strength with which a behavior occurs.

Outcome evaluation A method of determining how successfully a program is meeting its goals. Also called *program evaluation*.

Random sampling A process of selecting subjects from a larger group that allows each to have an equal probability of becoming a part of the sample.

Random assignment A process of distributing the subjects of a study into two or more groups. One of those groups receives the treatment being studied. The other does not.

Reliability Refers to whether the results of the measurement process would be the same if the measurement was taken again.

Research design The way in which an evaluation is structured in an attempt to control threats to its reliability and validity.

Sample The subjects included in a study; in the case of juvenile justice, the subjects are normally juveniles.

Single-subject design A research method that allows the practitioner to determine the degree to which specific behaviors have changed for a client.

Validity Refers to whether a study actually measures what it intends to measure.

REFERENCES

Bloom, M., Fischer, J., & Orme, J. G. (1995). *Evaluating practice: Guidelines for the accountable professional.* Boston: Allyn & Bacon.

Rubin, A., & Babbie, E. (1997). *Research methods for social work.* Pacific Grove, CA: Brooks/Cole.

Tripodi, T. (1994). *A primer on single-subject design for clinical social workers.* Washington, DC: National Association of Social Workers Press.

Yegidis, B. L., & Weinbach, R. W. (1996). *Research methods for social workers.* Boston: Allyn & Bacon.

Chapter 10

◆

Current and Future Issues

CHAPTER OUTLINE

Current Trends in Juvenile Justice
Probable Future Issues
Building an Effective Juvenile Justice System
Summary

Today's juvenile justice system has been shaped by a number of influences. The need to save troubled juveniles from a life of crime and imprisonment is one of those influences. Society's need to be protected from delinquent acts and future criminal behavior is another. As society and its ideas change, the juvenile justice system also changes. Sometimes the changes can be anticipated. This chapter discusses some of the changes the system may experience in future years. First, it examines the current trends in availability, treatment philosophies and approaches, interface with child welfare, and legal issues. Next, it looks at some of the issues that are likely to emerge in the future as a result of those trends. Finally, it considers what we know about how to build an effective juvenile justice system, and ways we can implement those procedures in the future.

CURRENT TRENDS IN JUVENILE JUSTICE

Several trends can be seen in the current juvenile justice system. These trends include increasing needs and dwindling resources, differing philosophies in the treatment of clients among members of the system, problems in cooperation and collaboration with child welfare workers, and the ethics of shared databases between social service agencies, law enforcement, educational institutions, and other organizations. In this section we'll discuss those trends and how they may affect practitioners.

Growing Needs and Limited Resources

In several chapters of this book we have noted the impact that lack of funding has had on the juvenile justice system. Programs have been overburdened, interventions have been compromised, and evaluations have been limited because practitioners have lacked sufficient resources. One of the challenges of juvenile programming is to ensure that sufficient dollars are available for prevention and treatment activities, and that resources are not redirected toward punishment and incarceration.

Many state youth authorities are severely underfunded, and legislatures appear reluctant to commit many additional dollars to them. This dearth of resources results in high caseloads, insufficient alternatives for assessment and treatment, and a lower number and quality of institutions for confinement. High caseloads make it difficult to see clients regularly to monitor plans that are developed, and intensive services can be virtually impossible to provide.

Some funding is made available for special projects through federal agencies such as the OJJDP. These dollars are limited and, therefore, also highly competitive. Federal dollars are often directed toward specific types of projects and require a rigorous evaluation component, something that can be very difficult for agencies without a trained researcher to provide. Practitioners who want to develop a program for families, for example, may find that dollars are being made available only for school-based intervention. Others may wish to intervene in the schools, but find funding only for home-based programming.

Other government dollars can be accessed through grant notices posted in the *Federal Register,* on Web sites, and through other media. Some of these sources provide long-term funding. Others offer only start-up dollars to fund programs for a limited number of years. Their intent is that the administrators obtain local support dollars during the period of federal or state funding. Sometimes local funding is simply too scarce to obtain, and very good programs either cease to exist or are downsized when the start-up period ends.

Some money is available from county or city government, law enforcement confiscation funds, or local businesses. Often the administrator must be very creative in accessing these sources, and with finding ways to use "matching" and "in-kind" resources to leverage additional sources of income. Grant writing is often very important to the life of not-for-profit agencies. Many have actually developed special departments to handle fund-raising. Many have used such creative strategies as hosting athletic tournaments, participating in media events, or purchasing fast-food franchises to raise money for their programs.

One additional source is private philanthropy, both from individuals and from charitable foundations. Grant writers usually approach these organizations with brief letters summarizing their program and asking for funding. Charitable sources that are interested in funding the proposed projects often respond with a request for more information or a personal visit.

Direct practitioners are rarely involved in fund-raising, particularly when they are employees of state agencies (although many such agencies have divisions that raise money). However, some direct practitioners in private agencies have to keep careful records of their activities in the form of "service codes" or numerical values that correspond to a type of service provided to a client. Each time a numerical code is recorded, this is regarded as a unit of service for which the agency is compensated. The agency bills the funding source at a pre-specified interval (often monthly). For example, the cost of one unit of in-home psychotherapy might be $75. If an agency provided 100 units of in-home psychotherapy to its clients in a given month, it would submit a bill for $7,500 to its funding source. This kind of billing involves the direct practitioner in financial processes. This is not fund-raising, but it does require an awareness of financial matters that has not been required of practitioners in the past.

Administrators are often very involved in fund-raising, particularly those in higher-level positions in private agencies. These practitioners often manage several sources of money to fund their agencies. They may have a contract with the state government to provide case management, assessment, or treatment to individual youth. They may also be able to bill Medicaid or state government insurance programs for some services. They may have internal programs run by program directors that are funded by grants from government sources or foundations. Many also receive yearly contributions from local citizens or businesses. Today's administrator must either have some training or experience with financial matters, or have a close lieutenant with those skills.

Advisors to the juvenile justice system may be shocked when they discover the nature of the funding problems in agencies. Often they become involved in the funding process in the local community. Often they must help make difficult decisions about what programs will be funded and which will not. It is important that advisors become knowledgeable about the manner in which agencies are funded, the manner in which funding is distributed, the goals of local programs, and the ways in which programs are evaluated.

Researchers are often fund-raisers, although their efforts are usually directed toward obtaining funding for their research. Program research and outcome evaluations are expensive to conduct, yet crucial to effective intervention. Many researchers either become expert grant writers or associate themselves with expert grant writers so that their important work can continue.

Advocates are crucial to the current funding situation in juvenile justice practice. In an age when the emphasis on punishment is great and more youths are being processed as adults, legislators often attempt to appease (or manipulate) their constituents by directing treatment dollars toward incarceration, surveillance, and other corrections techniques. Advocates must work to ensure that sufficient dollars are available for both functions: treatment and restraint (or confinement). The juvenile justice system must both rehabilitate the offender and help protect the public interest. Advocates can help to ensure that sufficient resources are available to help meet both goals.

Differing Philosophies in the Treatment of Clients

A second current issue has to do with the way in which offenders are treated. Current philosophies run from punishment only through approaches that call for treatment only. Many factors may incline practitioners toward one or the other of these alternatives.

Sometimes practitioners are urged toward a particular form of treatment, or a lack of treatment, by the disposition or preference of the court. Practitioners must follow the court's orders. If the court forbids certain alternatives, the practitioner cannot use them unless the court changes the order. Sometimes judges have preferences, but are ethically or legally forbidden from placing them in the form of an order. In such cases the judge's preference may be expressed in the order or simply stated in the courtroom. Practitioners are not bound to follow preferences that are not stated in orders. They do, however, risk incurring the judge's wrath in this and future cases. For example, one of the authors was once told by a judge in court that she could not order him to make a specific decision, but that if he chose to disregard her preference and things did not go well, she would consider having his agency investigated for criminal neglect. Needless to say, the author was very motivated to honor the judge's preference.

Agency policy may also influence treatment. Many agencies have specific protocols they expect practitioners to follow. They may also have individual practitioners who are approved for counseling and other services. The case manager should find out which of those approved practitioners is trained in empirically validated techniques. When none has training in those techniques, she can advocate that such practitioners be added to the list.

Unfortunately, political pressures often influence selection of treatment and placement alternatives. Decisions are sometimes made at the upper level of state agencies because a child's parent called a legislator who called an aid who called the agency's top administrator. Unfortunately, although these legislators and aids often truly have the best interests of the child in mind, they are usually not competent to make treatment or placement decisions. When faced with these situations, the practitioner can sometimes appeal to his administrators with an explanation of why the decision is inappropriate. Sometimes the administrator can convince the legislator that an alternative arrangement is better. Sometimes she cannot. When the administrator cannot persuade a powerful political figure like a legislator, the agency has no choice but to comply.

Another issue involving treatment may arise when the practitioner confronts issues of prior training versus effective practice. Some practitioners believe that once they have been trained in a specific technique or modality, they have no need to learn any other approach. This is an unrealistic belief that is potentially damaging to clients, since ongoing research provides a constant flow of information about what techniques are beneficial to juveniles. Practitioners should be constantly searching for new information on what works best for the kinds of problems the youths they supervise experience. They should also attempt to convince supervisors and other administrators who were trained in outdated techniques to allow them to utilize more recent approaches.

Cooperation and Collaboration with Child Welfare Workers

An ongoing issue for those who work with juveniles is the overlap between the juvenile justice and child welfare systems. In some states the systems operate under one head administrator. In others the systems operate separately. Other jurisdictions have some combination of these arrangements.

Regardless of the way the system is structured, some of the children who have been adjudicated dependent also commit delinquent acts. Conversely, children sometimes are adjudicated dependent because of investigations initiated by their delinquency case. These overlaps can cause systemic confusion that may ultimately have a negative impact on services to the juvenile.

Whatever the administrative arrangements between the two systems, some juveniles are caught in a struggle for control and others drop through the administrative cracks. In some cases each system wants the other to be responsible for the costs of care. This is particularly true for children with physical or mental disorders, because the cost of their care strains the agency's budget.

When juveniles do become involved with both systems, their lives can become very complicated. They may have a case manager from each system, two or more therapists, and two or more attorneys. They may be required to appear in a different series of court hearings for each system. One of the authors recalls being involved with a youth who spent most of a day running between floors in a courthouse to attend four different hearings with three different judges on various child welfare and juvenile justice issues.

Obviously, if the juvenile is served by neither system, none of the goals of either system is met. If services are duplicated, valuable resources are wasted and conflicting clinical input may actually be harmful to the youth and family. Practitioners should make every effort to see that children involved with both systems receive adequate services, and that the services they do receive are coordinated between agencies.

Communication and Shared Databases

One of the important issues within juvenile justice is its *fragmentation,* that is, the way its parts fail to work together. One example of this fragmentation is lack of information-sharing between agencies. Juveniles in state custody often pass through myriad agencies, both public and private. Many of these agencies assess the youth, and many ask questions already asked by other providers. When this occurs repeatedly, the juvenile and her family are subjected to long, repetitious, and often embarrassing questioning. Practitioners waste many hours collecting information that has already been collected elsewhere.

An example of this problem can be seen in the case of Theresa, a 17-year-old African-American female who was arrested for shoplifting. During her intake she was thoroughly interviewed by an officer of the court. She was diverted into a program run by a private provider, where she and her family were assessed and many of the same questions were asked. When educational needs were discovered, she was referred to a school psychologist for testing. He, in turn, referred her to a mental health practitioner. Each asked many of the same questions.

There are valid reasons that some information is not shared between agencies. Juveniles who have committed delinquent acts have many rights that should not be violated. One of those rights is the right to confidentiality. The agencies ask about areas of youths' lives that are relevant to their professional practice. Not all those agencies need the same information. For example, if Theresa is referred to a recreation program, its workers may not need detailed information about her educational or legal history. Her case manager, however, may find knowledge of her educational background (particularly any history of educational testing) to be invaluable in structuring a comprehensive intervention.

At the least, certain information is needed by each provider, and can be shared between agencies without a great deal of concern for the juvenile's right to confidentiality. Demographic data, for example, can be shared between virtually all the agencies involved. Mental health and educational testing information might be shared by the providers of those services and with the case manager who facilitates the overall treatment plan. Others might have access to various categories of information according to the client's need. In such a scenario, the issue becomes not what can be shared, but how and with whom it can be shared.

One answer to this question is a centralized computer database accessible to all agencies. In such a system various categories of information about clients can be warehoused, with access being granted only to certain agencies on a need-to-know basis. Information can be given various levels of security, according to its sensitivity. For example, demographic information might be given the lowest level of security. History of mental health treatment or sexual abuse might be accorded a greater level of security. Providers could not only receive data from the central database, but also print the information on their own forms.

Such systems are certainly not without problems. There are issues involving access and confidentiality. The degree to which any computer can be made secure is also an important question. Agencies whose cooperation is needed to make this kind of program work may be unhappy with the level of access they receive and may resist participation because of turf issues. Other agencies simply may not have the resources to purchase the equipment needed to participate.

Despite the difficulties involved in developing centralized databases, some jurisdictions have either installed such systems or are in the process of creating them. One of the authors was involved in such a project in the southeast Florida area. The project experienced many difficulties, primarily in the areas of funding, confidentiality problems, and consensus as to adequate content. The project is still in the planning process as this book is being written.

Legal Changes: Get Tough Policies

Several times during previous chapters we have mentioned the current trend toward tougher standards and sentencing for juveniles. This "get tough" approach places special demands on the concerned practitioner. As a state employee, she has a responsibility to obey the laws that govern her activity and to protect the rights and safety of the citizens she serves. As the juvenile's caseworker, she also has a responsibility to deliver competent, effective treatment.

"Getting tough" may mean closer surveillance or revoking probation for less serious offenses. It may mean that the worker will be increasingly involved in cases in which the juvenile is processed as an adult. "Getting tough" means different things in different jurisdictions, depending on the law, the court, and the administration in those areas. Some examples of what this tougher stance means in some areas are provided by Patricia Torbet and Linda Szymanski, as published in the *Juvenile Justice Bulletin* (1998).

The age at which juveniles can be transferred to adult court has been lowered, and the reasons for which they can be transferred have been expanded in some jurisdictions. For example, during the 1996–1997 legislative session several states modified their statutes regarding juvenile transfer. Four states lowered the age at which discretionary waiver could be exercised, seven added crimes for which it might be used, and four others added conditions related to prior arrest record. By the close of that legislative session, all but five states had *discretionary waiver* provisions, 14 had *mandatory waiver* provisions, and 14 had *presumptive waiver* provisions. Altogether, between 1996 and 1997, 24 states toughened their statutes that allow juveniles to be tried as adults.

Several states developed new sentencing alternatives aimed at more offense-based dispositions. This reflects a greater emphasis on punishment and incarceration. By the close of the 1995 legislative session, 17 states had passed blended sentencing options. By 1997 several had adopted juvenile sentencing guidelines. Several others had increased the age for extended juvenile court jurisdiction.

Corrections programming is also becoming tougher. Many state legislative decisions regarding corrections over the last several years have focused on public safety and the accountability of the offender. These statutes often emphasize institutional alternatives for serious offenders. For example, Louisiana recently passed a law requiring that juveniles who reach age 17 while incarcerated in a juvenile facility be automatically transferred to an adult institution.

A fourth "get tough" trend is in the area of confidentiality. More states are opening juvenile hearings to the public, publishing or releasing personal information of offenders, and broadening access to juvenile records. Some have forbidden authorities to *expunge* juvenile records or have increased the number of years youths must wait before their records are expunged.

Obviously, some very clear trends exist in the juvenile justice arena. Some have to do with funding. Some are organizational in nature. Others are related to the policies that govern the system. Current trends often have a way of continuing into the future. Sometimes they create other trends. In the next section we'll talk about where experts believe the current trends are likely to take us. Then, in the final section, we'll discuss some of the changes the system must make to be prepared for the future.

PROBABLE FUTURE ISSUES

Current trends often shape future issues. If we can predict tomorrow's issues by looking at the trends we now experience, the juveniles we serve can benefit. Unfortunately, future issues and problems in juvenile justice are notoriously difficult to predict. We must learn, however, to direct our efforts through anticipatory decisions rather than by reacting to events that have already occurred. In this section we will look at several issues that are likely to affect the future of juvenile justice. These issues include lack of resources, methods of processing, techniques of prevention and treatment, developing effective partnerships and collaborative efforts, effective professional communication, and the impact of all these influences on the client's legal rights.

Resources

We observed in the section above that juvenile justice programs in many jurisdictions already operate with inadequate resources. Specifically, we discussed funding, but deficiencies also exist in placement alternatives, staffing patterns, and poor relationships between some of the agencies that form the system. These conditions, combined with the effects of other trends, are likely to present significant challenges to practitioners at every level.

One trend that is likely to interact with limited resources is the potential for increase in violent crime by juveniles, discussed in chapter 1. If more juveniles commit more violent offenses, new programs and more secure facilities will be needed. More practitioners will need to be trained in management of potentially violent youth, both in the community and in institutions. Since home confinement may prove to be a more cost-effective alternative for many juveniles, agencies will need to purchase electronic surveillance equipment and will need to pay staff to monitor compliance with that equipment.

Although more white youth enter the system than do minority youth, minorities are disproportionately represented (Devine, Coolbaugh, & Jenkins, 1998). If, as experts expect, even more minorities come into supervision, training on interaction with minority groups will be increasingly important. Also, as minorities become more prominent in areas previously dominated by non-minorities, training will be needed for workers who have never interacted with minority clients. Ongoing research and intervention is needed to determine what factors contribute to this overrepresentation of minorities and to positively impact those factors.

The greater number of girls entering the system is also likely to impact resources. Gender-sensitive programming is clearly a must, as we discussed in chapter 7. Adequate housing will need to be made available for those who will be disposed to residential placements. Practitioners need more training in dealing with issues of physical and sexual abuse and with structuring group programs that use cooperative rather than competitive activities.

Since truancy rates are high or growing in many areas, intervention must focus on education and preparation for successful adulthood. Yet programs to educate youth may fall victim to legislation that redirects practitioners toward greater punishment. Administrators and advocates must find new, creative sources of funding for educational and vocational programs.

One of the reasons funding remains low for child and adolescent programming is the diversity of values regarding troubled children among the American voters. Some Americans believe very strongly that all offenders, regardless of their age, should be punished. One of their major concerns is ensuring that they and other law-abiding citizens are safe from criminal activity. Other Americans believe in treating offenders. They believe that punishment is actually counterproductive, and that it infringes on the inherent rights of individuals. Many Americans fall somewhere between these two extremes. Unfortunately, many people in each category have developed their beliefs without any scientific knowledge about what causes crime and what is effective in preventing it. They vote and contribute money to political campaigns to elect legislators that will represent those views. If citizens in a given geographical area oppose funding for programs, legislators are likely to oppose it as well. If public perception can be changed to support juvenile justice programming and adequate treatment, many legislators may be influenced to respond more positively to the system's need for resources.

Processing

Several new trends are likely to develop in the area of juvenile processing. Some are supported by federal sources, including the Coalition for Juvenile Justice (CJJ). Many revisions to the current court process are discussed in that organization's 1998 annual report.

The CJJ recommends increased use of mediation and dispute resolution services where they are appropriate. As we saw in chapter 8, these services have been shown to be effective in many settings and are very cost effective. The CJJ also recommends, however, that care be taken that no individual's or group's rights are violated when these interventions are used.

Another recommendation is that detention practices be altered. Despite the intent of federal law, statutory loopholes in many states allow juveniles to be detained with adults under certain circumstances. Also contrary to the intent of law, younger juveniles and those who have committed less serious offenses are often detained with older, more chronic juvenile offenders. This creates both a setting for potential abuse and for schooling in more serious crime. Future detention may include such alternatives as house arrest, electronic monitoring, and separate housing within facilities.

We have discussed transfer to criminal court in previous sections. Provisions for transfer are likely to become more broad, and mandatory transfer may become more prevalent. The CJJ suggests a direction for future legislation in this area: that transfers should be individualized and subject to specific statutory criteria.

Issues concerning the rights of juveniles are likely to continue to be debated. The CJJ urges that courts should fully protect the rights of juveniles. They contend that juveniles should be ensured that an attorney is available to them at every stage of the process. Conversely, they argue that court hearings should be open and that the records of juveniles should be available to any individual or agency that can clearly demonstrate the need to have that information.

New programs and funding opportunities for programs are likely to become available over the next few years. Government sources recommend effective early intervention; specialized programs for minorities, females, and disabled youth; stronger programs for those with mental health and substance abuse issues; and more competent evaluation of all these programs. Practitioners should actively participate in the development and implementation of these programs. They should base their efforts on the characteristics of effective programs discussed in earlier chapters.

Prevention and Treatment

Given the current federal emphasis on prevention, program development and evaluation are likely to continue in that area. Treatment seems to be moving in the direction of prevention as well, with recidivism defined as the activity to

Table 10.1 Prevention Principles

- **For infants:** Frequent home visits by nurses and other professionals.
- **For preschoolers:** Classes with weekly home visits by preschool teachers.
- **For delinquent and at-risk preadolescents:** Family therapy and parent training.
- **For schools:**
  —Organizational development for innovation.
  —Communication and reinforcement of clear, consistent norms.
  —Teaching of social competency skills.
  —Coaching of high-risk youth in "thinking skills."
- **For older male ex-offenders:** Vocational training.
- **For rental housing with drug dealing:** Nuisance abatement action on landlords.
- **For high-crime hot spots:** Extra police patrols.
- **For high-risk repeat offenders:**
  —Monitoring by specialized police units.
  —Incarceration.
- **For domestic abusers who are employed:** On-scene arrests.
- **For convicted offenders:** Rehabilitation programs with risk-focused treatments.
- **For drug-using offenders in prison:** Therapeutic community treatment programs.

SOURCE: Sherman et al., 1998

be prevented (tertiary prevention). A recent publication by the OJJDP (Sherman et al., 1998) summarized much of what is currently known about effective prevention programming. The "do's" and "don'ts" identified by these researchers are included in table 10.1.

Among the activities known to work are specific types of early intervention for infants, children, and pre-adolescents; certain school-based programs; specific types of training, monitoring, and surveillance for certain types of offenders; and several community-based law enforcement activities. Other efforts, such as drug education, "scared straight" programs, boot camps, arrest and punishment of juveniles for minor offenses, and certain types of school-based and community-based programs do not work. The OJJDP and other organizations are likely to continue funding programs and publishing results. Practitioners should familiarize themselves with this work and should develop their programs accordingly. A more detailed description of the current knowledge of effective prevention programming is included in table 10.2.

Minority Issues

Minorities are disproportionately represented at virtually every stage of the juvenile justice process. Despite greater awareness and intervention, this situation seems unlikely to be corrected in the near future. As a result, federal and state governments are likely to continue to sponsor efforts to correct these problems. The results of one such effort are reported in a document written by Devine and associates (1998) and published by the OJJDP. This document reports the results of an effort sponsored by the OJJDP to reduce minority confinement in five states: Arizona, Florida, Iowa, North Carolina, and Oregon.

Table 10.2 Characteristics of Effective Children's Services Organizations

Characteristic	Source
Low levels of conflict between employees	Glisson & Hemmelgarn, 1998
High levels of cooperation in the organization	
Clarity of employee roles	
Personalization	
Casework is individualized and nonroutine	Glisson, 1992
Caseworkers develop a personal relationship with clients	
Casework focuses on outcomes rather than processes	
Caseworkers are seen as available and responsive	Dozier, Cue, & Barnett, 1994
Practitioner/client interactions exhibit continuity	Wahler, 1994

The project identified four groups of underlying factors that contribute to minority overrepresentation in institutions. The four groups were factors in the juvenile justice system, factors in the educational system, factors in the family, and certain socioeconomic conditions. The individual factors included in each of these groups are illustrated in figure 10.1.

The project addressed minority overrepresentation at one stage of the system: incarceration. Important lessons were learned that may be applicable to other stages of processing. Researchers learned that five steps were necessary in the corrective process: (1) assigning organizational responsibility, (2) analyzing juvenile justice data, (3) identifying underlying factors, (4) creating and enhancing interventions, and (5) developing methods to measure the intervention's impact.

Minority overrepresentation is a serious and complex issue. It is clearly an important issue when considering its impact on the individuals, families, and communities it affects. Efforts to eliminate this problem are under way, and are likely to continue well into the future.

Collaboration and Communication

Interagency collaboration has been a hot issue in human services circles for a number of years. Collaboration refers to individuals and organizations that share common missions working together to help clients achieve their goals and improve their situations. Through collaboration, agencies expect to be able to reduce service costs and duplication and enhance service efficiency and outcome.

Although collaboration is a worthy goal, it has often failed to achieve its promise. Funding problems result in competition and turf wars between providers. Philosophical differences sometimes arise between agencies, preventing effective interdisciplinary treatment planning. Some have even questioned the value of interorganizational service coordination, producing data showing that some efforts have actually worsened the quality of services (Glisson & Hemmelgarn, 1998). Collaboration is a reasonable goal, yet results are elusive. In an

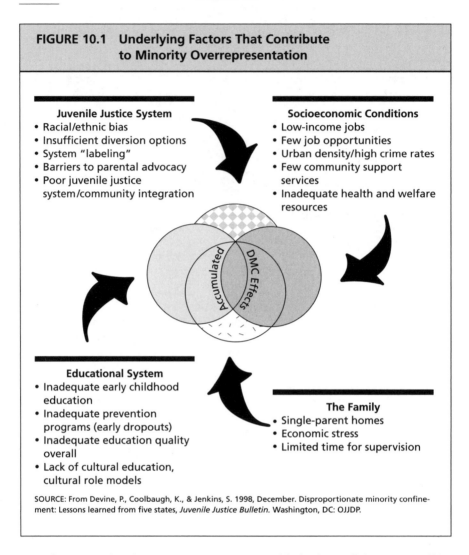

FIGURE 10.1 Underlying Factors That Contribute to Minority Overrepresentation

Juvenile Justice System
- Racial/ethnic bias
- Insufficient diversion options
- System "labeling"
- Barriers to parental advocacy
- Poor juvenile justice system/community integration

Socioeconomic Conditions
- Low-income jobs
- Few job opportunities
- Urban density/high crime rates
- Few community support services
- Inadequate health and welfare resources

Accumulated DMC Effects

Educational System
- Inadequate early childhood education
- Inadequate prevention programs (early dropouts)
- Inadequate education quality overall
- Lack of cultural education, cultural role models

The Family
- Single-parent homes
- Economic stress
- Limited time for supervision

SOURCE: From Devine, P., Coolbaugh, K., & Jenkins, S. 1998, December. Disproportionate minority confinement: Lessons learned from five states, *Juvenile Justice Bulletin*. Washington, DC: OJJDP.

age of great need and scarce resources, it seems likely that collaboration will be a discussion in the juvenile justice arena for many years to come.

Privatization

Privatization refers to the process through which services historically offered by government agencies are shifted through a contractual process to private agencies. Many private agencies have contended that they can deliver services more effectively, efficiently, and cheaply than can government agencies. Many services such as garbage collection and prison operation have been contracted to private providers in recent years. Most recently, several states have initiated the process of privatizing their children's services. Kansas has placed its services entirely in private hands. Florida is under a legislative order to place all child welfare services in private hands by the year 2003.

Privatization is not new to juvenile justice. Many jurisdictions have contracted with private agencies to provide a variety of service for many years.

However, no jurisdiction has totally privatized services. As pressure from the public and state legislatures mounts, increasing portions of the juvenile justice system may be privatized. The results of that process are a subject for future evaluation.

BUILDING AN EFFECTIVE JUVENILE JUSTICE SYSTEM

In order for the system we are building today to be successful in the future, we must use certain lessons as we plan interventions, write policy, and build the organizations that will serve juveniles and their families. In this section we'll talk about some of those lessons. First, we'll examine the objectives and elements of an effective system as proposed by the OJJDP. Next, we'll look at some alternatives for coping with unique offenses such as violence and sexual offense. Third, we'll review some proposed policy characteristics for an effective system. Finally, we'll talk about the characteristics that agencies need to be successful as service delivery systems.

Objectives and Elements of an Effective System

In order to develop a successful system, we as the designers of that system need to understand both what our system needs to do and the basic elements that allow it to accomplish its tasks. The former director of the OJJDP, Shay Bilchik, provides a summary of three crucial objectives and three critical elements that must guide the development of an effective juvenile justice system (Bilchik, 1998). Bilchik's objectives are (1) hold the juvenile offender accountable; (2) enable the juvenile to become a capable, productive, and responsible citizen; and (3) ensure the safety of the community. The three elements are (1) a mechanism for comprehensively assessing a juvenile, (2) the capacity to provide a range of treatment services, and (3) increasingly severe sanctions and enhanced treatment services.

The three objectives are much like the principles of the balanced approach discussed in chapter 4. Offenders must be held accountable by law enforcement, in the courts, and by the agencies who supervise them and provide them with services. For direct practitioners, this means ensuring that the terms of their behavioral contracts are met, that they complete relevant assignments and tasks, and that appropriate sanctions are administered at appropriate times. For administrators, this means ensuring that effective mechanisms are in place to support clinical and supervisory efforts, and that sufficient staff are employed to keep caseloads at manageable levels. Advocates, advisors, and researchers can emphasize the importance of this objective as they help plan and develop programs.

The juvenile justice system of the future must also develop prosocial competence in the offender and his social systems. Juveniles who leave the system should be better able to become productive citizens than when they entered. The responsibilities of various types of practitioners to facilitate this objective were discussed in chapters 4, 5, and 6.

Practitioners must also protect the community. The juveniles in their care have either violated the rights and safety of others or are at risk of doing so.

Protecting the community requires assessing the probability that individual youths will offend again, determining whether they are likely to commit particularly heinous offenses, and designing interventions that will prevent them from committing these offenses. To accomplish this goal, practitioners must employ the three elements listed by Bilchik: comprehensive assessment, a broad range of treatment services, and a system of appropriate sanctions and enhanced treatment.

Assessment was discussed in some detail in chapter 3. You will recall that we made a distinction between assessment as an overall process and two of its components: evaluation and diagnosis. We have learned a great deal about assessment over the last several years. It is important that we use what we have learned to improve our dispositional alternatives for juvenile offenders. Much also remains to be learned about assessment. We must continue to develop our knowledge of risk factors, need factors, and protective factors, as well as our ability to assess risk for specific offenses.

An effective system must also supply a wide range of treatment services to deal with the multiple problems experienced by juveniles who are disposed into state custody. Practitioners are often frustrated by recognizing a need in juveniles, understanding what services need to be provided, yet lacking a competent provider to whom the youth can be referred. Extensive knowledge of assessment practices will be useless to practitioners if sufficient treatment alternatives are not available.

Practitioners must also be equipped with a system of increasingly severe sanctions and enhanced treatment services for juveniles who do not respond to lower levels of treatment. Assessment is not likely to be a precise process any time in the near future. Given the difficulties involved in anticipating human behavior, accurate prediction may never be possible. Even when it is possible, some juveniles may not respond to well-conceived treatment plans. When this occurs, practitioners must be prepared with alternative sanctions to employ or to suggest to the court. They must also have a continuum of services to which resistant youths and their families can be referred.

Coping with Unique Offenses in an Effective System

Although problem behavior theory suggests that most juvenile behavioral problems are very similar, certain problems must be treated as unique. They can be considered unique because of their unusual recalcitrance to treatment and the degree of threat that they represent to public safety. There is no official list of such crimes, but, in the opinions of the authors, at least two clearly qualify: violence and sexual offense. Others may also belong in this category. Many experts believe that gang activity and weapons or drug offenses should be considered among those offenses. This section will discuss the two offenses identified by the authors.

Violent crime among juveniles has decreased somewhat over the last few years following a strong upward trend (Torbet & Szymanski, 1998). It is likely to increase again, given the number of children approaching the age at which violent offenses usually occur. Violent crime is particularly difficult to deal with for several reasons. First, although we know a great deal about the factors that place juveniles at risk for violent behavior, we are not yet able to predict very accurately which individuals will become violent. Also, experts have experienced some success in treating violent offenders, but the rate of success is still insufficient to ensure community safety. Third, violent crime has a strong impact on its victims and on society as a whole. This often causes policymakers to overreact, creating legislation that worsens rather than helps deal with the problem.

As the system struggles to learn to deal with violent offenders, some groups have made substantial progress. Borduin (1994) cited three programs that show promise: the Alaska Youth Initiative, Family Ties (New York City Department of Juvenile Justice), and multisystemic therapy. These three interventions are intensive, individualized, and use empirically supported intervention techniques in a family-preservation-like case management system. Practitioners will need to focus additional efforts on developing these kinds of programs in the years to come.

The OJJDP (1995) has published *Guide for Implementing the Comprehensive Strategy for Serious, Violent, and Chronic Juvenile Offenders*. The guide explains the strategy, provides a blueprint for its implementation, and discusses prevention, graduated sanctions, risk assessment, and other key issues. As with all juvenile justice technologies, the strategy requires further development. This and similar activities are likely to be among the trends of future years.

Sexual offense is another type of crime that is particularly difficult for practitioners. Like violent offense, it can be difficult to predict and many offenders have been resistant to attempts at treatment. Treatment programs often focus on incarceration and isolation of the offender in the interest of public safety. Effective interventions for sexual offenders must be developed. Such efforts are likely to be a part of intervention funding and research projects during the early years of the twenty-first century.

Policy Characteristics for an Effective System

Practice is shaped by policy on many levels. For the juvenile justice system, policy begins at the federal level, where broad guidelines are established by the Congress and the offices of the executive branch, such as the Department of Justice. State legislatures operate within these guidelines to develop specific statutes that create and control the system within their jurisdictions. Some local governments pass ordinances that make specific acts (such as curfew violations) criminal and actionable. Courts and agencies also make policy when they interpret policy and make daily operational decisions regarding policy delivery. In a sense, direct service practitioners also create policy as they develop individual operating procedures within those guidelines and make daily practice decisions.

Some of the policies that have shaped the system have been very good. Others have probably been more harmful than helpful. As new laws are written and procedures are developed, it is important that these policies are consistent with what we know about successful practice.

Aaron McNeese (1998) has summarized the three major shifts in juvenile justice policy since 1960. The first was during the 1960s, when community organization models were authorized and funded. These models were largely unsuccessful. The second shift occurred in the Juvenile Justice and Delinquency Prevention Act of 1974, which focused on prevention and separation of juveniles from adults in confinement. The third major shift was described in an earlier section of this chapter. This shift is a move toward a tougher stance with offenders.

Unfortunately, policy in many areas is more reactive than proactive. This means that it is formed in response to some perceived crisis that has already occurred, or to some highly publicized isolated event. This sometimes results in a "knee-jerk" response from lawmakers that appears designed to satisfy constituents rather than to improve the system. When these knee-jerk responses occur at the federal level, they are often very directive to state governments. This raises questions about whether the federal government has trespassed into areas of law constitutionally or traditionally given to states or local jurisdictions.

Effective policy development is a key to developing an effective juvenile justice system. Policy provides the guidelines under which the courts operate. It also provides operating procedures and funding for the public and private agencies that deliver services to youth. Practitioners often help to shape policy by participating in the preparation of proposed legislation, drafting agency operating procedures, and making daily decisions that interpret policy. Given what we know about successful intervention and treatment of juveniles, practitioners may wish to consider several points of information in their activities.

Since policy influences court processes, program development, funding, and other aspects of the system, practitioners' activities should emphasize the use of current theory and knowledge of effective intervention. Legislators may not have the time to familiarize themselves with these critical areas. Practitioners can help to make them aware of information that can inform policy development.

As we noted earlier, policy is often created reactively rather than proactively. A knowledge of past successes and failures, current conditions, and future trends can be very useful to practitioners who inform policymakers. Policy should be designed to address the conditions that trends are likely to create. Knowing what has worked and what has not can help to prepare for those conditions.

Policymakers must attempt to strike a balance between the rights of individual juveniles and public safety. This is a difficult, sometimes impossible balance, made particularly difficult by our inability to accurately predict the behavior of individuals. Future policy must address these issues, and must generate opportunities for research that can help us more accurately assess the needs and predict the future behavior of offenders.

Policy should emphasize diversion, prevention, and child welfare. The failures of the past do not mean that diversion and prevention do not work. In fact, there is evidence that they do work when they use appropriate programming. Further, many of the problems of families of delinquents are shared by families whose children enter the child welfare system. Policy that addresses common needs through consolidated program responses can address the needs of more children more effectively.

The juvenile justice policy of the future must both ensure adequate funding for programs and hold agencies that receive the funding accountable for effective, responsible service delivery. Dollars must be available to create programs, sustain programs, and pay professional personnel to staff those programs. Evaluation should focus on outcome rather than process, and should emphasize corrective activity before funding is withdrawn.

Legislators are influenced by votes and dollars. Because they cannot (and should not) escape the influence of the voting public, policy should generate dollars to inform the public of what works for juveniles. An informed public could support legislators in their efforts to develop effective policy.

Judges have an immense amount of power to decide the future of the juveniles whose cases they hear. Often they are asked to make clinical and administrative decisions regarding juveniles when they lack the training and preparation to do so. Future policy should create opportunities for judges to learn more about treatment for the families they see. Judges also have opportunities to abuse their power. Mechanisms should be put in place to control those who do abuse their power.

This list of considerations for future policy development is by no means comprehensive; nor does it constitute a legal opinion. It does, however, incorporate many of the ideas and much of the knowledge included in our current understanding of effective intervention and effective system operation. This list, along with others like it, might be a beginning in the development of a basic set of guidelines for juvenile justice policy practice.

Organizational Characteristics in an Effective System

Several researchers have examined the characteristics of agencies that deliver effective services to juveniles and their families. They have found some very interesting, as well as surprising, things. As the juvenile justice system continues to be built or rebuilt, organizations that serve children should incorporate these ideas into their structure and operations. The characteristics of successful children's services organizations are provided in table 10.2.

Recently, Glisson and Hemmelgarn (1998) examined critical factors affecting service delivery in several Tennessee counties. The researchers found that organizational climate, that is, the environment in which practitioners work, is very important to quality service. Specifically, they identified four characteristics typical of more successful organizations. These factors were low conflict between employees, high levels of cooperation within the organization, clarity of the roles of the employees, and personalization.

Low conflict refers to the presence of an environment in which discord and antagonistic behavior are minimized. This can make the workplace much more enjoyable, and can help to foster the second characteristic, cooperation. Cooperation is the degree to which practitioners work together to accomplish their goals. When workers are cooperating, information is freely exchanged between employees and practitioners support one another in the completion of their responsibilities. Role clarity refers to the degree to which the tasks of practitioners are delineated and defined. When employee roles are clear and tasks are clearly the responsibility of specific employees, the potential for conflict is decreased. Personalization is perhaps best explained as a lack of depersonalization; that is, employees feel valued as persons, that their ideas and contributions matter, and that they are more than just a cog in a machine.

Glisson (1992) also identified three important characteristics of casework in successful organizations. He noted that casework that generates positive outcomes is (1) individualized and nonroutine, (2) characterized by the development of a personal relationship between caseworker and child, and (3) focused on producing results rather than meeting processing goals. These characteristics are inconsistent with many of the practices of children's services organizations today.

Casework should be individualized and nonroutine. It should not be a canned approach or boilerplate list of services to be followed when juveniles with certain problems come into custody. This is consistent with our earlier discussion of the outcome literature on successful intervention. Unfortunately, many organizations do use routine approaches with children, and often sanction boilerplate treatment plan models to be used with children with specific types of issues and problems. Much to his discomfort, one of the authors served on a large committee that was ordered to develop just such a document. The final product was excellent, offering many alternatives and explaining that its content was only a guideline to help develop case plans. Unfortunately, some supervisors and members of the judiciary immediately began to require that case plans be virtually exact copies of the samples provided in the document.

Successful casework is also characterized by the development of a personal relationship between caseworker and child. It is important that the practitioner and the juvenile know each other and know what can be expected of each other. This requires regular visitation by and communication with the worker. Unfortunately this kind of regular contact can be very difficult to establish given the large caseloads and heavy workloads experienced by many practitioners. It does underscore the importance of regular contact with juveniles, even when some of that contact must be by telephone or in the form of drop-in visits.

Successful casework focuses on producing results rather than meeting processing goals. Many youth service organizations evaluate their success by process, looking at factors like the number of visits a juvenile received during his supervision. Although the number of visits may be important, it and similar process characteristics do not tell evaluators how much children have improved. Thus, a worker might visit a child regularly, make referrals to all the wrong organizations, and never facilitate any improvement in the child or his family. Successful casework looks at results such as improved psychosocial functioning, social skills development, educational improvement, reduction of recidivism, and improved family functioning.

Other researchers have identified additional characteristics of successful casework. Dozier, Cue, and Barnett (1994) found that children and families must see their caseworkers as available and responsive. This can be very difficult given the high caseloads and diverse responsibilities of many practitioners, but it is a key to effective service. In a related finding, Wahler (1994) found that interactions between practitioners and clients must exhibit continuity over an extended period. Continuity means that the practitioner's visits and calls must be seen as regular, helpful, and appropriate over an extended period of time. An effective system must guarantee that its direct service workers have sufficient time and resources to make these visits. It must also ensure that workers actually make these visits.

Several problems have plagued children's services organizations. Relatively low salaries, heavy workloads, difficult and demanding clients, insufficient training, a hostile judiciary, and insufficient service coordination have all been blamed at various times for system failure. Many have argued that these have resulted in a high level of employee dissatisfaction and turnover. One researcher (Solomon, 1986) confirmed that dissatisfaction and high turnover are problems in many systems. Glisson and Durick (1988), however, questioned the reasons for these problems. They found that worker dissatisfaction and turnover were not related to salary, client type, or education and experience of the workers. This suggests that although children's services workers certainly deserve to be well compensated for what they do and need to be well trained, other factors are more important to improve worker morale and service quality. On an individual level, this leads back to the importance of the work atmosphere. If it is not salary, client type, or preparation for the job that cause people to stay in these positions, what does make them stay? The answer, at least in part, was discussed in the first part of this section. Employees stay in children's services jobs because the organizational atmosphere is good, featuring low conflict between employees, high levels of cooperation within the organization, clarity of the roles of the employees, and personalization.

Another factor often believed to affect service quality is coordination of services. Obviously, smooth referral to a seamless system of providers that stands ready to meet a child's needs should improve the outcomes for that child; however, this does not mean that all efforts to improve service coordination will have that result. For example, in the study mentioned earlier by Glisson and Hemmelgarn, the researchers concluded that one effort at service coordination actually worsened outcomes for children in the geographical areas they sampled. The researchers mentioned several problems that may have contributed to the program's failure, but concluded that one of the more significant factors was that the new effort distracted workers from many of the tasks of case management.

Distraction of workers at all levels is likely to be a significant problem in today's children's services organizations. Although the authors have found little research in this area, it is a common theme when workers from various jurisdictions discuss problems within their system. The experiences of one of the authors as director of child welfare for a large district of a state child welfare organization will help to illustrate the problem.

The central tasks of children's services agencies are assessment and treatment of children and families. Assessment may involve many or all of the activities described in chapter 3. Treatment may include the activities described in chapters 4 and 5. Performing these tasks can often be difficult given large caseloads, demanding client situations, and other challenges. In addition to these core services, however, workers are often distracted by other commitments imposed by upper-level administrators, politicians, the judiciary, the press, and other groups. Even efforts at improvement can severely affect service delivery. In his former capacity as child welfare director, one of the authors recalls a time when the district was involved in nine separate studies, audits, or self-improvement tasks. Direct service workers were pulled from their daily tasks for interviews, committee participation, and report preparation. Middle-level administrators often ran from one organizational improvement meeting to the next, with little or no time to work with their employees. District-level administrators had a similar experience, except that their span of control included interviews, meetings, and reports for all these state-imposed functions.

Politicians can also seriously impair the functioning of children's services. It is important that citizens be able to exercise their right to speak through elected officials. It is also important that state agencies not be overwhelmed by contrived accusations from irate citizens who falsely construe the facts of individual cases in telephone calls or letters to their offices. Again, referring to the experiences of one of the authors, one call or letter from a public official can set in motion a series of events that might consume many hours of several employees' time. In the face of heavy schedules and large caseloads, the results of these political inquiries can be disastrous for children in care.

The judiciary and the legal system sometimes also impose a burden on the children's services system. Crowded court dockets sometimes have workers waiting in courtroom hallways for hours at a time, time that might be better spent in the homes of clients. Some judges, intending to compel compliance, frequently order middle- and upper-level administrators to appear in court, drawing them away from other important duties. Some judges also force children into specific placements that may not be in the best interests of children, perhaps severely affecting the well-being of those children and using precious dollars out of the state's placement budget for children whose needs are not appropriate for that facility.

The press can also have a substantial negative impact on children's services, even when the reporter or editor's intentions are good. The authors are aware of a recent case in which a judge hearing children's cases was forced off the juvenile bench by a misinformed editorial in a local newspaper. Political pressures influenced the newspaper to print incorrect information and accusations that undermined the judge's otherwise excellent work. A series of articles refuting the paper's error was too late to prevent the judge's resignation.

The problems described in these vignettes address a very important issue in children's services. Effective services for children require a cooperative effort by many community agencies. Administrators, politicians, judges, the press, and other groups can negatively affect service delivery while trying earnestly to help children. In an effective juvenile justice system, the component parts should work as a team, helping, not hindering, the efforts of the other parts.

The research projects and vignettes offered in this section tell us a great deal about what our juvenile justice system should not be and what it should be in the coming years. Administrators must focus on developing a positive work atmosphere where conflict is minimized, cooperation is rewarded, roles and responsibilities are clearly defined, and each employee feels personally valued and important to the work of the agency. Along with advocates, advisors, and researchers, administrators must find ways of dealing with the systemic problems that negatively affect services. For example, enhanced communication with the courts and an improved means of handling citizens' complaints to politicians could make a tremendous difference in the effectiveness of agency operations.

Characteristics of the Courts in an Effective System

The Coalition for Juvenile Justice (CJJ) (1998) has made a number of recommendations for improvement of the processing of juveniles. These recommendations should also be considered as plans are made to improve the juvenile justice system. The full list of their suggestions is included in the organization's 1998 annual report, *A Celebration or a Wake: The Juvenile Court after 100 Years*. We have included a few of those suggestions in this section. The suggestions are also summarized in table 10.3.

The CJJ has recommended that the various jurisdictions develop unified *family courts,* that is, courts that will deal with all family-based problems and issues in a single setting. This, the organization contends, will allow judges to deal with family issues more comprehensively and creatively.

A second recommendation is that greater care be given to the selection of judges and personnel within the juvenile justice system. Judges should have an interest in and commitment to children and families and should receive specialized, ongoing training for dealing with their issues. Juvenile justice personnel should also be more carefully selected and should receive comprehensive, ongoing training with gradual progression into full caseloads and more difficult assignments.

A third suggestion of the CJJ is that the system must be adequately staffed. Adequate staffing requires that a sufficient number of positions be available to administrators, that capable staff be recruited, that the staff be properly trained, and that employee turnover be minimized. They also urge that staff be adequately paid for the work that they do.

The CJJ also recommends that delinquency and child welfare services be integrated. This would be accomplished in part by establishing unified family courts. In addition, however, the service delivery systems should be integrated to ensure that service duplication is reduced and that communication is enhanced between practitioners.

According to the CJJ, innovative programs for status offenders should also be developed to reduce their contact with more serious offenders and focus on access to services. The current system allows too much interaction with serious offenders in which status offenders may develop relationships that lead to additional offenses. Some systems also focus on punishment, which is often ineffective with status offenders. Linkage to appropriate services can help less serious offenders avoid re-offense.

The CJJ also recommends that the jurisdiction of the court be extended to include the families of juveniles. If this innovation were implemented, parents could be held responsible for surveillance and monitoring activities, as well as

Table 10.3 Recommendations for Improving Courts and Processing

1. Unified family courts that handle all family-related matters should be developed.
2. Programs for status offenders that reduce contact with serious offenders and focus on services should be implemented.
3. Courts should be given jurisdiction over families of juveniles.
4. Professional court administration, data management, and caseload management services should be used.
5. Teen courts should be developed in more jurisdictions.
6. Greater use should be made of dispute resolution services such as mediation.
7. The detention system should be revised and improved.
8. Both an effective counsel and a competent prosecutor should be available for all cases.
9. Criteria-based transfer to adult court should be made possible at the discretion of judges only.

SOURCE: CJJ, 1998

for their part of the family contract. The possibility of legal action might motivate many resistant families.

Professional court administration, data management, and caseload management services are also among the recommendations of the CJJ. These professional services are crucial to the effective processing, yet they are absent in many jurisdictions. Professional services will also require appropriate training and financing.

The CJJ recommends that *teen courts* be established in every jurisdiction. Teen courts include juveniles as jurors, prosecutors, and defenders, and sometimes in a dispositional role. The CJJ also recommends careful monitoring and evaluation of these programs.

Another recommendation of the CJJ is greater use of dispute resolution services such as mediation. Many cases can be diverted from the conventional system using these alternatives. This could help to reduce the strain on some portions of the system. As we have seen in earlier chapters, mediation is a very effective intervention.

Juveniles should be guaranteed the availability of both effective counsel and a competent prosecutor. Juveniles should not be inappropriately influenced to waive counsel, and those who cannot afford an attorney should have one provided to them. Similarly, prosecutors should be experts in juvenile proceedings and should understand the mission of the court.

The CJJ suggests that juveniles should be transferred to adult court at the discretion of judges and based only on specific criteria. The organization believes that the decision to prosecute a youth as an adult should be left in the hands of the judiciary. It also believes that statutes should provide specific guidelines for those decisions.

The 1998 annual report of the CJJ makes a number of additional valuable suggestions that should be considered as the juvenile justice system is improved for the future. The publication can be obtained from the source listed in the "References" section of this chapter. Practitioners should obtain a copy and become familiar with its contents.

SUMMARY

In this chapter we looked at trends, policies, and programs that characterize the juvenile justice system today, and are likely to shape it in the years to come. The discussion is, of course, not comprehensive, and some of its assumptions about the future are likely to be inaccurate. The crystal ball is always a little flawed when it comes to policy development and human behavior.

Many of the trends discussed here are likely to continue, however. Many of the programs described are already in place. The suggestions for shaping the future system are likely to be valid as well, given our current level of understanding of the system.

This book was written to provide students with an overview of treatment philosophies, approaches, and issues in the juvenile justice arena. We hope that better prepared students will become better prepared practitioners. Better prepared practitioners, whether they are direct service workers, administrators, advocates, advisors, or researchers, can more effectively serve clients, and better help the system accomplish its mission: helping juvenile offenders become responsible citizens and preserving the safety of the public.

ACTIVITIES FOR LEARNING

1. In a group of three or four classmates, read the list of changes to the court and processing made by the CJJ and listed in table 10.3. In your group, discuss the following questions. Do you agree or disagree with each of the recommendations? Do you think each would improve or damage the system? Why? Do any of the suggestions seem to be particularly supportive of the rights of children? Are any particularly related to a "get tough" approach?

2. Obtain a copy of the OJJDP document *State Legislative Responses to Violent Juvenile Crime: 1996–1997 Update.* (Torbet and Szymanski, 1998). Look

at the seven transfer classifications on page 3. Which of these methods does your state use? If you don't know, how could you find out?

3. Make an appointment to visit the executive director or financial officer of a private children's services agency in your area. Use the information about funding offered in this chapter to prepare a questionnaire to guide your discussion. Ask how the agency is funded, what its sources are, and what kinds of activities its administrators use to access resources. Report your results to your class.

QUESTIONS FOR DISCUSSION

1. What do you think causes the over-representation of minorities in the juvenile justice system? What kinds of changes can be made to eliminate it?

2. One of the problems in the juvenile justice system is a lack of funding and resources. One of the reasons for this problem is a lack of awareness on the part of the public of the true issues in the system, and of the kinds of activities that are effective for troubled youth. What kinds of things could be done in your community to make

people more aware of the important issues in juvenile justice?

3. Review the elements of an effective juvenile justice system discussed in the section above. What factors do you think are most important to assess in a juvenile? Why? How can a community ensure that it has a sufficient range of services? What steps do administrators need to take to ensure the presence of a system of increasingly severe sanctions and enhanced treatment?

KEY TERMS AND DEFINITIONS

Discretionary waiver A means of prosecuting a juvenile as an adult: a juvenile judge waives jurisdiction and sends the case of a juvenile to adult court for processing.

Expunge To delete the records of a juvenile from official sources so that there is no documentation of any prior offense.

Family court A single court that deals with all family issues, including child welfare, delinquency, domestic violence, mental health issues, and others.

Fragmentation Separation, discontinuity, and lack of communication between community resources.

Mandatory waiver A means of prosecuting a juvenile as an adult: if probable cause exists to believe that a juvenile committed an offense specified by law, the accused must be transferred to adult court.

Presumptive waiver A means of prosecuting a juvenile as an adult: juveniles can be processed as adults unless they can show that they are likely to be rehabilitated through juvenile processing.

Teen courts Courts in which juveniles are involved as participants, for example, as counsel for the accused or prosecutor.

REFERENCES

Bilchik, S. (1998, May). A juvenile justice system for the 21st century. *Juvenile Justice Bulletin*. Washington, DC: Office of Juvenile Justice and Delinquency Prevention.

Borduin, C. (1994). Innovative models of treatment and service delivery in the juvenile justice system. *Journal of Clinical Child Psychology, 23,* 19–25.

Coalition for Juvenile Justice. (1998). *A celebration or a wake: The juvenile court after 100 years. 1998 annual report to the president, the Congress, and the administrator of the Office of Juvenile Justice and Delinquency Prevention.* Washington, DC: Author.

Devine, P., Coolbaugh, K., & Jenkins, S. (1998, December). Disproportionate minority confinement: Lessons learned from five states. *Juvenile Justice Bulletin.* Washington, DC: Office of Juvenile Justice and Delinquency Prevention.

Dozier, M., Cue, K., & Barnett, L. (1994). Clinicians as caregivers: Role of attachment organization in treatment. *Journal of Consulting and Clinical Psychology, 62,* 793–800.

Glisson, C. (1992). Technology and structure in human service organizations. In Y. Hasenfeld (Ed.), *Human services as complex organizations* (pp. 184–202). Beverly Hills, CA: Sage.

Glisson, C., & Durick, M. (1988). Predictors of job satisfaction and organizational commitment in human services organizations. *Administrative Science Quarterly, 33,* 61–81.

Glisson, C., & Hemmelgarn, A. (1998). The effects of organizational climate and interorganizational coordination on the quality and outcomes of children's services. *Child Abuse and Neglect, 22*(5), 401–421.

McNeese, A. (1998). Juvenile justice policy: Current trends and twenty-first century issues. In A. R. Roberts (Ed.), *Juvenile justice: Policies, programs, and services* (2nd ed.). Chicago: Nelson-Hall.

Office of Juvenile Justice and Delinquency Prevention. (1995). *Guide for implementing the comprehensive strategy for serious, violent, and chronic juvenile offenders.* Washington, DC: Author.

Sherman, L. W., Gottfredson, D. C., MacKenzie, D. L., Eck, J., Reuter, P., & Bushway, S. D. (1998, July). Preventing crime: What works, what doesn't, what's promising. *Research in Brief.* Washington, DC: National Institute of Justice.

Solomon, E. E. (1986). Private and public sector managers: An empirical investigation of job characteristics and organizational climate. *Journal of Applied Psychology, 21,* 247–259.

Torbet, P., & Szymanski, L. (1998, November). State legislative responses to violent juvenile crime: 1996–1997 update. *Juvenile Justice Bulletin.* Washington, DC: Office of Juvenile Justice and Delinquency Prevention.

Wahler, R. G. (1994). Child conduct problems: Disorders in conduct or social continuity? *Journal of Child and Family Studies, 3,* 143–156.

Index

Abandonment, 49, 50
Abuse, definition of, 50
  See also Child abuse; Sexual
    abuse; Substance abuse
Academic problems, 118–120,
  238
Accountability, 86, 205–206, 209,
  221
AD. *See* Adolescent Domain (AD)
ADHD. *See* Attention deficit hyperactivity disorder (ADHD)
Adjudication, definition of, 42
Administrative practitioners
  community social system inter-
    vention and, 137
  definition of, 26
  employment social system in-
    tervention and, 134–135
  fund-raising and, 259
  gang-related intervention and,
    141
  interaction in juvenile justice
    system, 33
  peer intervention and, 130, 133
  roles of, 15, 17
  schools and, 52
  in treatment facilities, 35
  See also Practitioners
Adolescent Domain (AD), 78, 80
Adolescent Problem Severity Index, 80
Adoption, definition of, 50
Advisors, 20, 259
Advocates
  community social system inter-
    vention and, 137
  employment social system in-
    tervention and, 134–135
  functions of, 32
  fund-raising and, 259
  gang-related intervention and,
    141
  interaction in juvenile justice
    system, 33–34
  peer intervention and, 130, 133
  roles of, 19–20
  school social system and, 126
  See also Practitioners
African Americans. *See* Blacks
*Aftercare for High-Risk Juveniles: An
  Assessment* (Altschuler &
  Armstrong), 220
Aftercare services
  case study, 221–223
  Intensive Aftercare Program
    (IAP), 219–224
  monitoring and, 221
  overarching case management
    and, 220–221
  as parole, 42
  programmatic action principles,
    222

publications about, 220
recidivism and, 58
termination and, 62
After-school programs, 121
Agency policy, definition of, 26
Aggravated assault, 3, 4, 6
Aggression
  antisocial personality disorder
    (APD) and, 13
  development of delinquency
    and, 8
  evaluation instruments for, 81
  as gang value, 139
  physical contact as, 230
  as risk factor, 10
Aggression Replacement Training
  (ART), 127, 129–130, 140–
  141
Alaska Youth Initiative, 271
Alaska Youth Services Needs Assessment Scale (AYSNAS), 80
Alcohol, 9, 23, 51
Alternative schools, 122, 142
Alternative-to-suspension pro-
  grams, 125–126, 251
American Indians
  communication techniques,
    181
  ethnic cleansing and, 179
  life story interview, 182–183
  racial identity of, 180
  rituals of, 180
  tribal differences, 170
American Psychiatric Association,
  13
AMI. *See* Associate Marine Insti-
  tutes (AMI)
Anger management, 128, 187
  See also Self-directed anger
Annsville Youth Center (New
  York), 216
Antidepressant medication, 148,
  167
Antisocial personality disorder
  (APD), definition of, 13, 26
Anxiety, 51
APD. *See* Antisocial personality
  disorder (APD)
Arizona, 266
Arrests, 4–5
Arson, 4, 6
ART. *See* Aggression Replacement
  Training (ART)
Asian Americans, 182, 184, 185
Assessing the Youthful Offender
  (Hoge and Andrews), 81
Assessment
  case study, 60
  for classification, 59, 61
  components of, 63–71
  definition of, 30, 55, 57
  demographic data and, 63–64

educational background and,
  64–65
effective juvenile justice system
  and, 270
family history, 67
importance of, 56
instruments for, 79–81
as intake, 43
for intervention, 57–58, 81–82
legal history, 65–66
medical problems, 70, 71
mental health assessment, 68–
  69, 72–73
purposes of, 56, 57–63
risk-based assessment, 76–79
sexual history, 70, 71
social problems, 69
specialized assessment, 72–76
substance abuse history, 68
for termination, 62–63
vocational training and, 65
  See also Classification; Evalua-
    tion
Associate Marine Institutes
  (AMI), 149
Attention deficit hyperactivity
  disorder (ADHD), 51, 72
Attorneys, 36–37, 38–40
Attorneys ad litem, definition of,
  37
Auto theft. *See* Motor vehicle theft
Avocational interests, 10
AYSNAS. *See* Alaska Youth Services Needs Assessment Scale
  (AYSNAS)

Balanced and restorative approach
  (BARA), 86–87, 88, 103,
  117, 209
BARA. *See* Balanced and restorative approach (BARA)
Baselines, 232–234
BB/BS. *See* Big Brothers/Big Sisters of America (BB/BS)
Beck Depression Inventory (BDI),
  80, 231–232
Behavior
  behavior problems in school,
    119
  daily behavior log (DBL), 231,
    232
  definition of, 229, 230, 256
  duration of, 230
  frequency of, 230
  intensity of, 230
  target behavior for single-
    subject design, 229–231
Behavioral contracts
  definition of, 115
  for delinquents, 93
  disciplinary problems and,
    120–121